Jewish Profiles

Jewish Profiles

Great Jewish Personalities and Institutions of the Twentieth Century

Edited by

Murray Polner

4764

Foreword by Irving Howe

JASON ARONSON INC.
Northvale, New Jersey
London

Production Editors: Bernard F. Horan and Leslie Block
Editorial Director: Muriel Jorgensen

This book was set in 11 point Goudy by Lind Graphics
and printed and bound by Haddon Craftsmen.

Library of Congress Cataloging-in-Publication Data

Jewish profiles : great Jewish personalities and institutions of the twentieth century
  [compiled] by Murray Polner.
     p. cm.
   ISBN 0-87668-793-1
     1. Jews—Biography. 2. Jews—United States—Biography. 3. Jews-
  -Politics and government—1948- 4. Jews—Intellectual life.
  5. Jews—United States—Intellectual life. 6. Judaism—20th
  century. 7. Judaism—United States. I. Polner, Murray.
  II. Present tense (New York, N.Y.)
  DS115.J38 1991
  920'.0092924073—dc20
  [B]   90-28237

Manufactured in the United States of America. Jason Aronson Inc. offers books and cassettes. For
information and catalog write to Jason Aronson Inc., 230 Livingston Street, Northvale, New Jersey
07647.

Contents

Foreword

by Irving Howe

Some shout and scream with the furies of fanaticism. Others speak calmly, in the tones of conviction and good faith. *Present Tense* was among the latter. With self-assurance and a merited warm response from its readers, the magazine steadily advanced liberal views and sentiments—not any sort of party line, not the monotonous reiteration of a single viewpoint, but a variety of modulated liberal opinions regarding sociopolitical and, especially, Jewish, issues.

It was not an easy task. During the Reagan years, when a sort of intellectual miasma spread across the country, there grew powerful within the American Jewish community a small group of intellectuals—mostly ex-radicals—with a venom that seems peculiar to those ex-radicals who came to be known as neoconservatives. As the ideologists of right-wing thought, these neoconservatives, who found their main outlets in the *New Criterion* and *Commentary*, exerted a certain behind-the-scenes influence in national affairs, especially in the form of a rather crude anti-Communism. One of the voices that remained steadfastly in contrast to the neoconservatives—less, perhaps, by polemic than by example—was *Present Tense*, a magazine that kept its sense of balance and good temper. The result was writing, both journalistic and essayistic, that was notable for its tolerance of manner and its avoidance of the party-line zealotry we find in a number of its contemporaries. In its variety and charm, the present anthology testifies to this achievement.

Jewish liberalism in America has a substantial history, in part as a tributary of an earlier Jewish socialism, in part as a pragmatic response to American circumstances. I am not one of those who tries to anchor Jewish liberalism in venerable Judaic texts and traditions. That seems to me a serious mistake, if only because those texts and traditions are so various and complex that they can be put to almost any use by anybody, whether of the left, right, or center, who is looking for usable (sometimes exploitable) ancestors. I think it much better that as American Jews we should base our politics on our own immediate judgments, and that we should defend our liberalism in the name of contemporary needs and experiences rather than to fall back on anything so amorphous as, say, "the prophetic tradition." Besides, as far as I can see, none of us these days qualifies as a prophet.

Everyone knows that during these last few decades Jewish liberalism has fallen upon hard times. In part, this is due to the larger difficulties of liberalism in the West, that is, of liberalism as political movement and body of thought. In America this means especially the exhaustion of the line of politics stemming from the New Deal. In a society increasingly subject to the world market and dominated by transnational corporations, some of the traditional reforms that worked (at least in theory) during the past several decades have become insufficient or irrelevant. But in part, the difficulties of Jewish liberalism are also due to specific circumstances. The victories of the right-wing parties in Israel and their intransigent position regarding the occupied territories necessarily strengthened the hand of those holding similar views in the American Jewish community. And the anointed leaders of the community, who probably hold fairly dovish opinions in private, have not always been exactly heroic in speaking their minds. There were of course also distinctively local circumstances—the passing influence that Reaganism granted the neoconservatives, and the growing friction in certain cities between blacks and Jews, for instance.

Yet it remains a notable fact in a time when the country as a whole drifted rightward (at least in presidential elections), the American Jewish community has by and large kept its liberal commitment. Not entirely, of course—we should not exaggerate. The liberalism of American Jews has become softer, weaker, less combative. It has become, I would say, a somewhat conservatized liberalism; and certainly it has lost some of its earlier self-assurance. Yet, as all polls and election results indicate, the politics of American Jews still tilts toward the liberal side.

Perhaps the most crucial issue currently facing American Jewish liberalism in particular and the American Jewish community as a whole is the attitude taken toward the Middle East conflict. Devoted as we all are to the security and survival of Israel, it becomes increasingly clear that there can be no end to the conflict between Jews and Palestinians, nor even an end to the Palestinian intifada, until there are negotiations between Israel and the freely chosen representatives of the Palestinians. The right to national self-determination that the Jews won for themselves by creating the State of Israel in 1947 must be granted to the Palestinians as well, with the proviso of course that Israeli security be insured. The only alternative to such a prospect is endless bloodshed, increasing militarization of Israeli society, and growing hatred and fanaticism on both sides. The greatest test for American Jewish liberalism in the next few years will be its readiness to speak out, despite predictable innuendos and assaults, on behalf of this outlook.

Meanwhile, here are some selections from the pages of *Present Tense*. Some are explicit in their articulation of the liberal outlook, some are implicit. And perhaps in these few remarks of mine, I have overstressed the political aspect of the liberalism of *Present Tense*. For what matters most is that the contents of this book embody the values, the styles, the *spirit* of liberalism, with a fine sense of pluralist openness, largely, I would say, in harmony with the best traditions of Jewish life in America.

Preface

It was a happy suggestion by Seymour P. Lachman, then director of the American Jewish Committee's Foreign Affairs Department, that led to my becoming the founding editor of *Present Tense*. It was 1972 and a propitious moment to launch a new magazine. The A.J.C. had been publishing *Commentary* since 1945, and that journal had taken a sharp turn rightward and generally ignored issues engaging Jews here and abroad. Similarly, the organization had for years pursued a "universal" approach, often emphasizing humane national and general concerns rather than a purely "Jewish agenda."

Elsewhere, Israelis had seemingly "come of age" following the exhilaration of their swift victory in 1967. And if the conquest of Jerusalem's Old City and the West Bank and the Gaza Strip was seen by many Israelis at the time as an act of biblical redemption, it was viewed here as an unparalleled act of heroism and, indeed, even as retribution for past Jewish agonies. Israel took on a new meaning for the vast majority of American Jews. It became their religion, a nearly idolatrous object of their affection. Once largely ignored by the bulk of their coreligionists in this country, Israeli Jews became Dayan's Supermen.

Israel's smashing triumph also led to a turning inward among Jews in this country. Suddenly, Orthodoxy became more confident, more out-spoken—although it has never numbered more than 10 percent of the American Jewish population. Adults returned to synagogues to be bar-

and basmitzvahed. Defense organizations abandoned their traditional emphasis on universal concerns and turned, more intently, toward "Jewish" interests. Some prognosticators even saw in all this activity evidence of a dawning of a new and great Jewish age. An over-optimistic hope, surely, but all the same a sure sign that many American Jews were beginning to shape a distinctly *American*-based Judaism, with the closest of ties to Israel, but otherwise indisputably American.

Armed, then, with a pledge from the A.J.C. of *absolute* editorial freedom, I became the editor of what soon became a liberal magazine dedicated to debate, discussion, and reportage. But we also took sides. The articles dealt with everything we thought mattered—from Israel to the Diaspora, from pre-Gorbachev Soviet violations of human rights and liberties to illegal secret American warfare against Nicaragua, from the status of the family to the plight of the homeless and impoverished. We were one of the first Jewish publications to call attention to the desperate situation of Ethiopian and Soviet Jews. We were among the earliest to challenge the war in Vietnam and the Israeli invasion of Lebanon in 1982. And we argued that Palestinians had rights, too, including the right of self-determination.

Present Tense, since its inception, sought to reflect the openness and tolerance that are the hallmark of liberalism and much of Jewish life. We tried to reflect the ethical and moral teachings of our faith, without which it becomes ritualized and vacuous. Our articles, our reportage, and, especially, our profiles of people and institutions gave evidence of the vast variety of the American Jewish experience. From *shtiebl* to *havurah*, from the left, center, and right, we are a variegated people with no center of infallible authority. Estelle Gilson's perceptive and thoughtful profiles of Agudath Israel, YIVO, and iconoclasts Arthur Hertzberg, Irving Howe, and Philip Klutznick, for example, give proof that all are legitimate claimants to the term, as "Jewish" as Ariel Sharon and Geula Cohen, here portrayed by Matthew Nesvisky and J. Robert Moskin.

Independence of mind and thought, the celebration of differences as well as common threads, our tradition's insistence upon moral behavior, and the pursuit of peace were, therefore, the components that made *Present Tense* what it was.

The profiles reprinted here have not been brought up to date. To be sure, some of the people have died and some of the issues have been resolved one way or another. Even so, the subjects discussed, the questions posed, and the people and institutions profiled remain fixed in time and are as memorable and significant today as they were when our writers first encountered them.

I would especially like to thank many of our authors, such as Estelle Gilson, Hesh Kestin, Stephen S. Rosenfeld, and Victor Perera, who were with us from the very start; Ira Teichberg and Judy Tirsch, our art directors; Leonard Kriegel, our literary editor; M. L. Rosenthal, poetry editor, and Gerald Jonas, who reviewed books for us; plus Susan Jacoby, Arthur Hertzberg and my friends and colleagues at *Present Tense*—Iris Goldman, Adam Simms, Gwen Lawlor, Hanna Desser, Seymour P. Lachman, Harry and Rita Hochman, David Gordis, E. Robert Goodkind, and Mark Amundsen—for their dedication and competence.

Regretably, *Present Tense* ceased publication in April 1990.

Contributors

Myra Alperson is a journalist and the author of two books.

Carol Ascher's most recent book is *The Flood*, a novel. Her essays and stories have appeared in *The New York Times*, *Ms.*, and numerous literary magazines. She is the recipient of four PEN/NEA Syndicated Short Fiction awards.

Isadore Barmash is a business writer for *The New York Times*. He is also the author of a dozen books.

Chaim Bermant is a British journalist and novelist.

Diane Cole is the author of *After Great Pain: A New Life Emerges* and *Hunting the Headhunters: A Woman's Guide*.

Anita Diamant is the author of *The New Jewish Wedding* and *The Jewish Baby Book*.

Mario Diament, an Argentine journalist and playwright, was executive editor of *La Opinión* until the paper was taken over by the military in 1977. He was a correspondent in Israel and the United States for the Argentine magazine *Siente Dias* and is now with the *Miami Herald*.

Jeremy Garber received an M.A. and an M.Phil. in Hebrew literature from Columbia University and has translated a variety of Hebrew and Yiddish poems. He is currently a lawyer for the American Jewish Congress and since 1985 has been poetry editor for *Reconstructionist Magazine*.

Estelle Gilson, whose articles have appeared in many magazines, is preparing a collection of short fiction for publication.

Andrea Jolles is a free-lance writer who lives in New York.

Richard Kostelanetz is a writer and artist who has authored many books of poetry, fiction, criticism, and cultural history.

Wendy Leibowitz has written many articles on issues facing Jews in the United States and Israel.

Robert Leiter is on the staff of the Philadelphia *Jewish Exponent*. He is also a contributing editor to the *American Poetry Review*. His short stories, essays, book reviews, and profiles have appeared in *The Nation, The New Republic, Redbook, Dissent, The American Scholar, The New York Times, Hudson Review, Partisan Review*, and other publications.

Diane Levenberg is a writer who teaches at Kutztown University in Pennsylvania.

Benny Morris, a reporter for the *Jerusalem Post*, is the author of *The Birth of the Palestinian Refugee Problem, 1947–1949* and coauthor of *Israel's Secret Wars: The Untold History of Israeli Intelligence.*

Jennifer Moses is a writer and editor.

J. Robert Moskin was the foreign editor of *Look* magazine and is the author of *Among Lions*, the story of the 1967 battle for Jerusalem, and *The U.S. Marine Corps.*

Matthew Nesvisky is an editor and feature writer for *The Jerusalem Post*.

Morton A. Reichek is a retired editor and writer for *Business Week*.

Jack Riemer, rabbi of Congregation Beth David in Miami, Florida, is the editor of *Jewish Reflections on Death* and the coeditor of *Ethical Wills: A Modern Jewish Treasury*. He was a student of Rabbi Abraham Joshua Heschel.

Sylvia Rothchild is the author of *Voices from the Holocaust, A Special Legacy: An Oral History of Soviet Emigrés in the United States*, and *Family Stories*, a collection of short stories.

A. James Rudin, a rabbi, is interreligious affairs director of the American Jewish Committee. He is a founder of the National Interreligious Task Force on Black–Jewish Relations, and is the coauthor of *Prison or Paradise? The New Religious Cults*, and the author of *Israel for Christians*. He has also edited four books on Christian–Jewish relations.

Marcia Rudin, the director of the International Cult Education Program, is coauthor of *Prison or Paradise? The New Religious Cults* and *Why Me? Why Anyone?*

Risa Sodi received master's degrees in French and Italian from the University of Massachusetts at Amherst, and authored a book on Primo Levi and Dante.

Robert Spero has written for many publications, including *Present Tense, The New York Times, Newsday*, and *Redbook*. He is author of *The Duping of the American Voter: Dishonesty & Deception in Presidential Television Advertising.*

Sheldon Teitelbaum is a Canadian/Israeli journalist living in Los Angeles, where he works as a public relations staff writer for the University of Southern California and as bureau correspondent for *Cinefantastique: The Review of Horror Fantasy and Science Fiction Films*. He also writes regularly for the *Los Angeles Times*.

Jewish Profiles

Agudath Israel

Estelle Gilson

Most of the stuff they write about Orthodox Jews is garbage. As if we were a bunch of esoteric kooks." The voice that booms over the telephone belongs to Rabbi Moshe Sherer, president of Agudath Israel of America and co-chairman of the world Agudah organization. "I want you to come down here and see for yourself the staff I have. It's huge. It's hip, alive, relevant."

"Down here" is 5 Beekman Street, an unprepossessing building just steps from New York's City Hall, where Agudath Israel of America administers not only a Torah education program, but aid to Russian immigrants, the elderly poor, displaced homemakers and businesses hurt by imports. It also runs a youth movement and public affairs office.

No one among the staff of more than 100 Orthodox men and women looked to me like an "esoteric kook." Some of the men, including the 63-year-old Sherer, were unbearded, and I saw stylishly dressed young women. As to "hip, alive, relevant"—this is Sherer's response to the call of Agudath Israel's founders to win Jews to "genuine Judaism" by the most modern means possible.

Agudath Israel was founded in 1912, at a conclave of Orthodox rabbis in Katowice, Poland, in response to the inroads made by secularist, Zionist and assimilationist Jews into the ranks of the Orthodox. As Rabbi Yaakov Rosenheim of Frankfurt, Germany, told his colleagues from Hungary, Poland and Lithuania, the organization's aim was "to

1

revive an ancient Jewish possession: the traditional concept of *Klal Yisroel*—Israel's collective body, animated and sustained by its Torah—that we seek to realize with our Agudath Israel and with the technical means provided by civilization."

Today's Agudath Israel—a worldwide movement of Jews whose lives are governed by Torah (Maimonides' Thirteen Articles of Faith are a concise statement of Agudist beliefs), with national headquarters in 12 nations and representation in nine North American cities—is still guided by a synod of Orthodox rabbis: Moetzes Gedolei Hatorah, or Council of Torah Sages. "This is the beautiful thing about Agudath Israel," says Sherer. "In all other Jewish organizations it's their boards" who make decisions. "And who are those people? Major contributors. Since when do real-estate operators or Wall Street tycoons have the Jewish background to make decisions for the Jewish people? We have big businessmen, too—some with thousands of employees—but they sit before the rabbis with humility and awe."

There are actually two Councils of Torah Sages, a 14-member group in Israel and an 8-member body in the United States. European Agudists can seek guidance from either council. Besides the United States, there are Agudah organizations in Argentina, Belgium, Brazil, Canada, Denmark, Britain, Israel, Italy, Mexico, South Africa and Switzerland. Six of the nine Agudah offices in North America have salaried staff. Three are directed by volunteers. Though each is autonomous, all depend heavily on the national office in New York for guidance. And all must subscribe to what Sherer calls Agudah's "theology and policy positions."

Sherer, who has been with Agudath Israel for 41 years, is an articulate and impassioned spokesman for Orthodoxy—whether in battling stereotypes or advancing the cause of Orthodox rights. His voice rises as he recalls the era when Orthodox Jews were "*nebechdich* [pathetic] lackeys of others who controlled the purse strings of Jewish life . . . and the Government considered the American Jewish Congress the voice of all American Jews. In 1961, when I appeared for the first time before a Congressional committee to testify in favor of Federal aid to nonpublic schools, it was a front-page story—a voice of dissent, speaking in a comfortable English style. Now, when I appear before Congress, it's two lines on page 62."

Agudath Israel grew slowly in the United States, and the way was difficult. The secularist and assimilationist pressures its founders had sought to stem in Europe were far stronger in the melting pot of America. In the early years, after its founding in 1922, the United States organization concentrated its energies on preserving centers of Orthodoxy and creating new ones for Torah study. With the help of visiting European scholars—among them Elchonon Wasserman, who influenced the teenage yeshiva student Moshe Sherer to devote his life to Agudath Israel—it created an Orthodox youth movement, summer camps and Bais Yaakov schools for girls modeled on those the movement had created in Poland. In the past two decades the carefully nurtured "transplant" has grown strong enough to try to win over other American Jews.

Agudah means "union" or "association." But at its inception Agudath Israel was opposed to Zionism. "The Agudah saw in Zionism the profanation of the belief in the coming of the Messiah," writes historian Celia S. Heller in "On The Edge of Destruction: Jews of Poland Between the Two World Wars." It also tried to remain nonpolitical. As the movement's official publication put it: The right "seeks to destroy the life and existence of every Jew as an individual." The left "seeks to destroy the Jewish people as a people." Agudath Israel, though wishing to avoid the tangles of Polish politics, tried to work with the Polish Government and, responding to initiatives of the Zionists and other Jewish organizations, even entered candidates in independent Poland's first legislative elections in 1922. It successfully elected six members to a Parliament in which there were 29 other Jews.

Yet when Poland's economy worsened, so did the situation of the Jews. By 1928 anti-Semitism was virulent. Jews—even those in Parliament—were subject to abuse. In 1936, when the Polish Government proposed legislation prohibiting kosher slaughtering as "inhumane," Agudath Israel finally changed its position on Zionism. "In the last few years before World War II," Heller writes, "Agudah . . . proclaimed that only through unity could Jews gain . . . strength and favored the creation of a Jewish state in Palestine."

During the war years, Agudath Israel of America gained support from spiritual leaders and scholars who had escaped the Holocaust. "The Struggle and the Splendor," the brief, emotional official history of the movement, describes the newcomers as "dynamic, totally selfless people who . . . had left Europe not simply to save themselves, but to do everything humanly possible to save those who had remained behind." The book describes "the official callousness and duplicity" and "the gullibility of the American Jewish establishment in allowing itself to be deceived into abandoning its brothers and sisters by accepting the priorities of the American government."

In 1941, Agudath Israel defied the Joint Boycott Council of the American Jewish Congress and the Jewish Labor Committee, which was advocating an American trade boycott of fascist countries, and continued to send relief packages to Polish Jews. "The Struggle and the Splendor" tells how American Jews allegedly placed "the priorities of the American government" before the needs of fellow Jews in Europe, and claims that Agudath Israel, with a few other Orthodox groups working to save Jews, might have been more successful had it not been a "maligned, isolated minority whose rescue work was impeded." Sherer agrees. "Most secular Jewish 'establishment organizations' sat on their hands during the Holocaust years," he says.

Though Agudath Israel is "the largest mass Orthodox organization in the world," according to Professor Seymour P. Lachman of the City University of New York, its 75,000 members in this country represent only a small percentage of the nation's estimated 500,000 Orthodox Jews. Yet when Moshe Sherer testifies before Congress, Agudath Israel is perceived by many as the voice of Orthodoxy. The primary reason for this is that it represents a coalition of Orthodox sects—including the Hasidim—with only three major exceptions; the Lubavitch and Satmar groups (though the Bobovitch, which it represents, has more members than the Lubavitch) and the modern Orthodox, led by Rabbi Joseph B. Soloveitchik.

The Lubavitch and Satmar, according to Sherer, find Agudath Israel "too Zionistic." The modern Orthodox, he adds, find it too "isolationist." But Rabbi Louis Bernstein, president of the (Orthodox) Rabbinical Council of America and a professor at Yeshiva University, believes Agudath Israel is "more concerned with the limited community with which they work, and (has) never come to grips either theologically or practically with the State of Israel." Agudists, for their part, believe modern Orthodoxy has succumbed, as Sherer put it, "to creeping compromises in its Judaism." And compromise on the tenets of Judaism is something Agudists refuse to accept.

Affiliating with Reform and Conservative groups is also something Agudath Israel will not entertain. "Affiliating implies we think that's an alternative form of Judaism," says David Zwiebel, director of Agudah's

Office of Government and Public Affairs. "We don't want to convey that impression." Nevertheless, Agudath Israel is willing to work with other Jewish groups on an ad hoc basis; for example, according to Zwiebel, it received support from Conservative Jews in backing New York State legislation requiring religious consent for divorce. Adds Zwiebel: "There are issues on which we even work with the American Jewish Congress"— still the epitome, it seems to them, of secular Judaism. However, American Jewish Congress assistant executive director Phil Baum can recall no projects on which the two organizations have cooperated.

Commenting on the tensions between Agudath Israel and other groups, Judah Gribetz, a Conservative Jew and friend of Sherer's, who was a counsel to former New York Governor Hugh Carey and a one-time Deputy Mayor of New York City, says: "Even though I don't agree with them on certain legislative issues, they do some terrific work. We have to understand them and we should hope they will understand us. The only beneficiaries of these tensions and conflicts are people who are unconcerned about the strength and cohesiveness of the Jewish community."

National Agudah organizations in other countries—with the exception of Israel, where Agudath Israel formed a political party of its own— do not take part in partisan politics, and no member would accept a political office requiring the administering of laws that run contrary to the teachings of the Torah. Yet the organization has proven adept at using the political process to its advantage. Under Sherer's leadership, the national organization has become increasingly aggressive in expounding its views on public policy, asserting its rights and demanding a share of public funding. Indeed, Rabbi Herman Newberger of Ner Israel Rabbinical College in Baltimore praises Sherer's "sensitivity to the political process."

The battle for minds—and money—is one that Agudath Israel is waging along traditional lines. "Any ideology, in order to survive," says Sherer, "must create practical projects. We must show there is a Torah way of doing things in a practical sense."

In charge of such projects is Rabbi Shmuel Bloom, administrative director of Agudath Israel, which has an estimated annual budget of $5 million. He is also responsible for the New York and California chapters. Previously, he headed Agudath Israel's Project COPE (Career Opportunities and Preparation for Employment), originally funded, in the early

1970s, by a grant from New York State. "We had to get [Jews] used to the idea of vocational training," Bloom says. "Jewish dropouts," he adds with a laugh, "are supposed to be people without master's degrees."

The project's original purpose was to train young Orthodox Jews who did not want to attend secular schools but needed to make what Bloom calls *parnassah*, a living. Today COPE serves both Orthodox and non-Orthodox Jews with a full range of services, from testing to job placement. It can place 80 to 85 percent of its graduates, a figure Bloom says is considered exceptionally high.

Another Agudath Israel project is the Southern Brooklyn Community Organization (SBCO), founded to reclaim the decaying Borough Park neighborhood that is home to one of New York's largest Orthodox communities. Rabbi Schmuel Lefkowitz, director of the organization since it began in a storefront in 1977, has seen his staff grow from three to 20 and funds for investment—initially underwritten by a Ford Foundation grant—increase from $100,000 to millions, with the help of the Federal Government, banks and other lenders.

Taking me for a drive around the Borough Park section of Brooklyn (SBCO now operates in Flatbush and Bensonhurst as well), which has nearly 100,000 Orthodox Jewish residents and more than 200 synagogues, Lefkowitz points to one of "his" houses, bought at a foreclosure sale for $13,000 and now worth at least $200,000.

There was poverty, crime and racial tension throughout the area when SBCO was created, he says. If the well-to-do had left, the entire neighborhood would have gone the way of many others in the city. He offered the example of Crown Heights and other areas that Jews had fled; yet they had nowhere to go. So the Orthodox community decided to make a stand.

SBCO grew out of a series of annual conferences initiated by Agudath Israel in 1975 to bring Jewish leaders, legislators and public administrators together to study community problems. "We literally went from door to door trying to get people to work with us and to raise money," says Lefkowitz, a social worker by training. "The day we opened our doors, Rabbi Sherer called his friend, [former Senator] Jack Javits. We also got to the Mayor's office immediately because no one was going to turn down an Agudath Israel request."

With volunteer help from attorneys, business owners and politicians, and funds from a wide variety of sources, SBCO demolished abandoned buildings, renovated others and built not only cooperative apartments—

with balconies for sukkoth—but a multiracial senior citizens center as well. (In fact, SBCO works closely with the local Hispanic, Italian-American and black groups.) Most of the housing is subsidized, and, to prevent speculation, owners of the low-cost cooperative apartments must offer them to SBCO if they contemplate selling within a specified number of years.

Not far from SBCO's cramped quarters is another Agudath Israel project begun in a storefront: the Fresh Start program, a multiservice center for displaced homemakers—women who have been separated, widowed or divorced. Begun in 1979, it is one of four such programs in New York City that are funded by the state and administered by ethnic and religious groups.

Divorce has increased among the Orthodox. However, because it is not usually sought or easily obtained, a woman may well have several young children to care for when she does separate from her husband, and may need counseling and financial assistance.

Of Fresh Start's clients, approximately 60 percent are Jewish (not necessarily Orthodox) women; 20 percent are other ethnic whites, and the remainder Hispanics.

Agudath Israel also continues to work to advance Orthodox education. It has positioned itself as "middleman" between most Orthodox schools in the nation—from the elementary to advanced Torah study level—and the local, state and Federal governments. Its Commission on Legislation and Government Affairs officially acts in behalf of Torah Umesorah, the association of elementary and secondary day schools, and AARTS, the association for Advanced Rabbinic and Talmudic Schools. Its director, attorney Steven Prager, and other commission members have had to become experts in local building and fire codes throughout the nation and in obtaining bus transportation for their constituents. For example, in New York, where the law offers students subsidized transportation to the nearest denominational school in their borough, Agudath Israel is also pressing for transportation to yeshivas on days when public schools are closed. In addition, it seeks bus transportation to special-education yeshivas, and a law enabling observant handicapped children to choose to attend such yeshivas even if special-ed programs are available in nearby public schools.

Agudath Israel has gained United States Department of Education accreditation for kollels, institutions for advanced Torah studies where students may be enrolled for many years. Many kollel students now receive grants given to graduate students at secular institutions.

Agudath Israel's government affairs office, aside from dealing with purely educational matters, presents the organization's positions on major national issues: school prayer (for); equal access to public buildings (against); the equal rights amendment (against). David Zwiebel, a young attorney who left the prestigious law firm of Paul Weiss Rifkind to join the Agudath staff, had favored the equal rights amendment before joining the Agudah staff in early 1984. He explains: Some scholars believe that by removing all classifications of sex, women could be drafted and that the state, as certifier of marriages, would be prohibited from discriminating against men who want to marry males.

"The language of E.R.A. is delightful," Zwiebel adds. "It's a principle in which we believe, but it raises too many broad, unanswered questions." He suggests that legislation be enacted to redress the shortcomings in current laws.

Two years ago, Agudath Israel scored major successes on the legislative front when, in the course of one month, the Governors of New York, New Jersey and Illinois signed into law Agudah-supported measures dealing with autopsy, divorce, Sunday burial and kashruth. Two of the signing ceremonies even took place at yeshivas.

Zwiebel has also sued New York City in behalf of Agudath Israel. At issue was a section of Mayor Koch's 1980 executive order instructing all organizations doing business with the city to refrain from discriminating against homosexuals in their hiring practices. The Salvation Army and the Roman Catholic Archdiocese of New York filed parallel suits.

New York's human rights laws had previously exempted religious organizations from compliance. Agudath Israel, claiming that the Mayor had no authority to issue it, asked the courts to declare the executive order unconstitutional. Last June, New York's Court of Appeals, the state's highest court, ruled that the Mayor did not, indeed, have the authority to ban sexual discrimination by the three organizations filing suit. The court said that religious groups cannot be held to the same standards as government.

The decision to bring suit against the city was made by Agudath Israel of America's board of directors, and was sanctioned by the organization's presidium, composed of Orthodox rabbis in their 50s and 60s. Whenever the presidium is split or deals with an issue of exceptional importance or sensitivity, the matter is put before the Council of Torah Sages, rabbis in their 70s, 80s and 90s. It was the council that had declared back in 1956: "It is forbidden by the law of our sacred Torah to be a member of and to participate in . . . any organization . . . composed of Reform and Conservative 'rabbis.' " In 1967, Rabbi Moshe Feinstein, chairman of the council, went further, denouncing Orthodox participation in ecumenical dialogues.

In the long run, says Sherer, "our hope is to self-destruct."

"Why not?" he says, when I laugh. "If we have an educated mass, we have fulfilled Agudath Israel's aim." He pauses. "I have faith."

Aharon Appelfeld

Matthew Nesvisky

Multiple ironies surround the fact that for thousands of readers Aharon Appelfeld has suddenly become *the* Israeli voice on the Holocaust.

Part of the irony is in the rapid rise of this acclaim. After laboring in Hebrew for nearly three decades, reaching a limited number of Israeli readers, Appelfeld only recently attracted worldwide attention when his translated work began to appear. Since 1980, four Appelfeld novels— "Badenheim 1939," "The Age of Wonders," "Tzili: The Story of a Life" and "The Retreat"—have been published in English and many European languages. Appelfeld says the publisher of the latter two books, E.P. Dutton, plans to print all 20 of his volumes of fiction and essays.

His works in translation have won a warm reception in both Jewish and non-Jewish circles. Moreover, after spending nearly all his adult life in Israel, Appelfeld is now frequently invited abroad to talk about himself and his writing. One result of this prominence is that the 52-year-old author has become identified as Israel's spokesman, or at least its representative literary figure, on the Holocaust.

However, Appelfeld insists he has no interest in or intention of being "a spokesman to the world," and is "not really a Holocaust writer." And a close look at what Appelfeld says—and doesn't say—indicates that actually he may not be the sort of writer who would endear himself to many of the overseas readers who enthusiastically embrace him.

"I am first and last a Jewish writer," he says emphatically. "That means I write for Jews, and, even then, only for a small, select number of Jews, a certain intelligentsia. I am not a popular writer. And I am not writing what is called 'Holocaust literature.' I view that term as a stigma. I'm just telling stories about Jews—to Jews—at a certain period in their history."

Appelfeld in conversation is remarkably like Appelfeld on the page: seemingly straightforward, brief and to the point, yet always suggestive of much more. His is a quality of exposition and narration that, despite his disclaimers, makes his work readily accessible to large numbers of readers. But while some critics suggest that Appelfeld's stories do not contain much more than meets the eye, many intellectual readers take the patent simplicity of his tales as proof of deeper meanings below the surface.

"I admit straight out that I am a minimalist," he says. "I'm as much interested in the unsaid word as in the stated word—perhaps even more. There happens to be a great tradition in Jewish literature concerned with the unsaid word. It begins with the Bible, which is probably my greatest single influence. I read at least a chapter of the Bible or Midrash every day.

"Now the Bible is well known for what it doesn't say. It doesn't go into much detail about setting and character, describing how people look or even how they think. It relates actions in a straightforward manner, and that's about it. It allows action, which is what we can observe, to reveal character, motivations and so on. This spare narrative technique is balanced stylistically with simple, short sentences and unadorned language."

He continues: "I find this a most effective way of telling Jewish stories. This is what I strive for in my own writing—first, to eliminate everything that isn't essential; second, to invest a proper function and significance in everything that remains. Why give 500 details when the correct 25 will do the job?"

Appelfeld, a professor in the department of Hebrew literature at the Ben-Gurion University of the Negev, teaches comparative Jewish literature. He has found that the pattern of spare narration is a long-standing tradition which he sees running from the Bible through Franz Kafka—a writer to whom Appelfeld is often compared.

"Yes," he points out, "I think my writing is influenced by two traditions, the biblical and the 20th-century European, of which I, of course, am myself a product. If my work has echoes of both Kohelet [Ecclesiastes] and Kafka, that's because I see them both in the tradition of Jewish minimalist literature."

The most striking "unsaid" element in Appelfeld's work is the horror of the Holocaust. He simply doesn't deal with it explicitly – and, for a writer whose work is labeled "Holocaust literature," this seems curious indeed.

"Badenheim 1939," for example, depicts a community of Jews in a state of anxiety on the eve of the outbreak of World War II. "The Age of Wonders" concerns an Austrian Jewish family reacting to the growing threat of anti-Jewish persecution. "Tzili" is about a Jewish girl who is separated from her family at the beginning of the war and spends the rest of the Nazi era in the forests, removed from the European nightmare. All the books share a paucity of detail concerning the "facts" of the Holocaust; in "Tzili" there is virtually no time or place reference, and the word "Germans" appears only once in passing. Appelfeld explains this by saying he is not the least interested in "documentations."

"Many other writers do that sort of thing," he says. "But, on the one hand, I don't think it is quite possible to convey the enormity of what we have come to call the Holocaust – on the other, there is a tendency among many writers of such literature to 'sweeten' the image of the victims and to 'demonize' the Nazis. I'm not interested in doing any of that, because I think it leads to distortions of the truth. It's bad art, and a kind of exploitation of the Holocaust, even if the writer's intentions are the best. What must be judged in the end is the quality of the storytelling, and its truth."

Appelfeld says his writing is not intended to provide either entertainment or information. Nor, he insists, is he trying to "work through" his own personal traumatic history.

"It's usually pointed out," he says, "that I draw on my own experience for my stories and novels. I acknowledge that. Yet I have no interest in writing autobiography. That would be merely memoir, and I don't want to be a slave to my memories. Memory is only one tool. Memory can't create a story; the artist must. So I objectify my own experience by recreating it in the stories of others."

Beyond that, Appelfeld observes that in truth he does not recall much of the Holocaust. He was only eight years old when the Nazis poured into his native Czernovitz in Romania. His mother died and he was separated from the rest of his family. (He was to find his father in Israel years later.)

Young Aharon fled to the forests and was adopted by a roaming band of older refugee boys. Later he spent some time as a cook's helper in the Soviet army. By war's end he was in Italy; from there he was sent by Youth Aliyah to Palestine.

Whether or not he was spared some of the worst experiences of the Holocaust is moot. The essential point is that he writes what he knows about and is uninterested in trying to recreate someone else's experiences.

In this sense, one does not come away from Appelfeld's books with an enhanced understanding of the Holocaust. And, even if this is the reader's expectation, it is not Appelfeld's intention.

"I am interested only in Jewish stories," he says, "things that happen to Jews, and how they respond, at a certain period in Jewish history. My stories are not necessarily set in this particular time and place because I happened to be there in my youth, but because this particular time and place were crucial in Jewish history, and in fact became the main issue of 20th-century Jewish life."

Herein lies the greatest of the incongruities related to Aharon Appelfeld. Though his work has been embraced by diaspora Jews more than that of any other Israeli writing about the Holocaust, it implies harsh criticism of the very idea of the diaspora.

The Holocaust, as Appelfeld sees it, was an inevitable event in Jewish history — or, conversely, this so-called Jewish "fate" was actually a result of the unnatural condition of Jews living as strangers in a strange land.

"We all know what the diaspora has meant," Appelfeld explains. "It has meant a perverted way of life, a confusion of identity, at its worst manifested in self-hatred. Imagine, self-hatred! It's not a condition that affects Frenchmen or Englishmen — just Jews. The response to this is the attempt to escape via assimilation, and we see where that leads. My family was 'assimilated.' My characters are usually striving for 'assimilation.' But aside from confounding their identity, it had no effect. It certainly was of no help in averting the fate that awaited the Jews in the *golah* [exile]."

Is Appelfeld suggesting that such a fate awaits Jews in the diaspora today? Understandably, he answers with even more than usual care in his choice of words.

"Look," he replies, "I can go only by my own experience. I came from

what was considered the most enlightened society of its time. My family
was as much of that culture as one could hope to expect. And look what
happened.

"But it's not for me to make comparisons. I'm a storyteller, not a
prophet. Readers can decide these things for themselves. I'm not a
preacher, or a teacher, or a propagandist or anything like that. I'm simply
a Jewish writer addressing myself to a Jewish audience."

For some, this may sound too oblique. Actually, Appelfeld's novels
often generate precisely that sort of reaction.

The Jews in the resort town of Badenheim continue their holiday,
even as the signs of their eventual doom loom larger and larger. The
father in "The Age of Wonders" insists that, because he is a respected
Austrian writer, anti-Semitism cannot touch him; his defense mechanisms range from denial to denigration of his fellow Jews to pathetic
attempts to flee from what is Jewish in himself. And Tzili, with only a
modicum of Jewish identity, wanders from place to place, buffeted by
events, kept alive only by a sort of animal awareness of the vitality in the
fields and forests where she lives.

All these stories, Appelfeld stresses, illustrate "the self-destruction that
preceded the destruction." Many readers may miss this "unsaid" point—
and at least one critic believes Appelfeld is more critical of the victims of
the Holocaust than of its perpetrators. Yet it would seem that, by
personal example, Appelfeld has suggested what he believes are two
proper responses to what he calls "the Jewish fate." The first is to remove
himself from the diaspora by living in the Jewish state. The second is his
religious observance.

"I've concluded," he says, "that one cannot be a Jew without being
religious. For me, it's simply a part of the definition of Jews. I don't
believe we can talk about a Jewish culture without including the element
of religious ritual and observance. [Though] I came from a totally
nonobservant family, I learned from what happened to Europe's Jews."

Appelfeld describes his level of religious observance as being akin to
that of America's Conservative Jews. He follows the dietary laws and
observes the Sabbath, but says that his daily reading of the Bible is
more a literary pursuit than a religious practice. For many years, he lived
with his Argentine-born wife, Yehudit, and their three children in
an Orthodox Jerusalem neighborhood, so that his family could

"experience the life of a Jewish street." For the past four years, however, the Appelfelds have lived in Mevasseret Zion, an exclusive suburb of Jerusalem.

"For me," he says, "being religiously observant is the only way of life for a Holocaust survivor. Every religious Jew who went through the Nazi period came out with his faith reinforced. Assimilated Jews either drew the proper conclusions, as I did, or deceived themselves by strange rationalizations. Not that I'm making any judgments; it's just the way I see things."

Readers of Appelfeld's works will find no such judgments. Nor will they find any didacticism in favor of religious tradition, or living in Israel. What they will find is a cool, detached statement: behold these Jews, behold how they lived, behold what befell them.

Uncritical readers, carried along by Appelfeld's strong linear narrative flow, perhaps will miss the message. Others may nod their heads and applaud Appelfeld for "telling it as it was." More sensitive readers may become uncomfortably aware that the author is clearly presenting a message: they may be moved to ask themselves how they measure up to Appelfeld's relentless depiction of how and where a Jew chooses to live his life.

Because this message is couched in severely economical prose, it may easily be overlooked. Early critics of Appelfeld dismissed him as having nothing to say; in the early 1960s at least one Israeli critic thought he had written himself out. Another critic even uncharitably suggested that Appelfeld was awarded the 1983 Israel Prize for Literature on the strength of his sudden acceptance abroad. His defenders, however, say such attitudes are a response to Appelfeld's preference for a subtle expression of ideas that are not readily comprehended by the average reader.

Appelfeld's translator, Dalya Bilu, finds that his prose is "a very simple rhythmic and poetic sort of Hebrew but, above all, a very personal sort of language. This makes it difficult to convey all his subtleties. And it makes for a deceptively easy kind of reading, especially because Aharon places so much meaning between the words."

Occasionally, Appelfeld produces a poetic figure of speech — not always with the happiest of results, as in this line from "Tzili": "The air and light kneaded her limbs with a firm and gentle touch." Such flights, however are rare. If a reader is halted or even mildly irritated by anything in Appelfeld's prose, this may stem from his resolute refusal to describe or explain more than he thinks is necessary.

Appelfeld's stories are as spare as a Giacometti figure—or, perhaps, in F. Scott Fitzgerald's more telling phrase, "as thin as a repeated dream."

Like dreams, Appelfeld's refashioned memories are conveyed with minimal detail, repeated patterns and flat characters. Aside from what his characters do, or what is done to them, we know little about them. And, as in dreams, these people and things around them sometimes take on symbolic significance, like the trains which figure so prominently in "Badenheim" and "The Age of Wonders."

Appelfeld rather typically comments: "I don't have to intentionally invest symbolic significance in anything. Our history, in fact, has given trains a symbolic meaning for Jews. Certain things have meanings for us that simply don't have to be stated."

Appelfeld's statement suggests how, like his dreams, his novels seem to emerge directly from his subconscious—and strongly resonate in the subconscious of his readers. For it is the unexpressed language of the Jewish condition that is the essence of Appelfeld's books.

Aufbau

Carol Ascher

I
t was 7:30 on a dark October evening, a time when most elderly New Yorkers remain in the safety of their apartments. Yet a crowd of well-dressed men and women in their 70s, 80s and 90s—still active physicians, lawyers, professors, journalists and poets—filled the wood-paneled hall of the Leo Baeck Institute, on Manhattan's Upper East Side, for the opening of an exhibit highlighting the 50-year history of Aufbau. Though some wore hearing aids and a few carried canes, every back was erect as they listened to the elegant German of tall, white-haired Will Schaber, the self-appointed Aufbau historian. Also listening were visitors from the West German Consulate. Standing in the rear were a handful of younger, second-generation German Jews like me.

Though they had come to celebrate their German-language newspaper's jubilee anniversary, for most this event was clearly an odd, bittersweet celebration—which, for all the pride they felt, recalled how long they have lived in exile.

Foreign-language newspapers created by immigrants are no rarity in the United States, or in any other country that opens its doors to newcomers. One result of the Nazi era was the founding of more than 400 newspapers-in-exile around the world, in such places as Amsterdam, Paris, Buenos Aires and Tel Aviv. Most, however, folded as their readers moved on to havens of greater safety or better prospects, or else assimilated into their new societies, where they found their heritage a source of pain and confusion. Yet, 50 years after its inception, Aufbau (meaning reconstruction or rebuilding) has a circulation of more than 12,000. (An issue mailed to a nursing home may reach 20 to 30 avid readers.) Though most subscribers live in New York, Chicago, Los Angeles and several Florida cities, a few thousand copies are sent by airmail each week to Argentina, Israel, West Germany and the Soviet Union. The paper even has a subscriber in Tasmania, an elderly Protestant missionary who fled Germany in the 1930s after he was put on a Nazi hit list.

Aufbau was founded in New York City in 1934, partly as the natural outgrowth of a decade-old, small but growing German Jewish club, and partly as a response to the growing dangers facing Jews in Europe. For the first 10 years, the club was devoted to social and literary activities, whose schedules were laboriously typed on penny postcards, then in brief monthly programs that carried advertisements. Shortly after the Reichstag elections in 1933, the club's officers decided to expand the circular into a monthly newsletter aimed at the increasing number of displaced German Jews arriving in New York.

"This was an exceedingly ambitious plan for a small group of young immigrants still struggling for their own existence," recalls Eric deJonge, then president of the German-Jewish club and one of Aufbau's founders. "A bare majority [of the club] was persuaded that a contemplated search list for friends and family members in this paper would have merit."

In its early years, the fledgling Aufbau subsisted on club-membership contributions and volunteer labor. (Significantly, it was banned in Germany in 1935.) By the late 1930s, it had become a prospering weekly, with a paid editor, Manfred George, formerly the chief editor of a small evening paper in Berlin specializing in theater and film. A robust figure, George was the paper's energetic and creative head until 1964.

Throughout the 1930s, the newspaper concentrated on ways to help its refugee readers: printing information about jobs and housing opportunities, opening its columns to those wishing to advertise their skills and wares, providing guidance on common American expressions and explaining financial rules and marriage and divorce laws, as well as strange American customs. (In an early cartoon, a woman in dainty underwear complains to her already savvy, top-hatted consort in a mishmash of German and English: "I don't know *wie ich mich* dress *soll* for *de maskenball* from German Jewish club." He replies, "*Das mach nix*, Selma.

Anything goes.") Clearly, an America vastly different from their Central European homelands astounded and delighted the refugees.

As the campaign against Jews in Central Europe intensified, Aufbau tried to stir American Jews to action by increasingly carrying news of events from overseas. A July 1942 headline read: "The Conspiracy of Silence." Reporting that one million Jews had already perished, the article warned, "Do not turn away, listen to the cries of the Jews of Europe." One Aufbau contributor, Robert Kempner, who worked for United States intelligence, broke the news of the January 1942 Wannsee Conference, the meeting in a Berlin suburb where Nazi officials first spoke openly about their plans for the "Final Solution." Throughout the war, Aufbau was one of the few papers to report on the Holocaust. It also found its way across the Atlantic. Hans Steinitz, Aufbau's editor since 1964, remembers seeing the paper more than once while an inmate in Gurs, a concentration camp in the French Pyrenees. In an environment where any news of Jews was treasured, he says, "It was a sensation—a revelation."

In this country, Aufbau also played an important role in developing the growing body of émigré writers. According to Will Schaber, who edited a collection of Aufbau pieces, "Aufbau/Reconstruction" (1972), "Manfred George had a special knack for discovering and using the journalistic talents of freelancers outside the staff." The working-class novelist Oskar Maria Graf, the pacifist Fritz von Unruh, the philosopher Karl Jaspers and the writer Stefan Zweig were among the many who used Aufbau as a platform for their views.

Increasingly, the paper became activist. During World War II it raised money to buy a fighter plane, collected maps of German cities from its readers for use in American aerial bombings, organized its women readers into Red Cross sewing groups and opened its columns to the campaign led by the philosopher-writer Hannah Arendt and Joseph Maier, author of the newspaper's weekly biblical interpretation column, for the establishment of an all-Jewish army. Aufbau also took a strong lead in insisting on the distinction between German Jews, who needed American help, and Germans, who were enemy aliens.

All the same, in urging wholehearted support of the war effort, the paper veered toward "uncritical patriotism," according to Will Schaber. Thus, when Presidential inaction prevented refugee-filled ships from landing in the New York harbor, the newspaper did no more than quietly report the incident.

Roosevelt's death in April 1945 was mourned with an admiring obituary by Thomas Mann, an occasional contributor, who wrote: "Here was someone who, for the first time, understood everything, knew everything, saw everything." (Aufbau's large boardroom walls are still adorned by three photographs: of Thomas Mann, Albert Einstein, who often attended Aufbau functions, and F.D.R.)

Yet Aufbau was fearless about its country of origin. While the war raged, Aufbau published articles by Mann, Arendt and the philosopher Paul Tillich on the future of postwar Germany. It was a wide-ranging and lengthy debate, centering around such questions as whether Germany should be decentralized, with its heavy industries banned forever, or whether a democratic Germany could be rebuilt, to which exiled German Jews might consider returning some day. For many Aufbau readers who refused to buy German products, travel on a Lufthansa plane (as a state-owned airline, it had been Nazi-operated) or ever consider returning to their native land, the debate was painful and at times acrimonious. (Indeed, my mother, a refugee from Berlin, would not drive a Volkswagen until the 1970s.)

Before and during the war, thousands of German Jews were separated from their families in the deportation process, in concentration camps and, in some cases, during hiding and escapes from country to country.

Aufbau offered survivors free space for notices aimed at locating lost relatives. "Jackobson, Ludwig, Jenny, Sylvia (deported to Theresienstadt from Berlin, Charlottenberg, Droyenstrasse, 1942) [sought] by Lotte Weiss, 26 Sandringham Drive, Moortown, Leeds, England," read a typical notice. Another, by two sons, one in Cuba, the other in Monaco, announced: "We are looking for our Mother: Bertha Mucke-Friedman, formerly from Breslau, deported from Beausoleil, France, 1942." In addition, Jewish agencies such as the Hebrew Immigrant Aid Society ran notices in the paper in behalf of long lists of individuals.

The paper also played a key role in the war-crimes trials of leading Nazis. As early as 1941, it began actively soliciting information from its readers on torture, forced labor and concentration camps under the Nazi regime, as well as on specific Nazis. Robert Kempner, then a member of the United States prosecution team at Nuremberg, who reported regularly on the trials for the paper, used much of the information collected from readers.

Several times, Aufbau's reports served as evidence for the prosecution.

When the trials ended, Aufbau demanded that untried war criminals be systematically tracked down. When the American High Commissioner in Germany began shortening prison terms for Nazis for good behavior, the paper reacted with outrage. (And, it was Aufbau's Kempner who, in 1969, revealed that a right-wing German organization was raising money to assist imprisoned Nazis.)

Aufbau hailed the creation of a Jewish state by the United Nations in 1947 as a "wonder." Yet, in an editorial which previewed its critical but deeply partisan eye, Manfred George wrote: "This is a beginning, not an ending . . . the land was the prerequisite. The rebuilding and its means of building remain the goal. It remains the goal not to form this Jewish land into any state, but into a model state, into a state of a people who have experienced . . . the mistakes and failures of so many other countries." By the Six-Day War in 1967, editor Hans Steinitz was cautioning Israel about the rights of Arab refugees. It was a position, like many taken since, that set the editors against the more conventional views of some of their readers. (I once wrote an article on censorship on the West Bank and in the Gaza Strip and Aufbau published it.) But it is generally agreed that many Aufbau readers like to find bold, even courageous opinions in the paper.

Aufbau had a circulation of 55,000, its largest, from the 1950s to the 1970s, when it was the newspaper which published news of West German Supreme Court decisions and changes in rules concerning reparation payments to those who had suffered at the hands of the Nazis. (It was, incidentally, a German Jewish psychologist writing for Aufbau who developed the theory of "post-survivor trauma," opening up an entirely new approach to restitution.) The concept of reparations, or *Wiedergutmachung* (literally, to make good again) may have provoked feelings of ambivalence in those who felt there was no way the Germans could "make good again." Yet lives, jobs, property and education had been lost, and some were gratified by the German government's willingness to compensate them.

For more than 20 years, until the late 1970s, Aufbau carried a biweekly legal supplement on restitution matters—a "must" for lawyers handling such cases. At the same time, the paper's analyses of reparation payments were regular, hurtful reminders to many Jews here and elsewhere that their only bridge to their homeland might, perhaps, be some kind of claim on their own behalf.

In the late 1960s, Aufbau began a campaign called "The Stepchildren of Restitution" that focused attention on Austria, which asserted it had no obligation to its former citizens, since the Nazi regime there had originated in Germany. Gradually, however, as a result of Aufbau's pressure, the Austrian Government relented, at first by including former Austrian Jewish citizens in its excellent social security system and later by agreeing to return confiscated art objects to their Jewish owners.

As the newspaper of German Jews, often mocked for their tendency to assimilate, Aufbau has had a record of longevity that may be inexplicable. Directed to a group whose members quickly mastered both spoken and written English, it has nevertheless continued publishing in German. Certainly, the paper's service role cannot be underplayed, from its search notices and restitution information, to its weekly page of religious information, including biblical interpretation, to its increasingly numerous death notices—complete with "formerly of Hamburg" or of another city under the name of the deceased. All the same, there are those German Jewish exiles who avoid reading anything in German— "Hitler's language," they call it—yet borrow worn copies of Aufbau when they learn it has printed new information about reparations.

Today's Aufbau continues to be intelligently written and edited, progressive and occasionally laced with a touch of sly humor. Reporting on Germany, Aufbau's coverage ranges from the antinuclear movement to the possibility of open borders between East and West Germany. Though it fully supports the struggle of Soviet Jewry (a Russian-speaking emigré covers the topic), the paper leans more toward detente than hysterical anti-Communism. Generally critical of Reagan, when the President was reelected last November, Aufbau ran an article with the double-entendre headline, "*Vier Weitere Reagan-Jahre*" or "Four More Years of Rain." Editor Hans Steinitz, a witty man who resembles Jean-Paul Sartre, came to the United States after the war as a foreign correspondent for several German newspapers. A thoughtful political analyst and independent thinker, whose editorials delight readers, Steinitz represents the best of the journalistic tradition. At a time when so much journalism in the United States is marred by shabbiness and sensationalism, Aufbau continues to represent dignity and caring to its readers.

In recent years, three new staff members, all born during the war and all non-Jews, have joined Aufbau. Gert Niers, previously a teacher and freelance journalist in Dresden, is now executive editor; Hermann

Pichler, who worked on a daily in Vienna, is in charge of city news, and Lisa Sparbrod, formerly a newspaper reporter in Hamburg, has taken over the women's page. Niers's and Pichler's fathers respectively were in the German and Austrian armed forces; Sparbrod's father was in the Nazi Waffen S.S. For all three, working at Aufbau is clearly making a kind of restitution; all are grateful for the absence of prejudice they've experienced as Christian Germans. Before moving to New York, Pichler lived in Israel for a year, where he met his American Jewish wife. Niers, who is also writing a doctoral dissertation on three exiled German-Jewish women poets, explained: "It's important for us to come to grips with what happened." And, gesturing at the busy, old Aufbau office, he added: "It's very rewarding to be here, like receiving a present you didn't really deserve."

"We're all here for the next 5 to 10 years—until the last person who made the trek from Hamburg to Shanghai to New York or Palm Beach dies," Sparbrod explained to me with a passion not usually heard in newspaper offices. Yet throughout its 50-year history, Aufbau has always engendered a rare and passionate dedication on the part of readers and contributors alike—a fact which is understandable when one realizes that, as Will Shaber said, "Aufbau *ist unser Heimat*"—or, loosely translated, "Aufbau has provided a home away from home." It's a home that has helped create a community out of a dispersed people. The active and energetic crowd of elderly German Jews who turned up to celebrate their newspaper's anniversary that October night in New York could easily be duplicated in Los Angeles, Sao Paulo or Tel Aviv.

Brandeis University

Sylvia Rothchild

N o school in the United States ever grew so fast," says Chancellor Abram Sachar. "When we started out in 1948 I thought it might take a century to put such a university together, but over eighty buildings were put up by one president in his twenty years of service."

Dr. Sachar, radiating energy and enthusiasm that belie his eighty-one years, was that president, and he is no more modest about his achievements than he should be. During his tenure he raised millions and became known as the nation's preeminent academic fund-raiser. He also was widely respected as the head of the only Jewish-sponsored, nonsectarian university in the United States, an institution which has always encouraged innovation and eagerly pursued excellence.

Ten years ago Dr. Sachar turned the presidency over to a younger man but he is still a presence on the campus, in a building that bears his name. He has no administrative duties but when asked what a chancellor does his eyes twinkle and he says, "He *chancelles*." Sachar still raises money for Brandeis. He's especially interested in scholarships and loans that will ease the tuition burden of middle-income students. Mainly, though, his door is open to students, parents, faculty, Brandeis contributors and journalists; he likes to discuss problems and complaints, to chat and reminisce.

And students like to talk with him. They see him as an empathetic grandfather figure who always understands and approves. "He's really interested in me as a person," said one young man. "He makes me feel he cares about what I do with my life." Sachar, in turn, boasts like a grandfather about how smart they are, how many graduate cum laude, how generous they are later as alumni.

His style of greeting visitors is flattering. The genial smile, immediate eye contact and firm handshake disarm those in awe of meeting so charismatic a figure, whose *A History of the Jews* is now in its twenty-sixth edition. He expresses special affection for the "concerned" and "compassionate" young people who have dared and still dare to confront the university and scold the trustees when they object to the university's policies.

When he recalls the turbulent sixties, he doesn't speak of rebels or radicals but of "gadflies." He remembers Angela Davis, a black philosophy student who was one of Brandeis' most famous rebels, as "a lovely girl and Phi Beta Kappa besides, who came under the influence of Herbert Marcuse." The late Marcuse is described by Sachar as, "the maverick in philosophy and politics who achieved national prominence as a radical guru."

Older faculty members share Dr. Sachar's nostalgia for the pioneering years. "Brandeis had to exist," said one, recalling its precarious beginnings. "It had to be excellent. It couldn't fail no matter how sorely it was tested." Others noted that Brandeis was most unusual in receiving accreditation in only five years and Phi Beta Kappa recognition in thirteen. Many describe the university's accomplishments as if they were personal triumphs. They recall the exhilarating first decade or so, when there were an unusual number of "stars" on the faculty.

Sachar's early faculty included novelist Ludwig Lewisohn, journalist-historian Max Lerner, psychologist Abraham Maslow, the Judaic scholars Nahum N. Glatzer and Alexander Altmann, Leonard Bernstein and Aaron Copland from the musical world and world-famous individuals such as Eleanor Roosevelt and Pierre Mendès-France, who lectured as faculty members.

Today, though Brandeis is still known as a high-powered intellectual place with high standards of teaching and research, few such "stars" shine on campus. The present administration under President Marver H. Bernstein—who came to Brandeis from Princeton—concerns itself mainly with balancing the budget, with stabilization and conservation. This inevitably inspires some faculty people to grumble about "slowing down," "loss of the spirit of adventure" and the like.

The history of the university is in the memories and the files of those who watched it grow. Sachar wrote about it in his book, A Host At Last, describing his administration from the conception of the university to its rapid establishment as a prestigious small university in which the Jews are hosts, not guests.

Brandeis' story begins with Middlesex College, a medical and veterinary school founded in 1926 on the present campus in Waltham, Massachusetts by Dr. John Hall Smith. A high-minded Boston surgeon, he was outraged by the efforts of the Massachusetts Medical Association to prevent aspiring Jewish doctors and veterinarians from entering a tightly held, largely Protestant monopoly. Smith committed his personal fortune to creating an institution with no racial or religious restrictions. Middlesex welcomed Jewish students and in its last years employed many professors who had fled Hitler's Europe. But the medical association withheld accreditation, and in 1946 the college was brought to bankruptcy and collapse.

When the director of the humanities department at Middlesex went looking for Jewish support in 1946 to try to save the school, he met Dr. Israel Goldstein, a rabbi of an influential New York Conservative congregation with experience in the councils of Conservative Judaism and Zionism. Like Smith, Goldstein was outraged by the unfair practices of many medical schools and their treatment of Jewish applicants and was looking into the possibility of developing a Jewish-sponsored college that could cope with the problem of discrimination.

Goldstein's committee and a counterpart committee in Boston negotiated for the ninety acres and the few dilapidated buildings that made up Middlesex College. Disagreements about style and objectives led to the loss of support of Albert Einstein, an early backer, Goldstein and the New York members of the committee. The Bostonians then took on the job of raising money for the school without their help—not an easy task in a period when people were also raising money for refugees in displaced persons camps and for the new state of Israel. Two years after the first steps had been taken, however, a liberal arts college named for Supreme Court Justice Louis Dembitz Brandeis was a reality. Sachar, then a member of the history faculty of the University of Illinois and national director of the B'nai B'rith Hillel Foundation, became its first president.

John P. Roche, a member of Brandeis' political science faculty in the early years, described Dr. Sachar as, "a strange mixture of scholar, dreamer and impresario," but his role in the birth of Brandeis was more like that of a midwife. The eight Boston founding fathers were unlike any other group of men who had ever committed themselves to establishing a university. Five of them had not attended any college; four were immigrants who had learned English in night classes. But all of them had made modest fortunes, prompting Sachar to describe them as "Horatio Alger types." Members of the generation that was driven to educate their children beyond themselves, they had great respect for learning, and philanthropy was part of their tradition. For them, supporting Brandeis was good for Jews, for America and for their self-esteem.

In his role as a fundraiser, Abram Sachar gave people opportunities to feel good about themselves, to see their names on doorways, libraries and laboratories, as donors to a distinguished place of learning. In his time men who had not graduated from high school marched in cap and gown in academic processions and their photographs appeared in the press next to those of scholars and celebrities. "Safaris to Boston" were arranged for businessmen from New York and other cities so they could share in the development of the university.

In the beginning there was much agonizing among the founders, the contributors and the faculty about Brandeis' image and objectives— about whether it should strive to be a Jewish version of Harvard, Princeton or Haverford—should be large or small, experimental or traditional, humanities or science-oriented, bookish or athletic, a Jewish university committed to Jewish life and learning or a non-sectarian school. Questions were also raised about the student body. Should Brandeis be a refuge for students who could not enter other universities because of restrictive quotas or should it accept only those with the highest academic and personal qualifications? Sachar believed the university could be a refuge for faculty members who had trouble in other places but should be very selective with students.

The university soon became a composite of all the possibilities open to it. Dr. Sachar found it ironical that Brandeis had an athletic center before it had a library. This came about because Abraham Shapiro, the man who subscribed the first $50,000 for Brandeis, earmarked the funds for the Shapiro Athletic Center. Shapiro, born in Lithuania, came to the United States via South Africa. He had come to affluence through hard work in a small shoe business in Worcester and later expanded his wealth through investments in real estate. His many philanthropies included an emergency fund for those who came into hard times in the shoe industry. Shapiro was convinced that the image of the new Jewish university would be irreparably damaged if it attracted only bookish students. He wanted Brandeis to be a "normal, wholesome American institution," not overburdened by Jewish intellectualism.

Fortunately, other patrons were equally passionate about science, literature, social service, Jewish study, music, art—and libraries. The Women's Committee organized by eight women in Boston in 1948 developed into the largest friends-of-a-library movement in the world, with 60,000 members in 115 chapters all over the United States. Women who have never seen the campus have raised $14 million in the last thirty years to buy books for the various Brandeis libraries.

Said Sachar in his role as fund raiser, "Money doesn't give you a great program, but a great program creates sources of money." The image of the university was created by its leaders, he believed, not by the mass of students or a changing faculty.

A case could be made, however, for Brandeis as response to a time and a constituency. Those who remembered the years when Jews begged for admission to universities and medical schools believed it was important that the university be a model of academic excellence and racial and religious nondiscrimination. To them, Brandeis symbolized a new time for Jews in America: the end of the immigrant era and the beginning of Jewish success and assertiveness. The original supporters and many of the alumni, who now number 13,000, still think of Brandeis as the university that represents the Jewish people to the world. "We hear from alumni as soon as anything goes wrong," said an administrator. "Any controversy or adverse publicity is taken as an affront."

Sachar and his older faculty and administration associates—and President Bernstein and his colleagues of more recent vintage—look back with pride at the university's accomplishments. This year 2,875 under-graduate and 657 graduate students are enrolled at Brandeis. There are 347 fulltime faculty members teaching in four undergraduate schools with thirty departments and programs. The university has a graduate school, a school of social policy funded by government grants, a major bio-medical facility and excellent programs of music, art and drama. The Rose Museum offers changing exhibitions of contemporary art. The American Jewish Historical Society with its library and Yiddish film collection is important for the research of students and scholars. Three chapels provide an attractive setting for religious services for Jews, Catholics and Protestants. The buildings inherited from Middlesex—including the Castle that was the major building, now a posh dormitory—are lost among the laboratories, classrooms, dormitories, performance halls, athletic facilities and student and faculty centers. The pleasant suburban campus, with rolling lawns and manicured gardens, is an open, accessible place, in some respects an extension of Boston's cultural life.

Brandeis University celebrated its thirtieth anniversary on October 4, 1978. There was a two-day celebration with receptions and exhibitions of Louis D. Brandeis memorabilia. The birthday cake was fifteen feet high, most of it counterfeit confectionery, made of styrofoam, covered with two hundred pounds of white and blue frosting. The issues that concern administrators and students today are, however, real. There is concern about being over thirty, no longer the precocious, rapidly growing school, and fear that the place will lose its special quality.

The newest change in curriculum includes the study of history which many students avoided in the sixties. Students and faculty are organizing a more structured curriculum around a common core of knowledge. The dean of faculty, Jack Goldstein, sees the trend as "redressing the laissez faire of the sixties." In the mid- and late sixties, when many American campuses erupted with protests, Brandeis was often in the news.

Professor Leon Jick, who was the dean of students in those years, speaks of them as "a turning point in America," blaming the often reckless behavior of some students on "the demise of a hundred and fifty years of confidence in technology and faith in the religion of progress." Other faculty members, however, remember the "bright—altruistic—energetic—politically astute" students, and miss the vitality and spontaneity of "the searching kids" capable of "messianic fervor."

Professor Jacob Cohen, who teaches a course called "The Sixties: Continuity and Change in American Culture," claims that campus radicalism was "more myth than reality." He believes that decade was a time of elaborate and outrageous gestures inspired less by ideology than by fear of being drafted to fight in Vietnam, a war they perceived as unnecessary and unjust. Further, he asserts, support for civil rights and opportunities for minorities, especially blacks, was a major factor.

In most of the protests, he thinks there was an element of "as Jews you should understand." And, he points out, demonstrations that seemed ominous to faculty members (who conceived of the university as did Professor Milton Hindus: "a privileged sanctuary for intellectual life, not attuned to the outside world") were not in retrospect as threatening as some thought they were.

To protest or not to protest is almost a moot question today. Some students claim that faculty members encourage them to be disturbers of the intellectual peace when an issue is involved. Others say that many teachers frown on protest as wasting class time and giving the university bad publicity—which can hurt fund-raising efforts.

A small group, with the encouragement of Rabbi Albert A. Axelrad, the Hillel director and Chaplain, encourages students to assert themselves and use their student power by speaking out against university holdings in South Africa, for Soviet dissidents and through projects bettering the community. And in the student paper *The Justice,* one finds letters from students who are opposed to strikes and demonstrations and threaten to sue the university if their education is disrupted. Still, the majority goes about its business as usual and the image of Brandeis as radical is entirely undeserved.

Most of the teaching staff agrees that teaching is more pleasurable now than in the recent past. Students often describe themselves in the words Professor Bernard Reisman, director of the Hornstein program in American Jewish Communal Studies, uses about himself: "I'm a reformer, not a radical. I believe in the system, in ideological commitment, in a perspective that values individuals and communities, and in the need to work with institutions."

Just the same, there is nostalgia for the days of idealism and protest. Even some of the most serious, responsible conservative young people have been heard to say lately that it must have been wonderful to be young in the sixties—"having solidarity with brothers and sisters fighting the good fight." Occasional efforts to test their power often end up like memorials to the mythical heroes of the previous decade. One such episode occurred last May when a group of 250 students—the Divestment Movement with the support of the student senate, some faculty and even one South African student named Ranuga—took over the Administration

Building for three days. Attendance was down in all classes, especially during a strike on the two days before the Administration offices were occupied. The students believed they were educating the administration and trustees on the evils of apartheid. As a result, the trustees rejected the option of immediate divestment but voted to exercise shareholder action against corporations involved in causing "severe social injury." "It was all very rational and unemotional," said one of the leaders. "We chose our cause, which was to force the trustees to divest themselves of the university's investments in corporations doing business in South Africa. Then we formed committees, got 550 signatures on a petition, made back-up plans and let the media know." Keith Jenkins, the black president of the Student Senate, announced that "the passive students of the seventies were now displaced by the new radicals of the eighties."

President Marver Bernstein walked past the Administration Building protestors as if they were invisible and also ignored the thirty others who spent the night in the hallway of his office. "If only he had stopped to talk to us," said one protestor plaintively. "That was all we really wanted, you know." And, a new twist: the 1979 "radicals" were so eager to leave everything in tip-top condition that they took up a collection to pay the maintenance people for working overtime.

President Bernstein said he'd have preferred that the students collect money to establish a scholarship for a South African student as a sign of solidarity. But other administrators spoke affectionately and patronizingly of the "good kids"—the black students and the "sociology nuts" who had not lost their social consciousness and sense of ethical behavior. The trustees meanwhile also agreed that apartheid is evil but only minor gestures would be made toward changing the University's investment portfolio. Divestment would cost the University $60,000 or so in broker's fees alone, they claimed.

The legacy of the sixties is also evident in several Brandeis programs, and students of that generation and the present one take pride in the role they played in convincing the university that these are essential. An outstanding example is the department of Afro-American studies which was formed after the student protests in 1968. It offers more than twenty-five courses in African and Afro-American studies, including history, sociology, political development, drama, literature and also such specific courses as Comparative Study of Group Oppression, African Religions and Philosophy and Political Economy of the Third World.

Then, too, Brandeis continues its Transitional Year Program for minority students of potential who were poorly prepared in high school. (The drop-out percentage is still much higher than that of students who enter in the normal process.) It is still operative because students exert pressure to keep it alive.

Another 1960s achievement, now a Brandeis tradition, is the Waltham Project, which began as a tutoring program for poor local children in 1966. Later a Tenants Association, Children's Center and an Alternative Placement Program to provide jobs instead of jail sentences for selected offenders (which has funding from the Department of Justice) were added. More than 12 percent of the undergraduate body has participated in the project.

Among less dramatic volunteer efforts are visits to nursing homes by a volunteer group that conducts religious services and holiday programs. Other major causes taken up by students include a ban on capital punishment, prison reform, abortion reform, opposition to a renewed draft and support for conscientious objection, Israel, and the freedom to emigrate for Soviet Jewry.

Brandeis monitors itself constantly and thus discovered last year that the ten most popular majors were psychology, politics, biology, economics, sociology, English, history, American studies, biochemistry and chemistry. Nevertheless the Judaica and Jewish communal affairs departments are the only ones now expanding. The Lown School for Near Eastern and Judaic Studies, for instance, includes undergraduate and graduate departments with intensive teaching and research in ancient and modern Jewish thought. The school includes the Center for Jewish Communal Service, organized to further research and seminars in contemporary issues.

The department of Near Eastern and Judaic studies started in 1950 with three students and Professor Nahum N. Glatzer of Frankfurt University as its head. He and Professor Alexander Altmann, both now retired, were eminent scholars, elegant models of a synthesis of Jewish and non-Jewish intellectual life and masters of the secular, academic approach to Jewish study.

The department, headed today by Professor Marvin Fox, has always been a rigorous one. Doctoral students are required to know Aramaic, Greek and Assyrian as well as Hebrew. No courses are given in liturgy, theology or Hassidism; Talmud is taught only part-time. Professor Fox, like the men before him, emphasizes the secularity of his program. "We are not here to proselytize. We are not involved in our students' adherence to any rituals or practices," he says. This year more than 800 undergraduates took courses in the department, though only 100 majored there. Eighty spent all or part of their junior year at the Hiatt Institute in Israel, which offers opportunities to study Hebrew and Jewish history.

More than seventy percent of the student body is Jewish, chosen primarily on the basis of their academic records. Though efforts are constantly made to broaden the geographic base, a third of the class of 1982 comes from New York. Many students don't think of Brandeis as a "Jewish community." It is their first choice for other reasons—because it's small, close to Boston, has a good premedical school program, and so on. But an increasing number come because no classes are held on Jewish holidays, pork products are kept out of the cafeterias, a kosher kitchen provides meals for Orthodox students and Sabbath, holiday services and *minyanim* are held for men and women of all Jewish persuasions. Many yarmulkes and even some ritual fringes are visible at Brandeis. Religious students feel at home there.

Not so the blacks. Keith Jenkins, a black student from Huntington, Long Island who was the president of the student senate in 1979, said, "It's a culture thing. It's a great school but you're always adjusting to the Jewish environment, and sometimes you feel suppressed by the overwhelming quality of it." Another black student added, "I'm getting a real good education but I'm always aware that I'm learning about another culture, and the people around me aren't sensitive to my feelings."

Some Jewish students also voice uneasiness about the "oppressive Jewish climate." "I was never so aware of religion," said Stacey Simon, a senior from Los Angeles and editor of the student newspaper, *The Justice*. Before her Brandeis days she had tried Scientology, visited Jehovah's Witnesses and occasionally gone to Jewish services. "You can't adopt a religion just because you're born into it," she said. "You have to shop around." She admitted feeling uncomfortable with Orthodox Jews. "I don't know how to handle myself," she said without embarrassment.

Another senior, a young man from New Hampshire, was similarly uncomfortable with students who wear yarmulkes and say prayers before meals. "And there I am, and I don't know how to do it. I'm not against it, but I think of Judaism as something that's here if I need it. I think of it like a bigger family that I'm part of, but don't need at this time in my life."

A Jewish student from the West described the effect Brandeis and Sachar had on her secular, liberal, "slightly anti-Semitic" parents, who had no Jewish affiliations. "But then they met Dr. Sachar and he really turned them around. They were so impressed with him and this place that they went back home and sent a contribution to the Combined Jewish Appeal. They even offered to do fund-raising for it." She spoke as if this were a mystery beyond her comprehension.

The Russian emigres who long dreamed of studying at Brandeis admit that the Jewishness of the place is a kind of balm for their initial culture shock. "It is the best place to enter American society," said Uri Wechsler, one of the students. They appreciate the faculty and are appreciated in turn. Robert Szulkin, associate professor of Russian, is their friend and guru. He says they are exemplary students and wishes more funds were available to bring more Russians to the school. They work very hard in an environment they find both free and safe.

At first a visitor to Brandeis sees a microcosm of American society, looking much as the founding fathers hoped it would. It appears to be a carefree suburban campus with pretty girls in jeans and spiked heels, incredibly young-looking boys showing off on skateboards, few outward signs of seriousness. In the lobby of the Administration Building is a trophy case with evidence of the athletic accomplishments of Brandeis students. The school's baseball team leads in New England; it boasts national champions in soccer and a national-rank fencing team. All the athletic stars are black, Irish or Italian.

What is special about Brandeis, however, is not its apparently all-American atmosphere but its success in changing Jewish self-concepts and its response to the shifting styles, values and strengths of American Jewry. Professor Reisman thinks of it as "a kind of synthesis, an example of Jewish diversity with a minimum of conflict and also an example of interaction between Jews and the general society—the best of Diaspora life."

Actually the Brandeis spectrum appears to be less of a "synthesis" than a collage of conflicting styles and objectives, coexisting in spite of irritations, misunderstandings and competition for funds. All the generations are there. Some older faculty and administration people still feel that Jewish institutions are somehow a breach of the unwritten contract of assimilation in return for emancipation. Some faculty members believe Brandeis' most important contribution is to link Jewish faith and commitment and higher education. Others say such things as "It's an outrageous privilege to be a professor teaching the message of a complex society," and "It's the next best thing to being born to an independent fortune."

A complex and contradictory place, but unquestionably a Jewish gift to American higher education.

Camp Kinderland

Anita Diamant

Brigadoon," a popular musical fantasy of the 1940s, begins with two Americans stumbling on an idyllic Scottish hamlet which comes to life every hundred years for just one day.

Life is sweet and simple in this place, where ideals of cooperation, fellowship and love animate its people.

There is something resembling Brigadoon about Camp Kinderland in Tolland, Massachusetts. For Kinderland comes alive once each year—but for only two months. Located in the lush Berkshire Mountains, it presents an idyll of fresh air, new friendships, softball, swimming and other vacation activities for urban children—most of whom come from New York City. Other camps do so too. But Kinderland is unique. Each summer since 1923, it has tried to create a society based on the dreams of its leftist, secularist, Yiddishist founders.

Elsie Suller, the camp's dynamic director for the past thirty years, describes the dream she's seen come to life every summer as: "A world where Jews will not fear anti-Semitism, where blacks will not fear racism, where women will not fear sexism—a society where children can grow up without fear."

To her definition might be added the words painted in English and Yiddish on a brightly colored mural at the handball court: "Peace/ Shalom. Human beings are family—black, white, brown and yellow. All that's different are the colors. But all are the very same by nature."

Originally situated in Hopewell Junction, New York, where it remained for 48 years, Kinderland was launched sixty years ago by a group of left-wing Jews. The founding generations were workers – bakers, printers, furriers and needle trade workers.

Many mortgaged their homes to get the camp started. Some were members of the Jewish People's Fraternal Order, one of the ethnic fraternal organizations involved in the International Workers Order, a body often regarded as a "front group" for the American Communist Party.

In those days, when New York's Jewish left was flourishing, there was a dizzying assortment of Jewish socialists; some even ran for public office. Communists helped form and lead labor unions. To many of these people, the promise of the Russian Revolution was then fresh, uncompromised and inspiring; many were convinced that a socialist utopia was on the horizon.

The political commitment to a thoroughly secular future among some Jewish immigrants – for religion had no place in their lexicon – was mediated by a desire to retain their cultural, ethnic and linguistic heritage. So they established schools where their children could study Marxism and Yiddish, but not Hebrew, which was regarded as the "*finsterish*" – dark – language of religion. Parents didn't want the lessons of the *schulerin*, or secular Yiddish after-school programs, forgotten during the summer so Yiddish classes were a regular feature at their children's summer haven, Kinderland. Thus the camp slogan: "*Foon schule in kemp, foon kemp in schule*" ("From *schule* to camp, from camp to *schule*").

Kinderland was "an odd political configuration," as one camper-now-counselor puts it, recalling how the camp attracted a wide range of people from the Jewish-leftist community. Heated political debate, reflecting the diversity of political opinion and affiliation, went on constantly, she says, among the counselors and in Lakeland, the adjacent adult colony, on Sylvan Lake.

Kinderland managed to stay solvent in its early years and, by the late 1920s, was serving nearly 400 campers each summer. The camp population was at its height during and immediately after World War II, when the American Communist Party claimed more than a million members. In 1946, with 700 children, Kinderland was full to bursting. On weekends, the camp was inundated by visitors – mostly parents, grandparents and other family members – who watched the children sing and dance and Yiddish artists perform, and themselves often sat in the shade and schmoozed.

"What an awakening," exclaims Elsie Suller. "It was the cream of Yiddish culture. A bunch of fascinating people!" Those were the years when Kinderland attracted some of the "worker poets" publishing in the then-lively Yiddish press. Members of the Artef, an avant-garde, Communist-inspired theater troupe, were regulars at the camp.

Among them for thirty years was Edith Segal, a choreographer of political dances for the masses. The daughter of a cigar maker, greatly influenced by Isadora Duncan, an early exponent of modern dance, she created dances and poems commemorating the death of Lenin, the Spanish Civil War, the plight of American blacks.

A regular feature of camp life until the 1950s was the "White Salute," a high point of remembrance for Judy Rosenbaum, a Kinderland camper, then youth counselor and staff member and a senior staff member since 1978, who brought her seven-year-old son to camp last summer.

"There was a lot of pomp and splendor on Sunday," she reminisces. "We were all dressed in white, and we wore white polished shoes and different-colored bandannas. We'd gather and line up in marching formations and group around the flagpole. There was a big band of kids and counselors; I still remember the tune. We marched to the gate, singing a song, usually in Yiddish. And there were the dances, the 'Spectacles,' Edith Segal's panoramic dances. I remember 'The Ballad of Stalingrad,' with 120 dancers."

A lively picture of Kinderland—and of Lakeland—appears in a booklet prepared for the 1976 camp reunion, which drew some 2,000 people to Madison Square Garden. In prose and poetry, in Yiddish and English, and in vivid photographs, life at Kinderland is lovingly chronicled. There are pictures of Madame Sholom Aleichem and Paul Robeson visiting the camp. There are numerous snapshots of plays and "spectacles" mounted by Edith Segal. In one photo, a group of boys clusters around a table festooned with signs saying, "Keep Olympics out of Germany, 1928–30." And in another, a group of girls and boys holding guitars sit under a banner that reads "Freedom School."

Kinderlanders were among the first to enlist in the American Abraham Lincoln Brigade, which in the late 1930s fought in the Spanish Civil War. And when world war engulfed the world, the camp mourned sons lost in the fighting, as well as families and friends destroyed in the Holocaust.

In the 1950s, when the Cold War and the onslaughts of McCarthyism dominated the American political and social scene, Kinderland was sorely threatened. The International Workers Order, long an important camp sponsor, was liquidated, leaving camp supporters scrambling to pay the mortgage. Some Kinderland administrators, including Edith Segal, were called to testify before the New York state version of the House Un-American Activities Committee (HUAC).

Says one long-time camper, "In 1955, every bunk was jammed. The next year, there were half as many campers"—a reflection of the fears instilled by the HUAC. And the Soviet references in Kinderland songs and dances vanished.

As time went on, Jewish Communists became increasingly disaffected with a party that refused to acknowledge the evils of Stalinism, the invasion of Hungary and finally the Soviet Union's anti-Israel and anti-Semitic positions. Many left the party, though some continued to profess Marxist political ideals. Still, the particular Jewish dream that characterized Kinderland hung on, and, unlike many other camps with leftist histories, this one survived.

In the process, Kinderland became more camp-like. The Yiddish classes ended. Newcomers from camps that had closed their gates came to Hopewell Junction and introduced such things as cookouts and sleep-outs. Says Judy Rosenbaum: "The programming was more secular, less Jewish, but still Yiddish. You still had to be a *schule* teacher to be a group leader. But it was always a struggle to keep Jewish culture alive."

By the early 1960s, the New York *schulerin* had begun to dwindle—and, as English-speaking generations were born, the numbers of the Yiddish-speaking generations diminished. But Yiddish songs continued to be taught at camp, and enough grandparents still visited Lakeland to speak to the children in Yiddish.

In the late 1950s and throughout the 1960s, Kinderlanders threw themselves into the civil rights movement. Programming in camp reflected total solidarity with the Freedom Riders in the South, among whom were camp alumni. Kinderland honored the grape and lettuce boycotts called by the United Farm Workers at that time and later celebrated the union's victories. The antiwar, black pride and women's movements also helped revitalize Kinderland, stimulating new energy and bringing in new campers with similar interests.

But by the beginning of the 1970s the original New York campgrounds were badly deteriorated and had become a tax burden. With great sadness, the home camp was sold and Kinderland began a period of diaspora, holding sessions at various locations until the present site in Tolland was purchased in 1976.

Throughout the 1970s and into the present, Kinderland has attracted children of New Left parents, as well as offspring of earlier generations, who want their children to learn something of a Jewish identity that isn't tied to religion. Still some of these parents expect too much of camp, wanting it somehow to provide the whole of a secular Jewish identity for children who learn little of it at home.

The program, meanwhile, remains self-consciously humanist, "progressive" (a term that seeks to avoid controversy and includes left-liberals and socialists alike), secular and Jewish. As throughout the years, Shabbat continues to come and go without any notice.

Kinderland's impressive and varied history hovers over its lovely new home in the Berkshires. Bunkhouses are named for heroes of many struggles, among them Anne Frank, Sholom Aleichem, Andrew Goodwin, Michael Schwerner and James Chaney (who were killed by Mississippi racists during the 1960s), Emma Lazarus, Joe Hill, Bar Kochba, Harriet Tubman, Hannah Senesh, Emmanuel Ringlebaum, Eugene V. Debs. The casino (an old camp name for the large recreation hall) is named for Paul Robeson. The kids decided that even the sports shack (which houses basketballs, softball bats and such) needed a name; they settled on Roberto Clemente, the Puerto Rican former Pittsburgh Pirate star baseball player, whose plane crashed carrying relief supplies to Nicaragua following a devastating earthquake. On Bunk Day, the children in each cabin present a skit or song about the person for whom it is named.

On Holocaust Day, the campers see films, sing songs, watch presentations, listen to stories and participate in discussions geared to their age groups about the destruction not only of the Jews, but also of Communists, gypsies, homosexuals and many others. Last summer, the staff decided to personalize the event—"It was easy to find six people in camp who knew the names and stories of relatives killed in the war," says program director Mitchell Silver. Because Holocaust Day emphasizes Jewish resistance, the program ends with the singing of "Zog nit Kaynmol" ("Don't Ever Say Never"), a resistance anthem. "It really worked," says Silver. Describing the effect of last summer's Holocaust Day program, he says, "The kids had been given so much, they were bursting. They sang that song with so much feeling, it was a thrilling moment."

On Workers Day—new this past year—the children learned songs of the labor movement, such as "Hold the Fort," "The Banks are Made of Marble" and "Dark as a Dungeon." Elsie Suller told them the story of the 1911 Triangle Shirtwaist Company fire, in which 146 women, many of them Jewish, died because the doors to their shop were locked from the outside. The fire galvanized support for the International Ladies Garment Workers Union in the Jewish community. And to give middle-class grandchildren of workers a sense of what human hands can accomplish, campers hewed and trimmed trees which they lashed together as a raft—and the raft floated.

During Kasrilevka Day—named for Sholom Aleichem's mythical town—campers dressed in costumes and used appropriate Yiddish phrases to reenact the bustle of a shtetl marketplace. On Hiroshima Day, the camp gathered by the shore of the crystalline pond and launched an armada of tiny paper birds to emphasize the terrible destructive power of nuclear weapons. Also, evening programs are always dedicated to the struggles and achievements of women, blacks and Hispanics.

But "special" programming isn't limited to special events and certain days. Added to typical camp goings-on—swimming, arts and crafts, softball and such—there is the daily "culture" activity. Last year, it was taught by Chaika Moran, a Lithuanian-born woman in her 60s, who shows the children how to write their names in Yiddish and tells them stories ranging from the works of the Yiddish writer, Isaac Leib Peretz, to highlights of the labor history in which she herself was involved. Chaika is "sensitive as a tuning fork," according to Elsie Suller.

And the children respond to her with affection and respect. A seven-year-old girl said solemnly, "Chaika told us about the scabs," and assured me that *she* would never cross a picket line, not even if her children were hungry.

Nothing is taken for granted at Kinderland. For example, the music counselor points out that "Fun is not enough. We never just sing songs. We talk about them. We discuss them on whatever level the kids are at." And she particularly likes this aspect of the place. "I never have to teach 'On Top of Spaghetti.'"

Traditional camp competitions such as "color wars" are transformed at Kinderland, where the three days of contests are designated as "Peace

Olympics." The camp is divided into three "countries" and, in addition to sports events, campers make banners and native costumes and learn songs and dances and a bit of the history of their respective nations. No cumulative scores are kept at the games, so competition is minimized. The point of the Olympics is to teach and to entertain, not to win.

There's another tradition at Kinderland called "kassa"—which apparently comes from a Russian word for sharing. When packages of goodies arrive from home for a camper, the food automatically becomes "kassa," the collective property of his or her bunk group. A 15-year-old counselor-in-training explained: "Kassa teaches us to be better people." Added Silver: "These are the kinds of things that make this a special camp. Otherwise, it's a regular summer camp with a lot of labor songs."

From what I saw and heard during a weekend visit, the Kinderland system works. The children have fun and learn a great deal—"painlessly," as one camper put it.

While there is no specific political line taught, certain kinds of attitudes are taken for granted and encouraged. The children learn, for example, that racism in any form is not to be tolerated. When a kitchen worker made a racist remark about a black camper, the children demanded to know why the offender wasn't fired. Camp songs are regularly rewritten to mention the president, as in "Reagan is our leader/He shall be removed." When I asked an eight-year-old what a socialist is, she replied: "Someone who is against war."

There really is no political "line" toed by the camp or its staff, though a general, unspoken consensus on certain issues prevails. For example, the Soviet Union is mentioned as little as possible. And while there is strong support for Israel, some of its policies and politicians come in for criticism.

Elsie Suller says that Kinderland teaches "a pro-peace philosophy." She continues: "The children will hear the word 'socialism' often, but we don't indoctrinate. We get them to think. We want to raise the consciousness of the children, but there is no particular 'ism.' We tell parents: 'Your child will get progressive secularism here, with a Jewish component.' Without the Jewish component, we've lost the soul of camp."

While about a third of the 135 campers last summer were not Jewish, the soul of Kinderland is still Jewish. "Staff discussions revolve around questions about what it means to be Jewish and progressive," Mitchell Silver says. Still, he and other counselors are convinced that Yiddish is a vital element in the equation and deplore the fact that Yiddish is vestigial at Kinderland today. Looking back, they believe that when the progressive Jews expressed themselves in Yiddish, the viability of a secularist world view was not so much in peril as it is now. Even though the children are still taught Yiddish songs, one camper confides, "It just can't mean that much."

The fact is that the culture which gave birth to Kinderland—including the *schule* movement, the Jewish labor movement, the various fraternal/political/cultural institutions of New York's immigrant Jews—no longer exists. In many ways, Kinderland has survived its own context.

And, says Silver, "From a broader perspective, you have to ask, can an ongoing Jewish identity be maintained apart from a religious component? If you take the longest historical view, the religious element is the common theme. But what makes Judaism such a rich tradition is that lots of different cultures have grown up in different places and become part of the stream of Jewish life. I hate to think that a concern with social justice would disappear from Jewish tradition.

"I believe that secularism can be part of and make a contribution to Jewish life. There is a way of being Jewish and not making a big deal of Shabbos. Kids have grown up here with a tremendous sense of Jewish identity. Camp provides a kind of optimism for Jews who feel uncomfortable with metaphysical beliefs; it shows that being an involved Jew can mean uniting with all peoples. Internationalism and universalism are important themes in Jewish life."

Silver, who holds a Ph.D. in philosophy and is currently studying to be a nurse, began as Kinderland's program director only last summer, relieving Elsie Suller of some of the many tasks she took on along with her other duties as director. He and the rest of the Kinderland community (staff, alumni supporters and parents) will wrestle Kinderland into the future, ever respectful of its past.

On the other hand, for Elsie Suller, Kinderland in 1983 embodies the principles on which it was founded. When she speaks of the camp's glory days, her eyes sparkle and her hands accompany the excitement of her words: "We had a dream and we hoped to carry it out. And we would bring it out in song and poetry. Oh, the songs! 'Throw off your chains. Get out of your *finstere caverne* (dark caves).' And the worker poets, the fiery poets—You would rise ten feet when you heard, '*Ich bin ein Yid!*' I have such a love for the language," she says, momentarily pensive. "It's sad for us not to have more Yiddish here. Yiddish was a reflection of the struggle."

Dressed in a full skirt, white hair piled into a bun circled with a bright-colored headband, lipstick ever red, eyelids cobalt blue, keys jingling, Elsie embodies the fierce energy which ensures another summer, another year for Kinderland. If one day there is to be a camp without her—and some people simply cannot imagine that—it will be a different place, a place that depends less on its history and more on new definitions of secular Judaism that will be set down in English rather than in Yiddish.

Certainly, life at Kinderland has changed from summer to summer, always reflecting the changing world outside. Inside its borders, the tension among respect for the past, devotion to the present and commitment to a better future have been major factors in keeping the camp alive.

And there is still that dream of a world where children can grow up without fear—a dream cherished by many Jews who insist upon the camp's Jewishness. As long as that dream is held as passionately by succeeding generations of Jews as it is by Elsie Suller, Kinderland will survive. No doubt it will change, but it will survive.

Arthur A. Cohen

Diane Cole

I n an era of specialization, he has specialized in being a Renaissance man – theologian, novelist, art historian, publisher, rare book dealer. But, says Arthur A. Cohen, "All I do now is write novels, study Hebrew, give lectures and run my bookstore."

At the age of 53, he asserts, "My energy and curiosity levels have never been higher." His theological interpretation of the Holocaust, *The Tremendum*, was published by Crossroad Books in New York in 1981. He is writing a novel called *An Admirable Woman*, and the plan for a new novel has already taken shape in his mind.

The author or editor of close to twenty books, Arthur A. Cohen is perhaps best known for his novel *In the Days of Simon Stern*, which received the Edward Lewis Wallant Award for excellence in Jewish fiction in 1973. Cohen describes that book as a "rag-bag" of Jewish history, literature and ideas. Actually, anyone who sets out to read Cohen's collected works will enjoy a thorough education in Jewish thought and philosophy, and will be immensely entertained by the four novels Cohen has published so far.

Cohen's work also includes a concise study of Martin Buber; a collection of essays titled *The Myth of the Judeo-Christian Tradition*; a short book on the Soviet poet Osip Mandelstam; a survey of modern Jewish thought called *The Natural and the Supernatural Jew*; *A People Apart*, a discussion of the Hassidim, with photographs by Philip Garvin;

and studies of the 20th-century post-Impressionist painters Robert and Sonia Delaunay. Cohen's interests are so diverse that publishing catalogues invariably add one book to the list that should not be there, for *The Communism of Mao Tse-Tung* was written by another Arthur A. Cohen.

"I've been trying to straighten that one out for years," Cohen says.

As he walks up Third Avenue near his Manhattan townhouse, where the first floor serves as the locale for his bookstore, Ex-Libris, Cohen carries himself with casual grace. He squints at the sun through horn-rimmed glasses and the glare hides his brown-green eyes. When he smiles, which is often, lines crease his cheeks. The brown hair is going grey, but the figure remains trim in informal, well-cut clothes. The mellow baritone voice invites questions. In spite of his air of self-assurance, he betrays a hint of nervousness. "If you can figure out how everything in my life fits together," he says with a laugh, "be sure and let me know."

Arthur A. Cohen was born in New York City in 1928 to an affluent, nonobservant Jewish family. His childhood was "far from eminent," he says. At boarding school he read, went to the theater and wrote plays. Then, while attending the University of Chicago, he found himself in the midst of a religious crisis.

He had never before thought seriously about his faith. But, confronted with the realization that, as he puts it, "Western culture is a Christian culture," Cohen wrestled with the idea of converting to Christianity. In his essay, "Why I Choose to Be a Jew," published in *Harper's* in April 1959 and anthologized in Nahum Glatzer's *The Judaic Tradition* (Beacon Press, 1969), Cohen confessed wryly that "I was rushed not to a psychoanalyst but to a rabbi—the late Milton Steinberg." Eventually, Cohen says, "I chose to be a Jew."

That choice pervades both his life and his work. After completing his studies at Chicago, where he gained B.A. and M.A. degrees, Cohen returned to New York to study at the Jewish Theological Seminary. There, he discovered that no one was prepared to teach him what he wanted to learn—Jewish medieval philosophy. Further, he recalls, after pursuing Ph.D. studies for two years, he was told that the only way to avoid being drafted for the Korean War was to enroll as a rabbinical student.

Cohen refused. "I never considered being a rabbi," he explains. "The position is too exalted. And I never have had the patience to deal with the daily sufferings of human beings. But I *did* want to spend my life in Jewish scholarship. J.T.S. betrayed me."

Angry and disillusioned, he left the seminary, but not to go to war. A childhood bout with tuberculosis had been serious enough to grant him a medical exemption from military service. He discovered a new career—publishing.

In 1951, Cohen joined with the poet Cecil Hemley to found the Noonday Press, which is today a subsidiary of the publishing firm of Farrar, Straus and Giroux and is known for its quality paperbacks. Cohen and Hemley's hardback book list was small but distinguished. Noonday published works by the poet Louise Bogan, John Middleton Murry's book on Keats, fiction by the experimental Brazilian writer Machado de Assis and the stories of a little-known Yiddish writer named Isaac Bashevis Singer.

By 1954, though, differences between the two publishers arose over the direction the company should take. Cohen sold his interest in Noonday to Hemley. In 1955, Cohen founded another publishing house, Meridian Books.

For Cohen, this was the most exciting part of his years in publishing. The Meridian imprint graced works by such luminaries as André Gide, Philip Rahv, Erich Auerbach, Edmund Wilson, Lionel Trilling and Jacques Barzun. Taking care to make the books attractive, Cohen hired his wife, the artist Elaine Lustig Cohen, to design them.

But as the company grew so did Cohen's administrative duties. Finally, he no longer felt he was a book publisher, but a businessman. "Then," he says, "it ceased to be fun."

So he sold Meridian to World Publishing Company, and in 1961 became director of the religious book department of Holt, Rinehart and Winston. Again, in his view, he was too successful. By 1964, he had become editor-in-chief and vice-president of Holt, Rinehart—positions he maintained until 1968, when he left publishing.

"Those were my falling-apart years," he says of the 1960s. "Throughout that time, I was very much involved in business. I was publishing relatively little of my own work. I worked at the office all day, then came home at night and began writing *The Natural and the Supernatural Jew*. I celebrated the Sabbath—I was very observant then. There were so many conflicting orders of obligatory structure that I lost touch with my own structure."

Then he came across a sentence by Franz Rosenzweig, the Jewish philosopher who, like Cohen, very nearly converted to Christianity before returning to Judaism. Rosenzweig, whose work continues to greatly influence Cohen, had written, "We have to smuggle Jewish ideas into general culture."

Cohen comments, "Now this is one thing that fiction is wonderful for. It's a smuggling device."

Soon Cohen began *In the Days of Simon Stern*, which successfully smuggles into its text a fable about the last Jew on earth, a lecture on the meaning of Purim and philosophical discussions on the nature of evil and the concept of the Messiah.

"It's the least subtle book of anything I've written," Cohen says. "In a way, it's an insane book. When I think back on it, I'm more dazzled by its invention than anything else."

The novel follows the peculiar career of Simon Stern, messiah. Brought up on the Lower East Side by immigrant parents, Simon earns a fortune in real estate. But that is not his real work.

At the end of World War II, as the horrors of the Nazi death camps become known, Simon resolves to use his millions to redeem a "symbolic remnant" of the survivors. His Society for the Rescue and Resurrection of the Jews, Simon declares, will be "a small Bene Brak as in the days after the destruction of the ancient Temple"—that is, a center of Jewish learning such as the ancient one presided over by Rabbi Akiva. Simon wants the Society's compound in New York's Lower East Side to be an enclave for a flowering of cultural and intellectual achievement. There the survivors' spirits will be healed; the Jews will endure. But at the same time the survivors' presence will, Simon asserts, "testify to the world that it is a monstrous place. . . . We shall hold up to the world the mirror of its desecration."

That is Simon's dream; its realization ends in holocaust. As the Second Temple was destroyed, so is Simon's compound, which was built to resemble it. Another historical pattern has repeated itself; another historical cycle is about to begin. And Nathan of Gaza, the blind scribe whom Simon brought from the death camps to New York, and who records the life and times of his literal savior, continues to hope for the advent of the Messiah. For all its rage and its portrayals of evil, the book remains, finally, optimistic.

At the center of all of Cohen's novels is what he calls "a hero of survival, someone who learned something from making it through." According to the author, everyone has this choice in life: "You can avoid conflict, or you can face it down." Invariably, Cohen's heroes "face it down."

This theme is most pointedly stated in the often satirical *A Hero In His Time*, published in 1976 by Random House.

In that novel, the minor Soviet-Jewish poet Yuri Maximovich Isakovsky must choose between his poetry — and the truth his conscience demands — and the material comforts with which the Soviet state rewards, and thus corrupts, those who survive by distorting the truth.

A Hero In His Time was written shortly after Cohen published his short book *Osip Mandelstam* (Ann Arbor: Ardis, 1974), in which he describes the Soviet-Jewish poet's determination to continue writing poetry in spite of political persecution. (Mandelstam disappeared during the Stalinist purges of the 1930s and is believed to have died in a Soviet concentration camp.) The fictitious Isakovsky's ambivalence towards his Jewishness reminds the reader of Cohen's evocation of Mandelstam, and Cohen admits to thinking about the one while writing about the other. An admirer of Mandelstam's poetry, Cohen corresponded with Mandelstam's widow, Nadezhda (known in this country for her memoirs, *Hope Against Hope* and *Hope Abandoned*), and sent her detective novels, a genre she enjoyed.

Are Cohen's novels "Jewish" novels?

"There's a point where Jewish madness intersects with the world's madness," Cohen says, "and there it becomes world literature. The real issue is whether or not you can make the connection — if you can transform the material and make the Jewish myth the world myth.

"There's a vast difference," Cohen continues, "between writing theology — which uses the systematic imagination, and writing fiction — which uses a non-systematic imagination. I hate didacticism. But I believe that fiction should smuggle something special into it. My novels are all tales plus something else."

Because Cohen's novels all do smuggle into their texts a variety of

philosophical, political, esthetic, historical and religious themes, Cohen
is often referred to as a novelist of ideas.

"That phrase is a compliment in Europe and a curse in America,"
Cohen comments, with a rueful laugh. "I think of myself as a European
novelist working in the American tradition. I'm working with materials
of American culture and with the great concepts of Western civilization.
I write novels about people who think, as opposed to people who do not
think."

His theological works are certainly intended for people who think. In
The Tremendum, Cohen wrestles with the meaning and significance of
the Holocaust. It is a short but complex work, both dazzling and searing
in its insights into language, history, religion and the nature of evil.
Cohen tells us that the enormity of the Holocaust demands a new
language, a new terminology in which to discuss it.

"We must find a language that allows us, as well as God, to go on
living," Cohen insists, summarizing part of his argument. "The function
of theology," he continues, "is not to distribute blame, but to find
possibilities to clarify human existence."

Because Cohen believes that "Where one stands on God really
matters," his theological works often rise to eloquent, impassioned
intensity. Readers may disagree with Cohen's conclusions; those unfamiliar with philosophical terminology may even have difficulty understanding some of Cohen's more erudite essays—but one comes away from
Cohen's work with great respect for the range of his knowledge and the
depth of his commitment.

Cohen describes his theology as "essentially Orthodox," though he is
different from many Orthodox Jews in his support of women rabbis. He
"disagrees fiercely," he says, "with all of liberal Jewish theology."

In spite of his orthodoxy, Cohen no longer observes Jewish ritual.

He attends the synagogue infrequently and asserts that he hates
synagogues. "They're a bourgeois enclave of middle-class values. Only
rarely are they transformed by the religious. The only reason to go to the
synagogue is to say *kedushah* or *kaddish*.

"My observance became conflicted," he says. "But the question of
observance is never closed, and I am non-observant today not without a
longing to return."

Nevertheless, Cohen says he "loves the liturgy." So much so that in his
next novel he plans to make extensive use of it. It will dramatize what

goes on in one man's mind in the course of the twenty-four hours that begin on the eve of Yom Kippur with *Kol Nidre* and end the next evening with the closing services of *Ne'ilah.*

Cohen admits to having no favorites among his many books. In fact, he says, he has never reread any of them. "Once a book is done, there's an authentic loss of interest. A published book is a document. It's a moment of self-clarification, and then it's time to move on."

With the publication of his first novel, *The Carpenter Years,* in 1967, Cohen did not really "move on" from his theological books and essays of the 1950s and early 1960s. He simply added the serious composition of fiction to his other activities. Today, besides being profoundly engaged in creating works of both fiction and theology, Cohen is also known for his published studies of artists Robert and Sonia Delaunay, who were important figures in the post-Impressionist, avant-garde and abstract art movements in the first half of this century.

Cohen's interest in art history, he says, derives from his wife, whose eye for color and design he cannot praise enough. "As language is to me, sight is to Elaine," he says admiringly. And perhaps this can also be said of their daughter, Tamar Judith, a college student.

In Ex-Libris, located on the ground floor of their elegant brownstone house, the Cohens' interest in art has been fused with the former publisher's love of books. Founded in 1974, this gallery-like bookstore carries on a flourishing international trade in rare historical art documents. Books and publications sold there are primary sources for early 20th-century art. A recent Ex-Libris catalogue offered a first edition of Guillaume Apollinaire's 1913 poetry collection *Alcools,* which features a frontispiece portrait of the author by Picasso. Price: $1500.

In addition to the areas of expertise Cohen has revealed in print, he harbors a secret passion—horseback riding, a pastime he pursues four times a week. "Riding's similar to writing," he confesses. "It's all about mastery."

"A writer has as many books in him as his energy, lust, time, or ideas allow him," Cohen explains. "One is always rewriting one's only book, which means that one is looking for more accurate ways of getting the job done."

Over the years, Cohen has found many ways of getting many jobs done. He set out to master several fields of knowledge and gives no sign of ceasing to face and conquer other challenges.

At his center, Cohen believes, lies his Jewishness. "The mission of Judaism is not to stave off disaster but to enlarge man's awareness of the Divine Presence," he has written.

If there is a unifying theme to Cohen's work, it is the expansion of the human spirit. In his novels, which give us, as he sees it, "a tale plus something else," and in his theological essays, his voice is a distinctive cry trying to rouse us. He awakens us not necessarily to faith, for we may have none to offer – instead, he makes us aware of a vast world of ideas. We may contest them; we may agree. But in forcing us to think, he has helped us prove that we live.

Geula Cohen

J. Robert Moskin

B old and outspoken, Geula Cohen stands on the extreme right of
Israeli politics. She speaks for a minority, and her vigorous,
uncompromising views are anathema to many Israelis and Jews
elsewhere, but she is forceful and demands and gets attention. What she
says jars most liberal Jews abroad; but in Israel, she is not alone.

Geula Cohen, according to the Western calendar, was born on
Christmas Day, 1926, and for more than 40 years she has given the
modern Jewish establishment almost as much trouble as Jesus of Naza-
reth gave the establishment of his era. In Israel's prestate days, she was an
active member of the underground Lehi (the Stern Gang), which battled
the British during World War II, when the Haganah made common
cause with Palestine's British rulers against the Nazis. More recently, she
backed the Likud when it first won power, and then as a Knesset member
fought the Camp David accords and giving up the Sinai Desert. She
opposes exchanging territory for peace.

As a girl, Geula Cohen found Menachem Begin's Irgun too mild for
her spirit and moved over to the more violent Lehi. Now she has quit the
Likud and helped form the political party Tehiya, even further to the
right. "I am always leaving the majority," she says. She is credited with
spearheading Israel's formal annexation of the Golan Heights in 1981,
and she has led illegal prayer demonstrations on the Temple Mount in
Jerusalem.

She says, "I not only pray in the synagogue; I fight in the Knesset. It is a battleground."

There is never any question about where Geula Cohen stands. She is more militant and more confrontational than even her fellow former Stern Gang member Prime Minister Yitzhak Shamir. A zealot who smiles easily, Cohen wants to hold on to occupied Judea and Samaria — the West Bank — even at the price of peace. She would settle the occupied territories with Jews from the diaspora and let the Palestinians have their state in Jordan.

Cohen refuses to compromise on territory. She says, "If you take out Hebron and Nablus and Judea and Samaria, you have to take them out from our songs and our prayer books and our history and our dreams. You are not taking geographical territories; you are taking spiritual territories." In this cause, she says, "I want to be Minister of Education. Very much so. I almost was. This dream doesn't leave me for one minute. I would push the Judaization of education — not religious but Jewish and Zionist education."

On her mother's side, Cohen's family came originally from Morocco, and her mother and grandfather were born in the Old City of Jerusalem. Geula is the fourth generation to be born in Palestine. Her father walked all the way from Yemen to Jerusalem. He became a follower of the militant Vladimir Jabotinsky. When she was 13, she joined Betar, Jabotinsky's Revisionist youth group. She says, "Our uniforms were brown, like the color of the earth, but our rivals said we were fascists." She joined the Irgun when she was 16, but when she found that it was not fighting the British, who "were closing the gates to the refugees from Germany," she joined the Lehi "freedom fighters" in 1943. She planned to be a teacher but instead became the Stern Gang's underground broadcaster and ever since has been a voice of the extreme right.

She was captured by the British in 1946. Imprisoned in Tel Aviv, she escaped but was caught again. She was sent to a tougher women's prison in Bethlehem and again she escaped. Fleeing toward the Talpiot section of Jerusalem, she took a bullet in her right leg and was thrown back in prison. She was finally sentenced to nine years. She told the judge he wouldn't be in Palestine in nine years.

After a year in prison, she escaped for a third time, and this time she succeeded with the help of Arabs who lived in the village of Abu Ghosh just north of Jerusalem. Last April 23, she celebrated the 40th anniversary of her escape by inviting the Arabs from Abu Ghosh to her home for a party. Some of them had served time in prison for helping her.

She says she never thought of herself as a terrorist but as a freedom fighter. "I felt my country was ruled by a foreign government. And it is my country. I wanted them not in my Jerusalem but in their London. I fought against them. I didn't want to destroy the British. I wanted them to leave my country, and when they would leave my country, they would be my friends."

That, she says, is the difference between the Stern Gang and the Palestine Liberation Organization: "We kicked out the British from here to their country; because they were foreigners, we succeeded. They [the P.L.O.] will never succeed in throwing us out of here because we are not foreigners and this is our only country."

In her small, neat apartment on French Hill, in a part of Jerusalem that became Israeli in 1967, Cohen sketched her vision of Israel's future. She does not want to annex the West Bank now but to settle it with Jews. She does not believe the Arabs of the West Bank will want to be citizens of a Jewish state. She adds, "Those who will be faithful to a Jewish Zionist Government and will swear to our flag and will be faithful to our laws, they can be citizens. The others will stay here; but if they cannot be faithful to the Government, they will have all the rights of inhabitants but will not be able to vote for the Knesset. This is not normal? I agree. What is normal in the history of the Jewish people? Nothing is normal. Coming here is not normal. But what is really not normal is committing suicide. To withdraw from the territories or to give all their inhabitants Israeli citizenship tomorrow is really not normal."

She says of the Palestinians: "They told the world that all they wanted is a home for the homeless, like the Jews before. They are the underdog, they said, and the problem is to form a state for the poor Palestinians. That's not the core of the problem. If they want a state for themselves, they have one [Jordan]. They want a second Palestinian state in Judea and Samaria, and afterward a third Palestinian state in Tel Aviv and Jaffa. The core of the problem is that the Palestinians did not want us to be here. And they want to destroy us. That is the core of the problem.

"They never had a Palestinian state here—never, never in history. Now they want to create one—but not in my state.

"The world is fooled in believing that a Palestinian state would bring peace to the area and that the Jewish settlements in Judea and Samaria are obstacles to peace," Cohen says. "But it's just the contrary. The only way to prevent war in the area is to settle Judea and Samaria with Jews because these settlements are obstacles to a Palestinian state. And everything that is an obstacle to a Palestinian state is an obstacle to war and promotes peace in the long run.

"This must be a Jewish state, or why did we come here?" she asks. "I prefer Reagan as my President and not Arafat. I am a great believer that we have a destiny here and that is why I am a great believer that one day Jews will come here. Not all, but many. Every morning when I get up, I am not thinking about how to get rid of a million Arabs. I am thinking about how to bring a million Jews here in 15 or 20 years. And I believe it is not an impossible mission. It is not a dream."

Cohen was formerly chairman of the immigration committee of the Knesset and she believes Israel should concentrate on attracting 10,000 to 20,000 new Jewish settlers a year. "We could triple [the number] in five years," she says. "I am a Zionist; I am going to bring others to live in Israel. That's Zionism."

She says solemnly, "If there are illegal settlements of Jews in the world, these illegal settlements are in Brooklyn, in New York, in Paris, in Buenos Aires; and these illegal settlements should be evacuated and planted here—in the territories. Without aliyah, we are finished here, even without a war. I think the real enemy of Israel is not the million Palestinians who are fighting us but the million Jews who don't come. The diaspora is our enemy—not the Jews."

She concludes: "I don't know if God agrees with me but I'll discuss it with Him if He is against me. Because I believe in my heart that I am right."

Lucy Dawidowicz

Diane Cole

In the summer of 1938, when Poland was mobilizing for war and thousands of refugees were trying to find an escape route from Europe to America, a young graduate student from New York City bought a steamship ticket to Gdynia in Poland. Her destination was the Yiddish Scientific Institute (YIVO) in Vilna; her purpose was to study a culture that has since been destroyed.

"I was there for a year and that of course explains everything," says historian Lucy S. Dawidowicz. Her words recall those of Hillel: "The rest is commentary." Her own commentary on Jewish life and history has included *The Golden Tradition* (Holt, Rinehart & Winston), *The War Against the Jews, 1933–1945* (Holt, Rinehart & Winston), *The Jewish Presence: Essays on Identity and History* (Holt, Rinehart & Winston), *The Holocaust and the Historians* (Harvard University Press) and *On Equal Terms: Jews in America 1881–1981* (Holt, Rinehart & Winston), all widely acclaimed. Recognized as the authoritative chronicler of Hitler's destruction of the Jews of Europe, she is now completing a brighter chronicle—the story of Jews in the *goldeneh medina* of America.

Dawidowicz tells her own story with thoughtful deliberation. It is the story of how a nonreligious, secular Jew born in America came to study Eastern European Jewry, and how—through her books, lectures, essays and reviews—she became one of the world's best-known historians of Jewish culture today.

Dawidowicz carries herself with dignity and warmth. Short and stocky, with simply cut brown hair and wide, attentive eyes behind tortoise-shell glasses, she wears a business-like plum-colored suit adorned with a single gold chain. Leaning far back in her chair, she weighs her words with care. After all, she began her academic career as an English major who wrote poetry and she knows that words count.

As we talk in her large, oblong living room, comfortably dominated by plants and books and cozy chairs, she crosses and uncrosses her arms, gestures leisurely, gazes out the window—from her apartment on New York's Upper West Side one can see the hazy outline of the World Trade Center in the distance—and pauses to pluck a wilted leaf from a luxuriant flowering plant. On the wall behind her, bookshelves provide the backdrop—the works of Eliot, Auden, Dickinson, Proust on one side; on the other, a stereo, with "Mostly Mozart" buttons from successive seasons of Lincoln Center's summer musical festival displayed among rows of opera recordings and musical biographies.

More bookshelves line her study, a darker, somewhat somber room, where her "working library" consists primarily of historical works. Dominating the room's solid, old-fashioned wooden desk is her new Eagle word processor, screen and printer. "I've had it for a year," she says, explaining how many bytes and rams the machine can manage, and praising the merits of the new technology. In the center of the room, a plain wooden table is neatly stacked with drafts and chapters of the book she is currently writing—a comprehensive history of the Jewish presence in America.

Above the desk, hovering over her, is a photograph of her late husband, Szymon, looking stern and sage. She speaks of him with an almost imperceptible crack in her voice. At his death is 1979, they had been married for thirty-two years.

Born in New York City in 1915, Lucy Dawidowicz started her academic career as an English major who read Wordsworth and wrote poetry, first as an undergraduate at Hunter College and then as a graduate student at Columbia University.

"It was 1937," she tells me, "and I remember sitting in a classroom, hearing the professor drone on about Wordsworth. It was a time when it seemed that the world, and particularly my Jewish world, was going up in flames. I looked out the window and thought, 'What is Wordsworth to me, at this time?' "

That is when she decided to undertake what she calls her "reverse" journey to Europe—"reverse in the sense of the track of history," she says—and go to Vilna's YIVO on a scholarship.

She had been there for a year, when, in 1939, Hitler signed his nonaggression pact with Stalin, and Americans living in Poland were warned to leave the country immediately.

"I went to Warsaw, leaving behind some of my things because I thought I would return," she says. "But of course I never went back.

"Leaving Warsaw was a journey of great drama. Poland was mobilizing everything that moved, including horses and wagons. The Polish port of Gdynia was closed. So I decided to go to Copenhagen, where friends from Poland had been stranded after the German invasion—but to get there I had to change not only trains but stations in Berlin.

"And then, somewhere near the Polish-German border, probably at Poznan, a German consul got on the train and sat in my compartment. We started talking in English. I told him I was an American; he didn't know I was Jewish. When we arrived in Berlin, a frightening city—everywhere soldiers, the military—he helped me get a taxi." The German consul had thus inadvertently aided the Jew. Dawidowicz adds, "I had a lot of *chutzpah* then."

The entire journey—from America to Eastern Europe and back to New York—was "the transforming experience of my life," Dawidowicz muses. "Everything that happened afterward, I suppose, was a consequence of what happened in Europe."

What happened first, though, was that Dawidowicz took "an unspeakably dreary job as a clerk" for the state government in Albany. Then Max Weinreich, who had headed Vilna's YIVO and, like her, had escaped from Vilna via Copenhagen, asked her to work for him at YIVO's new headquarters in New York. She also began graduate studies in Jewish history under the eminent historian Salo Baron at Columbia. And she met a young socialist labor leader newly escaped from Poland, Szymon Dawidowicz, whom she married in 1947.

"During this time, during the war, the world we lived in quite simply centered on what was happening over there, in Europe," she explains. And, in light of the various studies published during the war by YIVO concerning the Warsaw Ghetto—its history and its uprising—Dawidowicz says: "It's rather preposterous to say that American Jews did not care or do anything."

After the war ended in 1945, Dawidowicz continued her commitment to Jewish life. She went to Europe again, this time as a representative of the American Jewish Joint Distribution Committee. In Frankfurt, she recalls, as she helped identify the remnants of Europe's Jewish libraries— among them the "old" YIVO library from Vilna—to expedite their return to the "new" YIVO in New York, she derived "a kind of bitter compensation, closing the circle."

During her final six months in Europe, in 1947, she worked at Belsen, the Nazi concentration camp, which had become a displaced persons' camp for Holocaust survivors.

She helped supply school materials and other amenities, such as books and records, to the survivors. "Summer there is brief and cool," she wrote in her essay, "Belsen Remembered," published in *The Jewish Presence*. "In spring and fall the chill and damp penetrate your bones. In winter, I am told, ice formed in the corridors of the barracks."

In retrospect, it would seem that, having seen the death camps and their survivors at first hand, the future author of *The War Against the Jews* had already begun her research. But it would be twenty years more before the actual writing would begin.

First, Dawidowicz honed her research skills. She became a research assistant to novelist John Hersey, translating Yiddish tapes and documents relating to the 1943 Warsaw Ghetto uprising. Hersey used this data in his gripping documentary novel, *The Wall*, and in the preface wrote an acknowledgment to a "Mrs. L. Danzinger"—the fictionalized equivalent of Mrs. Lucy Dawidowicz.

Dawidowicz worked as a researcher for twenty years at the American Jewish Committee in New York. During that time, she began contributing essays to *Commentary* magazine and compiled and wrote her comprehensive, thoughtful historical introduction to *The Golden Tradition: Jewish Life and Thought in Eastern Europe*, a collection of autobiographical essays and memoirs spanning the last three centuries.

It wasn't until 1969, when David Mirsky, then dean of Yeshiva University's Stern College for Women, asked Dawidowicz to teach a course on the Holocaust that she realized that "There really wasn't a good book on the subject.

"I had been living with this all my adult life," she muses. "And so when people ask me, 'How long did it take to write *The War Against the Jews*,' I say, 'Well, it took four years.' But really, it was all my life."

In the introduction to that book, Dawidowicz wrote, she had attempted to answer three basic questions: How was it possible for a modern state to carry out the systematic murder of a whole people for no reason other than that they were Jews? How was it possible for a whole people to allow itself to be destroyed? How was it possible for the world to stand by without halting this destruction? Methodically and meticulously, she answers each question, painting a grim and chilling picture of Hitler's "Final Solution to the Jewish Question."

According to Dawidowicz, "Anti-Semitism was the core of Hitler's system of beliefs and the central motivation for his policies. He believed himself to be the savior who would bring redemption to the German people through the annihilation of the Jews, the people who embodied, in his eyes, the Satanic hosts." For Hitler, the Jews were a mythic enemy, Dawidowicz writes, and in waging World War II, "He engaged the real enemy along with the mythic enemy." Lies, deceit and terror were Hitler's natural allies as he promised new work and resettlement to the Jews he planned to slaughter.

The concept of Jewish passivity, she asserts, was as much a myth as any other. "Given those conditions of overpowering German might and terror, the wonder is not that there was so little resistance, but that, in the end, there was so much," she points out in The Jewish Presence.

No one can read Dawidowicz's country-by-country account of the fate of the Jews—in her 50-page appendix in The War Against the Jews— without visualizing the helpless civilian population against whom Hitler waged his bestial war. Here, she states, she has only a "partial" answer to the third of her basic questions.

"At bottom," she writes, "the success of the Final Solution throughout Europe depended on Germany's opportunities and resources to carry it out, that is, whether or not Germany had uncontested and supreme control of the country or territory. Elsewhere"—in countries such as Denmark and Italy, where many Jews were aided, concealed, or rescued—"the Final Solution was conditional upon a political tradition that held that all men were equal, that human life was valuable and that the Jews were human beings entitled to life."

Because the war of annihilation was waged specifically against the Jews, Dawidowicz is appalled by attempts to "universalize" the Holocaust or emphasize that "Everyone suffered." William Styron's novel, Sophie's Choice—which details the experiences of a Polish Catholic woman at Auschwitz—is "the most egregious example," she declares.

"I do not believe there is any historical foundation for Sophie's experience," she says. "If ever a non-Jewish woman was put in Sophie's position, there must have been some specific reason, some specific act she had done to bring on this particular sadistic punishment. But the fact is that *all* Jewish women, without any reason or cause other than that they were Jewish, were murdered. Styron's novel is a kind of gross misreading of history."

Dawidowicz also frowns on the "equalizers." These, she explains, "are people who ask, 'What's this big deal about the Holocaust? Look at the bombing of Dresden or Hiroshima.' They differ from the universalists, but their purpose is the same—the denial of the particularity of the Holocaust."

Unlike the Holocaust, she claims, such Allied bombings, odious and horrible as they were, actually were planned as a means to an end to the war. But "The murder of the Jews had as its end only the murder of the Jews. That is, means and ends were identical."

As for "revisionist" historians who claim that the Holocaust never happened, Dawidowicz dismisses them as "a bunch of crackpot anti-Semites." She says: "They're not to be taken seriously as revisionists or historians. They're not revising anything. They're denying the events of the Holocaust as a means of serving their anti-Semitic purposes."

Dawidowicz sees American Jews as the heirs of the Ashkenazic Jewish culture of Europe which was destroyed by the Nazis. To her, the American community seems at times to be all but assimilated, except for its interest in Israel and its preoccupation with the Holocaust.

She comments: "It may sound paradoxical, but I must say that I'm often distressed by the almost obsessive, ceaseless attention that American Jews seem to give to the Holocaust today. It's important for the Holocaust to have a place in our historical memory. We have to teach our children about it. As we teach children about Passover and our history of redemption, so we also have to teach them about our history of destruction. But we don't *live* for our history of destruction. One wants the right sense of proportion. I feel very strongly that, for the young, the continuing emphasis on the Holocaust is wrong. If we're a people that gets murdered, the young will flee from us. We have something more than that."

What, then, may be the "right proportion"? Is it too soon to see the Holocaust in perspective? "One can only speculate," Dawidowicz remarks thoughtfully, "but it may take its place in Jewish history as second to or equal to the destruction of the Temple.

"We live at a great crossroads in our history," she continues, "and whether we come out of it whole and creative and viable for future generations, we still don't know. We don't know what will become of us in America. We don't know what will become of us in Israel."

Currently, Dawidowicz is directing her vision to what has happened to Jews in this country since they first emigrated here. She describes her latest book, *On Equal Terms*, as "an interim report, a reflective pause in the course of my research toward a broad-gauged history of the Jews in America." For that comprehensive work, she says, "I still have a few years ahead of me of writing and researching."

Her work so far has done nothing to dissuade her from the belief that America is indeed the "golden land." She emphasizes that "Nowhere in the world or at any time in Jewish history have Jews enjoyed such an extraordinary situation of living in freedom as citizens on equal terms. And having the freedom to be whatever kind of Jews they want to be."

Dawidowicz tells me: "Jews are sufficiently comfortable in America now that they don't have to *prove* they're Americans. They no longer feel impelled to make strained equations between Judaism and Americanism. They're ready to accept differences that exist between themselves as Jews and other Americans. In an earlier time, Jews were less secure and less assured."

But with greater freedom and security come new choices and new dangers, she points out. "I think that we have to come to terms with the possibilities of freedom. We have to find new ways of continuing to remain as Jews, and do so creatively."

That, Dawidowicz says, means—for instance—finding ways to bring a Jewish dimension into the kind of cultural life one pursues. In the performing arts, that might mean going to see choreographer-dancer Pearl Lang's *Shira*, or hearing, say, composer Steve Reich's setting of *Tehillim*; or if one is a history buff, reading about Jewish history. The point is to "bring some aspect of Yiddishkeit into art and cultural enjoyment," Dawidowicz explains, "in addition to going to *shul*. In addition to reading *The New York Times* and worrying about Israel."

Today, after having grown up in a secular Jewish home—"The first time I ever went to *shul* was in Vilna, on Yom Kippur, when I was 23 years old," she confesses—Dawidowicz is by choice an observant Jew. "I'm not an Orthodox observer, but I do what I can," she says. The transformation occurred while she was working on *The Golden Tradition*, translating from the Yiddish an autobiographical essay by Nathan Birnbaum, appropriately titled "from Freethinker to Believer."

Dawidowicz concludes: "It's up to us to be what we want to be. We cannot continue to live as the Jews lived in Poland in the 17th century. It's preposterous to walk around in a heavy *streimel* in July! If we're not to become shriveled and withered, we have to learn to grow with the environment in which we live—but not be overtaken by it. That is the constant danger, the constant risk, the constant adventure. But that's also what the excitement of life is."

The legacy of Eastern European Jewry, the horror of Nazi Germany, the freedom of America—Lucy Dawidowicz has fixed her steady gaze on all three historical epochs. In so doing, she has shown us not only what we have lost but also why we continue to live.

Alexander Donat

Myra Alperson

L ast spring, when the word Bitburg began to call to mind far more than the name of an obscure German town, the phones began ringing more often than usual at the office of the Holocaust Library, in New York City. Arthur Pruzan, the executive director of the Holocaust Library's parent company, Holocaust Publications, found himself fielding not only requests for books, but expressions of support. "We were getting calls from veterans—non-Jews, too—who wanted us to know they wouldn't forget," he says.

Not forgetting is what the Holocaust Library is all about. It was founded in 1978 by Alexander Donat, a Warsaw-born journalist who had survived five concentration camps, to record, in print, the many forms the Holocaust took. At the start, first-person accounts, including Donat's own memoirs, "The Holocaust Kingdom" (first published in 1965), dominated the company's list. In time Donat expanded it with broader histories, such as Harold Flender's "Rescue in Denmark," the story of how the Danes saved most of their 8,000 Jews; more specific accounts, like Israeli prosecutor Gideon Hausner's "Justice in Jerusalem," a chronicle of the Eichmann trial, and books that singled out the bravery of non-Jews—"Janusz Korszak's Ghetto Diary," for instance. (Korszak, who headed the orphanage at Treblinka, walked to his death with the children there rather than abandon them.)

The Holocaust Library has also brought out the first English-language version of Ilya Ehrenburg and Vasily Grossman's "The Black Book," first prepared in 1946 but suppressed by Stalin. When the harrowing story of the Nazi slaughter of 1.5 million Soviet Jews, told through documents and eyewitness accounts, finally appeared in Russian in 1980, the Holocaust Library arranged for a translation by John Glad and James S. Levine.

Before Donat's death in 1983, the firm published 28 titles. A small and independent operation, the Holocaust Library has beat enormous odds in an industry where all but conglomerate-owned publishers seem destined to be absorbed or fail. In fact, its independence has been the key to its survival, and probably the reason it continues to be an innovative outfit. Nonprofit and lowbudget, the Holocaust Library was founded before the broadcast of the television series "Holocaust," before the establishment of a national Holocaust memorial, before the inclusion of Holocaust studies in academic curricula.

With the Holocaust Library (launched with a $50,000 trust fund left to him by friends), Alexander Donat was able to expand his own personal crusade to keep Holocaust experiences alive. His son, William, now chairman of the board, points out, "My father's willingness always to discuss his past and how lucky we were to be in the U.S. and start another life made us aware of our heritage. My children have grown up with it, and they feel strongly about the Holocaust." But, he adds, "Other families of survivors have tried to sublimate their experiences and forget."

Even in Poland, Alexander Donat, though an assimilated Jew, was an active promoter of Jewish culture. As the publisher and editor of *Ostatnie Wiadomsci* (The Latest News), the only Polish-language newspaper in Warsaw that was not anti-Semitic, he also published more than 200 Yiddish paperbacks, including biographies and fiction. But when the Nazis conquered Poland in 1939, he saw his livelihood destroyed and his own family divided and dispersed. Shortly before the Warsaw ghetto fell, Donat and his wife, Lena, placed their 2-year-old son, Wlodek (William), in the home of an elderly and sympathetic childless Gentile couple. Soon after, the Donats were deported to the Maidenek concentration camp; eventually they were sent to separate camps—Lena to Ravensbruck and Auschwitz, Alexander to four others, including Radom and Dachau, where he was liberated. Meanwhile, the Gentile couple—because of Gestapo pressure on those suspected of aiding Jews—put William in a Catholic orphanage, where he was baptized.

After the liberation of Poland in 1945, Lena Donat returned to Warsaw and found her son; they were eventually joined by Alexander. Several months after their remarkable reunion, described in trenchant detail in "The Holocaust Kingdom," the family moved to New York. Though he lacked a command of English, Donat turned to the field he knew best: printing. He established the Waldon Press in a loft in Manhattan's Chelsea district. The firm eventually thrived, and it was in a small office at Waldon that Donat founded the Holocaust Library.

As a one-man effort, the Holocaust Library struggled to become known. To start, Donat recruited a seven-member volunteer advisory board of survivors, including Elie Wiesel, to select manuscripts. As word of the company's existence spread, unsolicited material made its way to Donat's door. More than 100 manuscripts are now on file, according to Arthur Pruzan, who joined the Holocaust Library after Donat died and had been affiliated with several Jewish social service agencies. To accommodate the perceived needs of young Jews and non-Jews, a 13-member editorial board of scholars was formed in 1983 to develop new projects. William Donat explains that "what my father and his advisory board were committed to" was the plight of the survivors. But now the Holocaust Library is looking to serve a broader readership that includes the children of survivors, Jews with no direct connections to the Holocaust— and everyone else.

So while three books planned by Alexander Donat were being readied for publication in 1985, the Library was also actively seeking works that show not only what happened during the Holocaust, but what followed in its aftermath and how later events affected new generations of Jews and non-Jews. Works by non-Jewish authors, such as a reprint about the Christian protection of Jews, are being considered, as is a German-authored book on the history of Zyklon-B, the gas used in the extermination camps. Donat also plans to commission histories of lesser-known Jewish communities, such as the one in Bulgaria.

Books about the Holocaust are being developed for children, including a set of primers for the very young. "It's a very sensitive task," says Pruzan. "How do you teach the Holocaust to very young children without horrifying them?" To answer that question, the Holocaust Library has enlisted the help of Lisa Kumerker, a specialist in curriculum and sociomoral development at Hunter College in New York City, and

Helen Fagin, a professor of Judaic studies at the University of Miami, who is compiling interviews conducted with children immediately after the war.

The Holocaust Library has also collaborated with other organizations—notably Yad Vashem, the Holocaust memorial center in Jerusalem—on several projects. This year, a major work on the relationship between Polish Jews and non-Jews before the war will be published with Yad Vashem. There has also been discussion, says Donat, about their becoming the publishing arm of the United States Holocaust Council, and about a link with New York's planned Holocaust memorial. In the future, Pruzan sees the Holocaust Library becoming involved in film and video and computerized referencing of Holocaust literature.

A major achievement of the Library was the recent publication of "Against Silence: The Voice and Vision of Elie Wiesel." The three-volume set, compiled over a 10-year period by Irving Abrahamson, professor of English at Kennedy-King College in Chicago, contains previously unpublished stories by Wiesel as well as his speeches, interviews, book reviews, essays and one play, covering the gamut of Jewish concerns that have preoccupied him. In addition to the trade edition of the set, the Holocaust Library published 300 copies of a limited edition at $1,000 each, the profits of which will help finance future Holocaust Library projects.

Donat and Pruzan also envision an "Encyclopedia of the Holocaust," at a projected cost of up to $350,000, that would be a comprehensive reference for scholars and lay readers. Currently, however, the prospect of even embarking on such an endeavor is frustratingly remote, Donat says. Since its founding, the Holocaust Library has been a bootstrap effort, surviving on grants, donated office space and at-cost printing at Waldon Press, and has had to funnel the proceeds from the sale of one book into the production of the next. (In at least one case, Adam Starkopf's "There Is Always Time to Die," the author helped finance publication.)

With current production costs at around $12,000 to $22,000 per book (and average press runs of 3,500 in softcover, 1,500 in hardcover), the projected cost of the encyclopedia is daunting. And while Pruzan has succeeded in garnering more grant money for Holocaust Library and in raising profit margins since joining the staff, he complains: "In the Jewish world, there's light years between 'Oh, by all means' and when the check comes."

Yet both Donat and Pruzan point to the fact that their publishing company is still around after six years. For while President Reagan's visit to Bitburg proved how quickly some people have forgotten about the mass murders of the Nazi period, the Holocaust Library has learned from that incident how many others, Jews and non-Jews alike, want to remember.

Betty Friedan

Jennifer Moses

It is not easy to get an interview with Betty Friedan. In June, I called her at her New York City home and explained who I was and why I was calling. She told me that she would be in Sag Harbor, Long Island, for the summer, gave me the number there and instructed me to call around Labor Day. She sounded annoyed.

In late August, I called her in Sag Harbor. She said she was busy, but I should call back a week later. I called back in a week, but she said she was too busy to talk and hung up before I could say another word.

I called, again, a few days later. I think I woke her up. She said that she might be coming into the city the following week, and perhaps she could see me then. Then she hung up. I called her, as instructed, the following week, but she said she wasn't coming into the city after all. Perhaps, she said, we could get together on September 16: She would be coming to town to take part in celebrations attending the 200th anniversary of the Constitution. She was to appear on "Geraldo," a New York-based television talk show, and was scheduled to arrive at 5:30 P.M. "I'll be there," I said.

Then she asked: "Have you read my books?"

"Yes," I said.

"All of them?"

"I've read *The Feminine Mystique* and *The Second Stage*."

70

"All of *The Second Stage* or just the part that was in the *New York Times Magazine?*"

"All of it."

"Well, you must read *It Changed My Life*, too."

That weekend, I read *It Changed My Life: Writing on the Women's Movement*. Like her other works, it is wise, compassionate and deeply, fundamentally interesting. And on Monday, I called again: "I'm calling to confirm that I'll meet you this Wednesday at 6 o'clock."

"Yeah," she said. And then she hung up.

Later, on my way to meet Friedan in the Times Square building where "Geraldo" is taped, I found myself wondering whether the interview would be worthwhile. Friedan had been schooled in Gestalt psychology, 1940s liberalism and more than two decades of political action. I had a B.A. in English and was part of the generation of post-*isms* somnambulists. Friedan's biggest impact had occurred more than 20 years ago. I was 4 years old when *The Feminine Mystique* was published, in 1963. The world from which Friedan's ideas about women had emerged was long gone by the time I was old enough to date. And she had been writing and talking on the subject of women ever since. What, if anything, could she say to me that might be new?

Betty Friedan is a public figure. Strangers recognize her on the street. She is a prolific writer, and she likes to talk. To say that she is outspoken is to miss the point. One gets the feeling, when around her, that she believes that *not* voicing her thoughts would be a betrayal of her highest moral value—that shutting up would be tantamount to giving up. The mere mention of her name sends some people through the roof, and yet others say that she hasn't been a central player in the women's movement in years. She is a 67-year-old divorced mother of three grown children, the grandmother of two and the recognized founder of modern feminism.

On the phone, Friedan had mentioned some of the events she would be attending during her one-and-a-half day visit to the city—a public reading of the Constitution, a luncheon for Representative Patricia Schroeder, an awards ceremony or two. So I knew that she'd be hurried. Therefore I had prepared my questions with great care, numbering them 1 through 6 and making sure that they led naturally from one to the next. But when, at last, I was led into the greenroom, where Friedan was waiting to be called into makeup before the taping of "Geraldo," all my composure left me.

Before me sat a short, gray-haired woman wearing a blue dress and a rope of pearls, who very graciously introduced herself.

"How do you do?" she said. Then: "I need to get my hair fixed up. It's a mess. I never have time to do it properly."

The subject of "Geraldo" was feminism: Is feminism to blame for the problems that beset so many men and women today? The other panelists were Midge Decter, the neoconservative editor and writer who once wrote a book critical of modern feminism; Michael Levin, professor of philosophy at City College in New York City and the author of the recently published *Feminism and Freedom*, and Harry Brod, who was speaking for a group called the National Organization of Changing Men.

As she was being taken back to the makeup room, Friedan explained that she usually doesn't go in for TV appearances, but that as long as she was in New York for a couple of days anyway, she'd agreed to do the show. In a friendly, confidential tone, she said that, on occasion, she enjoyed a good fight. Seated before the mirror in the makeup room, she told the makeup artist: "You absolutely have to do something to my hair. Fluff it up or something, you see, on top." She then pushed her hair impatiently around her head.

The makeup artist asked Friedan what the show was going to be about. Friedan explained that it was on the subject of feminism. At this, the makeup artist began to talk, saying that it was nearly impossible to get a good man—much tougher than it had been in her mother's generation. Men, she went on, don't want commitment. In the old days, they needed women more, to take care of them and look after their needs at home. But now that women no longer play the housewife role, men don't need them.

"So they don't stick around," she concluded.

To me, this argument sounded similar to those put forth by antifeminists—those who claim that a working woman threatens the integrity of the family. I thought Friedan would let her have it. But she merely shrugged and said: "You think so?"

Then it was time for "Geraldo" to start. According to the show's producer, the hour would be divided into segments on such subjects as feminism and romance, and feminism and the family.

"Women now have much more complex, more interesting lives than they did before the movement," Friedan said in her opening statement. "They have more choices . . . but they still don't have enough real choices to put it all together. The needs of women for home and family are as important as ever. But we have to move into what I call the Second Stage."

Indeed, Friedan believes that women have made great headway in their quest for what she calls "full personhood," but that there is much that still has to be done. In her 1982 volume, *The Second Stage*, she called for a thorough rethinking of the women's movement. Though she continues to champion a broad spectrum of "women's issues," including the right of a woman to have a safe and legal abortion, equal pay for work of comparable value, economic rights for divorced women and support for women running for political office, she believes that the women's movement is stalled.

What the movement needs to do, Friedan says, is to redirect its efforts into a larger sphere of social action, beyond "self-serving feminist illusion," and to combat what she believes are the real dangers: the increasing feminization of poverty, the conservative backlash and the reluctance on the part of the younger generation to fight to retain hard-won rights.

Some of the figures are, indeed, dismaying. Although the wage gap is narrowing, in 1987 women made 70 cents for every dollar a man earned. In addition, while last year 55 percent of women considered themselves a part of the labor force, the majority continued to work in service and clerical jobs. Moreover, the Equal Rights Amendment (E.R.A.) was narrowly defeated, and many social programs designed to protect women and children have been dismantled. And the Reagan Administration, along with fundamentalists and other conservatives, has waged a crusade against abortion.

On "Geraldo," the accusations flew back and forth. Michael Levin, for example, claimed that feminism encouraged women to have sex "like a guy." "If," he maintained, "you didn't want to have sex, 'you must be repressed; you must be neurotic.' Women got used." Midge Decter said that the women's movement was born of two ideas—that women were victims of men and that there's no fundamental difference between the sexes. "This was a founding idea of the movement."

Friedan responded by saying, "I have a right to deny it . . . I want to correct the record right now." She said that the founding statement of purpose of the National Organization of Women (NOW), in 1966, called for "full equality for women in a fully equal partnership with men."

"The family is not the enemy," Friedan continued. "That came from a subversion of the women's movement. What we need now are real choices having to do with love, marriage, children. We're not finished. We need job care; we need E.R.A., provisions for decent housing and equitable divorce laws." The women's movement, she went on to say, is about opening up options, rather than shutting them down. But the subject of "Geraldo" was whether or not feminism is responsible for a whole host of problems, including the rise in teenage pregnancy, the dissatisfaction of the career "superwoman" trying to "have it all," the modern woman's much-publicized race with her biological clock and an alleged rise in the incidence of male impotence.

Yet Friedan kept insisting that the problems of women aren't sexual. In fact, Friedan has always focused on economic issues, despite constant publicity regarding, for instance, sex roles, the war between the sexes and pornography. Women's problems, Friedan believes, really concern such issues as wages, benefits, health care, child care and housing. The question of whether or not women should work, she said, is "obsolete." Women, including more than half of all mothers, *do* work. Thus she calls for the formulation of national policy concerning maternal and paternal leave, flextime, child care for families of all income levels and more flexible, individually tailored benefit packages. The idea that feminism created women's problems, she said later, is "ass-backwards thinking."

Under the bright lights of the studio where "Geraldo" was being taped, nearly everyone in the audience was reacting, asking questions, booing or applauding. At one point, during a commercial break, Friedan made a fist. Michael Levin had said something to her that no one else had heard – and it looked like Friedan would slug him.

But afterward, as she was walking west through the crowds in Times Square toward the first of a round of celebrations in honor of the Constitution, she was in high spirits.

Still, "Geraldo" had been one hour of constant yelling back and forth. Later, I realized why. First, each of the panelists had used the show as a forum. But more importantly, feminism itself – the focus of the show – is an impossible subject to define. For one thing, there is no single definition of what feminism is. If, in the 1960s, it was a popular and populist movement dedicated to eradicating discrimination in opportunity and wages based on sex, it's now several movements. Among those who call themselves feminists are women whose chief aim is fighting pornography, writers and theorists teaching at the finest universities in the land, radical separatists and members of groups such as the National Abortion Rights Action League and NOW.

More to the point, feminism is a difficult subject to discuss, because when you're talking about feminism, you're talking about women. Though it may be stating the obvious, the subject of women does not lend itself to narrow definition or easy answers, any more than does talking about any other large group—men, say. With unwieldy subjects, it's easy to slide from the complex questions of economics, law and justice to the emotional ones of sex and sexuality.

The day after the taping of "Geraldo" was the 200th anniversary of the Constitution. In a hired car heading down Manhattan's F.D.R. Drive, on the way to Federal Hall near Wall Street, Friedan reflected on the previous evening's debate.

"In some ways," she said, "women, the women's movement and the sexual issues are used as diversionary devices now, to take attention away from the really serious issues, like the distribution of wealth, economic survival, the educational resources of our country and the rights of the people to have a Government that addresses problems that affect their lives. It's the big-lie technique: The Government is serving big business, and yet the voices of reaction use the remaining viable movements of social change and call them 'special interests.' The term 'special interests' used to refer specifically to big business. Now the Government uses the term to mean the interests of the people themselves.

"The ones who now want to take away the rights of women are using antifeminism and abortion and the sexual issues to divert people from their economic exploitation."

Then she sighed, glanced at the first section of the New York Times, sighed again and said, "I really have to tell you that it appalls me that there are Jewish people using their brains and ingenuity to help reaction . . . to suppress the rights of the people. The social conscience and the morality of social conscience has always been the best of Jewish thinking. Such people not only betray the American values inherent in the Constitution, but the Jewish value of morality, in a specious attack on the women's movement."

She was born Betty Naomi Goldstein in Peoria, Illinois, in 1921, the year after women won the right to vote. Her father was an immigrant jeweler from Russia. When her mother, also the daughter of an immigrant, married, she gave up a career in journalism, as the women's page editor of the Peoria newspaper. Friedan was one of three children in an eight-room house.

The family attended a Reform synagogue, where Friedan went to Sunday school and studied to be confirmed. A week or so before her confirmation, she told the rabbi that she no longer believed in God. He told her to keep it to herself until after the ceremony.

She was not happy in Peoria. She described how she was excluded from local society because she was Jewish: "I had a miserable adolescence. Anti-Jewish feelings prevailed in the fraternities and sororities [in Peoria], and so I was an outsider. Believe me, I would have rather been eating hamburgers at the burger place with the other boys and girls than reading poetry and looking at tombstones. But it gave me the power of observation—the social consciousness of an outsider—that's vital for a writer."

At Smith College in Massachusetts, she became immersed in Gestalt psychology. It was there that she began to confront the implications of anti-Semitism. It was World War II. She became editor-in-chief of the college newspaper, wrote an honors thesis, won a fellowship to pursue graduate work in psychology at the University of California at Berkeley and graduated from Smith, in 1942, summa cum laude.

She moved to California to continue her studies but did not complete her degree. So she returned to the East Coast—this time to New York City—and got a job as a reporter. In time, she met Carl Friedan, and they married in 1947. (They were divorced in 1969.)

The family moved to Queens and then to Rockland Country. By this time, Friedan was a full-time housewife and mother of three.

"In Rockland County," Friedan said, "most of my Jewish friends were Unitarian. But my children had Hanukkah and Passover. When my oldest son was 13, I had a multigenerational party in the tradition of our ancestors. We sent out invitations: 'We invite you to celebrate the thirteenth birthday of our son Daniel.' My Unitarian Jewish friends called up and said, 'Oh, what do you want to do *that* for?' "

"And how did that make you feel?" I asked.

"Annoyed as hell. I always felt that my Jewish identity was important," she explained, "though many years ago, if I wasn't an 'atheist' Jew, I was an 'agnostic' Jew. What's interesting is that my feminism has brought me to a closer embrace of authentic Jewish roots, including an interest in theology."

Friedan is interested in the parallels between Judaism and feminism. I suggested that both antifeminism and anti-Semitism share contradictory rhetoric. For example, in Europe, from the Age of Emancipation—when, starting in the late 18th century, European Jews were granted equal rights as citizens—and onward, Jews were seen both as the social revolutionaries who wanted to tear down the existing order *and* as the bankers who controlled the world's coffers. So too, even now in America, women are portrayed as being both illogical and weak *and* pushy, loud-mouthed and castrating.

"Certainly there's an affinity between antifeminism and anti-Semitism," Friedan said. At the peak of the women's movement, she received anti-Semitic threats from people who addressed her by her maiden name and said that the E.R.A. was a Zionist plot to brainwash American women. She has written that "at the same time that Hitler was stripping Jews of citizenship, he issued decrees barring women from professional positions and political office."

But the real links between feminism and Judaism are, for Friedan, not negative. Friedan believes that the women's movement has given women power to fight for others and that this newfound sense of female power and responsibility is tied to Judaic tradition. She frequently quotes Hillel: "If I am not for myself, who will be for me? If I am only for myself, what am I?" And she takes these questions one step further: "And if I am not for myself, how will I have the power to be for anyone else?" The strength of the women's movement, Friedan maintains, is its origins in women gaining mastery over their own lives.

Thus Friedan sees herself as rooted firmly in the tradition of distinctly Jewish voices of social protest. "There's a sense of injustice that's built into our genes," she said, "perhaps from all the centuries of injustice, and I'm part of it. Many of the social thinkers and prophets have been Jewish."

By late afternoon, I was sitting opposite Friedan at a small table at the window of an Upper West Side restaurant. An hour earlier, she had been feeling slightly worn down from the day's events: the Schroeder luncheon, the public reading of the Constitution, the party afterward. But now she felt much better. She was expansive. She wanted to know about me. I told her about my mother, who started tap-dancing when she turned 50. I told her about the difficulties I'd had finding an apartment. She listened intently.

She began to explain how women's interests and Jewish interests overlap regarding the family. "Jews have always known that a strong family is important for both Jewish and human survival. And, in Israel, the strength of women is central to survival. Here, in America, the immigrant generation of mothers and fathers saw to it that their children got an education in a language that they couldn't even speak properly. Now that strength – the strength of the Jewish woman – has to be used in different ways."

While Friedan concedes that the patriarchal family structure may once have been necessary, she believes that the modern Jewish woman must be free to make her own destiny, in order to be free to give herself over to her family. Jewish men, too, must be encouraged to perform what has traditionally been women's work. The polarization of the sexes, Friedan maintains, weakens family life. Since the majority of women working outside the home do so not to "fulfill themselves," but rather to support themselves and their family, provisions for child care in the public and private sectors would strengthen the Jewish family.

Friedan is a founding member of an organization called the Jewish Awareness Group. She speaks frequently on the subject of Judaism and feminism. And she attends a Talmud study group in Los Angeles, where she lives part of the year as visiting professor at the University of Southern California. One senses that, like Yentl in Isaac Bashevis Singer's story, she dreams of immersing herself in the sacred texts. But unlike Yentl, she's too busy writing, lecturing, organizing, traveling and schmoozing to do so. She would never disguise herself as a man to be admitted into a yeshiva: She will only accept Jewish wisdom if it accepts her – as an equal.

"Every generation has a task," she said. "I think that the task for this time is to bring Judaism to the full embrace of the personhood of women. Whatever your concept of creation, mystery – whatever name you give to God – it must embrace the feminine as well as the masculine principle. That's what the women rabbis are doing. Once you've got the education and have broken into the field, once you're there, don't just sit still. The values, the definitions, the rubrics and standards of that field will come from the female as well as the male experience. Equality does not deny the differences between the sexes; equality ultimately must embrace the difference. But it must be equality. We must transform the terms; that holds for Judaism, too."

Judaism, she believes, must accept women as equal to men, grant women an equal place in ritual and encourage women to enroll in seminaries as rabbinical students.

Friedan ended the day as an honoree of the New York Civil Liberties Union, but she still had the whole evening before her. She attended a

Jewish Awareness meeting, the subject of which was the Vatican and the Jews. At well past 11 P.M., she was still going strong. As I got into a taxi headed downtown, I heard her voice. Twenty paces away from me, she and a friend from the Jewish Awareness group were arguing a point from the evening's debate.

Friedan is often impatient and distracted. She can be brusque, even rude. She does not always hear what others have to say, and from maintaining a posture of defense for more than two decades, she doesn't always detect the glimmerings of other truths that might be embedded in an opponent's argument. But she is also joyful, warm and compassionate, complex and brilliant. She laughs a lot. She thrives in the whirl and tumult of large gatherings. She is torn between sitting still, all alone with her thoughts and her pen, and stepping out into the world of political struggle. So she does both.

She told me a story: When he was a young rabbinical student, Friedan's maternal grandfather came to St. Louis from Hungary. In time, he made his way to Peoria. But before he got there, so the family legend goes, he amazed all his teachers by his brilliance: in one year, he supposedly finished grade school, high school and college. He went on to graduate first in his class from Washington University's Medical School.

He was in the Medical Corps in World War I and, upon his return home, was appointed public health commissioner of Peoria. At the outbreak of World War II, he was about to be retired. However, in the chaos that followed Pearl Harbor, he stayed on. "We never mentioned how old Grandpa was, and they didn't catch up with him until he was in his 90s. My sister and I, when we were in high school, used to take turns driving all over Illinois with him, to little towns, so he wouldn't fall asleep at the wheel."

One senses that Betty Friedan, too, plans to be driving all over the American landscape when she's in her 90s.

Chaim Grade

Morton A. Reichek

---

haim Grade, a 68-year-old Polish-born novelist, short-story writer and poet, has lived in the Bronx for the past thirty years. A short, bald man with an exuberant personality and a self-deprecating sense of humor, Grade (pronounced GRAD-eh) looks the way David Ben-Gurion might have looked with a haircut. He has a passion for the outdoors, a zest for good food and wine, and a hearty, convivial manner that masks the gravity of what he considers his personal mission in life: to commemorate the vanished religious civilization of East European Jewry and to preserve its memories.

Since his arrival in the United States in 1948, Grade has written and published seven books of prose, five volumes of poetry, and countless newspaper and magazine essays and stories—all in Yiddish—eulogizing the pre-Nazi world of the religious Jewish scholars and functionaries in the *shtetls* or ghetto towns of Poland and Lithuania, and resurrecting in literature a society that no longer exists.

Drawing his settings from his own years spent in the yeshivas or Talmudic academies of his birthplace, Vilna, and its environs, Grade says: "I have the feeling that it is the will of God for me to leave a monument for a world that perished. I don't want to seem melodramatic, but I've always felt that I remained alive to be able to describe what our life had been like."

Grade narrowly escaped from Vilna in 1941 as German troops entered the city. His mother and his first wife, a nurse from whom he had become separated while fleeing the city, both died in the Nazi death camps. Traveling eastward, Grade survived German dive-bombing attacks and the threat of execution by retreating Russian troops who mistook him for a German spy.

During the next four years, he worked on a Russian collective farm, wandered through the Soviet Asian republics of Uzbekistan, Turkmenia and Tadzhikistan, and was associated with a group of Moscow Jewish writers, most of whom were subsequently liquidated during Stalin's anti-Semitic purges. In Moscow, he met and married his present wife, Inna, while she was a college student there. She is sixteen years his junior. On the heels of the victorious Soviet forces, Grade returned to Vilna in 1945 with his wife. In despair over the city's devastation and the loss of his family and friends, they soon left the Soviet Union and settled in Paris. Two years later, they migrated to this country.

Among Yiddish readers, Grade has achieved the stature of a literary heavyweight. He has been honored with virtually every Jewish literary award available in this country and abroad. His most ardent devotees have compared him to such Western literary giants as Dickens, for his concern with the problems of morality and his deep-rooted humanity; to Bellow, for his skill in interweaving philosophy and narrative action, and to Faulkner, for his ability to transform his own provincial milieu into a universal setting populated by absorbing characters who are bigger than life.

As far as the American literary establishment has been concerned, however, Grade might as well have been writing in Icelandic or Basque. He has been virtually unknown until now to non-Jewish readers and even to Jews unfamiliar with Yiddish.

A handful of Grade's poems and short stories—including works he wrote before coming to the United States—was published in the Anglo-Jewish press and in English-language anthologies of Yiddish literature during his earlier years here. In 1967, a short novel, *The Well*, was published in translation by the Jewish Publication Society. Its plot, about two simple Jews who try to repair the half-ruined well in a Vilna synagogue courtyard, provides the backdrop for an extraordinary gallery of ghetto personalities ranging from religious fanatics and revolutionaries to beggars and nervous lovers. Five years later, an autobiographical sketch called *The Seven Little Lanes* – issued by Bergen Belsen Memorial Press – appeared, dealing with Grade's brief postwar return to Vilna. But both books gave Grade only limited exposure.

He started to gain more general recognition at the age of 64 on the strength of a novel, *The Agunah*, written in 1961 in Yiddish. The first of his full-length novels to be released in English translation by a major publishing house (Bobbs-Merrill), it is the tale of a woman whose soldier-husband is missing in action during World War I. Forbidden by Jewish religious law from remarrying because there are no witnesses to his death, her plan to wed again stirs up a communal furor that pits two rabbis against each other – one a gentle, humanitarian interpreter of the law and the other a strict constructionist.

Bobbs-Merrill also published the first volume of his two-volume novel, *The Yeshiva*, in 1976. The second volume of this epic work, subtitled *Masters and Disciples*, was released in English in December 1977. Much broader in scope, *The Yeshiva* presents a panorama of yeshiva life never depicted before in fiction. A saga about Talmudic students and their teachers, it is laced with plots and subplots involving brooding moralists consumed by guilt and doubts, and religious scholars grappling with secular temptations.

Irving Howe and the late Maurice Samuel, a literary scholar and translator who had much to do with the popularization of Sholem Aleichem here, have both acclaimed Grade as a major literary talent. Elie Wiesel, also a yeshiva student in pre-World War II Europe, calls Grade "probably the greatest living Yiddish writer. If he were writing in any other language, he would have been already recognized as the creator of masterpieces." Grade is well known in Israel, where his work has been extensively translated into Hebrew. One of his translators was the nation's late president, Zalman Shazar.

Grade's work differs markedly from the homespun vignettes of Sholem Aleichem and the erotic, mystical folk stories of the more contemporary Isaac Bashevis Singer – two Yiddish writers who have achieved universal renown through translation. His themes are more formidable, the settings more parochial. He writes novels of ideas that examine the ethical and legal qualities of Judaism and the confrontation between Orthodox and secular values. Despite his estrangement from Jewish institutional life, he treats religious traditionalists benignly in his stories. But more significant, Grade's writing represents a primary source of Jewish history.

He is an archivist who has assembled authentic source material for the future study of East European yeshiva life. Not surprisingly, the weightiness of his themes makes him more difficult to read, both in English and Yiddish, than Sholem Aleichem and Singer. He is also more difficult to translate because his Yiddish brims with esoteric Talmudic Hebrew references. Says Wiesel: "Grade's Yiddish is a more meditative, reflective language. Singer's is concrete, naturalistic." These problems have been responsible for the delays in bringing his work before a broader audience.

I recently visited Grade and his wife, Inna, in their five-room apartment in a housing cooperative near Van Cortlandt Park. The neighborhood is quiet and cheerful and surrounded by trees. The woodsy setting is important to Grade because he is infatuated with nature. (He has written several poems celebrating his frequent visits to national parks throughout the country.)

Many of the residents of Grade's neighborhood are elderly Yiddish-speaking people who hold him in awe as a literary celebrity. They know his writing largely through the *Forward*, New York's sole surviving Yiddish daily newspaper, which Grade—like Singer—has contributed to regularly for many years. In fact, the bulk of Grade's work appeared there and in two now-defunct Yiddish dailies before publication in book form. Grade now contributes to the *Forward* every Sunday, usually a piece of serialized fiction.

"First of all, we will take a drink," Grade said heartily in heavily accented English as he ushered me into his small study. I asked for a scotch. He grimaced as I added water and ice, then poured himself a glass of Israeli cognac.

The walls of Grade's apartment are crammed with close to 10,000 books in at least six languages. Like vines of ivy, bookcases are spreading into every room—even the bedroom and closets. Many of the books are what Grade describes as "Talmudic commentaries on the Bible and commentaries on the commentaries and commentaries on those commentaries." In addition to a massive selection of books on Jewish subjects, Grade's library is well stocked with Shakespeare, the great English poets, books on art and philosophy, and the Russian, German and French classics. Contemporary American literature is represented sparingly.

Several shelves are devoted wholly to Grade's personal hero, the seventeenth century Jewish philosopher Baruch Spinoza, who was an early rationalist critic of the Bible. Grade's favorite Western authors are

Dostoevsky ("the Shakespeare of the nineteenth century"), Victor Hugo ("a great humanist") and the Americans Whitman, Emerson and Melville.

"I need these books like a hole in the head," he said wryly. "It is bad to love so much books. I write only 10 percent of the time and read 90 percent."

Grade's wife shares his literary interests. She is a vivacious, erudite woman who earned a master's degree in comparative literature from Columbia University (her thesis was on Dostoevsky). Later, she taught Russian and French at C.W. Post College and other schools.

The Grades are childless and Mrs. Grade now busily functions as a literary factotum for her husband. She handles most of his record-keeping and correspondence, acts as his English interpreter when necessary, drives the family car, arranges his lecture schedule and helps edit the English and Russian translations of his work. Frequently he deferred to Mrs. Grade when I asked him a detailed question involving dates or numbers: "My wife will tell you better. She remembers more."

Mrs. Grade's parents were culturally assimilated Russian Jewish physicians. She learned to speak Yiddish only after her marriage to Grade. But she is still unable to read the language, which restricts her ability to translate her husband's writing.

Although Grade is preoccupied with religious matters in his writing, his life-style is distinctly secular. He belongs to no synagogue. Each year he spends the Jewish High Holy Days in the Adirondacks, where he and his wife rent a cottage for several months. Says he: "For me this is a strong emotional experience, to run away in the woods."

Born in April 1910 in Vilna, Grade was an only child. His father, an aged, impoverished Hebrew teacher whose first wife died after bearing four sons, was a *maskil*, a learned Jew whose religious views were tempered by secular inclinations. He wanted his son to learn a trade. But Grade's mother, a pious woman who supported the family as a fruit peddler, insisted that he attend the yeshiva and become a religious scholar. Grade's father died when he was 17 and for many years Grade and his widowed mother lived in a single, windowless room in a blacksmith's shop. At 22, Grade left the yeshiva, an ordained rabbi. At 26, he married a nurse whose father and grandfather were rabbis. Today he comments: "I never was a really good yeshiva *bocher* [boy], because I was interested in girls, in love affairs." He recalls: "So terrible! And then the books. All the time I was already reading secular literature in Yiddish and Hebrew. And then I have the big mouth to say what I think. So how can you be a good yeshiva *bocher* when you say everything that you think with such *chutzpa* as I did it?"

Caught up in Vilna's political ferment, Grade became a socialist and began to write poetry when he left the yeshiva. "All the time I had to fight whether I would remain a synagogue man and a *ben Torah* [religious scholar] while I was busy arguing about socialism, communism, nationalism, Zionism, and having a good time with the girls. It was too late for me to learn a trade, so I decided to become a writer. But how can you make a living from poetry?"

Grade's first published poem, written in 1932, was a melancholy tribute to his mother, who figures prominently in much of his poetry and prose. Says Grade: "Every writer, like every painter, has one face. In Rubens, with his hundreds of women, there is always one face. In Rembrandt, the most important faces are his father and mother. So I'm not Rubens and Rembrandt, but I too include my mother in all my work."

Some sample lines from Grade's "My Mother," read:

> Her face smolders, a fire pot,
> Her hands measure, weigh;
> She pleads, she calls,
> Till again she dozes with eyes half-shut:
> Her hand taps at the freezing air
> And stays there, stretched out.
> Just like
> A shadow on the snow,
> She sways back and forth the whole day long,
> Until late at night;
> She rocks herself like the pointer of her scale,
> To the left, to the right.
> Hunched up, one large hump,
> She rots in the snow flurries,
> Like the apples in her breast—
> And sleeps . . .

The poem was widely circulated in Vilna, and many of its admirers flocked to see Grade's mother at her fruit stand in the marketplace. "She was insulted and indignant because so many people came to watch her sleep," Grade says.

In 1936, he published his first volume of poetry, entitled *Yo* (Yiddish slang for "yes"), a collection of politically oriented pieces which present an affirmative, staunchly nationalistic stance in response to the growing oppression against the Jews in Germany, Austria and Poland. Although a recent article has implied that Grade was a communist, he refutes this: "I was never a communist. That was the one *chochma* [wise thing] that I did in my life, not becoming one. Because I made so many mistakes in my life that if God asked me to be born again and to make the same mistakes, I wouldn't accept it. We were radicals but not communists."

The book quickly established Grade as an important poet in Vilna and was acclaimed in Yiddish literary circles in far-off New York and Tel Aviv. "I never got as much recognition for anything, as I did for this little book," he says.

Disillusioned by the Moscow show trials of the mid-1930s and by manifestations of anti-Semitism in Poland's socialist organizations, Grade began to shift away from political poetry and to write: "like a learned Jew from the synagogue," reverting to the yeshiva for source material. His second book, *Musarnikes*, published in 1939, just before the start of the war, was a 150-page narrative poem inspired by his boyhood training in Musar, a Jewish religious movement popular during Grade's youth, which held that man is born evil and can only be redeemed through an ascetic life of self-denial. (This movement is clinically examined in Grade's later novel, *The Yeshiva*.)

His second book of poetry, with its severely religious motif, set the course for his subsequent work. His poems and novels project a wistful desire to recapture the religious belief and faith of his youth.

I asked Grade why he writes with such affection about a life which he no longer shares. "I know these people and these are the people I love," he responded. "They live a genuine life. I envy [observant Orthodox Jews] because I know how deep they feel. I envy anybody who can be happy. After all, who is rich? The man who is happy with what he has, especially if what he has is small."

Grade himself cannot explain why he abandoned organized religion. "I am busy with this question all my life," he comments. "But after all, Judaism is also a civilization. Religious people don't have to depend on a church. You know, it is impossible to find a poet who is not religious, who is not a mystic, who does not feel for things that do not exist and that we do not see. Officially, to be a Jew—or a Christian, for that matter—you have to do everything in accordance with official law and tradition. But that is not the same thing as being religious or not."

Grade still devotes considerable time to Talmudic study and wears a skullcap when he reads certain Biblical commentaries. "There are some books I can read without a hat," he says. "Even the Bible I can read without a *yarmulke*. I'm not afraid. But some commentaries—when I begin to read the Vilna Gaon [a legendary eighteenth century Talmudic sage], for example, it is very deep, and a lot I still don't understand. If I read it without a *yarmulke*, I begin to feel like my head is burning."

Grade subsisted in Russia by writing Yiddish patriotic poetry, receiving payments (per line of poetry) from the Jewish Anti-Fascist Committee and food rations from the Soviet Writers Union. "This small membership certificate was a matter of life or death for me" he says. "It made me like a prince in Russia and was enough to give me freedom."

Five volumes of Grade's work during this period were later published in the United States and Argentina, but the poems have never been translated into English. "I was clever with them," Grade says. "I didn't write one word against the Soviet Union and nothing about Zionism."

In his years in the Soviet Union, Grade became a close friend of many leading Jewish communist intellectuals who were later executed or died in prison during Stalin's final years. Among his Moscow friends was the Yiddish writer David Bergelson, who was one of twenty-four Jewish intellectuals killed on the night of August 12, 1952, in the basement of the notorious Lubianka Prison. Bergelson, with whom Grade had been a house guest for many months, had tried to dissuade Grade from leaving the Soviet Union.

"Chaim, why do you want to leave?" Bergelson asked him. "Is it because you feel you won't be able to write the way we want you to write?"

"No," Grade answered. "It is much worse. I am leaving because I am afraid it will be too easy for me to learn to write the way you want me to write."

Grade is still obsessed by the murder of Bergelson and the other Russian Jewish intellectuals who had befriended him while he lived in the Soviet Union. "In the entire thwarted and scarred history of modern Yiddish literature there is no chapter more tragic," Irving Howe and the late Eliezer Greenberg wrote in a recently published English anthology of

Soviet Yiddish fiction, *Ashes Out of Hope*. "Elsewhere in Europe scores of
Yiddish writers were destroyed by avowed enemies; here in the Soviet
Union a generation of gifted Yiddish novelists and poets came to its end
in the prison cells or labor camps of the very state to which they had
pledged themselves, sometimes with naive enthusiasm, sometimes with
wry foreboding."

In anguish over this tragedy, Grade wrote a poem entitled "Elegy for
the Soviet Yiddish Writers." Some excerpts translated into English by
Cynthia Ozick are:

> I weep for you with all the letters
>   of the alphabet
> that made your hopeful songs. I saw
>   how reason spent
> itself in vain for hope, how you
>   strove against regret —
> and all the while your hearts were
>   rent
> to bits, like ragged prayer books.
>   Wanderer, I slept
> in your beds, knew you as liberal
>   hosts;
> yet every night heard sighs of
>   ancient ghosts:
> Jews converted by force . . .
>
> Ghosts justify my despair, phantom
>   faces
> smile their lost mute shame.
> Through nights of fever and dream
> you razed your palaces
> to glimmering ruin. In your poems
>   you were
> like a pond — crooked mirror
> for the world of truth. The young
> have forgotten you and me and the
>   hour
> of our grief. Your widows receive
>   their dower

of blood money. But your darkly
    murdered tongue,
silenced by the hangman's noose,
is no longer heard, though the muse
again sings in the land. You left
me your language, lifted with joy.
    But, oh, I am bereft—
I wear your Yiddish like a drowned
    man's shirt,
wearing out the hurt.

Grade began to write prose at 40. His first work, a short story called "My Quarrel with Hersh Rasseyner," appeared in 1950. It revolves around a confrontation between two Holocaust survivors, one an Orthodox believer who has remained insular and utterly faithful, the other a writer, named Chaim Vilner, who is clearly the author's alter ego (he also appears as a major character in *The Yeshiva*), and represents the view of continuing Jewish creativity in a secular sense. In typical Grade fashion, the story presents no victor, but calls for reconciliation between Orthodoxy and Jewish secularism. After appearing in a Yiddish magazine, the story was published in English in *Commentary* three years later. It is now widely regarded as a Jewish literary classic.

Meanwhile, Grade had started to produce a steady flow of short stories and serialized novels for the Yiddish press. Much of this work has been privately published in book form, with the costs borne by Grade himself and by personal admirers. It was not until 1967, however, that the first of these prose volumes, *The Well*, was published in English. The book caught the attention of Curt Leviant, a professor of Jewish studies at Rutgers University, who contacted the editor of the *New York Times Book Review*, informing him that the first English book of a major Yiddish author had been published and recommending that the *Times* review the work. He was invited to do the review himself.

In his review, Leviant praised the book highly and subsequently translated the three other Grade books that are now available in English. Leviant eventually persuaded his own publisher, Twayne, which became a subsidiary of Bobbs-Merrill, to produce the English version of *The Agunah*. The book received highly favorable reviews in both the Jewish and non-Jewish press. More than 8,000 copies were sold, which was enough to convince Bobbs-Merrill to publish Leviant's subsequent translation of the two-volume work, *The Yeshiva.*

"Grade's books in translation have done well commercially," says Jacob Steinberg, Twayne's former president and currently publishing consultant for ITT, Bobbs-Merrill's parent company. "But it is a pity that Grade doesn't publicize himself in English. You need an articulate author to promote a book."

Grade is self-conscious of his limitations in English and refuses to speak in that language in public. In private discussions, he lapses into Yiddish when he has difficulty explaining himself. Nevertheless, he is a highly skilled orator whose jaunty style makes him an impressive public performer in Yiddish. "I have the blood of an actor," he explains sheepishly. In fact, the Yiddish lecture circuit has been the primary source of Grade's livelihood for many years. He has appeared before Yiddish-speaking groups in most major U.S. cities and in Israel, Latin America, South Africa and once even in Zambia. His principal lecture topic is Jewish literature and history. But in recent years he has curtailed his activities because of two heart attacks. Still another reason for his reduced lecturing, of course, is the shrinking of his Yiddish audiences. Grade is highly sensitive about the uncertain future of Yiddish as a living language. Says he: "It is a miracle that it still exists. History has been against its survival." But when I referred to Yiddish as a "dying" language, he snapped at me: "Don't say that to a Yiddish writer. If you come to my home, you are not going to tell me that I am going to die."

Many of our discussions were conducted over the dinner table. Mrs. Grade is an excellent cook, and on each of my visits she prepared dinner. Grade's favorite dessert is a dish of bananas, sherbet and a generous dash of Kahlua liqueur. Grade ate it heartily and joked: "I must thank you, for when I have guests it is the only time I eat good. I never get such things."

At least three novels, several novellas and collections of short stories, plus the bulk of Grade's poetry, still remain untranslated. For the past two years he has been reworking the longest of the untranslated works, *The Rabbi's House,* into novel form. The story ran as a serial in the *Forward* for three years during the late 1960s.

"I'm afraid to do it," Grade said. "It's a terrible problem. A new book is easier to write than converting from a serial to a regular novel. I see all the mistakes that I did. And then I am so busy writing poems for the newspaper, preparing speeches and quarreling with my wife and then making peace with her."

He is now trimming the original 2,000-page manuscript by about 50 percent and has changed the title to *Sons and Daughters*. He is also rewriting the ending, which now dissatisfies him. The book is written in the classic Russian style with an enormous number of characters and subjects. The story focuses on the rabbi's struggle to preserve religious tradition among his eight children and grandchildren. The prototype for the rabbi was the grandfather of Grade's first wife.

Grade's personal favorite among his untranslated writings is a collection of short stories, *The Silent Quorum*, which was published as a Yiddish book in 1976. "This is my best," he says. "But no one will translate it because there is not enough action."

Nevertheless, the stories are crammed with an extraordinary collection of personalities. A woodcarver makes a set of tablets of the Ten Commandments for a small synagogue and scandalizes the congregants by carving his own name at the bottom of the tablets. A distracted rabbi wanders from *shtetl* to *shtetl*, preparing what he considers a monumental book of commentaries on the Bible, and forgets where he deposited his wife and children. An observant Jew is infuriated when his son marries a non-Jew, and is even more angered—out of sympathy for his daughter-in-law—when the son deserts his Christian wife and their small child to return to his Jewish sweetheart.

Leviant, who recently published his own novel, is no longer available to work on Grade's untranslated material, and Grade has been unable to find a suitable replacement. Qualified Yiddish translators are scarce, the remuneration is modest and the technical demands to translate Grade's writing into English are exceptional.

The Hebrew poet Chaim Nachman Bialik once said that translation is like kissing a bride through a veil. In Grade's case, the barrier is even thicker. Isaac Bashevis Singer, to whom Grade is invariably compared, also writes exclusively in Yiddish. Singer, however, has lived in the United States more than a decade longer than Grade and has a greater command of English. Indeed, he knows the language so well that his translators function largely as copy editors.

Grade is saddened by his plight. "It is lonely," he says, "to have to publish a thousand copies of your own book, and if you sell 500 of them, you are a best seller. But there is the joy of creation. Does a Yiddish writer have less? I am conscious of a great duty to show the philosophy and psychology of the Orthodox Jewish people. Everything that I show is the Jewish *gestalt*."

The three decades in the United States have had no impact on the content of Grade's prose work. I asked him why he hasn't written about matters unrelated to Jewish life. Certainly, I said, his wide travels and personal adventures could furnish a tremendous amount of source material.

"I try to write about other things—things that are not so deep in Jewish civilization or so deep in me, not just Jewish problems," he responded. "But I can't go out. This is the life I know best. Not my years in Russia, in Paris, my travels in South America and South Africa. This is all superficial in my life. It comes and goes. What is really deep is the life that existed for 1,000 years—Jewish life in Eastern Europe. That is the life that will remain with me. I will never go another way.

"I have a complex. I don't know how to talk to the non-Jewish reader. I want to talk to him, but I don't know how to. I will never understand American psychology. Therefore, I don't write about America.

"That is what is so terrible for me. To be what I am in Yiddish life—a prominent writer—and to be a beginner in English. Who needs to begin again? It is too late. There is not enough time. I will never make it in *your* world."

Blu and Yitz Greenberg

Andrea Jolles

Blu and Irving ("Yitz") Greenberg have been called the most dynamic couple in American Jewish life. Blu has written *On Women and Tradition*, an eloquent and highly personal account of her attempts to reconcile her new-found feminism with her long-held orthodoxy. A second book, *How to Run a Traditional Jewish Household*, a detailed guide for the uninitiated, is filled with warm, humorous anecdotes about her family's observance of holiday rituals. Through Yitz's lectures and classes, he is credited with single-handedly bringing Judaism to lay members of the Federation of Jewish Philanthropies-United Jewish Appeal, and with making Jews everywhere conscious of the profound effect of the Holocaust and the rebirth of Israel on both faith and deeds.

The Greenbergs are the epitome of the modern Orthodox couple who have tried to integrate the best in contemporary society with their love of observance and tradition. And, with courage and conviction, they have spent the last decade explaining to the Orthodox how they can live halakhically with feminist equality, and to others how they can value authentic Jewish commitment. One of their goals is to help bring an end to the denominational wrangling which divides American Jewry.

Yitz says: "I am trying to scramble the lines separating the denominations. It is a *mitzvah* to scramble them, for they are misleading."

Their appeal for interdenominational harmony has attracted a large following among Reform, Conservative and even secular Jews, but not the Orthodox, who find their liberal interpretation of *halakha* close to heretical.

"The Greenbergs' attraction," says Arnold Eisen, assistant professor of religion at Columbia University, "lies in their combination of intellectual energy and openness. They are people who are complex and aware of conflicts in their own position—and that doesn't stop them from living or teaching the way they do. That combination is refreshing and reassuring."

They maintain an exhausting pace, attending and appearing at an endless round of conferences, discussions, lectures and symposia, some sponsored by the National Jewish Resource Center, which Greenberg founded and runs.

Arlene Agus, director of external affairs and planning for Yeshiva University's Cardoza Law School in New York City, and a friend of the Greenbergs, calls Blu "a pioneer, who has made real the great anguish of Jewish feminism felt within orthodoxy," adding, "She has made it possible for these women to say 'ouch.' "

On a recent afternoon, Blu, a pretty, small, dark-haired woman with warm brown eyes, had just returned from a three-day Women of Faith in the '80s conference sponsored by the American Jewish Committee in Washington, D.C. Sitting in her book-lined living room, her feet on an ottoman, she said she had told the group about her reaction to the omission of women writers from a series of magazine articles on the Jewish Sabbath. Her voice soft, her words precise, she recalled: "What passed through my mind at that moment were the labors of millions of Jewish women, every Thursday and Friday for three millennia, the trillions of plucked chicken feathers, the oceans of chicken soup, the tons of gefilte fish and kugel, the miles of linens washed and ironed for the Sabbath; the countless children with shiny hair, dressed in special Sabbath clothes—and in the magazine not one woman was called upon to reflect on the Sabbath." Then she began talking about her five children, who range in age from 16 to 22, and are scattered between Israel and the tidy, comfortable family home in the Riverdale section of New York City. "Our children are more worthy of interviews than we are," she said: "They're very strong personalities and we are very proud of them." Three of them—Moshe, 22, Deborah, 19 and J.J. (Jonathan Joseph), 18—are studying at yeshivas in Israel. The youngest, Goody, 16,

who is still at Ramaz, an Orthodox day school in Manhattan, and the
next to the oldest, David, 21, who is now studying at Yeshiva University,
are still at home.

How does she, as a feminist, feel about her children studying at
fundamentalist yeshivas?

"I wouldn't have it any other way," she maintained. "I want them to get
the best Jewish education they can where there is more emphasis on
learning than on ideology. The girls will be trained and have a sense of
themselves and a purposeful life, in addition to being wives and mothers.
And, though the boys' yeshivas are more fundamentalist and intransigent on women's issues, they can take the best of it, distancing themselves from certain parts.

"We try not to make them reflect our ideologies," she added.

Blu was born into the small Jewish community in Seattle, Washington,
forty-seven years ago. Her father, a rabbi who had gone into the family
men's clothing business, continued to teach Talmud. When her older
sister was invited to her first Christmas party, the family—unhappy with
the lack of Jewish educational facilities in Seattle—moved to Far Rock-
away, in New York City. Blu attended a yeshiva high school, Brooklyn
College and Yeshiva University Teachers Institute for Women.

After her marriage twenty-seven years ago, she "dabbled"—as she put
it—at part-time jobs for a while. Those included teaching Jewish studies
at Mt. St. Vincent College, a small Catholic institution near her home.
Describing herself as a "transition woman" during that period, she
explains that raising her family was her primary work for many years: "I
was lucky I could do that. I liked being at home and being available."

She added: "I had plenty of moments of ambivalence. The children
were close in age and there was a lot of activity. Sometimes I'd be in the
park with the kids and think life was passing me by, and other times I'd
sit in my office and have knots in my stomach. Women have to live with
that tension. Men don't have the best of both worlds, so they don't have
to live with that."

She dates her beginning awareness of other possibilities to 1973, when
she was invited to address the first National Jewish Women's Conference, an early effort to discuss Jewish feminism. There, she criticized
Jewish tradition for its failure to give women a broader role, and
feminism for its indifference to the human values of tradition. She was

applauded for the former and hissed for the latter. What she discovered then, she wrote, was that "You could be a mild-mannered yeshiva girl and a card-carrying feminist."

At the conference, she saw for the first time how directly involved women could be in conducting prayer – a turning point for her. This experience formed the basis for *On Women and Judaism*, in which she argued that feminism and Judaism could draw from one another. "An authentic Jewish women's movement must seek new approaches within *halakha* to absorb and express women's concerns and must seek to imbue women's concerns with Jewish values."

At her husband's urging, she gave up teaching at Mt. St. Vincent to devote herself full-time to writing and lecturing. He encouraged her, she said, to take her own writing and thinking seriously.

Now she will go on to complete her doctorate in religion at Columbia University; she plans to write her dissertation on some phase of modern Orthodoxy. Her future plans also include an historical novel about Rebecca, "a powerful figure," she noted, "who altered the course of Jewish history."

Blu has been most successful in explaining observance to the non-religious. She is, moreover, recognized by a growing number of non-Orthodox women as a voice of Orthodoxy. In *How To Run a Traditional Jewish Household* she wrote that modern Orthodox people are aware that "there are conflicts in being a citizen of the world and a member of the covenantal community, and conflicts in embracing universalist and particularist values almost simultaneously." But she also goes on to admit that "the tensions are quite bearable and the impasse generally negotiable." In the end, Arlene Agus pointed out, the quintessential Blu Greenberg is "a master harmonizer who tries to draw together the incompatibilities in modern life, bring together Jew and non-Jew, the Orthodox and the non-Orthodox, the feminist and the non-feminist."

In contrast to Blu's steady pace, Yitz is constantly in motion. An hour late for our talk, he apologized, explaining that a National Jewish Resource Center board meeting to settle the purchase of land for a retreat center had delayed him. At six feet five inches tall, very fair, with intense blue eyes, he looks more like a former basketball player than an ordained Orthodox rabbi with a Harvard Ph.D. in American history. He spoke quickly and quietly, his mind clearly outracing his vocabulary, his hands punctuating each statement.

Now 50, Yitz was raised in Borough Park, then an immigrant Jewish community in Brooklyn. His father was a ritual slaughterer and the rabbi of a small Orthodox congregation. He attended ultra-Orthodox yeshivas which, he said, gave him the security to confront the world beyond the Orthodox community.

"My friends who went to Yeshiva University spent their lives trying to be as religiously right-wing as possible," he explained, "whereas my yeshiva was so far out that it gave me the inner security of being so firm I didn't have to prove it." He attended Brooklyn College, graduating in 1953. That same year he was ordained at Beth Jacob Rabbinical Seminary.

Harvard, which he said was his "first real plunge into the gentile world," was one of several experiences which opened him up to the non-Jewish life in this country. At the university in the 1950s, he felt he could not wear a yarmulke, so instead substituted a hat.

"The first two or three years there," he said, "I felt I relived the immigrant experience in America. On the one hand, I wanted to be accepted so I wore the hat, not the yarmulke; on the other, I needed to assert my Jewish identity and particularity, so I couldn't go bareheaded."

The price was high, he admits now, and there was a lot of tension, but Harvard "was a very rich intellectual experience" which he credits with "opening my mind methodologically."

In the early 1960s, a Fulbright Fellowship took him to Israel for a year. What followed was a further series of revelations.

"I began reading about the Holocaust, sitting there in Israel," Greenberg reminisced. "It had an overwhelming impact on me and shook my feeling that the Orthodox had all the answers." The experience of Israel and the Holocaust became the basis for much of his later thinking in trying to bridge the gap between observant and non-observant Jews.

After a teaching stint at Yeshiva University, he accepted the position of rabbi of the Riverdale Jewish Center. He remained there for seven years until 1972, when he was asked to launch the Department of Jewish Studies at City College.

Both Greenbergs said their lives have been a series of happenstances. They have never applied for positions, nor have they had to strain for something they very much wanted.

Blu commented: "You can say we've been able to seize the opportunity when it came. But then, maybe we should have sat back and reflected on what our primary goal was. We were lucky that options came our way."

In the late 1960s Yitz began searching for some way "of enriching the Jewish content of lives and dealing with the open society." He thought, as he told me, that "There had to be some channel, or outlets, for identifying the critical areas and connecting the community to the scholars and the scholars to the community.".

He tried to persuade his Orthodox congregation in Riverdale to establish such a center. For the first time, he came up against resistance from his own community—and that was only the beginning.

"One of my stumbling blocks," he said, "was that the center would be more than just an Orthodox community. Many lay people in the congregation were excited by the idea, but they could not accept that it would be done by all denominations."

With a legacy left to the Jewish Studies Department at City College in the mid-1970s, Yitz and Elie Wiesel, whom he had hired to teach a course on the Holocaust, started a retreat, research and outreach center (which later became the National Jewish Resource Center) with the aim of renewing and enriching Jewish leadership. But when church-state conflicts arose over the question of whether, as a government-funded institution, City College could house such an organization, he left teaching to run the center independently. Now he serves as its president. Administrative tasks do not come easily to Yitz, who prefers to teach and write. One of the most painful experiences of the last few years, he said, has been to learn to live with his limitations.

"I realized that I can't take on a whole agenda. I have to take one step at a time. And I have to accept the difficulty of the process. Moreover, I had to learn that, as a rabbi and a professor, I overrated ideas, and I had to translate that realization into focusing on budgets and processes."

He would have quit "ten times over," he said, but for Blu, because "She has been the one major anchor in my life."

The prime goal of the National Jewish Resource Center, according to Yitz is to educate "all of Jewish leadership—rabbis, scholars, not just the rich, achieving Jews—and to give them the resources and exposure to the tradition through a short-term but highly intensive spiritual atmosphere at retreats."

In a series of pamphlets published by the Center, Yitz wrote about the struggle between faith and doubt in the modern age—a period he calls the third era of Jewish history. He believes that the devastation of the Holocaust made it difficult to have faith, yet the redemption of the founding and survival of Israel made it hard not to do so. He recognizes that a dialectic now exists between belief and non-belief, and that new forms of prayer which include women are necessary and possible. To have faith today, he writes, is to have a voluntary covenant with God, who because of the horror of the Holocaust "was no longer in a position to command, but the Jewish people was so in love with the dream of redemption that it volunteered to carry on its mission." Moreover, he makes clear, the establishment of the Jewish state has given Jews a power never before known in America or in Israel.

"Israel"—he wrote in "The Ethics of Jewish Power"—"is not the only expression of Jewish power. Increasingly, American Jews recognize that they must be involved in the American political process not only for Israel's sake but because government policies can make or break Jewish interests in the United States. This is why AIPAC's membership has doubled in the past fifteen months and why more and more Jews are involved in PACs, political fundraising, etc. Unfortunately, Jewish power is still too vulnerable and marginal but we must make the most of it. As Manes Sperber put it: After the Holocaust, Jews have a moral obligation to anti-Semites to be powerful so as never to tempt them into such evil behavior again."

Yitz Greenberg says that what separates him from thinkers such as Mordecai Kaplan, the founder of Reconstructionism, is that he is a post-modern Orthodox Jew. By that he means "that in many ways I've accepted the claims of Conservative, Reform and Reconstructionist, even though I may differ from them. Now I'm willing to admit there is growth and change in the tradition, and that many of the ethical criticisms the others have raised are true, and it's a challenge for the tradition and not to be dismissed."

He claims that anyone who recognizes the Holocaust and Israel as the central events in modern Jewish history "recognizes that what unites us is more important than what separates us. In the face of the Holocaust, all groups were unimportant but all carried on. In the face of Israel, everyone is a Zionist. If we are one in destiny, we can't be totally alienated spiritually."

Moreover, Yitz came to the conclusion that the Federation of Jewish Philanthropies was acting on many of the things to which the religious merely gave lip service.

"The priority of Jewish life was the sanctity of life," he insists. "But who was acting on it? The people who were raising money." He also discovered that these same people were spiritually bereft and almost totally ignorant of tradition.

Under a contract from the Federation, he began teaching a series of classes for its leaders on Jewish ethics, history and law. The classes met in offices all over New York City—before business hours in Wall Street board rooms, late evenings in Park Avenue apartments and during the day at the Federation. At first he attracted mainly women and the young leadership, but, as word spread, the older members began to attend as well.

Turning Federation on to Judaism may well be his most successful achievement. Susan Schlecter, who has been an active Federation fundraiser and regularly attends his original women's study group, praises Yitz for making her "more comfortable with God. He is a terrific teacher who gives us a lot of scholarly information and relates it anecdotally to what is going on today."

As a result of his larger responsibilities to the Center, he now teaches only one-fourth of the time there; the other Center classes are conducted by five program assistants. Currently, the Center has an executive director and an annual budget of $700,000, raised largely from private sources.

So far, the Center has been least successful in liberalizing the Orthodox viewpoint, a frustrating and painful experience for him.

Samuel Heilman, a professor of sociology and director of the Center for Jewish Studies at Queens College and author of several books on Orthodox Jews, says that Yitz "went out on a limb, fully expecting the [Orthodox] community to follow him—and when he looked back, he found they were sawing it off."

"I did go far out on a limb," he responds, "because I'm convinced that the true portrait of the Jewish community is not one community but the whole community. I think when the Orthodox community gains perspective—they've gone to the right in recent years—they will see I'm very much at the center, not in the wings. Meanwhile there is a certain loss of respect, so they've tried to write us off. I think they've failed. I love the community. I love the religious life. But I'm a critic of the community."

He says he relies on Blu to keep his own criticism of the community within bounds.

"In the struggle between affirming the present and holding to ideals, I find her independence, judgment and balance very helpful. Blu loves the tradition enough so that her own critique is not bitter, and she keeps me from letting my criticism drown her affirmation," he explains.

For her part, Blu has learned to live with her contradictions. She says: "Sometimes there is a discrepancy between my writings and my actions. For instance, I believe there should be women rabbis, but I wouldn't want my children to be married by a woman rabbi because there is no woman rabbi in the Orthodox community now. I've come to believe that I don't have to be apologetic for my inconsistencies, and can follow my intuition and not feel guilty that I'm not doing things at all levels."

The Greenbergs say they are not trying to push wholesale reform on the Orthodox community and create confrontation, but rather seek to bring about change slowly from within.

Blu attends a woman's service at the Hebrew Institute, another Orthodox congregation in her neighborhood. It is not a *minyan*, and certain prayers may not be recited by the women.

"There's a certain indignity in that," she admits, "and it's demeaning. But I don't find sitting in the *mehitza* [separate women's section] demeaning. When someone says I can't say the prayer with the name of God in it, I find that demeaning. And yet we can't make every issue a confrontation.

"We will push the next step when the moment is appropriate. I feel it's an incremental process appropriate to the community's religious life."

And Yitz adds: "Growth is a process, and we don't believe we have such truth that we can say what the exact outcome will be. What we think is important is to set the growth process in motion. Where it finally ends, let God and the Jewish people decide."

Arthur Hertzberg

Estelle Gilson

I t is 1 p.m. on a Friday afternoon and Arthur Hertzberg, rabbi of
Conservative Temple Emanu-El in Englewood, New Jersey, is
waiting for an elevator, surrounded by students in Columbia University's International Affairs Building, where he has an office and
teaches. Waiting is not Hertzberg's forte. You can almost hear his motor
running. Some of the students are in his undergraduate section in
American Jewish history, to which he has just lectured for two hours.

Within the next three hours Hertzberg will speak with me, consult
with students, speak with me again, receive phone calls about a World
Jewish Congress meeting and schedule an afternoon appointment. He
will lead a graduate seminar on American Jewish history in which Irving
Howe's, Nathan Glazer's and others' views will be discussed, speak with
me again, confer with an editor who has come uptown to discuss books
Hertzberg will write, arrange for someone to phone him at 4 p.m. and
make it back to Englewood by Shabbos.

In addition to his positions as Temple Emanu-El's rabbi since 1956 and
adjunct professor of history at Columbia (where he was awarded a Ph.D.
in 1966), he has also been a vice-president of the World Jewish Congress
since 1975. He was simultaneously president of the American Jewish
Congress and a member of the Conference of Presidents of Major

American Jewish Organizations from 1972 to 1978. And he served on the board of governors of the Jewish Agency for Israel and the executive of the World Zionist Organization from 1969 to 1978.

Two years ago, with seed money from a private donor, Hertzberg created the American Jewish Policy Foundation, an organization which he hopes will eventually have the prestige and influence of the Foreign Policy Association. All shades of opinion are said to be represented among the fifty carefully selected members who meet to discuss major current issues. Loosely associated with Columbia University, its roster includes historian Salo Baron, physicist I.I. Rabi and philosopher Sidney Morgenbesser along with political scientist Hans Morgenthau, Secretary of Commerce and former W.J.C. president Philip Klutznick, Edgar Bronfman of the liquor empire and Senator Jacob Javits, as well as some non-Jews. Among those who have addressed the group are Roy Atherton (currently United States Ambassador to Egypt), Undersecretary of State Harold Saunders, ex-World Zionist Organization president Nahum Goldmann, Egyptian Ambassador Ashraf Ghorbal and former United States Ambassador to the United Nations Andrew Young. Participants speak only for themselves and off the record.

Arthur Hertzberg's name also appears about a dozen times a year in *The New York Times*, where it is usually associated with controversial issues. Last September, a Hertzberg article supporting affirmative action for minorities—based on the view that Zionism is also a form of affirmative action—appeared on the newspaper's Op-Ed page. (According to Reby Evans, Hertzberg's secretary, he has a standing invitation from the *Times* to use this page whenever he has an important public statement to make.)

A descendant of rabbis—he says "rebbes," preferring the Hasidic overtones of the word—though he alone of his family left Orthodoxy for Conservative Judaism, Hertzberg expresses an almost reluctant, Moses-like obligation to "save the Jews." He says: "I am in 'Yiddishe' politics because I'm stuck with the Jews."

As a result, when he chooses an issue on which to make a stand, it is usually both important and political, and his voice is loud and solo. He does not sign statements. "I write my own," he says flatly.

Arthur Hertzberg's inability to remain quiet, coupled with his disdain for group statements and people who disagree with him, are regarded by many as arrogance. "Arthur Hertzberg will say anything to shock people." "Arthur Hertzberg likes to draw attention to himself." "He likes to shock the middle class and that gets in the way of his common sense." "He has no consistent political line," were some of the criticisms I heard.

He is incensed at the accusation that he has no central position. "You don't take on potent forces in your own congregation for effect." Speaking of a local election in 1966, he told me, "I got up in my pulpit the Friday before and I said, *chozzer* [pork] is forbidden. Racism is forbidden. To practice racism is to vote for the Republican ticket on Tuesday. I forbid it.'" Two of the town's leading Republicans, members of the congregation, asked its board to censure Hertzberg. It didn't.

Dr. Naomi Levine, senior vice-president of New York University and national executive director of the American Jewish Congress during Hertzberg's tenure, recalls that he opposed hard-line positions on affirmative action, state aid to education, the Jackson-Vanik Amendment (requiring that the Soviet Union permit Jewish emigration in return for Most Favored Nation trading status) and some of Israel's policies regarding Arabs. Generally, she said, "he felt compromise was to be encouraged." On Jackson-Vanik, she related, Hertzberg believed "that, the Soviets being rather hard-nosed, it probably was better to try to negotiate with them rather than adopt a piece of legislation to which they might react very negatively. They might take it out on the Soviet Jews. His main concern was to get them out. He didn't care what technique was used."

Though Hertzberg tried, during the decision-making process within the organization, to win others over to his point of view, Dr. Levine stated, "he was very disciplined but never went public" when he differed with the official position. Calling Arthur Hertzberg "intellectually stimulating and creative," she said that nevertheless it was not easy for some people to work with him. As she put it, "he has no patience with stupidity and demanded 'A' in the performance of those around him. Not a team person, he is very much a single operator."

Israel Singer, executive director of the American Section of the World Jewish Congress, who calls Hertzberg "a Hasidic Jew who is a Conservative rabbi by profession," is impressed by his "orderly mind." The rabbi's ability "to get up at the end of a three-hour meeting and synthesize it" he asserts, is evidence of this faculty. Citing Hertzberg's introduction to his *The Zionist Idea* (New York: Doubleday, 1959)—now a widely used text in high schools and colleges—Singer adds: "Only Hertzberg has had the capacity to take a seminal movement in the twentieth century and deal with it in such a way that one hundred twenty pages have captured Jewish modernity like no one else has."

Son of a Hasidic rabbi, Hertzberg probably was the smartest kid in his heder. He was born in Lubaczòw, Poland, in 1921 and brought to Baltimore in 1926 when his family settled there. Yiddish was his first tongue; it invariably pops through when he speaks English. His paternal grandfather, for whom he is named, was the teacher of the "Belze Rebbe," and his mother's father was the Rebbe's chief *shochet* (ritual slaughterer)— "a superstar among shochets," his cousin, Rabbi Wolfe Kelman, says.

Recalling Hertzberg's father from the Baltimore days, Kelman describes him as "a very scholarly man with a fantastic sense of humor. My memories of that home are of Arthur's mother just roaring with laughter at her husband's jokes." And Kelman remembers Anna Hertzberg "bringing in food all evening, and when I wanted to leave, forcing packages of food on me—they were poor. Oy, were they poor. I mean that was during the depression—stuffing a dollar bill into my back pocket in the dark hallway of the fifth-floor tenement."

Young Arthur remained "a little Belze Hasid" into his early teens, according to Rabbi Kelman. Kelman recalls Hertzberg's arrival to visit his own family in Canada, wearing *peyis* [earlocks] and *kipote* [long black coat] in the Hasidic tradition.

In 1940, at the age of nineteen, Hertzberg graduated Phi Beta Kappa from Johns Hopkins University. By 1943 he had been ordained a rabbi at the Jewish Theological Seminary. Eight years later, during the Korean War, though he was married and could have avoided service, Hertzberg volunteered for the "self-draft" of Conservative rabbis and served as an Air Force chaplain. Talking about it recently, he asserted: "Knowing from the very beginning that I was going to plow my own furrow, I was not going to give anyone the kind of handle which said, 'He ducked.' I don't duck. I do not duck."

He met his wife, Phyllis, who is English, in June 1949 in Paris when arriving by plane on his way to Israel, he found he had no place to stay. The Central Orthodox Committee of the Joint Distribution Committee offered to help and even assigned Phyllis Cannon, a young English-woman, to see to it that the young rabbi didn't get lost. "I instantly pretended that I didn't understand a word of French," smiled Hertzberg. After five days together in Paris and a transatlantic telephone courtship, the Hertzbergs were married in March 1950. They have two daughters, Linda who recently graduated Stanford University Medical School and Susan who studied at Harvard Business School and now lives in New York.

Discussing his published works, Rabbi Hertzberg told me: "My politics comes out of my scholarship." In his major scholarly study, *The French Enlightenment and the Jews,* published jointly by Columbia University Press and the Jewish Publication Society in 1968 (which won the first Amram Award in 1967 as the best non-fiction work in the field of Jewish studies), he sought to understand the reasons for European anti-Semitism. His major thesis was that: "Modern, secular anti-Semitism was fashioned . . . within the Enlightenment and the French Revolution." To Hertzberg this means that Western civilization, steeped deeply in Christianity and dominated by religious or secular powers, is chronically and endemically anti-Semitic.

Hertzberg's most recent book, *Being Jewish in America* (Schocken, 1979), reprints articles he wrote over a period of twenty-five years; many document his early and unpopular views. With great glee he declared that the title should really be "I Told You So." In the introduction, which is new, Hertzberg states the basic premise of his thinking about Judaism today, and offers an explanation of how his liberal positions which favor accommodation spring from conservatism with a small "c." "A generation which began in the 1930s, believing in its own capacity to succeed, is less confident now, more aware of problems than hopeful of their solutions," he writes. "The prevailing mood today is not thus going forward boldly to new adventure. It is rather one of defending a heritage which we [Jews] weakened in the boldness of the ardor of many of my contemporaries for grand solutions."

In his dark, paneled study in Englewood, not far from the George Washington Bridge leading to Manhattan, Hertzberg lets his swivel chair bounce suddenly forward and says: "The America we have known for the past hundred years is coming to an end, and those who don't draw the political consequences are heading for disaster. I know there are more goyim than yiddin," he adds sarcastically. "I can count. I know too that in the long haul of Jewish history we live by accommodation and '*Mir tur nit unreitzin alle goyim*' [We mustn't provoke all the gentiles] all the time."

Showing me a letter, one of dozens he says he's received from "young people all over the country" who supported his stand on affirmative action, Hertzberg continues: "I am willing to pay with some of the chances of my own children for social peace. Because if there is no social peace, then they have nothing. I do not want Jews to be the cheerleaders of the Cold War. I don't get my bangs out of being a defiant Jewish leader."

Jewish leader, writer, professor, scholar, polemicist and rabbi to a congregation of about six hundred families—juggling simultaneously more careers in the public eye than most people could manage in a lifetime—Hertzberg gives the impression of a man on a perpetual "high." Of medium height, round of body and face, wearing a brown or navy blazer, dark slacks and a light shirt on each occasion we meet, cheerful for all that his life is bound up with the world Jewish community, he speaks and moves vigorously. Yet he says: "I hope you won't call me anything but a suburban rabbi."

In 1966, he provoked controversy in a magazine article on the role of the rabbi in America, deploring the decline of great rabbinic careers. Citing famous American rabbis Solomon Goldman, Abba Hillel Silver and Stephen Wise as men whose careers took them beyond their pulpits, Hertzberg wrote: "There are no shared Jewish purposes in America grand enough to evoke" dramatic responses from individual rabbis. He meant himself, many believe. He was also pointing out that when the President of the United States wants to talk to an American Jewish leader, he is unlikely to choose a rabbi.

In 1975 he said, in an address to the Rabbinical Assembly, "In the contemporary situation the rabbi has only his biography, nothing else. He no longer has anti-Semitism to 'keep the Jews down on the farm,' he does not have an organized community, he has competition. With only himself, and what he is, he feels terribly cold and terribly lonely, and he would like to be able to say, like Moses, the very first rabbi and the greatest of them all, 'Go send somebody else.' But here *we* are. *We* are sent. *We* cannot avoid it."

This too sounds like autobiography. Those who know Arthur Hertzberg well believe that being a rabbi stands at the core of his being and, some think, accounts for the contradictions in his personality.

Rabbi Kelman, who is executive vice-president of the Rabbinical Assembly (Conservative) explains: "Most people don't like getting up in front of people and exposing themselves. To be a rabbi you have to be narcissistic. The real agony of the rabbinate is that you're attracted to it because of strong narcissistic drives. Nobody cares whether Frank Sinatra is nice to people. Every rabbi I know has this constant struggle. Arthur is super-endowed with psychic and intellectual energy. He has a high narcissistic impulse, more so than most rabbis, and a strong altruistic one. Reconciling these two is very tough."

Rabbi Seymour Siegel, professor of ethics and theology at the Jewish Theological Seminary offers another insight: "We have in this country three types of rabbi." They are, he explains, the rabbi-activist who is active "outside the boundaries of his congregation;" the scholar, usually associated with an institution of learning; and the rabbi-rabbi "who devotes himself to building up his synagogue as a significant institution."

Most rabbis choose one or perhaps two such careers for themselves, but Hertzberg has sought to be all three at once. That he has succeeded to the measure he has testifies to his intelligence, his restless energy, his drive and ambition. To the extent that he has failed—to the extent that he is not the Jew whose advice a President of the United States will solicit—to the extent a congregant can say, "My husband dislikes him"—to the extent that some students wrote in their evaluations: he is "condescending, intimidating, entrenched in prejudices, wastes too much class time on tales of his wonderful experiences and how great a guy he is"—to that extent he has failed to balance his ego and his altruism.

Everyone who knows Arthur Hertzberg talks about his ego first, then grants him the right to have a large one. What upsets people is a kind of cheerful arrogance demonstrated in the pleasure he takes in his intellectual superiority and the contempt he seems to display for his "inferiors." What did his graduate students think when he referred sneeringly to Golda Meir as "Saint Golda"? What is the effect on a visitor when he imperiously denounces those he disagrees with as "Jewish American *schreiers*" (screamers)?

Hertzberg is currently embroiled in Englewood in what he calls a "towering fight," in which his convictions as scholar, activist and rabbi merge. He has been a vehement opponent of a planned Jewish community center, which he disparagingly refers to as "Taj Mahal on the Palisades" and a "Yiddisher Country Club." Thundering that "twenty-first-century Jews won't need more lush recreational facilities," he adds: "In a community where we spend maybe $30,000 a year on the day schools, we're going to spend three-quarters of a million on the deficit of a recreational center? We're out of our goddam minds. It's an ego trip." It is also, he believes, "like many lay-led activities, a thinly disguised anticlericalism."

Both the president of the center and the chairman of the building fund have resigned from his congregation. Hertzberg says they have accused him of being divisive. "But do you know what I succeeded in doing?" he asks, gleeful again, "I split this congregation. I have kept $5 million out of their hands."

But a congregant, active in the drive for the center, interpreted events differently. "The center is being built despite his opposition," she said. "He lost."

Proponents of the center say it will bring now-scattered Jewish agencies and activities under one roof and will serve Jewish needs, and will also be able to serve others in the community. Hertzberg insists he is not against the center per se, merely against its "lushness."

According to Hertzberg, the center has already produced anti-Semitic attitudes. Englewood is a racially mixed community. "You Jews are always peddling us the Nazis," a reporter for a local paper told him, "and therefore we're supposed to be nice to you. In Bergen County you build the lushest buildings. From our point of view you're not victims, you're supercapitalists." He finds this particularly disturbing because he's convinced that American Jews must conserve for the future. And among the things they must conserve, he insists, are "allies" and the goodwill of "the guys whom you're going to have to deal with ten years down the pike."

Still, public quarrels don't seem to disturb Arthur Hertzberg. In fact he relishes them and recounts them with pride, as evidence of his integrity. He has exhibited disdain for the Jewish Telegraph Agency, the Jewish Agency and Israeli prime ministers. As a new member of the Jewish Agency, he objected publicly to Golda Meir's message to Richard Nixon in 1969 ranking herself beside the President on the Vietnam War. In 1971, in Israel, Hertzberg delivered a speech attacking Israel's treatment of its Sephardic "Black Panthers." Reports of the speech reached *The New York Times* and, as Hertzberg put it, Golda Meir "to all intents and purposes confiscated my passport—had me to her office and gave me hell for two hours while I stood my ground." Today, just as loudly and strongly, Hertzberg objects to the Begin regime's hard-line policies on the West Bank. "Arthur and Nahum Goldmann," Rabbi Kelman commented, "are the only two people I know who were members of the Jewish Agency and who attacked the official Zionist line."

What does his congregation think of his stand on national and international issues? "My congregation is the last congregation in America that has any sense" is his answer.

Most congregants I spoke to seemed pleased that their rabbi can say, "I saw Kissinger today," or "I had a fight with Begin." Many feel he gives a certain cachet to Temple Emanu-El.

Hertzberg has what he calls "an academic-type contract with Emanu-El—an appointment without limit of term, with two basic clauses." The first clause is that his salary be augmented by reasonable increases. The second is that if ever a dispute between rabbi and congregation arises, the chancellor of the Jewish Theological Seminary will be the sole arbiter. The contract was signed two-and-a-half years after Hertzberg arrived in Englewood, after he was offered an opportunity to serve a larger, wealthier congregation—what he calls a "cathedral"—in Chicago. He preferred to stay at Emanu-El with its smaller congregation and lower salary because there he has time to pursue his other interests.

After nearly a quarter of a century, some Emanu-El congregants love their rabbi and will continue to bring their troubles to him; others feel he lacks compassion and doesn't show enough personal interest in them and their children. For most, though, his sermons are often stirring.

People come from great distances to listen to Arthur Hertzberg. I heard a sermon that was both an education in Jewishness and a moving exhortation to prayer, in which he explained that the fringes of the tallis represent the 613 mitzvot. He went on to condemn a permissive society as "chaotic" and to insist "there are some things Jews don't do." "I will sell you a wilderness of books [about Jews] to come to shul every Shabbat. I will sell you a wilderness of [spiritual] poetry for a commitment to say a prayer," he concluded.

Another time, in an analytical mood, he said: "I know damn well that I have an enormous amount of power, a helluva lot more than my critics think. The source of that is simply that I belong to an older Jewish tradition in which you are rooted in continuing learning of what Jews are about. I cannot derive my Jewish opinions from the J.T.A. [Jewish Telegraph Agency]. I am not in debate with Charlotte Jacobson [chairman of the American section of the World Zionist Organization] or Menachem Begin. I'm trying to debate the Rambam. And I say this not for pose. I mean it. To really relax, I study *Daf Yomi*, the daily portion of the Talmud."

Hertzberg's current scholarly and Jewish concerns will result in several new books. He has already begun one on American Jews in which he asks, "Where do Jews fit in American history? What is it that this peculiar *galus* or exile, America, did to the Jews?" And he is planning another on the history of modern Jewish thought. "Having taught Zionism at Columbia, I have to ask the question: What about the other varieties of Jewish thought? The result will be a book I've been preparing myself to write for twenty years—from Spinoza, let's say, through Buber."

And history, Jewish thought and the urgency to speak out bring Rabbi Hertzberg back to politics. "One of these days someone will write a history of [present-day] Jewish America and will discover who said what. I have never changed my politics. I was a pragmatist and a Zionist in the '30s and '40s. I was not a Trotskyite and I'm not a hard-liner now. I was worrying about Jews a long time ago, and I'm still worrying about Jews. My politics remain the same, which are, if Jews stand up and say, 'We demand all.'" He stopped abruptly. "What do I have to give you, a speech? I'll quote you the Talmud.

"There's a passage in the Talmud, and if you quote nothing else out of this conversation, I don't give a damn, but this quote. On Tisha B'Av we're not supposed to study, as you know, because it's a very sad day. We do study *gittin* [tractate of the Talmud] the fifty-third folio of *gittin* because that contains some tales about the destruction of Jerusalem, and *gimmel* because there the question is asked over and over again: 'Why was Jerusalem destroyed?' And there are two answers which I want to quote to you." Hertzberg spoke them in Hebrew and translated: "Because they didn't give in to one another, and because they insisted on the last jot and tittle of their rights. When will the Jewish community be destroyed?" His face darkened and he slapped at his desk. "When some American Jewish organizations lead us together to insist on every last jot and tittle of our rights, and that's for quotation."

As for questions about his own future and the effect his controversial ideas may have on his career, Hertzberg responded with a combination of honesty and hubris. "What I have done in my life—and that's what I think I am resented for—has been practical enough to have accumulated enough security so that I can't be gotten at by the usual routes. I can't be fired. I can't be stopped. I can't be threatened. And the things which work generally, such as 'the prime minister won't have you to tea,' don't work on me either. I cannot be silenced. If I'm right, if I'm standing on principle, nothing's going to happen. What can they do to me? They won't make me chairman of the President's Conference? They won't love me? What will they do?"

Did he have aspirations to the President's Conference chairmanship, as I had been told?

"No, don't be silly. Let me put it this way. On my terms, yes, but on my terms it was unavailable. Why should this establishment, by whose rules I will not play, elect me?"

"Not a single American Jewish newspaper, Jewish weekly nor the J.T.A. – all of whom carry any handout from any Jewish organization printed on toilet paper – carried a single line of my Op-Ed piece in the *Times*," he said. But, he stressed, the Israeli press had reprinted it.

Hertzberg is determined that "American Jews understand that while it is in their interest to get what is available, the annexation of the West Bank is not. We must behave like intelligent tories, rather than stupid Mafia dons and move over a little when necessary." And in the Israeli daily newspaper, *Ma'ariv*, last April, an interview with him covered a full page. Among the things he told Israeli readers: "In Israel there is a mistaken impression that world Jewry and its leaders must not only support the political line of any Israeli government, but we must only regard the opinion of world leaders in terms of how Israelis would view it. We do not accept this position. We want to hear, to know, to test and to influence what goes on in Israel." He also predicted that whoever was elected American President "will have to find a solution to the Palestinian problem."

In *The Changing Rabbinate*, Hertzberg's address to the Rabbinical Assembly a few years ago, he spoke in all his voices. He began with a story about a rebbe and Hasid. By the sixth paragraph his listeners had heard more than a dozen Yiddish words. The seventh paragraph began: "In the days before I became a politician I wrote a book on the eighteenth century Jews in France." The eighth started: "As one who spends whatever time he can find on research in late medieval and modern Jewish history. . . ."

And the last sentence was this: "We are rabbis who have nothing going for us except our own passion, our own conviction, our own lives and what we are willing to put them on the line for."

In 1980, Hertzberg's talents still jostle each other for his time and attention.

"Sometimes I say to myself, 'You bloody idiot, if you really want to have a political career, why don't you go be Secretary of State?' I'm quite serious. Though sometimes I put it as a joke, if you understand shul politics, you understand international politics."

What will be Arthur Hertzberg's ultimate contribution to Jewish life? Clearly not even he can answer that question today.

Abraham Joshua Heschel

Jack Riemer

R abbi Abraham Joshua Heschel loved stories, so let me begin
with a story I found recently. It comes from Rabbi Sam Dresner,
one of Rabbi Heschel's disciples, who is at work on a book about
him. An excerpt from this book, which appeared recently in the Catholic
magazine *America*, contained this account:

Several years before Dr. Heschel—who was professor of ethics and
mysticism at The Jewish Theological Seminary—died, he suffered a
nearly fatal heart attack. Soon after, Sam came from Chicago to New
York to see him.

He writes: "He had gotten out of bed for the first time to greet me, and
he was sitting in the living room when I arrived, looking weak and pale.
He spoke slowly and with some effort, almost in a whisper. I strained to
hear his words.

" 'Sam,' he said, 'when I regained consciousness, my first feeling was
not of despair, or of anger. I felt only gratitude to God for my life, for
every moment I had lived. I was ready to depart, if need be. Take me, O
Lord, I thought. I have seen so many miracles in my lifetime.' Exhausted
by the effort, he paused and then added: 'This is what I meant when I
wrote in the preface to my book of poems: "I did not ask for success; I
asked for wonder. And You gave it to me." ' "

I did not ask for success: I asked for wonder. And You gave it to me.

This is the way Abraham Joshua Heschel evaluated his own life. Those who had the privilege of knowing him and of being his students can testify to the accuracy of his evaluation.

He was a man blessed with an extraordinary capacity for wonder, a remarkable ability to be excited, to be thrilled, to be exhilarated, to be uplifted. Whatever else he was, he was never dull.

To be with him was to be in the presence of effervescence, to be near lightning. He could be angry, passionate, satirical, meditative—but never pedestrian.

Things that other people took for granted, that they never bothered to notice, filled his heart with awe, his mind with excitement, his soul with joy.

Many of us remember how, before a seminar would begin, he would walk to the window, look out at the sky, and say to us: "Gentlemen, something wondrous happened tonight. Did you see it? Did you notice? The sun set!" And we would look at each other with embarrassment, for we had seen it but had not really seen it, until he called it to our attention.

I remember an experience with him in my student days. I had gone to a wedding, and when I came back I met him in the Seminary courtyard. He asked me where I had been and I told him. "What kind of wedding was it?" he asked. I started to say that it was a sad wedding because the groom had a physical handicap and the bride was up in years. I had gotten less than halfway through what I was going to say when he interrupted me with an exclamation. "How wonderful!" he said. Suddenly I realized he was right.

To me, the wedding had seemed sad, but when I saw it through his eyes I realized he was right. When two lonely people find each other— when two people, each of whom has little beauty, are able to discover the beauty in each other—how wonderful that is! I hadn't realized until he showed it to me.

I particularly remember the two stories he tells in *Man Is Not Alone* and *God in Search of Man*, about wonder—and about how we can crush the sense of wonder if we are not careful.

One story is about the educator who was walking with his daughter. The little girl turned and asked him, "Daddy, what is up there beyond the sky?" The father gave her a 'scientific' explanation. "Ether, my child," he said.

"Ether?" She held her nose.

Is that really all there is up there, beyond the sky? To give such an answer is to crush, not to enlighten; to block, not to teach; to limit, not to enlarge the horizons of a child's mind. Many of us have been the victims of such educators. Some of us were taught to paint what the teacher thought we should see, not what we saw. And some of us were taught the "primitive origins" of prayers, or "the real sociological meaning" of commandments. Heschel tried to teach us how to reach beyond ourselves, how to bear witness and not debunk, how to convey reverence instead of destroying wonder.

The other story is about what happened when the first electric streetcar appeared in Warsaw. Some old Jews simply could not believe their eyes. A car that moves without a horse? Some were stupefied and frightened. All were at a loss for an explanation of this amazing invention.

While they were discussing the matter in the synagogue, a man entered who had a reputation for being sophisticated. In addition to his knowledge of the Talmud, he was reputed to read books on secular subjects, to subscribe to a general newspaper and to be well versed in worldly affairs. They clustered around him and asked if he knew how the streetcar worked.

"Of course I know," he said. They hung on his every word as he began to explain. "Picture four large wheels in a vertical position in four corners of a square, connected to each other by wires. Do you get it?"

"Yes, we get it," they said hesitantly.

"Now, these wires are tied together in a knot in the center of the square and then placed within a large wheel which is placed in a horizontal position. Do you get it?"

"Yes, we get it," said the listeners cautiously.

"Now, above the large wheel there are several more wheels, each one smaller than the one before. Do you get it?" said the sophisticate.

"Yes, we get it," they said.

"Now, on top of the smallest wheel there is one tiny screw which is connected by a wire to the center of the car which lies on top of the wheels. Do you get it?"

"Yes, we get it."

"Now the machinist in the car presses the button that moves the screw that causes the horizontal wheels to move, which causes the vertical wheels to move, which causes the car to run through the streets. So you see, it is no wonder," said the sophisticate proudly.

"Ah, now we understand," said the old people.

But there was one old Jew who said: "By me it is *still* a wonder!"

For Heschel, the heart of religion was wonder. For him, the central issue was not that we have faith in God, but that God has faith in us—that, after all the times we have disappointed Him, He still continues to believe in us. Heschel taught that what we do with our lives is the response to that trust, that we love in response to the love with which we are loved. He said that to be the recipient of God's trust and to ignore it is a sin; that to be entrusted with the gift of life and waste it is a transgression; that to have eyes and not see, not really see, is a great loss.

In *The Earth Is the Lord's*, Heschel wrote: "What is the main objective of observance if not to feel the soul, the soul in oneself, the soul in the Torah, and the soul in the world?" Much of his writing was organized around these three rubrics. Let us consider each.

What, as he preferred to ask, is a human being? How shall we understand ourselves? In Germany, where he taught until 1938, Heschel was profoundly shocked when he found biology textbooks that defined a human being as a combination of iron, phosphorus and other chemicals worth so and so much money. He believed the road to Nazism began in those books: that one could draw a straight line between such teachings and the Nazi destruction of human beings; that people were dehumanized first in theory and then in fact, first in the classroom and then in the streets.

What Heschel found in those biology textbooks can be replicated in many American classrooms today—in philosophy classes where all values are said to be relative and all truths only a matter of opinion, and in science classes that speak of "programming people" and "turning them on," as if man were made in the image of the machine instead of the image of God. We have become so accustomed to such words that we are no longer even conscious how dehumanizing and how dangerous such language can be.

Heschel crisscrossed this country teaching and preaching that a human being must know who he is, where he comes from and Whom he represents. A person must know two truths: that he or she is dust and ashes, and is also made in the image of God. He or she must hold onto two insights: that everyone is mortal and at the same time immortal. All of us must constantly be aware that we can be here today and gone today, and that we can be gone today and yet be here ever after.

Some theologies exalt God by putting man down. Heschel never did. He constantly reminded us not only of our shortcomings but of our potential. What is said of nothing else on earth is said of man: Man, indeed every human being, is made in the image of God. How sad it is, he would lament, for people to forget who they are, where they come from and what they can be. "The Lord is your shadow," says the Bible, and Heschel liked to quote an interpretation of that statement which said that just as a shadow depends upon the person, so does God depend on us.

Heschel constantly tried to make us conscious of our cosmic significance.

In helping us to discover the wonder within the Torah, he drew on his great skill as a scholar, but took us beyond mere facts. Though he sought to know facts and dates and to teach them, he also wanted to capture the echo of the soul that reverberated in the words of a manuscript, to gain insight into the inner life of the historical figure he was studying. He wanted to understand the yearnings in the soul of his people. He wanted not only to dissect the words of a text but also to capture the melody within them.

Heschel taught us that there are many ways to read the Torah, and that what we get out of it depends on what we bring to it. To call the Prophets "literature," Heschel used to say, is like praising the manuscript of Einstein's theory of relativity by saying that he had a nice handwriting. Einstein may have happened to have good penmanship but that was not his goal, for his intention was to say something important about reality. So it was with the Prophets.

Heschel insisted that to focus on precisely when or where the Prophets lived, or on the exact spelling of their words, can be a digression—an escape—from hearing what they wanted to say. The Prophets *should* judge us, not be judged by us. As in the story about the brash young man who comes back to his first teacher after a stay in the yeshiva, in Heschel's *The Earth Is the Lord's*, the central question is not how much Talmud have we gone through. It is: How much has gone through us? That is what Torah study meant for Heschel.

Finally, we have Heschel's teaching about the wonder in the world. Heschel taught us to be sensitive to the difference between the Greek word for "world" and the Hebrew word. The Greek word is "cosmos," which means something complete in itself. The Hebrew word is "olam," which is a cousin of the word "neelam" which means mystery, wonder, something hidden. Heschel stressed that the world itself is a wonder and what we understand about the world is a wonder—and, above all, the fact *that* we understand is a wonder.

Heschel's views are filled with meaning because he lived with dynamism, with electricity, because he sensed the aliveness of all that is and responded to it.

He summed up his philosophy by teaching that there are two ways of looking at the world. One can say that the world is getting older every day, or feel sorry for the world that must arise every day for centuries, for millennia. In a way, one can wish that the world could retire and move to Florida to live on retirement benefits, as some people do. Or one can sense that the world is being born everyday. One can bend down and listen to the world's heartbeat and know that underneath everything there is pulsating life, coming to expression in the grass, the birds, in everything.

In one sense, Heschel's last years were the years of his greatest fame and glory, but, in another, they were the years of his greatest isolation and loneliness. The question is: Why, at this point in his life, did he turn to activism, investing much of himself in social causes? Why did he choose to spend his last energies in a race against time, juggling tasks, commuting between worlds, finishing his book on the Kotsker (a 19th-century Polish Hasidic rebbe), carrying on political activities—and hearing so much harsh criticism from fellow Jews, students, peers? He must have known how precarious his health was, how precious his time, how much writing he still needed to do.

The key may be found in a comment of Heschel's about Maimonides. Responding to the question of the relationship between Maimonides the philosopher and Maimonides the physician, he suggested that for Maimonides the practice of medicine was not instead of religion, or in addition to religion—it *was* religion. "It was prayer in the form of deed," he wrote, arguing that Maimonides's life moved in stages, his metaphysics leading him to the love of God, and the love of God leading him to the healing of God's people.

In his book about Heschel, Byron Sherwin writes that what Heschel said about Maimonides can also be said of him. In the 1960s, he wrote about the Prophets, producing a work that is a lasting contribution to biblical scholarship. In the process, the Prophets deeply affected Heschel, for, as he lived with them in his consciousness, a change came over him. This man, who could have lived out his years in a scholar's study, instead became more and more deeply involved in social issues. The pain of the blacks in the South, of Jews in the Soviet Union, of human beings in Vietnam penetrated his soul and gave him no rest.

So he became a guide and a goad to all of us on the controversial issues of our time. He went to the White House to speak up for the rights of the aged, became a central figure in the civil rights movement and was one of the major voices in the protest against the Vietnam War.

He journeyed to Rome in the hope of bringing about a change in the Catholic Church's understanding of the Jew – and, though he had some effect there, he was harshly criticized by some within the Jewish community for this act. He journeyed to Selma to stand with Martin Luther King, Jr. "Father Abraham" they called him there, for they sensed in him more than a spokesman for the Bible – rather, an embodiment of the Bible. But, a few years later, when the civil rights movement fell apart, and some blacks robbed and pillaged Jewish-owned stores, he was mocked by cynics for what he had done. The day before he died, he went – in the cold, and despite ill health – to the gate of a prison to greet Daniel Berrigan, the Catholic priest and pacifist being released after an anti-Vietnam demonstration, and his Seminary students found fault with him for canceling classes to do that.

Others have studied the Prophets and not come away so deeply affected. If so, perhaps they did not really study the Prophets but only the details that surrounded them. Heschel studied the Prophets and came away from the experience transformed. Speaking up in the name of God against evil became for him not a digression from religion, but its essence.

So began the last lonely years, when he won so much admiration in the Christian world and so little appreciation in the Jewish world. Some of his students and his peers could not understand why he did these things "instead of Judaism." Like the Prophets of old, he was alone at the end, isolated and misunderstood. And yet in those years he brought to fruition all that he had studied and taught and become until then.

In a eulogy he once gave for a friend, he said that there are three levels of mourning. The first level is with tears. The second and higher level is with silence. And the third, the highest of all, is with song. Ten years have passed since his death in December 1972. It is time to turn our mourning into song. And may his spirit continue to live in us, with us and through us for many more years to come.

Irving Howe

Estelle Gilson

I rving Howe, best known to the American public as the author of *World of Our Fathers*, is a busy man. He answered my letter asking for an interview with a one-sentence postcard. He set the time for our meeting at his East Side apartment in New York in a sixty-second telephone call. Half an hour into our talk, he waved a pink-shirted arm over my tape recorder and said, "I should think you have more than enough material now."

I didn't think so, but I didn't argue the point. I was betting that Howe, who has authored or coauthored, edited or coedited almost half a hundred books still in print, including essays, anthologies and biographies, who lectures and teaches, cares earnestly about what the world thinks of his viewpoints. I asked another question, and at the end of an hour we were still talking.

We sat in a comfortable living room, painted white, which, while not austere, gave the impression that it contains nothing superfluous or frivolous. The west wall is lined with books; beneath a bank of windows are a large desk and a typewriter. My coat had not been hung up, but thrown across a floral-covered upholstered couch; the armchairs we sat in are covered in the same fabric. As we talked Howe leaned back, frequently with his arms raised behind his head. A dark-blue knitted necktie punctuated the pink shirt, its top button open. His cheeks are round and ruddy; gray hairs curl at the nape of his neck. Every so often looking up at Howe's half- or three-quarter profile, I thought I was looking at Senator Daniel Patrick Moynihan.

World of Our Fathers, for which Howe and his publishers, Harcourt Brace Jovanovich, had modest hopes when it was published in 1976, was a surprise best seller. It is dedicated to his wife, Arien. In 1977, it won the National Book Award.

The book's subject, as described on its dust cover, is "the journey of the East European Jews to America and the life they found and made." Familiar, even banal though this theme may be to some—especially older Jews who themselves were immigrants—it proved fascinating to millions of readers. Well-written, crammed with facts, evoking names, places, objects and ideas that formed the essence of the Eastern European immigrant experience, it represented for non-Jews, in the words of an Anglican Church friend of mine, "a part of American history I knew nothing about." For some Jews it was equally novel, for others a nostalgic journey into the almost forgotten past.

To Howe himself, *World of Our Fathers* marks the meeting place of the three broad roads of his life as a writer. He has been a lifelong socialist, a literary critic and a secular Yiddishist. In varying degrees, all these elements have been evident in his writing—his more than a quarter-century as editor and coeditor of *Dissent*, a socialist quarterly magazine— his teaching in colleges across the United States—his current work as Distinguished Professor of English at New York City University's Grad-uate Center—and many lectures delivered over the years up to the present.

Yiddish came first in Irving Howe's life. He was born in the Bronx, in New York City, in 1920, the only child of David and Nettie, who had emigrated from Bessarabia in 1912. "They were quite ordinary," he told me. His father had a grocery store; when it went bankrupt in 1930, he became a door-to-door "customer peddler" of linens. Later both parents became garment workers. To save rent during the difficult Depression years, the family often lived with relatives. Howe spoke only Yiddish until he was old enough to go into the streets and to school. He attended DeWitt Clinton High School and was graduated in 1940, with a BSS, from the College of the City of New York—in those days the "Harvard" of brainy but poor New York boys.

As the child of immigrant parents, Howe said, he missed certain "physical aspects" of growing up, an experience not unique to him. This happened because "You were taught to be afraid, not that your mother set out deliberately to teach you. It was just communicated. Fear was handed down. Fear of the physical world, fear of the external world. Fear of sports, fear of getting hurt, fear of catching cold."

By the time he entered college, Howe was a committed socialist. He had joined the movement when he was fourteen years old, after reading a series of magazine articles by Sherwood Anderson about hunger among North Carolina textile workers. "The realization of what it meant to be poor I had first to discover through writings about poverty," he told me. At City College, Howe was active in the Young People's Socialist League, a Trotskyist group, sometimes neglecting his studies to serve the socialist cause. Among those he recruited into the League was Irving Kristol—now, in Howe's words, a "conservative ideologue." Writing in 1977 about Howe during those years, Kristol described him as "thin, gangling, intense . . . always a little distant as he enunciated sharp and authoritative opinions."

Aside from the reading he'd done at college, he "discovered" literature when he was a soldier during World War II in Alaska, he recalled. What was he doing in Alaska? "If you ask that question, you were never in the Army. You're not supposed to be doing anything in the Army, you're just in the Army. It was quiet. There was no fighting. There was nothing to do." He read more than 400 books in this period.

During a leave from the Army, Howe hitch-hiked to Anderson's home town. "There it was. Nothing special. Nobody knew him."

"Was it disappointing?"

"As Andy Warhol said, 'In America everybody is famous for fifteen minutes.' "

After his discharge, Howe wrote for *Labor Action*, a socialist newspaper. Later he had a job as a part-time assistant to the noted philosopher-writer Hannah Arendt, then an editor for Schocken Books. During this period he began a free-lance career doing reviews "here and there—and that's the way I broke in."

His first important book was an English revision of an earlier translation of Leo Baeck's *The Essence of Judaism* (Schocken, 1948). Other early books were *The UAW and Walter Reuther* (Random House, 1949), *Sherwood Anderson: A Critical Biography* (Sloane, 1951) and *William Faulkner: A Critical Study* (Random House, 1952).

Early in 1953, Howe and Berlin-born sociologist Lewis Coser began to plan a magazine that would express their dissent from (in Coser's words) "the abysmal political and intellectual atmosphere" of the McCarthy period. They hoped for four issues. *Dissent* just celebrated its twenty-fifth anniversary. Howe is still a coeditor, now with Harvard professor Michael Walzer.

In the early 1950s, Howe began to be seriously involved with Yiddish literature. Eliezer Greenberg, a Yiddish poet, wrote suggesting a collaboration which began almost immediately and continued for more than twenty years. Together they translated and coedited various anthologies of Yiddish writing. Currently Howe is working on the *Oxford Anthology of Yiddish Verse* with Ruth Wisse of McGill University, and Chone Shmeruk, a Yiddish scholar in Israel.

I had been surprised to read in Howe and Greenberg's *A Treasury of Yiddish Poetry* that some of the translators knew no Yiddish. Howe explained that translators were given literal translations and separate descriptions of each work's verse scheme, meters, rhymes, rhythms, and so on. An extremely complicated process, it sometimes yielded better results, because, he said, "The important thing with a translator is how well he does in his own language. And if you have people who can write verse in English even if they don't know Yiddish, the result may be better than with 'kalyakes' [another version of schlemiels] who do know Yiddish but can't write English." Nevertheless he tried it both ways and decided that "It's a question of which failure is more bearable."

In a literary career as long as Howe's, changes in critical judgment are bound to develop. And they are still more likely when the judgments were based initially on political thinking. Howe's books are often reissued with new introductions in which the contemporary Irving Howe encounters his early self. Coolly, he measures the younger man, finds some of his thoughts understandable but no longer acceptable and attempts to clarify his present attitudes. Speaking of *Politics and the Novel*, first published in 1957 and reissued as a paperback in 1967, Howe said, "When I wrote it I thought of myself as more of a Marxist than I do today. And Marxism as a system doesn't terribly much interest me any more. I suppose there are elements of it that one has absorbed in one's bloodstream just as in a way by now we're all Darwinists. The Marxist intellectual framework which I think is visible in that book I had sort of moved away from, but the underlying socialist ethical view I retained." Howe also moved away from his Trotskyist ideas.

"Has it been difficult," I asked, "to maintain a consistent viewpoint on literature and politics as the world—and Irving Howe with it—changed?" "I think," he replied, "I have a method of writing which is to some extent self-cannibalizing, self-dependent," he explained. "When I do something on a topic, I will go back to what I had done on that topic before, pull out a little bit of it, repeat it, maybe change it, vary it. There is a sense of continuity which I was brought up with. You don't start afresh. You look at what you've done on something before and you develop it, vary it, change it. Some people criticize me for this and claim that I repeat. Sometimes maybe this is so, but by and large it's not repetition. I would like to think it's development."

Equally important to him is a sense of being coherent and logical. For the success he's had in achieving this, he credits socialism. "You see, I was brought up in the socialist movement where there's a very considerable stress, a high valuation, on coherent presentation, logic, a systematic, orderly development of ideas."

In his writings Howe continues to refer to himself as a socialist and a radical.

When I asked what he meant, our conversation went as follows:

"You also refer to yourself as a radical."

"Yes, that's what I mean, as a socialist."

"Would you define socialist and radical?"

"Well, I can't do that offhand." Nevertheless he did.

"A radical," said Howe, "is someone who wants to make deepgoing social changes in the society. I'd say I'm a democratic radical with a small 'd.' That's what I mean by a democratic socialist—someone who wants to maintain political democracy."

"Would you say the terms are almost equal?"

"As I see them, they're necessarily ambiguous because everyone has his own political language. But I would say in America it means a great stress upon egalitarianism, upon ending the extreme results of wealth and poverty. It means the extension of democratic rules and regulations into economic corporate life, where they don't exist at the present time. It means greater control and participation by workers in corporate life. It means an extension of social legislations—in other words an extension of the welfare state and then going beyond the welfare state."

And a liberal? "A liberal is first someone who believes in political liberty, in civil liberty and things like that—in that sense, I'm a liberal too; I believe in that very strongly—but whose desire for change and social reforms doesn't go beyond modifying the existing system. The liberal accepts the continuity of the capitalistic economy which I, in principle, don't. There are possibilities, in my judgment, in America for collaboration between liberals and people like myself."

As for the welfare state, Howe declared: "It isn't as if there is something you define. You move closer to the model of the welfare state or you move further away from it. The Scandinavian countries are obviously closer than we are. England is closer than we are to a welfare state. And there's been a considerable retreat in the seventies."

Howe has strenuously attacked conservatism and neo-conservatism in his writings. Among others, he wrote *The New Conservatives* with Lewis Coser (Quadrangle, 1974); and in an article, "The Right Menace," which appeared in *The New Republic* in September 1978, responded to the conservative argument that the welfare state implies a loss of personal liberties as follows: "Despite all the cries about encroachments on liberty, we have not suffered any serious loss of liberties that can be attributed to the welfare state. . . . The erosions of our liberties—McCarthyism, loyalty checks, FBI and CIA escapades—have come not from the growth of the welfare state, but rather from political misconduct by elements of society that bitterly oppose the welfare state."

He believes too that "The conservative argument that democracy requires capitalism is as simplistic as the argument sometimes advanced by socialists that democracy is 'fully' possible only under socialism."

Howe thinks conservatives today ostensibly accept the welfare state but will try to "starve" it. In *The New Republic* essay, he wrote: "The primitive conservative ideology, as it proposes a return to laissez-faire that never was, will crumble to nothingness. This is because it *is* nothing, a mere ideological phantasm. The sophisticated conservative strategy of enduring elements of the welfare state while steadily trying to cripple it will be a far more formidable antagonist."

And Howe threatens to be out there fighting. "When I consider how very much my father's old age was eased by those bureaucracies which chaps like William Buckley find it so easy to sneer at, I want to go out into the streets and join some sort of demonstration . . . against the current menace from the right."

Howe's essays, literary criticism and political works, well written but often dense and uncompromisingly dry, are clearly addressed to people able and willing to cope with their subject matter and style. The questions arise: Is he addressing only intellectuals? And how does he characterize them?

"Intellectuals," said Howe, "are people who are concerned professionally and systematically with ideas. By professionally I don't mean in terms
of earning a living, but people concerned with ideas for their own sake,
who believe in the importance and values of ideas. And so you can have
a garment worker of a certain kind in the recent past who could be called
an intellectual. It is a question of a certain attitude, a certain set of values.

"In America," Howe went on, "there is no mass socialist movement as
there is in European countries, so that we are confined, unfortunately by
necessity – say in a magazine like *Dissent* – to speaking essentially to other
intellectuals and more or less educated people in the hope of changing
current opinion. If one were writing in other countries, there would be
the possibility of a wide audience and so you could write in a more
popular fashion for that audience. Other kinds of things, like literary
things or certain kinds of political theorizing, are necessarily confined to
an intellectual audience because that's the only audience which is
interested and capable of getting it."

Howe has written of the gulf between intellectuals and union leaders,
and their inability to understand each other's problems. He feels there's
been improvement in this area, citing "people like Doug Fraser [president
of the Auto Workers Union] and Vic Gotbaum [top official of New York
State, County and Municipal Employees Union], who are very serious
people, who read and have intellectual interests, with whom it's possible
to have a serious discussion."

In a complicated man like Irving Howe, many subjects that interest him
become inextricably intertwined. So the interview proceeded from socialism to literary criticism, to problems of Yiddish writers and being
Jewish in America today.

Talking about what makes a good literary critic, he said that "One
must have a knowledge of the history of literature, about the way
language is used in a given historical epoch. Presumably you should
know everything – not that anybody does, you would be a monster if you
did – but you should know something about other disciplines, social,
historical." He is less interested in methodology than in the "intuitive
powers of the critic's mind. When I read Edmund Wilson or Lionel
Trilling, what I was interested in finding out was what does this extremely bright, intelligent, sensitive mind think about this."

Howe remarked that he considers himself "in the tradition of people
like Wilson, who, in addition to literary criticism, had more explicit,
open or social or political interests." (Interestingly, Howe's affinity for

Wilson was noted by *Newsweek's* reviewer of *World of Our Fathers,* who called Howe "our most capable man of letters since Edmund Wilson.")

Just as political ideas are found in Howe's literary criticism, so Jewish references can be found in his other works. In his book (co-authored with Lewis Coser) *The American Communist Party: A Critical History* (Beacon 1958), in which he refers to Eugene Debs, the Socialist Party leader, as a moral prophet, he recalls an occasion when Debs apparently mixed up his papers and read the first part of a speech twice, to resounding applause. Howe reminds readers of "the sly wisdom of the old Hasidic saying that what matters is not the words but the melody."

In "New Styles in Leftism," a 1965 essay in *Steady Work* (a collection of Howe articles, subtitled *Essays in the Politics of Democratic Radicalism,* published by Harcourt Brace Jovanovich in 1967), discussing people "with whom to identify in the Communist world," he writes: "We identify with the 'revisionists,' those political *marranos* who, forced to employ Communist jargon, yet spoke out for a socialism democratic in character."

And in a *New York Times Book Review* article on D.H. Lawrence early this year, Howe likens Lawrence's scheme for a Utopian community made up of writers Middleton Murry, Kathleen Mansfield, E.M. Forster and others to a "kibbutz of prima donnas."

When I asked whether there was a time when he would not have used such an association in writing about Lawrence, Howe answered, "No, I would. I don't see why not. People naturally use the references which are in their imagination."

"Even so, it has to mean something to the person who reads it."

"Well, by now," Howe explained, "everyone who reads the *New York Times Book Review* knows what a kibbutz is. It was meant sort of half-jokingly."

But Irving Howe is an essentially humorless man. Jokes and half-jokes are not often found in his works. And now too he felt compelled to explain. "By its very nature a kibbutz is not supposed to have prima donnas."

Intimations of what was to come in the monumental *World of Our Fathers* appeared in *Steady Work* in a memoir of the thirties called "How It All Began." Here the writing "takes off." It is warm and evocative, and, as if heeding Howe's own critical criteria, shows the reader the world in which immigrants' children were growing up forty years earlier through the workings of an active, individual, distinctive, interested sensibility.

(Hannah Arendt presented a copy of *Steady Work* to the Columbia University library.)

When I asked if further writings of this kind were forthcoming, Howe said he is working on a "public autobiography." "It's not about my life and loves. It deals with the political, cultural and literary experiences that I've been in or near," he said.

It is not likely that anything Irving Howe writes for publication will be very personal. For one thing, his use of the word "I" sometimes carries a strangely detached quality. He says: "I was friendly to Breira," or "I am not friendly to *The New Yorker*," or "I am not a friend of the Begin government," as though he were an institution or a state himself. For another, he seems to share the attitudes he ascribes to Yiddish writers— "a sort of shyness and puritanism," as he puts it.

"There are things you don't talk about," he elaborates. "There have been some Yiddish writers like Schneour, to some extent Weisenberg, both brothers Singer, who began to put sexual material and motives into their fiction, but still the Yiddish tradition is very reticent on this matter, and though Isaac Bashevis Singer is a great hero to the external world, among Yiddishists there's a considerable ambivalence toward him. There's a feeling that he often brings in things that are not so nice. A great master of style, but some of the attitudes and values he has leave them very uncomfortable."

Howe ascribes this puritanism of Yiddishists to the fact that they have traditionally perceived marriage as sacred and sex as something organically connected to marriage, not as a form of play. "Sex as play was alien to Yiddish culture," he asserted.

Discussing another aspect of American Jewish writing, he said: "The immigrant experience was an absolutely compulsive subject for most of the so-called American Jewish writers." It is not merely a matter of Graham Greene's quip, he added, that an unhappy childhood is a writer's gold mine, but that "The childhood and adolescence of these writers left so organic a mark that it can't be easily escaped. For the American Jewish writer, the sense of having grown up in a different world—better, worse, but different—has stamped their work." In Howe's desire to preserve, record and explain to himself as well as to others the world of his father and the world of his own youth, he too seems to be impelled by this emotional need.

Explaining some of his "I" statements, he said that though he had not been a member of Breira, he was friendly to the organization to protect it from the "very nasty sort of witch-hunting campaign against them in the Jewish world," and because he felt it was important that "These people should be able to speak freely without assault inside the Jewish world." (Breira—the word for "alternative" in Hebrew—sought ways to establish peace in the Middle East, its ideas often counter to Israeli policy and the concepts of American Jewish organizations.)

As for why he was not friendly to *The New Yorker*, Howe did not say, but he once wrote, "For every short story writer who has survived *The New Yorker*, one could point to a dozen whose work became trivialized and frozen after they had begun to write for it."

He is critical of the Begin regime, he said, because he deplores Begin's view of the West Bank as "something the Bible gave him," and because he believes it is "politically and morally deplorable and dangerous for Israel to try to rule over 800,000 Arabs and to adopt an imperial stance." Though Israel has every reason to insist upon adequate guarantees if it gives up the West Bank, Howe believes the Begin government "did not think out the whole autonomy business and did not realize that this clearly was a way toward creation of an independent Palestinian state, which they were against. They fell into a trap there, I suspect."

This led us back to *World of Our Fathers*. Some critics had complained that Howe did not give the Zionist movement its due in the book. To him this would have been "a projecting backward" of a later occurrence. Zionism, he asserted, was only "a very weak marginal phenomenon in the immigrant world." He believes Zionism "is finished now, anyway in America. If the whole idea of Zionism is the ingathering of the exiles, what does it mean," he asks, "to be an American under eighty and over eight, to have the cost of a one-way ticket and to call yourself a Zionist?" He considers himself not an ideological Zionist but rather a supporter of Israel.

Howe dismisses another criticism of *World of Our Fathers*—that he gave relatively little attention to the Hebrew language, the Hebrew writings of men like Peretz, Schneour, Zeitlin and Mendele Mokher Sforim, and the Hebrew-language press in the immigrant world. "A very tiny, marginal phenomenon," he remarked. "Besides, there's no obligation to write about everything."

Still Howe concedes that there is more substance to comments that the book emphasizes secular life and neglects immigrant religious beliefs. He laughed when he recalled a clever, but "accusing" review in Yiddish in an Orthodox journal, where he "was lambasted for knowing the names of all the Yiddish poets, but not the rabbis." Historians, he said, "are drawn to what is dynamic and changing. In the immigrant Jewish community it was the secular. If you ask yourself, in terms of what was working, what was creative and fresh in the immigrant world, it was theater, literature, the labor movement. Orthodoxy had very little to do with it. You can't write a book about the constancy of that."

Howe went on to paraphrase his Orthodox Yiddish critic. " 'Look,' he said, 'after all, what complaint do we have against him? He never pretended to be anything other than he was and if we want a book written from our point of view, then one of us should write it.' " Howe thought this was both sensible and amusing. He sent the man a postcard saying, "You're absolutely right."

Irving Howe, not yet 59, has assumed the role of an elder statesman. He is concerned about the future and a legacy for future generations. In "The Limits of Ethnicity," an essay adapted in June 1977 from his commencement address at Queens College, Howe said: "Sentimentalism is the besetting sin of the Jewish turn to ethnicity—a sentimentalism that would erase memories of ugliness and pathology, disputation and radicalism." And still turning Jewish words and concepts loose on the world, he offered his young audience the word "mensch." "It suggests," he told them, "a vision of humanity and humaneness; it serves as a norm—a possibility beckoning to us. You don't have to be Jewish or non-Jewish, you don't have to be white or black, in order to be a mensch."

And writing in the Winter 1979 anniversary issue of *Dissent*, Howe states, "I hope the magazine can keep going for a few more years. We need to pass on to our younger friends not so much a particular crux of opinion as a ranging style of criticism."

An hour had passed. To the one or two speculative questions I had posed, Howe's reply had been "That's for others to decide." Now I asked: "Is there anything important still left unasked or unanswered." Almost reluctantly, he turned toward the desk . . . "Just ten minutes before you came," he said, "I finished an essay called 'The End of Jewish Secularism,' in which the word 'end' is used in its double sense as 'purpose' and 'conclusion.'

"I've come to feel, very sadly," he told me, "that the Jewish tradition from which I come is really reaching an end. Yiddish is coming to an end. The immigrant culture in which it subsisted is coming to an end, and the distinctive Jewish secular world which was based on the labor move-

ment—secular schools—that also is coming to an end." He believes that a
small, serious religious component in American Jewish life will persist,
but to him most religion is "unserious," with temples and synagogues
becoming increasingly secularized institutions. People whose Jewishness
is not based on religion but on habit, style, an inherited way of life, will
have problems maintaining their Jewish identification.

The problem, he predicts, "will become more acute insofar as there's a
hope for peace in the Middle East. Maybe 85 or 90 percent of Jewish
activity in America is directed toward Israel, but, if you can imagine a
situation in which that's no longer true, then you can no longer define
yourself as Jewish just by writing a check. You have to ask yourself 'What
does it mean to me?'"

Will American Jews ask themselves this question? He doesn't know.
"There are all these exhortations about being Jewish, but nobody speci-
fies what that means. The only people who have a clear answer are the
religious ones. Everyone else is in trouble. But of course there is nothing
more vulgar, morally and intellectually, than to turn to religion in order
to, quote, keep Jewishness alive. The only reason to turn to religion is
because you believe in God. If you don't, that's an act of insincerity and
bad faith. Anyway, this is the problem I'm trying to explore."

"Do you have children?" I asked.

"Yes, but they're grown up. I don't want to get into that." His hands
waved over the tape recorder. (He has two—Nina, a clinical psychologist
and Nicholas, a medievalist.)

"I mean in terms of their being 'Jewish.'"

"It's a general problem. It isn't just a personal problem with me, and I'm
trying to face that question."

Turning again to the Middle East, he said: "If there were a happy
conclusion to the Middle East conflict, and it is conceivable that it will
happen, the internal spiritual conflict in American Jewish society will
become more acute."

"And you have no solution for it at this point?"

"As soon as I do," said Howe, then hesitated.

"You'll call me up?" I asked.

And Irving Howe said he would.

Jewish Daily Forward

Isadore Barmash

Occasionally young journalism students or graduates, eyes eager, manner hesitant, come to the *Jewish Daily Forward*'s editorial offices in New York City. Most ask three questions: Can they make a living as Yiddish journalists? Can they get a job on the *Forward*? And inevitably, if the response is encouraging, will the newspaper survive?

The man they usually talk with—editor Simon Weber, who joined the *Forward* forty years ago—answers with a sort of Jewish shrug. When I asked about the newspaper's prospects, he sighed and told me: "Even though our circulation today is substantially lower than it used to be, if there were more Yiddish writers, I would hire them. Each Yiddish journalist is a treasure. But can we be competitive on salaries for new young writers, if and when we find them?" His voice trailed off.

Ever since its first issue appeared on April 22, 1897, the *Forward* has been this country's most important medium for the dissemination of Jewish culture, pioneering not only in interpreting major news events but also in publishing the best and most enduring Yiddish fiction. On another level it served scores of thousands of Jewish immigrants from the shtetls and cities of Europe as the passage-way between their *mamaloshen*, or mother tongue, and old customs and habits, and the strange language and ways of America.

Jacob C. Rich (byline: Ya'akov Reich), now eighty-four years old and for nearly six decades a member of the *Forward* staff, summed up the paper's purpose and achievement: "It isn't and wasn't a newspaper but a movement, a cause, a support for socialism and an aid to the sweatshop workers. It taught them dignity and concern for each other."

The *Forward* was launched by the Forward Association, an organization of Jewish immigrants of socialist persuasion, as a publication designed to function freely within the Socialist Labor Party of those days. This group had decided to break with the dictatorial Daniel De Leon, the party's dominant figure and editor of a labor newspaper, who had coerced union members to strikebreak and otherwise violate union ethics. Abraham Cahan, a well-known journalist and socialist, was induced to become the editor. It was named the *Forward* because Cahan had been told that the *Vorwärts* of Berlin was the world's most eminent socialist daily and probably hoped that the German journal's prestige would rub off on his.

From the outset the *Forward* was notable for its particular formula. Cahan stressed the interpretative article with such style and impact that it became known as a paragon in the field and an example to larger, more prosperous newspapers. Starting under Cahan's editorship and continuing with those who followed him, the Yiddish printed by the *Forward* reflected changes in usage.

Cahan's stamp was total. He juxtaposed serious socialist articles with human-interest pieces. He wrote about each Saturday's Torah reading, drawing relationships to socialist philosophy. He urged workers in every industry to unite, stressing that they lived in a free country. He campaigned for tolerance between religious and non-religious readers. He sought to make the *Forward* a vehicle to brighten and elevate the lives of its readers. And, day in and day out, he insisted on lucidity and clear, vernacular language.

One of the most popular features, which helped thousands to adjust to their new home and to solve burning personal problems, was the "Bintel Brief" column, which published information, advice, guidance, even solace about practically everything under the sun. For example, a self-confessed "atheist" wrote to ask if he could say *kaddish* for his father, because otherwise his mother would be unhappy. (Cahan said "Yes, of course.") Another atheist, also a socialist, asked if his beliefs would be violated if he sat with his family at a seder. (Cahan said "No.") Others wrote about mixed marriages, sweatshop problems, whether a birthmark on the face represented a curse, family quarrels, even pinochle disputes. (Cahan admitted he knew nothing about pinochle.)

Eagerly awaited each afternoon by the immigrant, the socialist, the working man (and woman), the small businessman, the housewife and many others, the newspaper thrived. In 1924 it reached a peak circulation of 220,000, one of the highest of any newspaper in New York. But, as Yiddish declined as a spoken language and many Yiddish-speaking readers died, the circulation figure headed downward; today it totals about 40,000. In 1943 it became a morning paper. It is now published only five times a week, on Tuesday, Wednesday, Thursday, Friday and Sunday. With advertising also dropping off, the last two decades have witnessed financial losses each year.

In the past four years, the Forward Association has conducted three fund-raising campaigns which have produced a strong flow of gifts, 70 percent of them from individual readers. From 1976 through 1978, the amount raised was $730,000, just about enough to cover that period's deficits—which heartened both Simon Weber and Harold Ostroff, the general manager, considerably.

Here's how Ostroff summed up his reaction: "There is a strong commitment in the community. Many believe that, in addition to the wealth of Jewish literature, we must continue to have a Yiddish newspaper to help preserve our culture. Frankly, before our volunteer campaign we were in danger of having to close down. But now we feel that the turnout in the campaign is a good sign and we must hang on."

Today's *Forward* is put together in a place which is a far cry from its original location on the Lower East Side. That building at 175 East Broadway, with its huge neon *Forward* sign on the roof, was in its way as much a beacon to the "tired, poor, huddled masses" as the newspaper itself. In June 1974, after sixty-two years there, the management sold the building to a Chinese organization and moved uptown to the red-brick Workmen's Circle building on East 33rd Street.

Whether one is a young journalism student or a nostalgic adult seeking Yiddish *kultur* symbols, this locale—a modern setting, about average for an insurance firm, with Weber in one office, senior writers in another, and the city room in a third—produces a letdown feeling. Where, one wonders, are the trappings, shabby but reeking of culture, of the great Jewish journalists and novelists? Gone, perhaps, with the old building. But the editors and senior writers, almost all elderly men, remain. Among the seventeen editorial people who do the work that seventy did in 1939, when Simon Weber joined the *Forward*, one finds lingering and potent memories of an Abraham Cahan, a Sholem Asch, an Abraham Reisin, an I. J. Singer.

Their thoughts erupt with enthusiastically recalled detail or sweet-sour edges as they recall the old days: "Abe Cahan, one of America's greatest journalists, insisted on Yiddishe Yiddish but allowed the use of American words if they were commonly used by the immigrants. The *Forward* would be the vehicle for assimilation, but maybe he was too zealous and helped precipitate the decline of Yiddish itself."

"Sholem Asch, a fine novelist but difficult, demanding, always seeking obeisance from colleagues and so disdainful." "Chaim Grade? I think he's lonely. He will talk you deaf and dumb. But he's quite a storyteller and also a very decent man. Isaac Bashevis Singer gets a marvelous translation, but his Yiddish is infinitely more colorful, juicier."

"I remember when Singer first came in, a poor young slouch. He was very upset when someone told him his grammar could be better, but today every Jewish writer is jealous of him."

Reflecting the passage of time and readers, assimilation, economics, the advent of television and new publishing technology, the *Forward* has changed in many ways. Most important was its political repositioning. Though in the paper's early decades it hewed to the American Socialist Party line, its editorial policy seemed to shift, perhaps stumble, toward more independent thinking as first the American Labor Party (organized in 1936 so that socialists could have their own designation on election ballots) and then the Liberal Party underwent changes in composition and policy. These days the *Forward* is generally independent but often reflects Democratic Party thinking in its editorials.

It's unlikely that the *Forward* will ever abandon its original socialist orientation. Friends and critics cite its fervent, sometimes shrill nationalism ("Israel right or wrong") and its edging toward a complete tolerance for religion and an inclination to cater to the religious reader. But the boxed homilies that flank the masthead are from Karl Marx's *Communist Manifesto*: "Workers of all lands, unite. . . . The freedom of the workers depends upon the workers themselves." These homilies, which some readers like and others don't, are retained, says Weber, because certain older members of the Forward Association insist on it.

The *Forward*'s opposition to communism created some problems, most sharply in 1922. After a fruitless effort by Socialist Party left-wingers to unite with the then-underground Communist apparatus, several staff members broke away and established a rival Yiddish daily, the *Freiheit*, which followed the communist line. It has since repudiated the Russian variety and follows its own vaguely communistic beliefs. That paper still publishes three times a week, but as a result of the party's decline has lost most of its readers and much of its sting.

What does the *Forward* look like these days?

The emphasis is on culture, commentary, interpretation, service. In his early years as editor, Simon Weber, who is now sixty-eight, sought to emphasize news coverage, but discovered it wasn't feasible. Summing up this experience, he said: "I tried to develop a couple of news reporters since we were rich in 'think' pieces, but I failed. It is very hard to compete with radio and television. One of our special problems is that there aren't enough Yiddish journalists who can interpret politics or know enough about America. Everyone wants to write about Israel. So we decided that the area where we could be strong was culture."

With Isaac Bashevis Singer already in the fold and achieving worldwide recognition (he remains, after his Nobel Prize, a salaried *Forward* writer), Weber added Chaim Grade as a writer of poems, short stories and novels. He brought in others—among them Mordecai Strigler, a Talmudic scholar who writes on ethics and philosophy; Dr. Elias Shulman, who covers current books and literature in general; J. Shmulewitz, an expert on the Holocaust and survivors, and Abraham Shulman, a news writer who also turns out a humorous column, "Yeden Tag" (Every Day). Weber also has three rabbis writing regularly—Orthodox Rabbi Aaron Ben Zion Shurin, who covers religious and community affairs; Rabbi David Graubart, a Conservative who discusses the Talmud; and Orthodox Rabbi Abraham Hefterman, who takes up special questions such as mixed marriages. No Reform rabbi on the contributing staff? "If I found a Yiddish-writing, Reform rabbi, I would gladly hire him," replies Weber. "But Rabbi Graubart never forgets there are other religious movements," including Reform and Reconstructionists.

Weber also started a column, "Pearls of Yiddish Literature," a sort of guessing game. Readers are given four lines of a poem and asked to name it—or several paragraphs from a short story or novel to identify—or a Yiddish crossword puzzle. It has become a popular feature with hundreds of *Forward* readers.

As for news, it is largely rewritten from the wire services, incorporating a special blend of Jewish consciousness. The Jewish Telegraphic Agency or United Press International provide coverage on local Jewish stories; the *Forward* supplements these with its own "specials."

Continuing Cahan's insistence on keeping the paper's language current, Weber has spurned what he calls a "eunuch Yiddish" or Yiddish without Hebrew. He has removed the Germanisms and Anglicisms. Thus, he says, *efsher*, is acceptable but not *fileisht* for "maybe," and *a sach* for "a great deal" is better than *fiel*. So Hebrew diction has been retained, Weber said, since "Yiddish without Hebrew is like serving food without seasoning." But in the interest of removing phonetic dross a *boychick* is now *yingle* or *yunger man*. *Obwohl* (although) is *chutch*; *dese* (these) is *dosiga*. And "constitution" is *constituzie*; "administration" is *administrazie*; and "collection" is, perhaps not so fortunately, *gelt zamlung*.

The *Forward* staff is rich in background, talent and seniority, short on youth and knowledge of the American scene, and displays a tendency to brood upon the Holocaust. No doubt this last is to be expected, for most of the editorial staff and mechanical and composing-room personnel were born in Europe.

Jacob Rich, the oldest staff member, was a child prodigy who received a Harvard scholarship and was graduated in the class of 1919. He started on the *Forward* an unbelievable fifty-eight years ago and is still going strong with four columns a week. He writes smoothly about politics, education and even gardening (under the pen-name of Yoseph Rachlin). Formerly a successful free-lancer whose work appeared in the *Saturday Evening Post* in its heyday as well as in H. L. Mencken's *American Mercury* and *The Nation*, Rich wrote a series for the *Forward* on the Southern textile strikes during the Depression. Along with Cahan, he covered the Bruno Hauptmann trial after the Lindbergh kidnapping. "Abe, of course, did the commentary," he told me. "I wrote the news stories."

Shelomo Ben Israel, another senior writer, is an expert on the Middle East. He does a Sunday news commentary on New York's radio station WEVD-AM and FM, which is also owned by the *Forward*. (Recently, the Forward Association agreed to sell the AM facility but the deal is still pending.) Like others on the paper who started out with other forms (Simon Weber, for example, began his career writing Yiddish short stories), Ben Israel originally wrote articles on the Middle East for the *Boston Globe*, simultaneously producing detective stories for the *Forward*.

In 1946, when the *Forward* offered him a political affairs post, he joined the paper full time and retired his fictional Jewish private eye, David Almog, and Almog's canine companion, Gibor (Hero).

Tzirl Steingart, who was a member of the Jewish resistance movement in France, writes a daily column on food, education, fashion and family problems. She also writes under such pen names as Sarah Berkowitz (her younger sister, who was killed by the Nazis at the age of twenty with her husband and child) and Hana Lasmar (her mother, who was also murdered by the Nazis).

A medical advice column by Dr. Paul Weinsaft appears on Sundays. Mitchell Lokiec, an efficiency expert with the International Ladies Garment Workers Union, writes a weekly column on economics and government. Boris Smolar, editor emeritus of the Jewish Telegraphic Agency, writes a weekly column on Jewish community life, as he has for the last fifty-five years. And the durable "Bintel Brief" still runs four times a week.

Weber shares the writing of editorials with other staff members. Recently he ripped into a Vietnamese defector who described the treatment of Vietnam's ethnic Chinese as "worse than Hitler," asking why, if so, the Vietnamese haven't built gas crematoria or death camps. "Why make the Holocaust a metaphor?" he demanded. He also recently charged that, though President Carter insists that he hasn't changed his Israel policy, "Everyone can see that there is a tilt toward the P.L.O." But in another editorial, he disputed Israeli policy of cutting back on food subsidies, saying it was "taking the bread out of the mouth of the poor."

Will the *Forward* continue *biz a hundert un tzvanzig*—for another 120 years?

"The paper's financial health is precarious," Harold Ostroff said. "Readership has been declining for a long time, as has advertising, so we have been hit from both sides. The Forward Association, our readers and such unions as the International Ladies Garment Workers want to preserve a Yiddish newspaper."

Yiddish is now taught at some fifty American colleges as well as in Israel, Ostroff pointed out, which makes for at least some glimmer of hope for future circulation. "We also find that more people want to read the literature in the original for both nostalgic and intellectual reasons, and that's a good sign," he added.

And, Simon Weber mused: "We already help educate readers by

publishing listings of Hebrew words used in Yiddish with their definitions. Why not the same for Yiddish words? Perhaps we are coming full
circle with third- and fourth-generation American Jews. Yiddish needs
the same educational stimulus that Hebrew did."

Philip Klutznick

Estelle Gilson

At 76, you might expect a man who can look back on a career of over forty years of service to the Jewish community to retire on his laurels and rock slowly on the front porch.

Not so, if that man is Philip M. Klutznick, lawyer, self-made million-aire and a man endowed with phenomenal energy and drive. Klutznick, who served seven Presidents of the United States, was most recently Jimmy Carter's Secretary of Commerce. His positions in Jewish life were equally eminent. He was international president of B'nai B'rith and president of the World Jewish Congress (WJC). Despite the fact that he is no longer in a position of executive power in Jewish organizational life, Klutznick has by no means lost interest in its causes.

Throughout his long career, which encompassed many years of service to the American government and to the Jewish community here and elsewhere in the world, Klutznick has often expressed views which stirred heated, contentious debate. Commenting on the impact of some Klutz-nick concepts, a friend recently told him: "You go from strength to strength. For many years you were described as 'wise.' Then you gradu-ated to 'brilliant.' And now you have achieved the superlative – you are regarded as 'controversial.' You can't do better than that."

There are many notable examples of his tendency to stimulate fresh thinking about vital problems. One of the most important occurred in

141

July 1982, following the Israeli invasion of Lebanon, when Beirut was under siege.

Earlier, Klutznick and his wife had visited former WJC president Nahum Goldmann at his Paris apartment, along with former French Premier Pierre Mendès-France. They discussed the possibility of issuing a statement calling for immediate peace in the Middle East; Klutznick offered to begin formulating one. Though Mendès-France had never before signed a statement about a Jewish cause, Klutznick welcomed his participation, for he believes that those who have held high government posts possess a kind of political sharpness which persons in voluntary organizations seldom develop.

After the statement was written, the three signers decided it would be useful to add a response from the PLO. Eric Rouleau, a French Jewish journalist, was entrusted with contacting Dr. Issam Sartawi—assassinated by Palestinian killers in April 1983—who was known as a "moderate." Sartawi responded immediately, praising the Jewish initiative.

The statement appeared on the front page of the leading Paris newspaper, *Le Monde*, and on front pages throughout the world. Its first sentence read: "Peace is not made between friends, but between enemies who have warred and suffered," and it called on Israel to raise the siege and begin negotiations with the PLO.

According to Klutznick, "The thing became a sensation overnight. It was called 'the Paris declaration.' The mail was enormous, five to one for it. The number of Jewish people who found something they could be 'for' that wasn't 'disloyal' would shock you. You know, we've learned to hate too. We keep talking about those who hate us. One of the great sadnesses of this terrible extended period of enmity is that people who should know each other better now hate each other."

American Jewish reaction was swift. Rabbi Arthur Schneier, chairman of the American Section of the WJC (which was then meeting in Paris), announced that Klutznick's views were unrepresentative of the American Jewish community, and that "While no one questions their [Klutznick's and Goldmann's] motives, they speak for themselves and themselves alone. Their pronouncements can become self-deluding and misleading."

Though most Jewish leaders have disagreed with him publicly, Klutznick claims he doesn't feel alienated. "I'm perfectly comfortable where I am," he asserts. "I'm powerless, except to the extent that I can influence others. I do it when I feel I have to. I'm a selfish person. When I feel I can't live with myself anymore, I say what I want to say."

Discussing the Paris statement in New York some time ago, Klutznick said he'd been asked to defend the declaration, but—referring to the mass protest demonstration in Israel following the massacre of Palestinians in West Beirut—had refrained, because "400,000 marching in Tel Aviv spoke louder than any words of mine, and they spoke for me."

This dramatic episode was not Philip Klutznick's first major brush with organized Jewry. In 1978, he alone among American Jewish leaders agreed to meet with Anwar Sadat while the late Egyptian president was in this country. During 1981 he was the only Jewish member of the four-person Seven Springs Center study mission to the Middle East, which included former Assistant Secretary of State for Near Eastern Affairs Harold H. Saunders; Merle Thorpe, Jr., founder of the Foundation for Middle East Peace; and Joseph N. Greene Jr., president of the Center, a "think tank" on public issues in Mt. Kisco, New York. After conferring with high officials in Israel, Egypt, Jordan, Saudi Arabia and Syria, the group issued its recommendations—including one stating that the United States would need to deal directly with the PLO—which disturbed many Americans and produced sharp denunciations of Klutznick. As a result, Elsa Solender in *The Baltimore Jewish Times* reported: "Philip Klutznick was called just about everything short of traitor." " 'Naive,' 'uncritical,' 'intellectually weak' were a few of the terms used," says Solender, adding: "B'nai B'rith was urged to repudiate him." Moshe Decter in *Near East Report* accused Klutznick of "passing along without challenge the cynical historical distortion of Arab propaganda that the Palestinian Arabs are 'a special people . . .' "

Klutznick met with me in his New York apartment, which is elegantly furnished in pale greens and golds. A man of medium height, round-faced, wearing dark-rimmed glasses, he was immaculately groomed in dark-blue business suit, dark tie and white shirt. Speaking with a flat Middle Western accent and with the smoothly controlled speech of one for whom politics is second nature, he gives an interviewer little insight into his private personality. Judging by what he chooses to say and how he chooses to say it, however, it is clear that he is a man who expects to be listened to. One senses power even in his assertions of powerlessness.

Because this man, who once spoke for tens of thousands of organized Jews, has been criticized by the very organizations he once led, I asked him to explain how his ideas had changed.

"I never changed," Klutznick told me. "I never was a follower of the routine. People suddenly discovered I had ideas that to them were outlandish. It's the environment in which I work today that has changed.

When I was a youngster, I wrote a speech that won the high school award. It was about race, creed, color and war. I hated war from the time I was a youngster. When I was ten, during World War I, I had a fist fight with a boy who was bigger than I was because he said the Jews had caused the war." Klutznick lost that fight—which, he says, was the first and last fist fight he ever had.

Klutznick was born in July 1907, in Kansas City, Missouri. His parents, Morris and Minnie, were observant Jews, and sent him to cheder—but, Klutznick reports, he was "a very poor bar mitzvah."

He attended elementary and high schools in Kansas City and went on to the University of Kansas, completing his undergraduate work at the University of Nebraska in 1926, after the family had moved to Omaha. Three years later, he earned a Bachelor of Laws degree from Creighton University in Lincoln, Nebraska. He helped organize a junior B'nai B'rith group, later known as the B'nai B'rith Youth Organization, when he was 16 years old, and held the title of assistant executive secretary of the organization. By 1925, when he was 18, he had become second international president of Junior B'nai B'rith.

"You started early at the top in international Jewish affairs," I commented.

"No, no," Klutznick waved his hand, laughing. "We became international overnight because we'd gotten a chapter in Canada."

While he was at college, Klutznick traveled the country organizing chapters of Junior B'nai B'rith. When he went to law school, he was asked to help out on a part-time basis. Klutznick agreed, his salary was set at $50 a month—and here, in a fleeting glimpse into the private recess of his personality, he felt compelled to explain that "The salary was later adjusted."

Philip Klutznick left Junior B'nai B'rith when he began to practice law. He later became chairman of the senior group and eventually took the post of international president of the entire organization. (Currently, he is honorary international president.)

"I also was president of my Zionist district in Omaha," he told me.

"You were a Zionist at that time too?" I asked.

"I am a Zionist," Klutznick said vehemently. "I think I am as good a Zionist—or better—as some who go to the meetings of the World Zionist Organization. But I see things differently from some who were not around years ago. We speak of Zionism as if it were an accepted phenomenon in the American Jewish community. It wasn't. It was a minority. It was looked upon as a step down in Omaha when I became president of the Zionist district after I'd been president of B'nai B'rith. It was a B'nai B'rith town."

"I felt then and I feel to this day," he asserted, "that Zionism was an effort to reclaim the people as much as the land. You can't redeem the land unless you redeem the people. What's the use of a state of Israel if it's going to be like every other state? It has to respond to the culture, the history of our people. That's our greatness."

Klutznick ended his participation in what he calls "the Zionist mechanism" when American Zionists no longer supported Chaim Weizmann (Israel's first president, whose program of cultural Zionism he favored) and turned his attention to other Jewish cultural and educational affairs.

Today, Klutznick warmly recalls two mentors he encountered when he was on the threshhold of his career. One was Reconstructionist philosopher Mordecai Kaplan, who, Klutznick said, "clarified for me the challenge facing an American Jew who willingly lives in two civilizations—that of his people and their needs, and that of America and its needs. A man has multiple loyalties; his task is to try to do justice to all."

His second teacher was Louis Te Poel, a Catholic and his professor in law school, who was Omaha's corporation counsel in 1933. Te Poel chose Klutznick, then a young lawyer, from a list of more experienced attorneys to serve as his assistant. One day, he explained his unusual choice, telling Klutznick that, while he'd not been the most brilliant student, he had demonstrated the ability to see both sides of an issue and to find points of agreement between opposing views.

"He urged that I not lose that quality," Klutznick remembers. "There is no greater service a lawyer can render than to bring peaceful adjustment between conflicting claims. I have tried to live that way in all walks of life ever since.

"With two such teachers, however, I have managed to step on some toes over the years. Now and then, trying to see both sides causes one to become controversial; but it has brought me much happiness and peace of mind."

Philip Klutznick became involved in government activity when the federal bureaucracy was still relatively small. One of the Roosevelt administration's first pieces of legislation was the National Industrial Recovery Act of 1933, which provided funds for slum clearance and new housing. Like many other cities during the depression years, Omaha was bankrupt. Under Te Poel's guidance, the young assistant corporation counsel went to Washington to press Omaha's needs. "Out of sixty projects that were first allotted funds," Klutznick said, "we, the little town of Omaha, got two. I became deeply involved in the program. I found that it helped clear up problems and also provided work. And I kept on, and housing became a kind of obsession with me."

Not long after the United States entered World War II, Klutznick— then a partner in an Omaha law firm—was spending a quarter of his time on housing matters in Washington at President Roosevelt's request. For six years Klutznick was in Washington full time, heading programs first for defense housing and later for housing for war veterans.

During his youth in Kansas City, Klutznick and his family knew Harry Truman. In fact, as a young man, Klutznick had made a speech for Truman when he was running for local office.

After Roosevelt's death in 1945, Klutznick, then commissioner of the Federal Public Housing Authority, a presidential appointment, submitted his resignation to President Truman, according to custom. "And, typical of the President," he recalled, "the phone rang the next morning, and Matthew Connelly, his secretary, said, 'The boss wants to talk to you.' Truman got on the phone. He said, 'Come on over here. Right now!' " Klutznick, conducting a meeting at the time, turned it over to his assistant and went to see Truman, who demanded: "What's this business of resigning? We haven't won the war or the peace yet."

"I said, 'Mr. President, it's customary when there's a change in the presidency for presidential appointees to resign.' But," said Klutznick, laughing, "I was so embarrassed. He said, 'You're not a presidential appointee, you're my friend.' So I stayed on."

One of Klutznick's special concerns during the war was housing for civilian war workers. "For example," he explained, "when we suddenly had to provide rocket powder for the military, the only place you could provide it was out in the wilderness. Overnight, we had to create a community with all the facilities. When the country needed small aircraft carriers to reach Japan as well as to protect the country's western coast, we had to build a town for 65,000 people virtually overnight. I was out there when the ground was broken. Eighteen months later aircraft carriers were available."

Throughout his years of government service, Klutznick continued his association with B'nai B'rith and other Jewish organizations. When, during Truman's administration, he learned that contributions to the United Jewish Appeal from federal employees were sought on an informal basis, he got together with Leon Keyserling, chairman of the Council of Economic Advisors, and obtained Truman's approval to organize an official campaign.

Klutznick remained in Washington after the war to help plan for urgently needed housing for veterans and their families. In 1947, President Truman awarded him the Certificate of Merit for "rapid-fire construction of half-a-million housing units."

When he returned to Chicago, Klutznick was 40 years old and not only had contacts in the highest levels of federal and state government as well as the American Jewish community, but also broad expertise in housing. And he had a particular dream: before resuming the practice of law, he wanted to build "a town that managed itself," putting into effect what he'd learned in his years of federal service.

One of the most important things he had learned was that the morale of war workers—in effect, the sense of well-being and the efficiency of civilians—depended not only on the type of shelter they had, but on ancillary community services such as access to food supplies, entertainment and social opportunities. "Rosie the Riveter," said Klutznick, "was only as good as the hairdresser who was available when she had a day off and could dress herself up a little bit."

One result of Klutznick's dream was Park Forest, a suburban complex built on thirty acres of farmland south of Chicago. It houses 30,000 people and has been called a "model of intelligent planning." Thereafter, Klutznick never returned to the law. In the ensuing decades, he put together an empire of vast real estate holdings which in 1968 became the Urban Investment and Development Company. The Klutznick family still directs the company, which in 1970 was sold to Aetna Life and Casualty Company for more than $52 million. In the 1970s, Klutznick carried through a major project: construction of Chicago's Water Tower Plaza, a seventy-four-story, $195-million complex, which includes the Ritz-Carlton Hotel, 150 shops and forty floors of condominiums. His offices are in one of the buildings, his and his wife Ethel's home in an upper story of the tower. He's been known to refer to this arrangement as "living over the store."

In addition to ever-expanding involvement in business, he was active in government and in Jewish affairs. His three "careers," all international in scope, were interwoven one with another—and he relished all of them.

In 1957, President Eisenhower appointed Klutznick a delegate to the United Nations. Later, President Kennedy appointed him ambassador to the Economic and Social Council of the U.N., a position he retained until 1963 under Johnson's presidency. He also served on the President's Advisory Committee on Indo-Chinese Refugees.

At the same time, Klutznick was appointed chairman of the American Housing Committee for Israel by Prime Minister David Ben-Gurion. In the 1950s, he helped plan construction of the deep-water port and industrial center of Ashdod in Israel. He continued to be active in a gamut of Jewish associations, was a founder and first president of the Presidents' Conference—a group representing leading American Jewish organizations—and was chairman of the Institute of Jewish Policy Planning.

Of his international travels, Klutznick told me, "I never went to a foreign country without visiting the Jewish community." As a result, in 1966—before most other Jews were aware of the gravity of the situation—Klutznick first spoke out against Soviet anti-Semitism. "The first reaction is to get mad, and to attack frontally," he said in 1977. "I think that's wise in a limited way. On the other hand, one must take a look at 3 million Jews in the Soviet Union. Are there other alternatives to frontal attack?"

In 1976, *Who's Who* cited Klutznick, then 69 years old, for "four decades of immense public and private accomplishment," and as a man who has "tempered a businessman's practical goals with the vision of a humanitarian." Since then, he has gone on to further achievement. In 1977, he became president of the World Jewish Congress, succeeding Nahum Goldmann. In 1979, when Klutznick was 72, President Carter appointed him Secretary of Commerce, and Klutznick took a leave from the WJC to accept the post.

When he took his position, Klutznick became the oldest member of the Cabinet. *Business Week* speculated that Klutznick's appointment was designed to smooth Carter's way with the American Jewish community, then wary of the President's push for peace in the Middle East. Others pointed to Klutznick's important position in the Chicago business community as a possible factor on the eve of Carter's primary battle with

Senator Edward Kennedy for the Democratic Party nomination for the presidency.

Klutznick's tenure at Commerce, which lasted until the end of the Carter administration, was a fairly quiet one. A report on the front page of the *Wall Street Journal* noted that he had "airily addressed an administrator in his 50s as 'young man.' " He was also reported to be often away from his desk, "speaking to Jewish groups when important decisions are pending." In response, Klutznick denied being a spokesman for the President in the Jewish community and declared that he saw more business groups than Jewish organizations on trips outside Washington.

Klutznick supported Carter's Camp David peace negotiations. In 1981, he wrote that the Camp David momentum "should now be accelerated in an attempt to draw Palestinian representation into the negotiations."

On June 28, 1982, while Israel's Lebanon offensive was going forward, an article by Klutznick, titled "Israel's Moment for Compromise," appeared in *The Christian Science Monitor*. In it, he stated that a majority of Americans and American Jews concurred with the statement that "There must be a way to guarantee Israel's security and also give the Palestinians an independent state on the West Bank." He pointed out that "With Israel's military action against the Palestinians and others in Lebanon, with its firm grip on the West Bank, it may seem to some that Israel need no longer contemplate compromise." But instead, Klutznick urged, "At this moment of Palestinian weakness, it is imperative that Jews face the simple truth that it can no longer be reasonably denied that the Palestinian people are entitled to self-determination. Now is the crucial moment for that historic offer of peace coming from the Jewish people to the Palestinian people."

Even as Klutznick continues to believe that Israel's security is not debatable and that the United States must continue to provide Israel with military equipment, he presents a beguiling vision of Israel at peace. From the financial point of view, he stresses, the cost of maintaining Israel's security before the Lebanon offensive was $7 billion annually, or one-third of the nation's gross national product. Simply by reducing military spending, and not calling up the work force for emergency military service, Klutznick argues, there would be more profit for Israel in peace than in war. Within one year of an established peace, he believes, Israel's economy would grow as much as 50 percent. Also, peace would bring increased immigration to Israel, less emigration and a higher birthrate. And, Klutznick contends, all of Israel's neighbors could be its trading partners. With Israel's genius in agriculture, manufacturing and banking, he foresees a role for the country as "the Switzerland" or "the Japan" of the Middle East.

Recalling the 1982 "Paris declaration," Klutznick said recently: "If anything, the evidence is that it [mutual recognition] was the proper thing to encourage and it is proper even now—especially now, when there is evidence of weakness on both sides. The decline in Israel's situation, economically and governmentally, and the decline in the Arafat position indicate that both may have missed the boat."

Is Philip Klutznick being fooled? Is he being used by the enemies of Israel? Dr. George E. Gruen, the American Jewish Committee's Middle East specialist, who attended some of the Seven Springs sessions, says: "I heard him being very tough on the Arabs, demanding the Arabs make concessions to show good faith. Those who think he's naive or a tool of the Arabs are being unfair to him. I don't question his honesty, integrity and loyalty." But, Gruen added, "Some people say: 'He doesn't have to declare these views publicly. He could get them heard privately.' It is an issue of group solidarity and dissent, not the question of the right to speak."

Klutznick concedes, "The voluntary society offers advantages to those who stay within the accepted norm. Those who are seeking the opportunity to serve—and I don't deprecate this—are very careful about what they say. You didn't hear me saying these things when I was president of the WJC."

Today, disagreements among Jews on the questions Klutznick has raised are no longer swept under the rug. They are expressed openly and strongly. For this, the American Jewish community owes Philip Klutznick a debt. Few people could have said what Klutznick did and have continued to serve that community.

Klutznick's present convictions are as clear and sharp as ever. He strongly urges support for human rights for all peoples. He opposes "escalation of armaments" and "militarism" everywhere in the world. He insists, "There is as much danger as potential in the power Israel has. Power is corroding." He continues to be willing to represent a polarized position, to publicly state unpopular views and at times to go counter to the position of those for whom he once spoke.

One need not always agree with Philip Klutznick to recognize the courage it has taken to speak out over and over again, when he might have collected his awards, citations and the honorary degrees he has received from almost every Jewish university in the United States, and rocked silently on his porch.

Klutznick still serves on the executive committees of many Jewish organizations, including the WJC and B'nai B'rith. He is active in Chicago affairs and is a member of the board of its Lyric Opera Company. He is now collecting his public and private papers, and is writing what he calls "memoirs." But, he says, "I will not publish. I will leave what I've written.

"I still try to attend to things as much as I can," he tells me. "I'm not trying to make money, but I have to be sure my investments don't deteriorate. We have a big family."

There are five Klutznick children, for whom he set up a partnership in the family business when he retired. Three of the five, including his only daughter, live close by in Chicago. The youngest, an unmarried son, divides his week between New York and Chicago. Another son, whom Klutznick calls "the white sheep of the family," runs a school for children from broken homes in Boulder, Colorado. He and his wife have fourteen grandchildren, whose accomplishments Klutznick enumerates, like any doting grandfather.

When he speaks of Israel's future and the continuing risks of war, he refers to grandchildren—his own and others. "I want them to be part of Jewish generations to come who can enjoy the treasure of a Jewish world with a Jewish state at its core," he insists. "If the Jewish people want a state, they will not have it for their grandchildren if it's in constant war. That's the history of human experience."

Teddy Kollek

J. Robert Moskin

Teddy Kollek, now 77, has held for 23 years the job of Mayor of Jerusalem, arguably the toughest mayoralty in the world. For more than a year now, he has governed the city during the Palestinian uprising. He has kept Jerusalem peaceful compared to the West Bank and the Gaza Strip, but it has been a time of extreme tension.

This increases Kollek's inherent stubbornness. He says, "We have before ourselves a very simple principle. Jerusalem will remain one and will remain the capital of Israel. Within the city, everybody has the same rights, and we will fight that everybody should have the same rights."

At his age, the responsibility begins to show. Kollek's phenomenal energy still outpumps that of most men, but he is slowing down. Nevertheless, he can still withstand the pounding of an 18-hour battle-filled day, and he will stand for reelection once more this spring. And he still cares passionately about Jerusalem.

Because this Judean hilltop city is of intense emotional importance to millions of Christians, Jews and Moslems, Kollek has struggled to encourage Jews and Arabs to want to live in Jerusalem together. (Arabs make up 30 percent of the city's population.) He has tried to inject some zing into the life of the city despite the fanatical opposition of ultra-Orthodox Jews, who condemn as sacrilegious showing movies on Friday evenings and playing soccer or driving a car on Saturday. And he has modernized, with health and social facilities, parks, playgrounds and museums, a city that was for centuries a dusty, provincial backwater.

The Palestinian uprising that began in December 1987 to force the birth of a Palestinian state in the West Bank and in East Jerusalem has endangered everything Teddy Kollek has done over all these years. Until the uprising began, no Jew or Arab was afraid to walk in any Jerusalem street day or night, whether that street was in Jewish West Jerusalem or in Arab East Jerusalem.

But now the level of hostility has risen. Violent rallies have erupted on the Temple Mount, especially after Moslem worshipers were aroused to action at Friday services in the Al Aksa Mosque. Jews of both Peace Now and ultra-Orthodox persuasions have demonstrated in the city's streets. Yeshiva students and Arab youths throw stones. On both sides, fundamentalism grows more virulent. Nevertheless, Kollek points out with gratitude, only one person has been killed in Jerusalem—while, according to the unofficial Associated Press count, over 300 Arabs have been killed in the West Bank. "But with all this," Kollek says reflectively, "it certainly isn't the same Jerusalem anymore."

Still, Jerusalem is part of Israel now and under Israeli law. "We have all the national Arab institutions in Jerusalem, mainly because the law is more open; it's part of Israel," Kollek says. "We have a democratic law and you can apply to the courts. If the nationalistic institutions were in Ramallah or Bethlehem, they would be under military law."

Tourism, which is crucial to Jerusalem's economy, has been ruined by the uprising. Kollek blames the many American Jews who stay away for this decline, calling them "absolutely shameful." "People from the United States are afraid to come," he says. "We had a tremendous drop in American Jewish tourism. I think American Jews, who have been supporting us all the time, have a right to criticize; but they do not have a right to stay away and become scared, ghettoized Jews. American fundamentalists, and Christians from all over the world, come to Jerusalem as before. The only ones who stay away are the Jews, particularly the American Jews."

Kollek finds it irrelevant that some American Jews may stay away because of their horror at the Israeli Government's brutality in the occupied territories or because Israel today is hardly their choice for a relaxed vacation. He says in simple disgust, "They are scared."

In his Haganah arms-smuggling days and now in his Jerusalem days, when with astounding effectiveness he gathered $200 million through the Jerusalem Foundation to modernize and beautify the city, Kollek has depended heavily on American friends and supporters. To see American Jews staying away now because of the actions of a Government he opposes makes him angry.

He says, "I think the whole situation in Israel is extremely uncomfortable to people in the United States—even more so than to us. It is a very complicated situation that will not find an answer quickly. It is partly our fault because we created an impression we could do everything. We owe a great deal of gratitude—but also some disappointment—to Leon Uris and to his novel *Exodus*, because everyone expects everyone in Israel to be a hero." His temper rising, Kollek adds, "I don't know why you bastards are pressing us to solve all this immediately. It can't be solved."

And he says, "We are very tolerant, more than anyone else, but there is a limit to this tolerance too. It is very annoying for many people who do not take the long historic view to be nice to Arabs and nice to Christians and nice to everybody all the time and not get any return or recognition for it. We are not Christians giving the other cheek and we never will."

All the work he has done over many years to help Jews and Arabs to live side by side in the city is now threatened by the exploding hostility between the two peoples. As Naomi Shepherd writes in her recent and knowledgeable book, *Teddy Kollek, Mayor of Jerusalem,* "Jerusalem now lies on the fault line of the Arab-Israel conflict." Shepherd accurately portrays Kollek as the mayor of a beautiful but troubled city in which Arab is fighting Jew and fanatical Jew is fighting secular Jew.

To express his determination, Kollek tells the story about showing the late columnist Joseph Kraft through the city. Kraft asked him why he kept up his furious activity, building community centers and health centers and parks and kindergartens, when all this might be destroyed. Kollek told Kraft that he was like the ants. "We try to build the most beautiful anthill possible; and if some giant foot smashes it, we'll build it again. That's what we are here for."

The situation has been better in Jerusalem than in the West Bank. Kollek says, "I believe our policy [in Jerusalem] over 20 years of mutual respect and various educational activities that lead to a certain amount of tolerance has had an effect. But maybe I'm too optimistic."

During the uprising, demonstrations, rock-throwing episodes and tire-burnings have disrupted Arab villages on the outskirts of East

Jerusalem and on the roads leading to the West Bank. Shops were closed during commercial strikes in East Jerusalem. Moslem youths burned Israeli and American flags on the Temple Mount, and the police used tear gas to disperse the crowd and rescue a policeman who had been dragged into the mosque and injured. Molotov cocktails and rocks have been hurled at Jewish cars and homes.

With his traditional Labor Zionist faith, Kollek continues to call for Government improvement of Arab housing, education and employment in the city. He says, "Now, no one can claim that there is no need to do anything because Jerusalem's Arabs are happy with their situation. A peaceful Jerusalem is not to be taken for granted."

Before the uprising, Kollek used to say that his toughest problems were with the ultra-Orthodox Jews, who were stampeding movie houses on Friday nights, smashing bus kiosks with advertisements of women in bathing suits and preventing the city from building a soccer stadium. He was also concerned about the departure for more lively and secular Tel Aviv (and for Los Angeles and New York) of many young Jerusalemites fed up with attempts by the ultra-Orthodox to extend their mores and life-style beyond their own neighborhoods and to impose them on the entire city. If the Arab-Jewish problem should ever be solved or quieted, Jerusalem will still have to resolve its tension between Jew and Jew.

I ask Kollek how he feels about the violent means by which the Israeli Army puts down the Arab stone-throwing demonstrations. With sudden passion, he replies, "So why not? We should bash their heads in." On the word "bash," he slams his fist on the table. Surprised, I ask him if he really means that. He answers, still angry: "Absolutely. And we'll do it one day, because you can't keep it up all the time—being spat at and having stones thrown. So one day someone explodes."

Then he pauses and says thoughtfully, "All these 20 years I warned people that things cannot be taken for granted. All the time I spoke about the fact that we have to even out services and conditions and, even so, it may take some time. At the same time, things were going smoothly and maybe it would go on like this. Now, suddenly, we woke up to the fact that it just won't continue smoothly all the time, that you have situations in Jerusalem that you have to confront. I am not too dejected about this." He understands the fragility of Jewish rule in East Jerusalem.

Would he do it over again? "You have no other choice. I don't see another route. Basically, we can only do more of the things we did. It is a clash of cultures, and we haven't invested enough thought, and we haven't done enough. Recently, we were sitting with 150 senior Arabs and had long discussions. We never had this before. We see that we took things for granted that we shouldn't have taken for granted. Now we don't take things for granted."

This man will go down in history as the great leader of modern Jerusalem. Teddy Kollek has never held national elected political office, but he played a significant role in saving Jews from the Holocaust and in creating and building the State of Israel. He grew up in Vienna where his father worked for the Rothschild bank, and as a young Zionist he landed in Haifa when he was 24. He and his wife, Tamar, were founders of Kibbutz Ein Gev on the eastern shore of the Sea of Galilee, under the Golan Heights. On numerous missions he saved Jews from the Nazis. In a face-to-face meeting in Vienna in 1939, he convinced Adolf Eichmann to let young Austrian Jews go to England and eventually to Palestine.

During World War II, Kollek worked under cover for the Jewish Agency in Jerusalem, Turkey and England. And in 1947 he headed the Haganah mission in New York, smuggling arms, planes, money and men to Palestine. Repeatedly, he took great risks to save lives and to support his Zionist cause. In 1950 David Ben-Gurion appointed him Minister to the Israeli Embassy in Washington, and two years later Ben-Gurion called him home to become Director General of the Prime Minister's office. As the young nation's ranking civil servant, he virtually ran the Government on a daily basis.

After Ben-Gurion was replaced by Levi Eshkol, Kollek resigned in 1965 and directed the building of the magnificent Israel Museum above the Valley of the Cross in Jerusalem. At the end of that year, Moshe Dayan, Shimon Peres and Yitzhak Navon convinced him to become the candidate of Ben-Gurion's Rafi Party for Mayor of Jerusalem. Kollek won an unexpected personal victory.

During his first term in office, the city—which had been divided by battle in 1948—was reunified by the Six Day War of 1967. Kollek quickly discovered two things: Jerusalem's Arabs felt that the Jordanian Government, which had governed the city since 1948, had neglected Jerusalem. And Palestinian nationalism had taken strong root under Jordanian rule.

Kollek says most of the Arabs did not support the sporadic terrorist acts that began to shake the reunited, Jewish-ruled city. But he wrote in his autobiography, *For Jerusalem*, "I was certain that the moment the Arabs of Jerusalem believed they could get rid of us, they would do so.

Certainly, improved economic conditions carry less weight than national feelings." And he added, "Today, of course, many have come to share my belief that we wasted opportunities immediately after the Six Day War."

The Israelis should have compromised then with the Arabs, he says, "because we don't need a million and a half Arabs." He remembers that at the end of the 1967 war, he escorted Ben-Gurion to the Western Wall from which the Jordanians had banned the Israelis. "When we came home from the Western Wall, Mr. Ben-Gurion came back to our house. Everyone said the Arabs were badly beaten in a war that they started; surely they will make peace now. Mr. Ben-Gurion said a proud people can't make peace when they are beaten and humiliated. He maintained we cannot give back Jerusalem—for this we have prayed all our lives—but all the rest we should give back.

"My feeling all these years was we should not take it [the West Bank] because we don't need it," Kollek says. "But today you have such strong feelings, and people will certainly not want to give in to the United States, the strongest country in the world. All these things you cannot measure."

Kollek made certain that Jerusalem's Arabs had water, electricity and jobs. Under Jordan, they received virtually no municipal services and paid virtually no taxes. Under Israel, they had both services and taxes. He says, "I think we behaved in many ways much better than any other country would have behaved." The Arabs could remain Jordanian citizens (and did). They could travel to Jordan, an enemy country, and their children could go to college in the Arab world. Still, the Arabs could vote for the Jerusalem City Council (which some did) and run for municipal office (which none dared).

Kollek constantly opposes Jewish groups trying to settle in the Moslem Quarter of the walled Old City. He says, "They wanted to be close to the Temple Mount when the Messiah would come. If the Messiah was in need of their support, it would be a tragedy. I also knew this was a provocation that would cause a lot of trouble one day, and, of course, recently it has."

Ariel Sharon moved into the Moslem Quarter and raised a howl. Kollek says Sharon had every right to move there; the building had been bought by a Jew from Russia in 1880. "But [Sharon] did not do this because he was short of living space. It was meant to be provocative. He did it in order to show he is a strong man who can do anything he likes.

I don't think it had a terrible effect. He doesn't show up there very much. He had a party there, and now he sleeps in a hotel." Kollek adds, "He did it only to get votes."

Kollek is not surprised that democracy needs to be learned in Jerusalem. He says, "You have to remember: Practically everyone in Jerusalem has not been educated under democracy. Sixty-nine percent of the children in school come from countries between Morocco and Afghanistan, between Turkey and Yemen. And all the Hasidic Jews who are educated under their rabbis are certainly not educated in a democratic way. Even the refuseniks who come out [of the Soviet Union] with great convictions are far away from any democratic principles.

"We have for the past three or four years been trying to introduce basic grass-roots democracy in certain districts of the city. So far, we have three Arab districts and seven or eight Jewish districts, and it starts working. But it is a long way off."

Kollek continues, "There has never been an Arab leadership in East Jerusalem. You have no democratic tradition among the Arabs." But Jerusalem's Arabs have learned to use Israeli freedoms to their own advantage. Those freedoms are often violated by Israeli forces, but they would not even be available anywhere in the Arab world.

Kollek blames the Israeli Government for failing to build sufficient schools for the city's Arab children. "Sixty percent of the schools are private, and this is mainly because the Government hasn't built schools. If every year they would add another 10 or 12 classrooms, we wouldn't be in that position. But we are roughly 200 classrooms short, and these children go to schools that have been financed by Jordan and the P.L.O. There, they start with a nationalistic anthem in the morning and end around noon with a [nationalistic] story, and what can you expect?"

As mayor, Kollek tries to avoid the tangled debates over Palestinian statehood and concentrate his activities on the concerns of the city. "If there is danger of trouble on the Temple Mount, I speak to the Moslem Council, which is responsible for the Temple Mount. We have tension in a certain quarter and I speak to the inhabitants of the quarter. If we have problems with schools, I speak with the teachers.

"The problem of the Israeli Government or the political parties is that they need two to tango and they don't have a partner. The P.L.O. may look as though they are in charge; they are not in charge. I don't know whether there is anybody in charge."

Jerusalem's Jewish population has large numbers of families that came originally from Arab countries and many religious Jews. Except for

Kollek's charisma and record, the people of Jerusalem would overwhelmingly vote for the right-wing Likud Party. After Kollek retires, many expect the city to be run by a Likud mayor. It will be a totally different city.

When this tolerant, energetic, impatient man is gone from the scene, Jerusalem will no longer be the vibrant, pluralistic, hopeful, beautiful city that Teddy Kollek has built out of the rubble of the battles of 1948 and 1967. Then it will be time to pray for Jerusalem—which has been prayed for over generations—in quite a new way.

Kollek will not guess what Jerusalem might be like in his grandchildren's day. "We have a daily struggle. We understand Jerusalem is not only a city but also a symbol. We have to work hard for tolerance and for understanding. But where it will all lead to, why should we know?"

Yeshayahu Leibowitz

Matthew Nesvisky

Israel is not a fascist state yet, but it is heading in that direction. Without withdrawal from the occupied territories and an end to the Nazi atrocities being committed there, fascism is inevitable. And that will mean concentration camps—not only for Arabs, but for many Jews as well."

The speaker is not some wild-eyed anti-Semite or anti-Zionist. He is an Orthodox Jewish Israeli. Nor is he some youthful rabble-rouser. In fact, he is an octogenarian. Similarly, he is not given to flinging about inflammatory language with careless abandon. Rather, as befits his European training in science and philosophy, he is uncommonly precise in his choice of vocabulary. If the speaker shocks, it is because he intends to shock. If his rhetoric sounds hyperbolic, it is neither out of ignorance nor malice. He witnessed the rise of Nazism in Germany. That's part of his credentials.

Yeshayahu Leibowitz is probably the most outspoken, wide-ranging and consistent social critic the State of Israel has yet produced. Were it not for his indisputable intellectual brilliance and his long and distinguished service to the country's academic community, Leibowitz might be ignored. As it is, many Israelis do not quite know what to make of him. Some, including a good many young people, revere him as a fount of wisdom and inspiration. Others patronizingly dismiss him as a social gadfly or colorful old curmudgeon. A few consider him downright

160

dangerous. "May God grant Professor Leibowitz a full 120 years," wrote one of his kinder opponents, "and may he put the professor's ideas to rest as soon as possible."

Social critic is a role to which anyone may appoint himself; prophet, a title which some have applied to Leibowitz, is something else again. Modern Israel has handily replicated such biblical archetypes as the farmer and the fighter and the poet—but while it has no shortage of intellectuals and thinkers, it has been notably lacking in prophets. Not since Martin Buber died a generation ago has any figure of preeminent moral and spiritual stature arisen in Israel. Does Yeshayahu Leibowitz, a man who, incidentally, dismisses Martin Buber with a snort of contempt, qualify as a genuine modern prophet? Or has he simply stepped into the vacuum and assumed the mantle by default?

Says his long-time colleague Natan Rotenstreich, retired Hebrew University philosophy professor and current vice-president of the Israel Academy of the Sciences and Humanities: "Professor Leibowitz is a true phenomenon, as deeply rooted in the sciences as he is in Maimonides. It's true, he doesn't follow the German dictum of being 'modest in your style and pointed in your meaning.' But he has such a profound understanding of the nature of values and of the nature of knowledge that . . . yes, there often does seem to be a kind of prophetic inspiration in his thought."

Prophet or not, Leibowitz is clearly an iconoclast. It is also widely agreed that he is a thoughtful rationalist driven by a strong moral imperative. Yet it seems apparent that he enjoys stirring controversy and rather relishes being a focus of controversy himself; hardly a week goes by without Leibowitz appearing in a public forum, publishing a diatribe in the press or sounding off on radio or television. Beyond these general observations, however, it is very difficult to evaluate the man. Yeshayahu Leibowitz won't hold still long enough to pinned down to anyone's satisfaction.

Part of the problem lies in the intimidating range of the man's erudition and expertise. Born in Riga, Latvia, in 1903, Leibowitz earned a doctorate in chemistry from the University of Berlin and, "just for the knowledge," a degree in medicine in Basel. As the Nazis rose to power, Leibowitz fled Europe for Jerusalem. Eventually he headed the Organic Chemistry Department at Jerusalem's Hebrew University, retiring fifteen years ago.

Since retirement, he has taught in the university's philosophy department on a voluntary basis as professor emeritus (most recently courses in Kant and in the philosophy of biology). For twenty years he was also editor of the *Hebrew Encyclopedia*, Israel's equivalent of the *Britannica* (he once threatened to resign that post over the censorship of a single word from an entry on politics). In addition, Leibowitz is recognized as a talmudist whose profound insight and understanding were displayed for many years in a series of popular radio and television programs.

Armed with such a formidable background, Leibowitz over the years has spoken out publicly on virtually every aspect of Israeli life, from the religious establishment to the national health system. And because he is fiercely individualistic, because he thrives on taking unusual or unpopular positions, and because he is as idiosyncratic in style as in substance, hardly any sector of Israeli society has failed to be alarmed or offended at one time or another by Leibowitz's withering criticism.

Yet on no issue has Leibowitz stirred more passion than that of the occupied territories. This is of course the most divisive issue in Israel today. It is perhaps no coincidence, however, that in this area lies the professor's strongest claim to the prophet's mantle. Immediately after the territories fell into Israeli hands in the Six Day War of 1967, Leibowitz was urging the government to withdraw. While other Israelis were jubilant at the "liberation" of Judea, Samaria and Gaza, Leibowitz was raising the specter of the moral cost of occupation. Within weeks of the war, he was predicting that maintaining control of the territories would require "Israel turning into a nation of secret service agents and security men." And that, he added, "would only be one manifestation of the fascist state."

Few listened to Leibowitz in 1967 or, for that matter, as he continued to condemn the occupation in the ensuing decades. As long as the territories were quiet, Israelis in the main found it easy not to think about them. But with the advent of the Palestinian uprising, they have had to think again. To be sure, the political leadership has hardly embraced the views of Yeshayahu Leibowitz; but he never had great expectations in that regard anyway. What does hearten the professor is what he perceives as the growing consciousness of the problem among the younger generation. He is particularly fond of those who have refused to do military service in the territories—which as a movement is virtually unprecedented in Israel. In the first months of the intifada, Leibowitz publicly called for thousands to refuse to serve.

"Military service in the territories turns our youth into murderers against their will," he told a rally in front of the prime minister's office. "I call upon them to refuse to serve there and to refuse to obey the illegal orders of the government . . . [to prevent] Israel from becoming a fascist country conducting an eternal war with all the Arab states."

Right-wing extremists responded to this by labeling Leibowitz a traitor and demanding his arrest for sedition. The authorities discreetly declined to pursue the matter.

In private conversation, the lion in his den proves no less incendiary. Leibowitz lives in a modest apartment in the center of Jerusalem with his wife, a retired mathematics teacher. The couple has five children and twenty-one grandchildren; among the few photographs in Leibowitz's book-crammed study is one of a sixth child, a son who was professor of neurology at the Hebrew University and who died at age 35 of cancer.

"The young people in this country are our only hope," Leibowitz mutters, his restless eyes fixing momentarily on the photograph. "It's public knowledge that some seventy young reservists have been jailed for refusing to serve in the territories. What's less known is that several hundred more have also refused but have simply been assigned elsewhere by sympathetic commanders. That's encouraging. Each refusal is a blow against impending fascism"—and here in a typical Leibowitz rhetorical leap the professorial mumble is abruptly replaced by fiery exhortation— "*and each refusal is rejection of the Nazi atrocities taking place right now in the West Bank and Gaza!*"

Does the professor mean this literally? Isn't such terminology just for shock effect? Given the experience of the Jewish people, could Israel actually be following the road to fascism?

"You're a fool to think otherwise," Leibowitz snaps. "No people is immune to the disease. Shamir may be a disaster, but he's *our* disaster, we can't blame anyone else. Because we're no different from anyone else. A German philosopher identified the progression as early as 1848—from humanism to nationalism to bestiality. Israel's tragedy began on the Seventh Day—that is, the day immediately following the Six Day War. That's when the leadership decided that the territories were going to be part of the 'Greater Land of Israel.'

"And that's what set us on this evil course. It has nothing to do with who we are or what we aspire to. Once we accepted rule by force over another people, once we accepted the apparatus of oppression, all other values fell by the wayside. It doesn't matter in the least what we suffered in the past at the hands of others. Man's course of action isn't determined by historical precedent but by present circumstances."

Then let's stay with the present. It's agreed on all sides that the current situation is intolerable; where does Leibowitz see possible rescue?

"There's only two avenues," he answers promptly. The first is from a strong opposition within Israel. The second is an imposed solution from the superpowers."

How likely is the first, considering that the political opposition has largely been co-opted into the so-called national unity government?

"I recognize that's a problem," he acknowledges, the perpetual frown deepening on this perpetually angry man's face. "But if enough of the public gets fed up with the territories and demands change, well, there's our hope. The force for change must come from below. We're not going to have some figure come galloping in spontaneously to save us, the way Charles De Gaulle extricated France from Algeria. The leadership we have right now is a valid reflection of public sentiment—just as Hitler was a true and legitimate expression of the German people. If the Israeli public wants to change its leadership, then we can extricate ourselves from this quagmire."

Does Leibowitz see a will for change?

"Some," he grunts. "You would not believe the number of anguished young people who come to see me, people from all political orientations. They say their party leaders—including the Citizens Rights Movement and the far-left Mapam—aren't listening to them. So they come to me for encouragement. All I can say is that if enough people organize and speak out, the leadership will have to listen, because it will no longer be a legitimate leadership. But I know this is a lot to ask. It requires heroism to oppose the establishment. Most people aren't heroes. The opposition is there, and it's growing, which is good. But how large it will grow, or how rapidly, I can't say. And meanwhile the atrocities continue."

For this reason Leibowitz would be just as happy with a solution imposed from outside.

"This is a terrible irony," he says, "because my entire definition of Zionism, the whole reason I favored Jewish national independence, was that we were fed up with being ruled by the goyim. The time had come for us to have the ability and the right to commit our own follies, crimes and disasters—*and to be responsible for them*. But if we can't take the responsibility, we may just need the Gentiles to save us."

And how likely is that?

"It's quite possible," Leibowitz says. "If Mr. Gorbachev and Mr. Bush find it in their common interest to change things in the Middle East, we could see an imposed solution. America certainly has the power to bring it about. It could decide it doesn't need us any longer as a watchdog against Communism. It could tire of pumping billions of dollars into Israel. It could conclude, as it did in Vietnam, that the effort simply isn't worth the cost. Then we'd have a solution."

And in Leibowitz's vocabulary, whether it comes from opposition pressure within Israel or via economic and political pressure from without, that solution can take only one form: partition.

In theory, dividing the Land of Israel between the two people who lay claim to it indeed seems the most rational course of action. But the very word "partition" sticks in the throat of most Israelis, not the least because many of them believe partition would not satisfy the appetite of the Palestinians. But here Leibowitz brushes all doubts and hesitations aside.

"Making partition work," he growls, head weaving with impatience on its fragile-looking neck, "is merely a matter of details—demilitarization, international policing, whatever. The only thing to remember is that the alternative is war—war between Israel and the entire Arab nation from Morocco to Qatar. That's insanity. I refuse to accept that."

The reason Leibowitz can accept partition where so many others cannot is a matter that goes deeper than mere politics. Surprisingly, it has more to do with his religious convictions. And here we come to the philosophical foundation on which the more visible political gadfly and social critic rests.

As a scientist, Yeshayahu Leibowitz has no difficulty in his Orthodox commitment to the commandments of the Jewish faith; for him it is an existential leap made possible by the conviction that observance of the *mitzvot* connects men and women to God, and to ignore that connection is irrational to the point of self-destruction. Accordingly, Leibowitz is a passionate adversary of whatever contradicts the commandments. Primary among these is the practice that Judaism from its very origins has consistently opposed: idolatry.

One form of idolatry, Leibowitz maintains, is nationalism. "The state," he says, "has its social function. But it is not a repository of values. It's a mistake to expect the state to be better than any other human institution. And once we overvalue the state, or think that its interests can override those of the individual, or become willing to die for it, we're guilty of idolatry.

"I, for example, was one of those Jews who shared in the wish and desire and will to reconstitute the political status of the Jewish people. But unlike many, I had no illusions that statehood would be any more than what I said, an instrument of social organization. A 'light unto the other nations'? A racist idea! A state isn't a framework for values. Believing it is isn't merely misguided—it's dangerous! It's the kind of idolatry that yields Nazism!"

For Leibowitz the framework of values exists elsewhere, not formulated by men but given to the Jews by God. For this reason he argues, much to the dismay of most of the other Orthodox Jews in Israel, for the strict separation of church and state.

"Religion and state have nothing in common," he explains. "In fact, they are in opposition to each other, because their interests are so different. At the very least, religious Jews should not want secular Jews regulating their way of life, disbursing their funds, or enacting civil laws to enforce the so-called Jewish character of the state. Such a partnership is a total anomaly. At the same time, history shows repeatedly that involvement of the religious establishment in the civil conduct of the state can only lead to corruption. This is why I call the religious parties the concubines of the state. It's an idolatrous relationship."

It was just this unholy union, he says, that was responsible for the Who-Is-a-Jew? crisis. "I don't have the answer to that question," he admits. "For eighty or a hundred generations it wasn't a problem, because Halacha (Jewish religious law) contained the solution. But since the mid–19th century the majority of Jews haven't accepted Halacha, and so the halachic view is meaningless to them. In the face of that, I don't know what to say.

"But from the battle in the Knesset, at least one thing should be clear: we're not going to get a satisfactory resolution through the expedient of religious factions trying"—again the voice rises alarmingly—"*trying to blackmail secular Jews into legislating a definition into the Law of Return! That's immoral no matter from what direction you look at it!*"

By the same token, Leibowitz considers fanatic attachment to the Land of Israel a kind of idolatry. Just as he has condemned making a fetish of the Western Wall—his term for it is *disco-tel*, a portmanteau of discotheque and Kotel (Hebrew for Western Wall)—so Leibowitz decries excessive devotion to territory.

"This is, of course, the place where our history is rooted," he says, "and I prefer to live here. But not having sovereignty over all the land is hardly the worst thing that could happen to us. Even total exile didn't prove disastrous for us. In many ways, the Jewish people continued to thrive in the Diaspora.

"That's why," he continues with rising passion, "the Gush Emunim settlement movement is the greatest catastrophe to befall the Jewish state. In their blind determination to cling to land, they're dragging us into the worst degradations. It's always been the way with messianic fools, those who are so presumptuous as to think they know God's will."

And now, suddenly, Yeshayahu Leibowitz's voice takes on a re-sounding timbre that in a secular age may be as close to the voice of sheer prophecy as we are ever likely to hear:

"My only consolation is this," the octogenarian thunders. "If Israel comes to its senses and gets out of the territories, the Gush Emunim superpatriots will be the first to abandon this country! Just as the followers of the false messiah Shabbtai Zvi were the first to convert to Islam, so the idolators of Gush Emunim will lose their raison d'être for remaining here if the territories are returned.

"Because that's the sum total of their impoverished concept of Juda-ism. They're not interested in Jewish values, only in the power of the state as a tool for their messianism! And if they don't have the state dancing to their tune, then nothing in secular Israel will be of interest to them. They'll be happier in Brooklyn. Let them go there! That would be a step toward salvation for us all!"

Primo Levi

Risa Sodi

When Primo Levi opened the door to his apartment in Turin, Italy, on June 19, 1986, and led me into his sitting room, all the trepidation I had felt on meeting a famous author dissolved. He was a small man, with a shock of white hair receding to just the right authorial degree. His inquisitive glance and easy laugh made the tone of our conversation pleasant, just as the content was serious.

After a half hour, Levi got up to prepare a caffè, and I had time to take in my surroundings. The living room of his fourth-floor apartment was furnished with the sort of fin-de-siècle chairs and sofas and cool stone tiles one would expect to find in the salon of one's grandaunt. Levi, in fact, had been born in that very apartment, in 1919, and perhaps it had been in the family for generations. The pictures on the walls, the small statues on the tables, the color of the furniture were all unobtrusive. One's attention was therefore drawn to Levi's desk, the double window and the two massive bookcases behind the desk. One bookcase was devoted entirely to Holocaust-related writings in all the modern European languages (including Yiddish) and Hebrew. The other had a shelf on which Levi kept his favorite books, dog-eared and annotated. The one incongruous element in the room was the word processor on Levi's desk, plastic as opposed to the wood, stone and linen of the rest of the house.

When Levi fell down the building's stairwell, just nine months after our interview, the world was stunned. The police report ruled it a suicide, but many of those who knew him have not accepted — indeed, have vociferously rejected —

that thesis. I remember the low balustrade in his apartment building. I remember Levi's lively demeanor and his undiminished enthusiasm. All who knew him remark on his reticence, his abhorrence of la grande geste. *They ask, Isn't it possible that Levi, who had just undergone minor surgery and was still taking medication, suffered a momentary, tragic dizzy spell and, in calling down to the concierge who had just brought him the day's mail, lost his balance and accidentally fell? That is my belief.*

Whether suicide or accident, Primo Levi's death means that a mighty voice was silenced much too prematurely. In the 1950s, after republication of his first book, Survival in Auschwitz, *Levi was acclaimed as a writer of superlative Holocaust literature. With his subsequent novels and his poetry, he took his place among the masters of contemporary Italian letters. I have no doubt that, with the passing of time and wider dissemination of his works, Primo Levi will come to be regarded as one of the great authors of 20th-century literature.*

Risa Sodi: Your latest book, *The Drowned and the Saved*, contains some things that are more personal than your previous works and some reflections that your other books don't contain. [Published as *I sommersi e i salvati* in late May 1986, the book received considerable attention in the Italian press because its considerations of the "gray zone"—a sort of purgatory of Nazi victims who in turn became oppressors—seemed so appropriate to the Waldheim case, which was just then breaking. In fact, Levi called Waldheim *un grigio*, a "gray zoner."] In your chapter "Communicating," you said: "[At Auschwitz] I was given the rare good fortune of being able to exchange some letters with my family . . . I know that this was one of the factors that allowed me to survive . . ."

Primo Levi: Yes.

Sodi: Considering this and the other privileges you enjoyed, such as being able to work at your own profession [as a chemist] or meeting the Italian "volunteer worker" who gave you an extra ration of soup every day, could you still say it was possible to survive on one's own in the death camps?

Levi: Without outside help? I'd say it was technically impossible, and primarily for physiological reasons, given the condition we were in. The amount of food they gave us was not enough to survive on. We needed an "extra," some sort of privilege, whatever its form—legal or illegal, stolen, extorted or donated. I pointed this out often in *The Drowned and the Saved*.

All of us survivors had some sort of lucky break. Mine was in the form of Lorenzo, the Italian volunteer worker you mentioned and whose story I told in *Moments of Reprieve* [1986]. Others . . . for example, I remember a prisonmate of mine from Breslau, a German Jew. Now the *Lagerälteste,* the "dean" or internal commander of the camp, was a common criminal who also happened to come from Breslau. These two knew the same beer halls in the city. And the German Jew survived. He survived because when he was hungry, he went knocking on the door of the Lagerälteste, who was a powerful man. Similarly, in *Survival in Auschwitz* [English edition, 1961], I told the story of a certain Hungarian engineer who invented the job of caring for the other prisoners' calluses. He too survived (though I'm not sure he made it till the end) because he found a way to round out the balance of calories. You know, it takes at least 2,000 calories to survive in a resting state. But we worked, so we needed at least 2,600. They gave us 1,400 or 1,500 a day. Those who didn't get those extra calories couldn't survive.

Sodi: Those are physical concerns. But what does receiving letters have to do with survival?

Levi: Receiving letters was fundamental because it meant reestablishing contact with the outside world, knowing that your family was alive. Obviously, by the time I got the letters, I could only be sure that my family had been alive two months earlier. But that was still something. Better than nothing.

Sodi: Were you afraid of repercussions against your family?

Levi: I was completely irresponsible. I didn't fully realize how dangerous it was to send those letters. My family wasn't in Switzerland; they were here, outside Turin. They were in hiding, but they could have been captured at any moment. My father was already dead at the time, but my mother and my sister were here. They were in danger, and I knew it. My sister was a partisan, so she was doubly in danger. All the same, in August, when I received the first letter, I was sure that in June she had still been alive. I've saved all the letters that Lorenzo mailed for me. Each one bears the stamp "Zensor"—[verification] by the censor stamped right on them—and yet the censor didn't realize what they were. Lorenzo rewrote them in his own hand for me—a man who could barely write, a bricklayer. If the letters had been discovered, it would have been very serious for all of us—for Lorenzo most of all because, you see, it was forbidden to speak to us. It would have been the gallows for me because anyone who tried to get a letter out was suspected of being a spy. And, besides, letter writing was prohibited.

Sodi: And what about the ones who never heard from their families?

Levi: You mean almost everyone. For the most part, my campmates were Polish, Czech and Hungarian Jews whose families had been totally wiped out. I've never heard of anyone else who was able to get a letter out and receive mail as well. I even received a package. You must have read that in *Moments of Reprieve*. I consider myself an extremely lucky person for that. Those were extremely rare occurrences.

Sodi: So it took luck to survive.

Levi: Luck was the first virtue.

Sodi: You write at the beginning of *The Drowned and the Saved*: "The oppressor remains what he is, and so does the victim. They are not interchangeable. The former is to be punished and execrated (but, if possible, understood)."

Levi: Yes, of course.

Sodi: But how to understand the oppressor? In what way? Historically . . .

Levi: In all ways: to understand how a man could reduce himself to that. Because, as I wrote and as I saw, they weren't monsters. They weren't born monsters. They were normal people. I don't know if you've read a beautiful book by Gitta Sereny [*Into That Darkness: The Journey from Mercy Killing to Mass Murder*. London: Deutsch, 1974]? You must read it! Do you know the story of Stangl? No? Are you interested? I'll tell it to you in brief.

Stangl was a modest functionary, the son of a post office official—I don't remember now whether Austrian or German. Anyway, he was a very modest man who was offered the chance to create a career in the SS. He got to be commandant at Treblinka after climbing the career ladder rung by rung, but he was also pushed by his wife's ambition. She was a sort of Lady Macbeth: Never satisfied with her husband's salary, she always wanted something more. He ended up commandant at Treblinka, which was a real extermination camp. It wasn't like Auschwitz where some, a few like me, 5 percent, managed to survive. No, Treblinka was one of those camps from which no one got out alive. After the war, Stangl was tried in Germany, sentenced to life imprisonment and became a model prisoner—just like before. [In 1948, Stangl escaped from an Austrian prison to Brazil, via Morocco. Captured in 1967, he was tried and convicted in Germany in 1971. Stangl died in prison six months later.] He had always been obedient; he'd obeyed all his orders. And he agreed to be interviewed by Gitta Sereny, the Hungarian-American journalist.

Now, I think her book is fundamental to understanding just who the

Nazis were. They were completely shielded from their work. It's not that they liked their work: In fact, they didn't like it. But it was part of an order that they had accepted and that they wanted to carry out well. Stangl insisted on the fact that under his direction, order reigned at Treblinka—the same thing [Rudolph] Hoess says about Auschwitz. Stangl agreed to the interview, which lasted, I believe, 20 or 30 sessions— months on end. Once a week, Sereny went to the prison and obtained permission to speak with him. He spoke freely, obviously. There was nothing left to hide. I think his statements were sincere enough.

Stangl had been saved by the Vatican, as had many Nazis. The Vatican used the same chain of convents to save Stangl and others that had been used to save the Jews from the Nazis. This is really very Italian. The same organization and this sort of chain of convents brought them to Syria or Egypt or South America; Stangl, I believe, went to South America. Just a few hours after the last interview, Stangl had a stroke and died, as if he had finished saying everything he had to say.

Sodi: Do you think the Nazis feel the same need to bear witness?

Levi: Perhaps. The other example I mentioned was Hoess. Hoess was the commandant at Auschwitz. He and Stangl came from a similar background. Hoess was in the Freikorps, that is, those right-wing volunteer assassins. He had even been found guilty of murder in the 20s. Then he made a career for himself in the SS, becoming an extremely diligent commandant. He bragged about how everything ran like clockwork, perfectly. He was the one who invented the gas chambers with hydrogen cyanide. Previously, they had used carbon monoxide. And he was always proud of his . . . invention, right up until the end.

When he was arrested, he was examined by a group of psychiatrists, who found him to be of mediocre intelligence, but normal nonetheless. I believe it was the English who called for the death sentence, and he was hanged at Auschwitz. But before hanging him, they asked him if he would be willing to write his memoirs. He snapped to attention, replied, "Yes, of course," and wrote his memoirs under those conditions—with a certain dignity, I might add. He always tried to find excuses, but the thrust of his writing was to point up a job well done.

His boast until the very end was, "In my own way, I was a good commandant." It seems that wasn't true. For example, it seems that he wasn't at all honest. He had a whole freight-car full of stolen goods. He wasn't even faithful to his wife (although he describes himself as a scrupulously faithful husband); instead, he had a prisoner-lover. But the point is that he may even have believed the fabricated truths he created for himself. It was his salvation. He wanted to be happy with himself until the day he died, at least proud of having been a good husband and an honest administrator – two things [that] he was not.

Sodi: Would you put Stangl's need to see himself as a good commandant together with what you write of the prisoners themselves, who even when ordered to build a wall, tried to build a good, solid one – although this was against their own interests?

Levi: Yes, yes. Solzhenitsyn noticed this too. It's one of man's fundamental needs: that when he does something, he must do it well.

Sodi: From *The Drowned and the Saved,* I seemed to understand that the great injustice of the camps was that it was possible for the Nazis to fabricate or at least modify their own truths and hide behind them, while it was impossible for the survivors to find the same oblivion.

Levi: Certainly. There were some who tried to flee the truth. I've told the story in *The Drowned and the Saved* of my friend Alberto who, when faced with his father's death, closed his eyes and said: "No, this time I won't see."

Sodi: I was also struck while reading *The Drowned and the Saved* that you considered being stripped, being naked, such a shock. You say that it was an integral part of the whole process that the Nazis deliberately created to make the task of killing the inmates easier for the guards.

Levi: It was Stangl himself who devised that offense. In the very last sentence of her book, Sereny asks Stangl why so much useless violence was committed. He says that it simply made the guards' task easier.

Sodi: What weight did these offenses to your dignity carry – the nakedness, having to defecate in public or urinate from the train? What weight did they carry in the struggle for survival? To my eyes, today, they might even seem minor compared to the struggle for physical survival.

Levi: They carried some weight at the very beginning, exactly because they occurred before our imprisonment began – the train episodes, at least. And even being stripped and having to defecate in public were things that happened the first few days, before all the other things overtook us. In short, it was a sort of prologue. Then, clearly, and I've said this before, we got used to it. It became routine. But not being naked. Being naked, especially without shoes, is always extremely debilitating, even in our culture. If you imagine yourself shoeless, not on the beach, but in the city, especially with your feet in a sorry state, it's very offensive.

Sodi: You place a great deal of emphasis on the impossibility of

communication, whether with the outside world or even among your-
selves [the campmates]. Besides German, was there a lingua franca at
Auschwitz?

Levi: At first it was Polish and Yiddish. Then so many Hungarians
came that we all spoke Hungarian. It was the most common language. I
spoke German with them since not all but many Hungarians knew a little
German. Except for the peasants, that is. The peasants didn't know
anything, and there were so many of them! I didn't know there were
Jewish peasants, but there I saw Jewish peasants from Hungary. They
spoke only Hungarian and Yiddish. They were small landowners, with
two or three hectares [five to eight acres] of land. Slovaks, too. Some
Slovaks even brought their sheep with them! The Germans asked them
if they had any animals and said, "Bring your animals along." They
plundered themselves.

Sodi: What was your internment at Fossoli like? [A village of several
thousand outside Modena in Italy's northeastern Emilia-Romagna region, Fossoli was the site of a Fascist, then Nazi, internment camp in the
1940s.]

Levi: It was very much Italian-style. I was captured by the Fascists,
not the Germans. First, they put me in a military barracks in Aosta [the
capital city of the northwesternmost region of Italy, Val d'Aosta.] Then
they handed me over to the *carabinieri*, who treated us very well, after
their own fashion, that is, and then they in turn transported us to
Fossoli. Fossoli was administered by the Italian police in a bungling,
humane way—the way things are done in Italy. There was a camp
commandant who was a Neopolitan policeman and, as such, corruptible.
We could get things from him. I remember, for example, that some of the
girls who were with me got permission to go with him to Carpi, which
was a town nearby. There were public baths there, and they even went to
get their hair set. All this was very *all'italiana*.

Sodi: Then you weren't treated as enemies of the regime.

Levi: No, not at all. I even remember a boxing match between the
commandant and a robust friend of mine who boxed. The commandant
challenged him, and they had a public match. It was all "family-style"—a
sporting encounter, mind you, not a beating. Then one day, suddenly,
the SS arrived and said, "Italians out! We'll administer the camp now."
Within three days, they had deported everyone.

Sodi: Did you foresee what was coming next?

Levi: I was almost sure of what would happen, but not completely.

Sodi: Did you know anything of the death camps?

Levi: I knew very little. I knew that falling into German hands was fatal. With us at Fossoli was a group of Croatian Jews who had a strange story to tell. They had been persecuted and even killed by the Germans, but some of them had fled to Italy, and it seems very strange that they fled to a country that was under a Fascist regime. They were taken in by the regime and interned in various villages in Veneto and Piedmont, hoping that things would continue *all'italiana* until the end (that is, that the Germans would respect Italian sovereignty), something [that] did not happen.

Sodi: And before you were captured, were you aware of the diatribes of the Italian racialist writers like Orano, Preziosi, etc.?

Levi: Of course.

Sodi: What effect did they have on the Jews?

Levi: They were alarm signals, especially when *The Defense of the Race* was published. [A manifesto issued in September 1938 by a group of "Fascist scholars," *The Defense of the Race* listed the various racial provisions against the Jews that were subsequently enacted into law.] Orano's early writings didn't make much of an impression because Italy wasn't yet allied with Germany. They just seemed like one man's stand. But in 1938, when the racial laws were promulgated, we began to hide behind convenient truths. I was still a boy. I was very inexperienced. But even my father, for example, used to say, "Ah, but in Italy, since the Church and the Vatican are right here, they won't do anything to us." And yet, my father was a man with a great deal of experience. During the First World War, he was in Hungary, i.e., in enemy territory. When Italy declared war on Austria and Hungary, he was very humanely repatriated. The Hungarians gave him a travel order and sent him home. He used to say, "That's the way it will be this time. We're Italian citizens, we're not German citizens, and they'll treat us as such." This tendency to create a convenient set of truths is very widespread.

Sodi: Very few Jews left Italy.

Levi: Yes, relatively few. It wasn't easy. It wasn't easy at all. It was costly, and it took a lot of courage. You had to be . . . [both] very rich . . . [and] very intelligent. At the time, some were rich but not intelligent; others were intelligent but not rich. And so very few left. To leave took intelligence, money and courage.

Sodi: I'd also like to ask you a few questions about Jewish life here in Turin, or in Italy.

Levi: In Turin or in Italy? It makes a big difference, you know!

Sodi: Let's say in Italy. You say in *The Drowned and the Saved* that you're not a believer, that you weren't a believer before you went to Auschwitz. Did you have a Jewish upbringing?

Levi: Yes, I was bar mitzvahed.

Sodi: And you speak Hebrew.

Levi: Yes, but very poorly.

Sodi: Well, you must speak at least a few words because you quote them in several of your books!

Levi: I had help! I know maybe 200 words.

Sodi: And Yiddish?

Levi: I learned a little Yiddish in the *Lager*, and then I have four books right here that I studied to write *If Not Now, When?* [Levi's homage to the bands of Jewish partisans that fought in Poland and Russia toward the war's end, published in 1985]. I bought myself a grammar, a dictionary and so on, and I studied a little. Although I can read it haltingly, if someone speaks to me in Yiddish I can barely understand. As for Hebrew, well, at this point maybe I'd be able to read the *Derashah** with the aid of a dictionary, but I'm not sure. Once my bar mitzvah was over, it was all over.

Sodi: If you consider yourself a nonbeliever, can you consider yourself a Jew?

Levi: Yes, I have no doubt about that. Culturally, I'm a Jew because in my own way, in my own partial way, with gaps and lacunae, I've followed and still follow Jewish culture. Not all my friends here in Turin or Italy are Jews, but most are. I married a Jew. My children are Jews. Out of loyalty and as retaliation for the racial laws, I feel that in the same way that I am Italian, I am a Jew. I was born in Italy, and I was born a Jew. Why should I try to construct a different identity for myself?

Sodi: This seems the opposite of Jean Améry. [Jean Améry, born Hans Meyer, was a German philologist and philosopher, and a thoroughly assimilated Jew. He fled Germany for Belgium, was later captured and tortured by the Gestapo for belonging to the Belgian resistance, and then was deported to Auschwitz as a Jew, where for a time, he and Levi were confined to the same barracks. In 1978, Améry committed suicide. "The Intellectual at Auschwitz," a chapter of *The Drowned and the Saved*,

---

*My tape is unclear here regarding the exact word Levi used. —R.S.

considers Améry's story in more detail. Some have pointed to Améry's story in commenting on Levi's own apparent suicide last year.]

Levi: No, not exactly the opposite. Améry also mentions the "necessity and impossibility of being a Jew." He suffered a much more severe trauma than I did. He was a German philologist and was in all respects part of the surrounding society when he was forced to emigrate.

Sodi: But didn't he also feel Jewish and later try to build himself a Jewish culture?

Levi: He didn't construct a Jewish culture for himself. He only *says* he did, when, in fact, he didn't even try. Améry declared in one of his essays that you can't construct yourself a culture out of opportunism and, in fact, he was a man who knew nothing about Judaism. No, for me it was different. There was a trace of Jewish culture in my family; there was even a certain amount of tradition. My grandmother, for example, celebrated the Pesach with 40 or so of her nieces and nephews, and I remember those seders well. Those things didn't happen in Améry's house—why, they even had a Christmas tree! My childhood was Jewish to a large extent. Did you read *The Periodic Table?* In Italian? Do you remember the first chapter, "Argon"? My mother still speaks the half-Jewish, half-Piedmontese dialect I use in that chapter. [Originally published in 1975, *The Periodic Table* appeared in English translation in 1984.]

Sodi: You did a mitzvah by writing down that dialect! Otherwise it might have disappeared completely.

Levi: Of course I did—I did it on purpose!

Sodi: Do you think Jewish culture in Italy is disappearing?

Levi: [Pause] I don't think it's disappearing. I believe that strange things sometimes happen. Let me digress a moment. Here in Turin and in Piedmont, we speak a thick dialect that's hard to understand. It's almost like French. By now, very few people speak it anymore, maybe only a quarter of the Turinese. But in spite of that, Piedmontese dialect theater is undergoing a renaissance. The theaters are almost always full, and many, many poets now write in Piedmontese dialect.

I think the same thing is happening to Italian Judaism in general. Modern Italian Jewish culture is a revival culture. Showing interest in it is a little like attending to a dying man. [The moribund] get a lot of help; they always attract a crowd. Exactly because Jewish culture is disappearing numerically in Italy, it's attracting a great deal of interest. People are flocking to it in the same spirit that I did that mitzvah you were talking about—preserving a Judeo-Italian dialect that's disappearing. Many non-Jews in Italy are interested in Judaism. I receive a great many letters from non-Jews who have read my books and ask for information. In fact, I get more letters now than some time ago. It's an enigmatic sign because this interest, and Jewish culture along with it, may very well die out. Did you know that there are little more than 1,000 members of the community now in Turin? There were 5,000 of them before the war— 5,000 of us. Today there are 1,100.

But there's also a critical mass that stands apart from any numerical considerations. Mixed marriages are the norm today. For example, the State Registry Office lists my children as Jews. They're dues-paying members of the congregation, but they take no interest in it. If they get married, they'll almost certainly marry Christians. And then there's also the other side of the coin. There are men and women who have asked to join the synagogue. As you know, this is an extremely favorable moment for all sorts of sects.

Sodi: Do you mean that they consider Judaism a sect?

Levi: Well, they're searching for truths, especially the young people. They seek revealed truths, and they go looking for them in the strangest places, like with the Jehovah's Witnesses, the Mormons and so on. And some of them even come to us. They write to me—and I'm not even a good teacher!

Sodi: Something similar is happening in America. There are now Yiddish courses on many college campuses, and they have a good following. Yiddish culture is also disappearing. My grandparents spoke Yiddish, my parents understand it, and I don't know anything about it.

Levi: Nothing!

Sodi: Maybe the students in the Yiddish courses are like me: They remember their grandparents . . .

Levi: And they're trying to recover the past. It's clear that, by so doing, they're constructing something that's very different from a living culture that grows along with us: They're rebuilding a culture that is historical more than anything else. I'm sure that if there were a Jewish theater in Turin or Milan or Rome for that matter, it would attract an extraordinarily large audience. In fact, every time foreign troupes come through (Israeli companies, for example), the theater here is sold out. Yes, this means paying attention to a culture, interest in a culture, but it's not the kind of renewal that living cultures experience.

Let me tell you that even though there are so few of us in Turin, the

Jewish cultural life here is pretty intense. Right inside the synagogue, we have a cultural center that many non-Jews participate in as well. There's a beautiful library, open to all. There's a school that's called a Jewish school but that really isn't because three-fourths of the pupils and teachers aren't Jews. We fought a battle with the rabbi over that, and we won. He wanted the Jewish school to be for Jews only, but he had to give in to our request, to what the members wanted. Every school needs a certain number of teachers, and there just weren't enough; it needs students too, and there weren't enough students. Now it's a pretty good school, where Jewish culture is taught to whoever wants to learn it, but where three-quarters of the students are non-Jews.

Perhaps the two communities of Milan and Rome will survive. In fact, I'm sure that Rome will, given its particular, popular character. Milan, as you know, is experiencing a strange tug-of-war because at least half of the community is made up of new immigrants and there are very strong tensions between the Italian Jews and the Iranian immigrants. The Iranian Jews are not very happy with how the Italians are running the synagogue. They consider them too relaxed, not Orthodox enough. It's similar to the situation in Israel, with the exception that in Milan there are many Iranian Jews, they're very rich and they carry a lot of weight.

Sodi: Do you think you will come to America soon?

Levi: Let me tell you, my wife and I are in a disastrous state here in Italy. We have two people to take care of: My mother is 91 (she's in the next room); my mother-in-law is 95 and blind. We can't go anywhere because even though we have help, they go on vacation in the summer. So for us, instead of being a break, the summer is always a problem. Although I was invited to go to the United States in November [1986], when *The Monkey's Wrench* is scheduled to appear, I wrote that I won't be able to accept. If I go, I leave the whole burden on my wife's shoulders. By a miracle, we were able to get away for 12 or 13 days in April, but only by asking my sister to come up from Rome, and she also has her own burdens. We can't go anywhere. I've done nothing but turn down invitations right and left.

Sodi: Your mother and mother-in-law are very long-lived.

Levi: My mother-in-law is 95, but she has two sisters in the United States: One is 97, and the other is 96. The youngest lives here and she is 89. It's a strangely long-lived family.

Sodi: That bodes well for you!

Levi: It depends on *how* you age. My mother-in-law is blind. She's been completely blind for 15 years. We really need someone around the clock. My mother isn't blind, but she's very senile. We have to do everything for her as well. As a result, I can't make any plans. In fact, my plans are not to make plans. I can only write. I've had invitations from everywhere. I had an invitation to go to Germany. I am very interested because a German editor has just signed a contract to republish all my books in their entirety. Discussions with the Germans could be very interesting. But for now I've said no. Then I've had the invitation to go to the United States in November. My American editor is frenetic. He proposed a schedule (which I wouldn't have accepted in any case) to go to the U.S. for 14 days with stops in New York, Chicago, Boston, Houston . . . I don't remember the rest, but eight East Coast cities and the whole Pacific Coast, plus an undetermined number of interviews.

Sodi: You have to watch out for "undetermined" numbers!

Levi: You're right. In fact, last year, I was there but I came away half mad. I gave 25 interviews in 20 days—and I don't speak English that well. Well, I speak it well enough, but I understand it very poorly. Twenty-five interviews, six conferences and nine flights. I was in six cities. Everything was in a hurry. And I'm no longer a young man. Then back at the hotel, we had to keep the phone off the hook because otherwise we would get phone calls at all hours of the night—pleasant ones, to be sure, but it was impossible to rest. What's more, it was the first time I had been in America. So, it was a fairly . . . interesting experience, but . . .

Sodi: If you want to remain anonymous, you can stay at our house.

Levi: Thank you, but if I come to America, it's because I'm not anonymous!

Mordechai Levy

Wendy Leibowitz

E very Jew should have a gun," said Mordechai Levy. "A good
slogan is, 'Every Jew a .22.' A better slogan is, 'Every Jew an M-1,'
but it doesn't rhyme." He took a bite of pastrami on rye and
smiled.

Levy, 25, looks like an overworked accountant, which he is. He is also
the leader of one of the newest "defense" groups in the United States, the
Jewish Defense Organization. He frequently sits in Ratner's delicatessen
on Manhattan's Lower East Side, in New York City, wearing a rumpled
gray business suit and a knitted blue skullcap. His large brown eyes peer
out foggily from behind thick lenses covered with fingerprints. His voice
is high and reedy; the accent, Brooklyn. His organization, he said,
numbers 3,500 members.

Levy's successful launching of another Jewish defense group raises
questions about the existence of Jewish extremism in the United States.
Ever since Meir Kahane founded the Jewish Defense League in 1968,
radical Jewish groups have sprouted and persisted in the United States, a
country relatively free of the political terrorism that plagues Europe and
the Middle East.

The number and activities of Jewish militant groups rise and fall with
the tides of bigotry, fear, prejudice and hatred, and their names change
to suit current fashion. In 1976, "The Jewish Armed Resistance" claimed
responsibility for a midnight explosion outside the Manhattan offices of

the Soviet and Czech airlines to "protest recent developments in current
Middle East talks." In 1981, "Thunder Out of Zion," an organization
never heard of before or since, called a newspaper to say it had bombed
the Four Continent bookstore on Fifth Avenue to protest its selling of
books published in the Soviet Union. In 1984, a Soviet diplomatic
residence in the Bronx was firebombed by a group calling itself "Jewish
Direct Action."

Mordechai (born Mark) Levy started the Jewish Defense Organization
in 1982. His purpose was to harass Soviets, arm Jews and confront former
Nazis. The J.D.O.'s membership application form, filled with grammat-
ical errors, lists "fields of activities" as "nazi-smashing, karate, knife-
fighting, and office work."

As Levy sees it, "The J.D.O. exists to help Jews help themselves fight
against their enemies in the United States: anti-Semites, Nazis, the Ku
Klux Klan, the Communists. Lyndon Larouche and Louis Farrakhan
have no right to talk, no right to walk, no right to live."

Levy's pale, scholarly looks belie a violent past. A former member of the
J.D.L., he was arrested in September 1981 in connection with a bombing
near the Soviet Mission in Los Angeles. In New York the same year, he
allegedly attacked reputed Nazi war criminal Boleslavs Maikovskis. He
paid a small fine for the latter offense, but has never served time in jail.

The progenitor of the J.D.O. was the Jewish Defense League, founded
by Brooklyn-born Rabbi Meir Kahane. Sheldon Engelmayer, managing
editor of New York's *Jewish Week*, worked with Kahane at *The Jewish
Press* when Kahane was organizing the J.D.L. "It was a volatile, explosive
era," he explained. "The J.D.L. was born in an America ripped by race
riots, LSD, assassinations, student uprisings and anti-war protests. There
was a lot of anti-Semitic rhetoric and violence against Jewish stores and
schools. Many people felt a need for Jews to protect themselves. Into that
need stepped the J.D.L."

A New York attorney, who requested anonymity, said he was drawn
to the J.D.L. in 1968: "This was right after the Six Day War, when you
had a new feeling of pride in the Jewish state's military power. I remember
the outpouring of joy. It was the first time since the Maccabees that we
could celebrate such a Jewish victory. Then came Kahane, talking about
Jewish militarism. It didn't seem farfetched or dangerous to me. It was an
expression of Jewish pride."

Rabbi Eugene J. Lipman of Washington, D.C., well remembers his
first encounter with the J.D.L. "The Jewish Community Council of

Washington held a meeting of Jewish merchants who'd been burned out in the riots," he said, referring to three days of rioting that took place in the capital in 1968 and left 10 people dead and much of the downtown business district gutted. "We wanted to help get them back on their feet. People from the Small Business Administration, the Anti-Defamation League and the mayor's office were there, setting up low-interest loan programs, arranging for building repairs. In the middle of the meeting, some thugs stood up and shouted, 'Let's break their black butts.' A lot of people who'd been destroyed financially shouted their angry approval. The meeting broke up."

The J.D.L. grew to more than 10,000 members in its early years—or so it claimed—but started to decline after Kahane moved to Israel in September 1971. Some of his more devoted followers went with him to Israel and in 1984 he was elected to the Israeli Knesset. Much J.D.L. money was drained by his anti-Arab political party.

The State Department stripped Kahane of his American citizenship in October 1985, and it became difficult for him to return to the United States to raise money and J.D.L. morale. But he appealed the decision. On February 20, 1987, in a Federal court in Brooklyn, Judge Leo Glasser restored Kahane's American citizenship, ruling that Kahane's acts and statements "show beyond a doubt that he wanted very much to remain an American citizen."

Kahane, a brilliant fund-raiser, is now able to travel easily to and from the United States. But even though he visits frequently, his departure for Israel was seen as betrayal by some of his American supporters, who speak of him bitterly, and Levy no longer calls himself a Kahane supporter.

"Farrakhan is spreading his anti-Semitic poison to thousands of blacks in hundreds of cities and college campuses, neo-Nazis like Lyndon Larouche won over six election primaries, Tom Metzger of the Ku Klux Klan got over 50,000 votes in California [where he was a Democratic Party Congressional nominee in 1980], Jewish kids are being attacked every day and where is Kahane?" Levy asked. "Talk about the abandonment of the Jews."

Without Kahane to control them, former J.D.L. members split into various vigilante groups that operate independently. Law-enforcement authorities believe the J.D.L. and its splinter groups are responsible for numerous violent acts, including murder.

In January 1972, two bombs exploded within moments of each other in Manhattan offices of organizations that brought Soviet performers to the United States. The first, at Columbia Artists Management, injured no one. The second exploded in impresario Sol Hurok's office at the corner of 56th Street and Sixth Avenue. The 83-year-old Hurok was unhurt. Iris Kones, who worked in the accounting department, was killed instantly.

The J.D.L. denied any involvement. With an eye on the police, the group has a policy of publicly denying any illegal activity. Meir Kahane, commenting from Israel, said it was done by another group to discredit the J.D.L. After a five-month investigation, three J.D.L. members were arrested and indicted on murder charges.

Harvard University law school professor Alan Dershowitz defended Sheldon Siegel, who was accused of making the bombs. Dershowitz had grown up with Siegel in Brooklyn. In his book, *The Best Defense,* Dershowitz wrote, "How could I turn down a case involving someone I'd known as a kid? . . . But how could I represent a bunch of Jewish hoodlums? . . . But aren't Jewish hoodlums entitled to representation?"

All charges were dismissed against the three J.D.L. members because the Government had used illegal wiretaps to gather its information. As Federal Judge Arnold Bauman dismissed the charges, furious at the Government's mishandling of the investigation, he said, "They have literally gotten away with murder."

On April 5, 1982, the Tripoli, a Lebanese restaurant in Brooklyn, was destroyed by a fire that started at 1 A.M. At 2 A.M. a man called United Press International and said the J.D.L. had set fire to the restaurant because it was "the undercover headquarters of the Palestine Liberation Army in New York." Randy Medoff of the J.D.L. said that his organization had no role in the arson attack.

In early August 1985, Mordechai Levy cursed and threatened Tscherim Soobzokov in a speech in a New Jersey synagogue. Soobzokov had successfully defended himself in a 1980 lawsuit alleging he had concealed his membership in the Nazi SS in order to gain admission to the United States. The court ruled that Soobzokov had not concealed his war record.

At 4:30 A.M. on August 15, a telephone caller wakened Soobzokov in Paterson, New Jersey, telling him his house was on fire. When he stepped outside to check, a bomb exploded. Soobzokov was killed; his wife, daughter, 4-year-old grandson and a neighbor were injured. As before, Jewish terrorist groups denied that they had carried out the attack.

"Whoever did it, did a righteous act," was all Levy would say.

A day after the New Jersey bombing, an identical bomb was found outside the office of the American-Arab Anti-Discrimination Committee in Roxbury, Massachusetts. A police officer was injured while trying to remove it. Jewish defense groups said they didn't know anything about the bomb.

A month later, on September 6, 1985, a bomb exploded at 4 A.M. at the Long Island home of Elmars Sprogis, a 69-year-old former policeman in Latvia who had successfully defended himself against allegations that he collaborated with the Nazis during World War II. A passerby spotted a fire at the Sprogis home; his legs were blown off when he tried to open the front door to help evacuate the family. Sprogis was only slightly injured.

Shortly afterward, an anonymous telephone caller told the newspaper *Newsday:* "Listen carefully. Jewish Defense League. Nazi war criminal. Bomb. Never again." A spokesman for the J.D.L. in New York denied that the league took part in the Sprogis bombing, but called it "a brave and noble act."

The latest death occurred on October 11, 1985, in the wake of the hijacking of the Italian cruise ship *Achille Lauro* by Arab terrorists. Alex Odeh,* the regional director of the American-Arab Anti-Discrimination Committee, opened the door of his office in Santa Ana, California, and a bomb exploded. The 41-year-old Palestinian immigrant and father of three was killed; seven others were injured.

The F.B.I. classified the Odeh slaying as "a terrorist attack." Lane Bonner, a spokesman for the F.B.I., publicly accused the J.D.L. In response Irv Rubin, head of the J.D.L. in California, said: "We had nothing to do with the bombing. If they have any evidence they will make an arrest rather than try and slander us." No arrests have been made to date.

The present head of the J.D.L. is 30-year-old Victor Vancier, also known by his Hebrew name, Chaim Ben-Yosef. He was arrested in New York on May 8, together with two other people said to be J.D.L. members, Jay Cohen, 23, and Sharon Katz, 44. The three were charged

---

*See "The 'Quiet' Death of Alex Odeh," by Mark I. Pinsky, *Present Tense*, Winter 1986.

with conspiracy to violate Federal explosives statutes in connection with six incidents: the firebombing of four Soviet cars in 1984, 1985 and 1986, a 1986 bombing at Avery Fisher Hall in Manhattan and the releasing of a tear-gas grenade at the Metropolitan Opera House on September 2, 1986, during the performance of a Soviet ballet company.

The arrests came after the police received tips from an informant, identified by the police only as C.S., who wore a wire with which he recorded Cohen saying that Katz entered the opera house on September 2 carrying the tear-gas cannister in her handbag.

"People ask, 'How can you attack innocent people?'" Ben-Yosef said when he was featured on a radio call-in show after the incident. "I tell you, the people attending that ballet were not innocent. They were guilty of supporting Soviet-Nazi oppression of Jews. To see a ballet, they will pay to support the greatest persecution of Jews since Hitler. Well, maybe now they will go to see an American ballet. There wasn't one innocent person in that place."

Ben-Yosef said he would take a jail term in stride, "part of the price you pay for doing your duty to your people." He has already served two months in the Rikers Island penitentiary for the firebombing of a Soviet diplomat's car in 1974 and a year and a half in Federal maximum-security prisons for a series of firebombings of Egyptian diplomats' cars and residences. He admits that J.D.L. membership is down to less than 500, but he hopes his forthcoming trial will revitalize the league.

Ben-Yosef was arrested on the way to mailing a letter to another J.D.L. member, Murray Young, a 59-year-old electrician from Long Island, who was arrested in April after an F.B.I. raid on his home uncovered 17 firearms, including an Uzi semiautomatic carbine and materials and tools used in making explosives. J.D.L. records and documents were also found and taken by Federal agents in the search. Young is charged with illegal possession of a handgun and silencer, a Federal offense. He has pleaded not guilty, and was released on a $1 million bond. His family says he is a gun collector.

The letter Ben-Yosef was mailing to Young, according to Assistant United States Attorney Gregory O'Connell, read in part, "Keep your mouth shut because the government doesn't have enough evidence, and if everyone keeps their mouth shut, everything will be all right."

While these arrests may disable the J.D.L., Levy's J.D.O. is there to pick up the slack. The Joint Terrorist Task Force, composed of detectives from the New York City Police Department and F.B.I. agents, believes the bombings in New Jersey, Massachusetts and California are "the work of a different faction."

Mordechai Levy is skeptical that the J.D.L. will ever reach its former strength. He said Ben-Yosef's J.D.L. is "dead. Long live the J.D.O." The J.D.O. is active at the moment, he added, recruiting people who have never been involved in such a group before. Members of the J.D.O. in New York speak with a desire for vengeance against former Nazis, a mixture of religious and political antagonism toward the Soviets, contempt for Arabs and, most of all, fear of blacks. Almost all of the dozen people at a recent J.D.O. meeting felt that blacks were anti-Semitic. "All blacks detest Jews," said one woman in her 20s. These Jews feel particularly vulnerable to violent attacks on the street by black criminals.

"I've been mugged," said one J.D.O. member who is a mailcarrier. "If I were Italian or Hispanic, no one would pick on me. But because I'm Jewish, I'm a target. That's why I joined the J.D.O. That's why I think every Jew should join."

"The J.D.O.'s attitude is: If *they* carry knives, *we'll* carry knives," added one of Levy's supporters, a young man studying in a Manhattan yeshivah.

Levy is sensitive to charges that his group is racist. "I've never said a word against black people, white people or yellow people," he said. "How could a Jewish person, who's been the victim of discrimination for generations, be a racist against other people?"

All the people I spoke with requested anonymity when speaking of Jewish-black tensions. "I'm a social worker, not a bigot," said a middle-aged women from Queens who said she was "very active" in the J.D.O. "I go into the ghetto all the time, not like a lot of liberals who are divorced from reality. The liberals are naive and sweet and think everyone else is too. Well, the black is not a product of Eastern Europe like us. He's a product of urban disorder. Jews have to learn to be tough, to be streetwise. Blacks respect that. You can eliminate a lot of anti-Semitism by carrying a gun."

Rifle and shotgun license applications are available at all J.D.O. meetings. The J.D.O. carries out its weapons-training classes at police target ranges, completely within the law. "You can learn guns in three weeks," said Levy. "It's a how-to course. In three Sundays you know how to load, fire and use your weapon."

The classes are held weekly at the Mitchel Athletic Complex in

Nassau County, Long Island. Twenty people showed up last December for the beginner's class. About half were immigrants from the Soviet Union, Israel and Iran. They paid a $5 fee and listened to Levy lecture about what he called "dark clouds facing American Jews" and his own prowess with a gun. "No one knows more about guns than I do," he said proudly and repeatedly. "You should know not just how to fight, but what you're fighting for," he exhorted the class.

Then, after a brief safety warning, the class practiced loading rifles, shotguns and an Uzi submachine gun. An hour was spent firing. In their training camps in the Catskills, the Jewish defense groups use swastikas, pictures of Adolf Hitler, Yasser Arafat, Muammar el-Qaddafi and Vanessa Redgrave as targets. At this Long Island police range, a more orthodox bull's-eye was provided.

"Jews have been taught to fear guns. Well, I'm the first to say guns are bad things," said Levy. "But it's better to know how to use them and not need to, than to need to and not know how."

Michael Goldstein, a member of the J.D.O. since its inception, agreed: "Having a gun is dangerous, not having one is even more dangerous."

Other slogans were repeated throughout the two-hour class: "Better to be picked up in a paddy wagon than a 'morgue wagon' "; "An unarmed Jew is an unprotected Jew"; " 'Turn the other cheek' is not a Jewish expression."

Americans over the age of 18 are allowed to keep a gun at home, as long as the gun is licensed. A license is obtainable if you have never had a felony conviction or been institutionalized for psychological reasons.

Sergeant Timothy Ganun of New York City's Firearms Control Board points out that on Long Island, these restrictions on rifle and shotgun permits were abolished in 1980. "Just show some I.D. and they'll sell you anything you want," he said. This has been a boon to the Jewish defense groups.

The J.D.O. has also benefited from an increasing acceptance in mainstream America of the legitimacy of violence under the guise of self-defense or vigilantism. The outpouring of support for Bernhard Goetz's 1984 shooting of four blacks in a New York City subway is one example. Indeed, the J.D.O. contributed $500 to defend Goetz.

"Jews have been brainwashed into thinking that pacifism is a Jewish idea," said Levy scornfully. "Well, if violence isn't Jewish, then Israel isn't a Jewish state and Hanukkah [which commemorates an ancient Jewish military victory] isn't a Jewish holiday."

In his speeches Levy frequently draws on incidents in which Jews have been the victims of violence, such as the 1985 murder of Denver radio talk-show host Alan Berg by a neo-Nazi group. Levy combines these occurrences to present a pattern of anti-Semitism in the United States, equating America of the 1980s with Germany of the 1930s. This outlook is symbolized by the J.D.L./J.D.O.'s preemption of the once-proud Jewish slogan "Never again," meaning, "Never again will Jews submit to the terrors inflicted upon them by the Nazis."

"Forty years ago in Germany, Levy would have been a prophet," said Monroe Rosenthal, a retired anthropology professor and J.D.O. member. "If an organization like the J.D.O. had existed in Hungary, Poland or Romania, Hitler would not have succeeded in wiping out a third of the Jewish people.

"It [a holocaust] can happen here, in the United States," he continued. "This country is in severe economic, political and ethnic turmoil. Jews have got to become aware that there is danger on all sides. It just takes one thing—another Vietnam, this 'Iranscam' that Israel is in the middle of, some Ivan Boesky on Wall Street—to set off riots and unrest. And Jews should be prepared. Paranoia on a personal level is unbalanced. But on a national level, a little paranoia is a good thing. I do Tai-Chi and I belong to the J.D.O."

After a yeshivah student, Chaim Weiss, was murdered by unknown assailants on Long Island in November 1986, Levy and nine J.D.O. members showed up outside the yeshivah with four rifles, several shotguns and three attack dogs. Police checked that all the rifle permits were in order and did not confiscate any of the weapons. The J.D.O. was gone two days later, but they had made their presence felt. After such an incident, Levy usually launches a local recruiting drive.

A former J.D.L. member, now a graduate student, remembers why he joined. "I wanted to fight back," he said. Appalled by his former activities, he spoke on condition that his name not be used: "I felt like I was at war. As in all wars, the creation of a common enemy—neo-Nazis, anti-Zionists, leftists—united us so we felt more powerful than we really were. There was a thrill of pleasure, of shared power, that belonging to the J.D.L. gave me. It was more emotionally satisfying to call for revenge than to try to understand compromise. It felt *good* to be one of them."

He understands the motivation of many of the young men who join militant groups. "Being in the J.D.L. for me was a very masculine thing," he said. "It was part of a search for machismo that I and a lot of guys my age went through during high school and college. The J.D.L. was forceful. Shouting down Arab speakers, rallying against Vanessa Redgrave—I saw it as standing up for my rights as a man."

Sheldon Engelmayer of the *Jewish Week* believes the Jewish defense groups reflect the insecurity that many Jews feel in America. "To a certain extent we are still ghettoized, still running for cover," he said. "When you hear of a shooting, your first thought is, 'God, I hope it wasn't a Jew.' There's a real fear of some kind of blame attaching itself to the Jewish community. It's partly a racial memory. But it also indicates a mistrust of American society as a whole."

A J.D.O. member who refused to give his name disagrees. He believes militant Jewish groups are not a result of mistrust of American society, but simply a result of exposure to American life. "The J.D.O. is sort of a by-product of democracy," he said. "When Jews emerged from the ghetto to live among people with different values—and America values violence, from the cowboy to Rambo—some of it rubs off. When in Rome, do like the Romans and know how to stand up for yourself. What's wrong with that?"

Irving Levine, national affairs director of the American Jewish Committee, has a different view. He notes that mainstream Jewish organizations run far-reaching programs to improve black-Jewish relations and confront the fears that fuel extremist groups in America.

"Our main function is to improve community relations," Levine said. "You don't do that by providing gun-training classes. You do that by sponsoring encounter groups on campuses, education programs in schools, legislation in the government. Farrakhan is an isolated figure because of what mainstream Jewish groups have done. You have to isolate extremists like Farrakhan, not imitate them."

Malcolm Hoenlein, executive director of the Conference of Presidents of Major American Jewish Organizations, who has known Mordechai Levy for about 10 years, said: "He's a very smart guy, and not as irresponsible as he's sometimes perceived to be. His motivation is sincere. I don't think, when you're dealing with young, dedicated people, that you can afford to say no. You should try instead to direct their energy toward legitimate goals. Mordechai Levy should not just be dismissed."

Levy, however, ridicules the methods of mainstream Jewish organizations.

"When Moses saw an Egyptian smiting a Jew, did he set up Egyptian-

Jewish encounter groups? Did he form a committee to study Egyptian-Jewish relations?" Levy asked in disgust. "No! He smote the Egyptian. That means he killed him."

Even so, in February 1986, at the National Jewish Community Relations Advisory Council's annual meeting at the Waldorf-Astoria Hotel in New York, Levy participated as a paying delegate.

"He set up an information booth, and tried to distribute leaflets," recalled Kenneth Bandler, the council's director of information. "He made a bit of a nuisance of himself when he tried to corner people. He comes across as a young, extremely emotional kid. Almost unstable. It was obvious that he desperately wanted to be accepted."

And Rabbi Charles Sheer of Columbia University says Levy calls him regularly "to let off steam."

"We're actually on pretty good terms," said the rabbi.

Levy attempted to rent space a year ago to speak at Columbia but was barred. Rabbi Sheer said that Columbia students view Levy as someone who would provoke anti-Israeli and anti-Jewish feelings on campus.

"Now at Yeshiva University, I think Levy has a lot more support," said Sheer, a Yeshiva graduate. "Students who are deeply involved in Jewish issues, or who just dress more traditionally, are sensitive to the fears of anti-Semitism that Levy talks about."

"Levy just says what everyone has been whispering to themselves for a long time," said one Yeshiva student, who pointed out that the Lubavitcher rebbe now has his own armed security force. "Levy doesn't advocate illegal activity as far as I know."

"If he organizes a guard at the request of a community, then this is legitimate," said another Yeshiva student. "The J.D.O. just shouldn't impose itself where it's not wanted."

Levy frequently draws on the Bible for ideological justification for the use of violence. The Jewish militants ask the Jewish community: How do modern Jews refute, ignore or repudiate biblical violence?

"Under Jewish law, only a government is allowed to use violence, and then only during a time of war," said Rabbi Eugene Lipman of Washington, D.C. "Otherwise the normal processes of law should be used to deal with criminals. 'An eye for an eye' means monetary compensation for damage done. This has never been contradicted in all of rabbinic literature."

On the need for revenge, which Levy calls "a God-given right,"

Lipman countered: "Revenge is a divine privilege. It is not a Jewish motive. Human justice is administered by the courts."

Questions surrounding the legal rights of the militant Jewish groups continue to divide American Jewry: Should they be allowed to speak in community centers? Should their activities be covered in Jewish newspapers?

"We have a problem with the J.D.L.," admitted Sheldon Engelmayer of the *Jewish Week*. "If we deny them coverage, we actually generate sympathy for them. We give them space on the op-ed page if what they say is factual and within the realm of good taste. If they organize a march down Fifth Avenue with 1,000 people in support of Soviet Jewry, we'll cover it. The only thing I know is, we refuse to list 'arms and weapons training' under singles events."

Last year Teachers College of Columbia University was thrown into an uproar when the Columbia Barnard Debate Council invited Levy to speak. "They wanted someone controversial," said Dean Storelli of the college's public relations department. "Well, they sure got controversy." Various groups launched protests, and Levy's invitation was revoked by the Room Assignments Committee, which determined that "Mr. Levy's goals were neither cultural nor educational." Levy then tried to rent space at the college, but was again refused. And despite repeated efforts, Levy says no other group at Columbia University will invite him to speak on campus.

Just as Levy insists on his right to speak, so does Vanessa Redgrave insist on hers. Because of her public support for the Palestine Liberation Organization, the British actress is frequently threatened by militant Jewish groups. In 1982, the J.D.L. threatened to disrupt a series of performances she was scheduled to give with the Boston Symphony Orchestra. The threats were so dire that symphony officials canceled her contract because they said they were worried about the safety of the performers and the audience. Redgrave filed a $1.2 million lawsuit against the orchestra. Recently, the highest court of Massachusetts ruled in Redgrave's favor, saying her civil rights had been violated when the orchestra "acquiesced to outside pressure." The case is now before the First United States Circuit Court of Appeals.

The Soviet United Nations Mission, another target of the J.D.O.'s hostility, has become more complacent about the group. "We receive the obscene phone calls and report them to the police," said Anatoly Khudyakov, a representative at the mission. "We know these are only a few people shouting. No one believes that these few people represent the

American people, or American Jews. But when the threats get worse, we increase security."

Making threatening phone calls takes up only part of a Jewish Defense Organization member's time. Mordechai Levy's typical week is very busy. Sundays he runs the weapons-training classes. Monday nights he reserves for speaking engagements. Tuesdays he distributes J.D.O. leaflets in various Jewish neighborhoods. Wednesdays, he meets with the 14 other members of the Jewish High Command at J.D.O. headquarters on Bleecker Street in Greenwich Village to plan future events. Thursday nights he runs karate classes. And on the Sabbath, he rests.

There are those who say that it's best to ignore this handful of people and let the police handle the occasional bomb. But others feel that to ignore them is to refuse to recognize the feelings of alienation and insecurity that many Jews experience in America.

The most difficult argument to face is that the rise of Jewish militancy is the result of legitimate pent-up needs in the Jewish community. "What has happened to our fury, our need for revenge and satisfaction?" asked the writer Anne Roiphe. "It has resurfaced in disguised form among our politicians and leaders."

Roiphe argues that the extreme reaction to Jesse Jackson's use of the word "hymies" caused many Jews to "assume that all his people are out to get us and that the poor among them are no longer worthy of our concern and effort. . . . The anger stirred in the Jewish community tells us how enraged we still are and how frightened that our hard-won middle classness could be stripped away."

As long as that fear persists, so will violent Jewish organizations.

The London Jewish Chronicle

Chaim Bermant

The Anglo-Jewish community is small, numbering about 410,000 and most of its members belong to an Orthodox congregation or at least are eventually buried in Orthodox cemeteries. There is also a strong Reform movement. At least three major factions divide the Orthodox, and the Reform group is split in two, but all of these elements have this in common: practically everyone "takes" the *Jewish Chronicle*. This is not to say that the *Chronicle* is regarded with universal affection. Hardly a week passes in which it is not denounced from an Orthodox pulpit. Indeed, some ultra-Orthodox rabbis have gone so far as to issue a formal interdict banning it from Jewish homes—but to no avail, for it is too ingrained a habit.

Now 132 years old, the weekly *Chronicle* has become as much a part of the Anglo-Jewish Sabbath as candlelight. While journals once regarded as national institutions have faded away, the J.C. has not only survived but prospered. It is one of the oldest newspapers in Great Britain and the oldest Jewish newspaper in the world.

Among the reasons for J.C.'s longevity are its independence, its adaptability, the essential conservatism of the Anglo-Jewish community (which it has helped keep that way) and the accomplishments of a brilliant editor at a crucial phase of its existence. He was Leopold Greenberg, of whom more later.

Another factor is the growing prosperity of Anglo-Jewry. The economics of newspaper production are such that an increase in circulation can mean a loss of revenue. The nineteen cents which the J.C. costs wouldn't even pay for the newsprint of an average forty-eight page issue. Everything depends on advertising, especially on its quality. Since most J.C. readers are in the sought-after AB (top quality) advertising category, the paper can charge about $1,200 per page. This is extraordinary for a British weekly with a circulation of 70,000 – including about 5,000 in the United States – and some 300,000 readers. Also, the J.C. has probably benefited from the common belief that Jews are more prosperous and more numerous than they actually are. (When I told an editor of a national daily that there are less than half a million Jews in Britain, he said: "Come off it, there's *millions* of you.")

Advertisers of quality goods and services flock to the J.C. like pigeons to their cote. The display ads would lead one to believe that the average British Jew smokes Havana cigars, drinks Moet and Chandon champagne, drives a Daimler, swathes his wife in minks, frequently visits Israel, buys his kosher chickens pre-packaged and frozen, and is chronically short of rabbis.

Actually, the "Classified Announcements" are the *Chronicle's* major source of revenue. Every Jew in Britain who is Bar Mitzvah or Bat Mitzvah, becomes engaged, gets married, has a child or adopts one, celebrates a silver wedding, dies and acquires a tombstone pays tribute to the J.C. – directly or through his heirs – in the form of an ad. Not unusual are annual insertions on the anniversaries of deaths, in some cases for as long as forty years after the events. A single death can be a gold mine for the J.C., producing columns of paid condolences from relatives, friends and neighbors.

Equally lucrative is the J.C.'s "Social and Personal" column, a monument to Anglo-Jewish snobbery. Usually taking up at least a page, it carries the traditional "hatch, match and dispatch" ads found among the "Classified Announcements," but at more than twice the charge. Yet everyone who wants to be among the elect pays up cheerfully. As one wit put it, if the dead could ever rise again most of them would probably announce their return in the J.C. – and on the "Social and Personal" page rather than the common one.

The *Chronicle* began in 1841 as a four-page paper, price twopence. The Jewish community was tiny, some could not read English, others could not afford twopence and there was already a rival in the field, *The Voice of Jacob*. The two merged to save each other from extinction. When another rival appeared some ten years later, the J.C. merged again. So it struggled along with varying fortunes until the early 1880s, when the first of a series of pogroms occurred in Russia, Poland and Lithuania.

During the previous decades, while the Anglo-Jewish community was waging the battle for emancipation, the J.C. was largely a family news-sheet padded out with theological essays. With the pogroms there came a quickening of Jewish life as English Jews sought to aid their stricken brothers. Soon thereafter mass immigration from Eastern Europe began, and what had been a small, staid, inbred and largely Anglicised commu-nity was transformed into a teeming immigrant society.

The old community saw in the new a threat to its Englishness, a reversion to the ghetto. Many established Jews supported the fierce agitation against mass immigration that quickly developed. But the *Chronicle*, which had been regarded as the mouthpiece of the old guard, took an independent stand and championed the cause of the alien. In 1891 it inaugurated a monthly supplement, *In Darkest Russia, A Journal of Persecution*, which helped greatly to open British eyes to tsarist barbarity. In place of foreign news largely lifted with due acknowledgement from other newspapers, it began to print dispatches from J.C. overseas corre-spondents.

The J.C.'s alertness to happenings abroad was not matched, however, by awareness of the transformation taking place at home. During the last years of the nineteenth century, the paper sometimes read as if it were written for a Kensington dowager with private means, a charitable disposition and an insatiable interest in the life and works of Anglo-Jewry's own royal family, the Rothschilds, or such lesser royals as the Montefiores and the Sassoons. The lives and works of these personages were often, if subliminally, put forth as examples of the heights to which English Jews could aspire. As they began to marry out of the faith, the J.C. reacted with an almost personal sense of betrayal.

When Hannah Rothschild, daughter of Baron Meir and then the wealthiest woman in England, married a Christian, the Earl of Rosebery, the *Chronicle* found no consolation in his being one of the foremost peers of the realm and a rising politician—in fact, a future prime minister. It was convulsed with grief, as witness this excerpt from its comments:

If the flame seized on the cedars, how will fare the hyssop on the wall? If the leviathan is brought up with a hook, how will the minnows escape? . . . was there amongst the millions of brethrenin-faith all over Europe no one of sufficient talent, sufficiently cultured, sufficiently high-minded to be deemed worthy to be received in the family circle, that this honour must be bestowed upon one who must necessarily estrange the partner from her people? . . . A sad example has been set which, we pray God, may not be productive of dreadful consequences.

(The term "leviathan" was particularly unfortunate, for Hannah was a bulky wench, or "heavy baggage," as her husband once described her.)

In 1873 the paper was shaken by the appearance of the *Jewish World*, produced by Lucien Wolf, Laurie Magnus and Meyer Spielman, a trio of journalists well known in the newspaper world and with ready access to the skills of Fleet Street. The newcomer's innovations were quickly imitated by the J.C. The J.W. had lavish illustrations; the J.C. followed suit. The former had a Yiddish page for immigrants; the latter produced a Yiddish supplement. One courted small-town readers with more provincial news; the other issued provincial supplements. One Friday the *World* came out with a "Children's Column." The following week the J.C. appeared with "Aunt Naomi," forerunner of the present "Junior Chronicle."

The pace of the competition was wearying and expensive. The *Chronicle* got into difficulties and was acquired in 1906 for a mere £13,000 by Leopold Greenberg, a journalist who had worked on the liberal *Daily News*.

Greenberg had been a close associate of Theodor Herzl and was a founder and secretary of the English Zionist Federation. He saw the paper mainly as a vehicle for Zionist propaganda. Up to then the J.C. had described Zionist events and reported Zionist polemics, but had seldom expressed its own opinions. In 1896 it had published Herzl's *A Solution of the Jewish Question*, which contained most of the ideas later incorporated in his *Judenstaat*, but this did not reflect any commitment to Zionism by the J.C. Altogether, there was a soggy ambivalence about the paper's attitude.

Greenberg knew where he was going and was determined to take the community with him, to the dismay of the older families. The J.C. had for many years received a monthly subsidy from the Rothschilds and no major matter of policy had been settled without a meeting at New Court, the head office of the Rothschild bank. Greenberg dispensed with the subsidy and the meetings. When Lord Rothschild protested about something in the paper, Greenberg retorted: "I can't call in the edition now, but I'll give you back your two-pence if you like."

Greenberg's Zionism brought the immigrant masses into the *Chronicle's* orbit. There were a number of ephemeral Zionist Yiddish papers, but a well-established "Englischer papier" voicing Zionist sentiments was very reassuring. However, for a time during World War I the J.C. alienated a great many newcomers.

The war was going badly for the Allies; Britain and France were being bled white on the Western Front. In 1916 Britain proposed to augment the size of its armed forces—up to then composed of volunteers—by conscription. Most of the Jewish immigrants were Russian subjects. They were to be given the choice of enlisting in the British army or being deported for service in the Russian army. This was regarded as eminently fair by the general public, which probably was not aware that many had fled from Russia for their lives and were being asked to fight for their persecutors. The J.C., while unhappy about the prospect of deportations, supported conscription. To the embarrassment of the paper, already known as "the voice of Anglo-Jewry," the worried newcomers found a champion in the *Manchester Guardian,* which argued that the proposed act would violate their right of asylum. The J.C. thought it would do nothing of the sort, stating that:

> The Russian Jew may still come here. But in coming he must be prepared to abide by what is on his arrival, or what may subsequently become, the country's law. To ask the privilege of settlement here, and to demand exemption from the burdens that weigh on other residents, is, in our view, to set up an impossible claim and to bring the whole principle of asylum into disrepute.

The resentment against the J.C. on this issue was soon forgotten in the face of a larger one: the Balfour Declaration, which first saw the light of day in the form of a letter from Lord Balfour to Lord Walter Rothschild. The old families feared that the basic premise of Zionism would expose their loyalty to question, and tried to prevent the Declaration from being publicized. Greenberg, who played an important part in the negotiations leading to the Declaration, insisted they were speaking only for themselves. The idea of a Jewish state, he declared, had fired the imagination of world Jewry.

The Rothschilds and others attempted to counter his arguments by publishing an excellently-written newspaper, *The Jewish Guardian*, but it petered out, mainly because non-Zionist Jews were not sufficiently interested in Jewish life.

In recent years, the *Chronicle's* solitary eminence has occasionally tended to limit its freedom of expression. To create the impression that it is not part of the ruling Establishment, the paper often goes out of its way to attack the powers-that-be. But whether it appreciates the honor or not (and one suspects it does), the J.C. is generally considered to be the official voice of Anglo-Jewry. This has made for some delicate situations.

Following World War II, for example, when the Jews of Palestine were in open rebellion against the British, the editor, Ivan Greenberg, son of the great Leopold, ignored the directives of his Board and applauded the rebels in near-Revisionist terms. This produced consternation in the Anglo-Jewish establishment, of which the Zionist Federation was by then an important part. There were threats that another journal would be started (and one almost certainly would, but for paper rationing), and Greenberg was finally dismissed. For the next decade or so the J.C., careful not to offend anybody, took a middle-of-the-road attitude on controversial issues.

During and shortly after the war, paper rationing held the circulation to 15,500. It increased to 22,400 the week that rationing ended in 1947, reached 51,500 by 1949, and thereafter moved steadily to its present level. The Holocaust heightened Jewish consciousness and a series of dramatic events during the second half of the 1940s—the UN debates on the future of Palestine, the massacres in the Jerusalem corridor, the illegal immigration, the War of Liberation—brought a succession of new readers.

Since the time of Leopold Greenberg, the foreign news service has been the heart of the *Chronicle*. Able correspondents report from centers of Jewish population throughout the world and capable analysts in London comment on events abroad. The very quality of the foreign news service highlights the deficiencies in local news coverage, but there is no dichotomy in treatment or approach. Overseas reports deal with "hard" news, while practically all the happenings at home are "soft" news, or no news, or gossip. The farther the J.C. goes from London into the provinces, the more gossipy the items become. No week passes without columns of snippets such as this:

The fourth annual speech day of the Newcastle Jewish day school was held at the Imperial Hotel, Jesmond, with Mr. A.S. Science presiding. Mrs. Ray Guttentag of Sunderland, formerly of Newcastle, distributed the awards.

There is also a restless quest for *naches*, for assurance that Jews are still making it one way or another in the great world. Twice a year, on the Queen's Birthday and the New Year, half the staff is sent searching through the Honours List to try to unearth a new Jewish Baron or Knight, or even a humble MBE (Member British Empire). More often than not, those who turn up have no connection with Jewish life. But no matter, their names are blazoned forth.

On the other hand, the arts and culture pages rank with the best in British journalism today. In recent years, the J.C. editor has responded to the tastes of his subscribers by bringing together an outstanding team of theatre, film and music reviewers and critics, among whom are some of England's most gifted writers. A favorable review of a book can have a dramatic effect on its sales.

There was a time when J.C. critics felt impelled to sniff out a "Jewish" angle and to praise any Jew involved at any level in the arts, but today works are approached entirely on their merits. There are still a few weak spots in the J.C.'s coverage, but if the current trend continues many readers who are disinterested in or tired of Jewish affairs may take the paper solely for its pages on the arts.

The main body of the J.C. is a continuing celebration of Jewish tradition. Every event in the Jewish calendar is marked by commemorative and descriptive essays and memories of how *zeide* and *bubbe* did it. "Junior Chronicle," read avidly by the young, is today, as in Aunt Naomi's day, a primer of Jewish religion. The women's pages discuss issues of interest to women generally – and also print recipes which are thoroughly checked so that every ingredient will be acceptable to the most Orthodox housewife. When a steak house advertises in the J.C., it must include the assurance that "omelettes and fish dishes are always available." No advertisement announcing an event on Friday night or a *Yom Tov* is ever accepted.

Actually, the J.C. is both newspaper and parish magazine; this may be another reason for its longevity. It is also a constant challenge to William Frankel, the present editor.

Soon after he took over in 1958, he decided that real news could be found on the home front, but it had to be dug out. Reporters who had been content to accept handouts from communal institutions were sent forth to ask questions. More important, Frankel found a Cause with a capital "c". Before we examine the Cause we had better first examine the proprietorial structure of the J.C., and the not uncomplicated nature of its editor.

When Leopold Greenberg bought the *Chronicle* he was helped by three leading Zionists acting in their private capacity. One was Leopold Kessler, a prosperous mining engineer who had led the El Arish expedition early in the 1900s to investigate the possibility of a Jewish settlement in the Sinai. Kessler eventually became chairman of the company and his shares were inherited by his son David, the present chairman and managing director.

David Kessler, now sixty-six, lives the life of a rather urbane country squire in The Buckinghamshire near the Vale of Aylesbury, an area known as Rothschild country because of the numerous residences once occupied by Rothschilds in the surrounding hills. He and his wife, who is a local judge and a social worker, are popular figures in local country society. Their spacious house breathes the spirit of Olde England. It is hard to believe that his forefathers did not land at Hastings with the Conqueror, but came from Silesia. A major in World War II, he has the soldier's staccato manner of speaking and still looks martial, even in mufti. He is a member of the Liberal synagogue, his wife is a convert, and he wears his Judaism lightly. He is intensely interested in Israel, but finds it difficult to discuss events at home without suppressing a yawn. He occupies a different universe from his readers.

William Frankel, on the other hand, is in some ways the J.C. reader writ large. He was born fifty-six years ago in the East End, the son of a *shamos* in a Hasidic *shtieble*, who through great perseverance went from the bar to a highly successful career in journalism and considerable public eminence. His is in many ways a typical East End success story. What is untypical, and endearingly old-fashioned, is his passion for things English—English ways, English mores, English attitudes, English tolerance, the English sense of fair play, and, above all, English cricket. On an ideal Sabbath he will go to *shul* in the morning, (possibly officiating as *Baal Tefillah*), then to a quick lunch and finally to Lord's (London's leading cricket ground), with nothing to disturb his rest save the click of bat on ball—truly a Lord's day. At the beginning of his editorial career he was a member of the Reform Club. He has since gravitated to the Atheneum, a meeting place of bishops, High Court judges and dons. He is a Justice of the Peace and a CBE (Companion of the British Empire) and will one day no doubt become a Knight. But he is shrewd enough to realize that even as Sir William he will never enter Kessler's Olde England, for his past exerts too strong a pull.

He has tried to make the Anglo-Jewish community more attractive, which is to say more English. This was his Cause, and in 1961 he thought he had found his instrument. In that year the Chief Rabbi vetoed the appointment of Louis Jacobs—possibly the ablest rabbi to have served Anglo-Jewry since the war—as principal of Jews' College of London University, because he thought Rabbi Jacobs' views were not in keeping with traditional Jewish teaching. When Jacobs was invited back to the synagogue he had left to join Jews' College, this appointment was also vetoed and his followers were expelled from the United Synagogue.

Here was a Cause if ever there was one, indeed a whole complex of causes. Involved were the right of free speech, the right of congregations to appoint rabbis of their choice, the question of whether an institution of London University has a right to impose theological norms, and finally the question of whether Rabbi Jacobs' ideas placed him outside the Orthodox pale. In an American context, these ideas would have put him in the right wing of the Conservative movement and possibly even beyond it. They were shaped by a number of distinguished rabbis in the United Synagogue and elsewhere. But the United Synagogue, up to that time a very English institution, had shifted away from the traditions of tolerance. In a campaign that went on for several years, William Frankel set himself to check this. And he lost, for the bulk of the Anglo-Jewish community regarded the conflict as essentially one of Louis Jacobs versus the Chief Rabbi. Anglo-Jewry is not a concourse of theologians, and few of the J.C. readers understood the basic conflict of principles involved. Had Jacobs challenged God in his heavens, they might have been disposed to side with him, but he was challenging the Chief Rabbi and they could not.

The campaign for the Cause was also handicapped by both Anglo-Jewish and J.C. history. The concept of a Chief Rabbi is basically alien to Jewish tradition, but when the United Synagogue was formed by a private Act of Parliament in 1870, it was decided to appoint a dignitary who would bring unity and discipline to all elements in the community – and also perhaps to satisfy the Anglo-Jewish craving for a King of Israel.

So over the years the J.C. built up the Chief Rabbis, printed their speeches, reported their movements, echoed their exhortations, applauded their actions. On the whole, it had good material to work with. What the J.C. had done for almost a century, it could not undo in a relatively short time.

After Rabbi Jacobs was out of the United Synagogue, Frankel (who frequently visits the United States and is an admirer of the Jewish Theological Seminary) hoped to make him the leader of a new English-style Conservative movement. He envisioned a situation in which different rabbis would be free to follow their different ways, with everyone working for a true synthesis of all that is best in English and Jewish life. Again it did not work, and again because of the attitudes instilled over the years by the J.C. itself. For whatever criticisms of the religious leadership are published in the opinion columns, and they are frequent and outspoken, conservatism is still the J.C.'s hallmark.

English conservatism has tended to preserve Jewish conservatism, and the J.C. has helped to preserve both. It gives an occasional frustrated kick against the ghetto walls, but on the whole it has helped to maintain them, and in maintaining the ghetto it has maintained and enlarged its readership.

Marshall Meyer

Robert Spero

igh noon on the nouvelle West Side. Today's oysters at Docks are Chesapeakes, Apalachicolas and Belons for another buck. Docks is the hottest restaurant on upper Broadway since the old Tip Toe Inn, which, God forbid, never served such *trayf* to the Eastern European lefties who lived around here. Across the street, the Boulevard, doing a passable imitation of St. Germain now that the chains protecting its sidewalk tables from nocturnal crack scavengers have been removed, offers shoppers fresh from the local Banana Republic mahi-mahi, mako shark and, for $14.95, the ubiquitous grilled tuna.

The tuna served around the corner at Congregation B'nai Jeshurun is out of the can. It is free. But for homeless blacks and Hispanics, driven from their rooms in the neighborhood by million-dollar yuppie condos named after southern cities and states far to the west of the Hudson, lunch is delicious and the homeless dine with dignity. This is no soup kitchen. The food is served on china by volunteers from the congregation. There are flowers on the tables, there is music in the air. Many of the homeless will spend the night in the synagogue. The linen will be fresh.

The idea for the shelter and its humane touches are typical of B'nai Jeshurun's rabbi, the man the former Argentine military junta, out of anger, and the Jewish establishment in Buenos Aires, out of fear, called *el rabbino rojo* ("the red rabbi").

Recalling the slander, Rabbi Marshall Meyer smiles with the self-assurance of a man who has made a career out of thumbing his nose at the establishment, particularly the Jewish wing, whether over the issue of the homeless, homosexuals, fascists, fellow rabbis, ritual, Israel or the Conference of Presidents of Major American Jewish Organizations.

And still Meyer is all but worshiped for his strongly held beliefs by thousands of congregants on two continents. His help is eagerly sought by dozens of causes from New York and Buenos Aires to Jerusalem. Universities, synagogues and sometimes the establishment he rails at beseech him to lecture. Indeed, he sometimes sits on the establishment's boards.

The rabbi clearly loves the limelight – as a young man he seriously considered a life in the theater – and he knows how to play to the crowd to advance his agenda, beginning with building a sense of community in a congregation so depleted and spiritually moribund two years ago that getting a minyan was all but impossible. More material was the problem of keeping even 10 men warm in winter: The synagogue had no heat.

B'nai Jeshurun, the oldest Ashkenazic synagogue in New York, architecturally breathtaking in its expansiveness and attention to detail when it moved to its present location on West 88th Street in 1918, had literally become a dump. Rooms were piled high with trash and broken furniture. The roof leaked. Floors were missing. The vestry, where the homeless now eat and sleep, was flooded. Stained glass windows were dangerously bowed. Many of the synagogue's most precious objects had been removed and no one knew where they were.

"When I came to B.J. I sat down on the first floor in the middle of the hall," Meyer remembers as he smokes a Rothmans with a practiced flourish. "There was no table, no lights, no secretary. I put an old bridge table next to the public phone booth – that was the only thing left – and every time I wanted to make a call I put a quarter in. I loved it, but it was hard as hell."

B'nai Jeshurun hardly seemed a step up for the American who had been perhaps the most prominent rabbi in Argentina – for that matter in all of South America – for 25 years, the last seven filled with both international acclaim and personal threats because of his impassioned words and deeds on behalf of the thousands of persons kidnapped and murdered by the junta, as well as his support of imprisoned writer Jacobo Timerman.

By 1984, exhausted by the years of battling the junta and then by his work as the only American to serve on President Raul Alfonsín's National Commission for Disappeared Persons (where he helped write *Nunca Más*, the 50,000-page report of the torture and kidnapping), Meyer pulled up stakes and moved back to the United States with his wife.

After a stint as vice president of the University of Judaism in Los Angeles, Meyer realized how much he missed having a pulpit. He could have had his pick of wealthy congregations and received a large salary, but, he says, "I realized to my chagrin that there didn't seem to be very many synagogues that I could take seriously. There is such a lack of imagination and poverty in American Jewry—and this the center of world Jewry demographically. The more I spoke to young Jews on college campuses, the more I realized how *starved* they were. When you'd sit down with them and listen, they had this extraordinary spiritual hunger."

Rebuilding B'nai Jeshurun from nothing was the sort of challenge Meyer was looking for. But like his mentor, Abraham Joshua Heschel, he was more concerned with the architecture of time than the architecture of space.

"How do you sanctify time in a world where the concept of sanctification and holiness is almost impossible to define in any terms that are meaningful to modern man and woman?" he asks, his eyes flashing with energy and feeling. "How do you translate spiritual goals into action?

"People say: 'We don't want to talk about the homeless, we want to talk about spirituality.' It's true, the Bible says: 'Man does not live by bread alone.' But damn it," Meyer says, raising his voice, "You can't live *without* bread either! It's a major luxury to say let's talk about the sanctity of the Sabbath *only*.

"When you give real food and nourishment to a woman or man starving on the streets of New York, and you do it with love and care, or you give them a place to sleep, you are translating the Torah into reality. That's why the first thing I did to build the B.J. community was not to concentrate so much on the surfaces as it was to make sure there was a shelter and food program because saving human life is more important than praying."

If Meyer was attracted by the possibilities B'nai Jeshurun offered him, his concept of social justice, community and worship was a magnet to Jews who had never been affiliated with a congregation.

Although B'nai Jeshurun had an organ, he purchased a better instrument to enhance the aesthetic qualities of the service, a particularly unpopular move for many Jews who equate the organ with Christian worship. Meyer scoffs: "People forget that almost a hundred instruments were utilized in the Temple."

Hearing music coming out of a building that had been dark for so long, people wandered in from the street, found the synagogue a sanctuary from the anonymity and loneliness of the golden ghetto they had once fought so zealously to preserve, and began bringing in their friends.

Once inside, the new congregants were in for an even bigger surprise. Unlike so many of his rabbinical colleagues (whom he likes to twit about it), Meyer was not a master of ceremonies, presiding over the worship service. "I wanted to get away from this idea that the rabbi blesses," Meyer says. "The rabbi leads the congregation in prayer because he supposedly and hopefully knows a lot more about Judaism. But he asks God to bless – the source of blessing is God." There was no cantor at B'nai Jeshurun because Meyer believed all members of the congregation should be cantors if they had beautiful voices. Women, who weren't counted for a minyan at the old B'nai Jeshurun, chanted the services and read from the Torah and one became the first new president. There were no sermons except at High Holidays (at which time a member, who happens to be the world's greatest *klezmer* clarinetist, plays the Kol Nidre). Instead, Meyer introduced issues and goaded the congregation into no-holds-barred dialogue. It all caught on. B'nai Jeshurun now has over 350 members who, he says, "have a joyous sense of community."

Carrying the message of the Torah into the streets is not the career that would have been predicted for the youngest son of the first man in America to manufacture long pants for boys. Born in Brooklyn in 1930, Marshall Meyer was raised and educated in Norwich, Connecticut. He was the kind of 16-year-old who was equally at home in an Eagle Scout pup tent ("I was awarded two Palms and the Order of the Arrow," he reveals in all seriousness) and the local radio station where he had his own opera program.

At Dartmouth College Meyer was another philosophy major without a philosophy until he studied with Eugen Rosenstock Huessy, an intimate friend of Franz Rosenzweig, who, along with Martin Buber and Hermann Cohen, was striving to evolve a Jewish philosophy within Western tradition. Rosenstock Huessy (a Christian convert from a very assimilated Jewish family) forced Meyer to clarify his Judaism to himself. "Either I could really defend my Judaism as a philosophical as well as a spiritual pursuit, or I could consider the alternative, as Rosenstock Huessy had. He challenged the very inner core of my being."

But it was a new professor at the Jewish Theological Seminary who got Meyer to think seriously about the rabbinate. He had won a senior fellowship in 1951 to study the source of Rosenstock Huessy's basic tenet: Without Jesus there is no love for Jews. "The old sore," Meyer says. But there was no one at Dartmouth to guide him. So Meyer, who would never be accused of lacking chutzpah, simply walked into Abraham Joshua Heschel's office at J.T.S. and persuaded the scholar to come up to Hanover to tutor him.

For the next eight years, except for a year of study at Hebrew University, Meyer rarely left Heschel's side, first as a rabbinical student of the man he considers to be the most significant Jewish thinker of the 20th century ("if not several other centuries"), and then as Heschel's private secretary.

Studying at J.T.S. brought Meyer into contact with Paul Tillich and Reinhold Niebuhr, who were teaching Christian theology at Columbia. "I felt that a rabbi today just couldn't limit himself to Judaism, although I could study five lifetimes without knowing enough about Judaism. I *had* to know a great deal about Christians and Christianity."

Still, the liberal rabbinical student might well have ended up with the kind of Conservative pulpit he now deplores had he not been crushed by the sudden death of his parents while finishing his doctorate at J.T.S. "I just had to leave the country for a year or two. I asked the World Council of Synagogues, 'Where do you need a rabbi?' They called Singapore, but the line was busy. They called São Paulo, but nobody answered. They called Buenos Aires and lo and behold they said, 'Yes.'"

He sailed for Argentina with his wife, Naomi, in 1959, without knowing a word of Spanish. By the time they left, 25 years later, Meyer had translated some 70 volumes into Spanish, including works by Salo Baron and all of Abraham Joshua Heschel's books.

Actually, the 28-year-old assistant rabbi of Congregación Israelita de la Republica Argentina could have gotten along quite well without knowing much Spanish since the sermons at the upper-crust synagogue were in German—which made sense since the rabbis were German and Swiss and 90 percent of the aging congregation was German. (One rabbi was married to a Christian who had a crucifix over the bed!)

Meyer's apparently eternal battle with the Jewish establishment began soon after he arrived at Israelita. Against the wishes of the board of directors, he founded Camp Ramah. It was an instant success. Besides Hebrew, the camp taught Jewish philosophy and history, as well as theater and ballet. Children from Uruguay, Brazil, Bolivia and Chile had to be turned away. Everyone in South America wanted a young rabbi. Overnight, the charmingly aggressive Yankee became a star.

It seemed obvious to Meyer that without a rabbinical seminary—there had never been one in South America—there was no future for Argentine Jewry. So in 1962 he founded Seminario Rabinico Latino-Americano and served as its rector for the next 22 years.

But Israelita's insularity, not atypical of synagogues in Buenos Aires and throughout South America, was beginning to stick in Meyer's craw. He believed it was a historical necessity for Argentina to have a modern synagogue, with roots in the country, which not only addressed itself to Jewish and Zionist issues, but also wouldn't hesitate to involve itself with Christian society, not as a synagogue with a ghetto mentality, but as one carrying the prophetic Jewish message. Three years later he founded Comunidad Bet El.

He coaxed his new congregation to enter into a genuine interfaith dialogue with its neighbors—it was the time of Pope John XXIII and the Second Vatican Council. He started the first ecumenical group on the continent, which met monthly for more than two decades. "We had some very, very rough moments when we were threatened because of what we were doing," Meyer says. "The roundtable discussion we put together on Argentine television with a priest, a minister and a rabbi was *scandalous.*"

From a handful of members, Bet El grew to a thousand families, replacing Israelita as the largest synagogue in Buenos Aires, if not as the citadel of the Jewish establishment. Yet when it came to Zionism, Meyer outdid the crème de la crème he often criticized. "Nobody could be a member of our congregation unless they donated to the U.J.A.," he says, dismissing the apparent contradiction. "If you wanted to be a member, you had to be involved with the greatest adventure of the Jewish people in the 20th century."

The years in Argentina passed. Juan Perón and his followers came and went and came again and went again. Marshall Meyer plunged ahead with his own crowded agenda, founding and editing a Spanish-language Jewish quarterly and the Library of Science and History of Religions,

teaching Midrash and theology at his seminary, serving on committees
for mental health, planned parenthood and human rights. Naomi Meyer
bore three children, who today consider themselves more Argentine
than American. Indeed, home *was* Buenos Aires, with its splendid
Parisian-style boulevards and plazas. The Meyer family summered at
Camp Ramah on the sea or in the mountains. The United States seemed
far away. Had Isabel Perón not been overthrown by the fascist junta in
1976, the Meyers might still be comfortable expatriates.

But this was no ordinary Argentine military junta. Within a few
months the "disappearances" (Argentina's tragic contribution to world
vocabulary) began. Using the rooting out of left-wing thought as its
pretext, the junta treated the country as its private preserve—plundering,
kidnapping, torturing, raping, murdering at will. Over the next seven
years, 9,000 people disappeared, although Meyer believes 15,000 is a
more accurate figure. More than 1,500 of these men, women and
children were Jews. And Marshall Meyer, believing that acquiescence in
the junta's rule would betray not only the essence of his Jewishness but
the mandate of the Prophets as well, found himself in open opposition
with the wishes of the D.A.I.A. (Delegation of Argentine Jewish Associations), the body that officially represents Argentine Jewry to the
Government.

"As people began to disappear, the Jewish establishment position was
'You're better off not making a habeas corpus,'" Meyer says, anger rising
in his voice. "They [the D.A.I.A] had cordial relationships with the
junta. They said they required those cordial relationships because if they
had not had them many more thousands of Jews would have been killed.
I was an inveterate opponent of that position. I don't think you have
cordial relations with Hitler. They said this is a local problem. Fifteen
thousand people murdered is not a local problem.

"If we have learned one thing, you only aid a fascist government when
you have one address for the entire Jewish community. The D.A.I.A. has
a right to speak, but that doesn't mean Marshall Meyer or Chaim Yonkel
can't speak." (When reminded that he wasn't exactly Chaim Yonkel,
Meyer said frostily, "The point is you have to build up your own
credibility.")

Despite receiving written and telephoned death threats almost daily,
Meyer spoke against the junta at every opportunity, marched with the
Mothers of the Disappeared in the Plaza de Mayo, operated the family
apartment as a station on the underground railroad to save people before

they disappeared—"Many were Jews. There was a way to get them to Israel"—and suffered embarrassing body searches in order to visit Jews held illegally in Argentine prisons, particularly his old friend, the writer Jacobo Timerman, who was among those who were savagely tortured for years by the violently anti-Semitic army and police.

The D.A.I.A. accused Meyer of blackening Argentina's image by using the world media to talk about the disappeared. Of course he used the world press and television to reply: "The only individuals responsible for blackening Argentina's image in the world are the killers and the torturers, not the people who are defending justice and the due process of law."

Timerman's highly personal account of his torture in *Prisoner Without a Name, Cell Without a Number* triggered as much anger within important segments of the American Jewish establishment as it did within the D.A.I.A. A surprising number of American Jews were quick to agree with the position of conservatives Irving Kristol, Jeane J. Kirkpatrick and William F. Buckley Jr. Writing in the *Wall Street Journal* in May 1981, Kristol used Timerman as the stalking-horse for what he called the "current debate about the place of 'human rights' in American foreign policy" and attempted to draw a "distinction" between what conservatives viewed as friendly authoritarian governments (such as Argentina's) and unfriendly totalitarian governments (such as that of the Soviet Union).

The nasty debate was well documented at the time in both the Jewish and the general press. Marshall Meyer says he paid little attention to it. Portions from Kristol's article were read to Meyer at his office in B'nai Jeshurun: "Jews in Argentina today lead lives that are not very much more nervous and afraid than those of non-Jews. . . . Moreover, all synagogues, all Jewish communal organizations, all Zionist organizations (including the left-wing Zionist organizations) function freely and openly without harassment. Rabbi Marshall Meyer of Buenos Aires, a distinguished fighter for human rights to whom Timerman has dedicated his book, is in the process of building a $20 million rabbinical seminary. That, too, presumably tells us something."

"Ridiculous," said Meyer. "Besides, the seminary only cost $3 million."

Each year to mark the birth of Israel a gala parade marches up New York's Fifth Avenue. This year, crowds, waving tiny Israeli flags, lined the streets to celebrate the state's 40th anniversary. The Jewish establishment dutifully cheered the attractive marchers. Politicians, knowing what was good for them, were all smiles. The only harsh words were reserved for young Palestinian rock throwers.

Across town, Israel's anniversary was marked by a very different event. Five thousand people jammed the street in front of B'nai Jeshurun for the first rally ever sponsored by a coalition of 19 national and international Jewish peace groups. The only harsh words were reserved for the policies of the present Government of Israel.

Marshall Meyer spoke eloquently. Had anyone from the Jewish establishment bothered to attend (the event, he says angrily, was reported briefly on but one local TV station and not at all in the *New York Times*, although it sent a reporter and a photographer), it is not likely Meyer would have endeared himself to them with such speechmaking as "We believe that there must be an end to the occupation of the West Bank and Gaza . . . an end to second-class citizenship . . . The forces for peace that are at work in Israel are not naive, unsophisticated parties that are playing into the hands of our would-be exterminators, but rather they represent the individuals steeped in Jewish and world history who have learned their lessons well: that no nation can continue to exist based upon the oppression and exploitation of others."

Why does this rabbi seem to go out of his way to confront the Jewish establishment at every turn, in every country?

Meyer claims he doesn't do it gratuitously. "I am certainly not antiestablishment, not by nature," he says. But when a visitor says, "I suspect you may be," he roars with laughter and replies "I suspect you may be right!"

A tall, well-built man with a quick sense of humor, Meyer is by nature extremely serious and can dramatically change the mood in a room when he discusses such subjects as social justice and due process of law—and almost everything Marshall Meyer says or does sooner or later is concerned with justice and due process.

"Establishments," he says almost sadly, "Jewish, Catholic, any establishment, don't risk. They stand for status quo, which impedes progress. They have institutions to protect. They don't have the commitment to necessary change which is so vital for dynamism and creativity."

Meyer's frequent displeasure with and sometimes, it seems, his outright distaste for the Jewish establishment begins at the top, with the Conference of Presidents of Major American Jewish Organizations.

"How do you get to be the president of these major organizations?" he asks, perhaps as bewildered as he appears to be. "Who the hell do they represent? I don't know if they really represent all these organizations. Are they really speaking for 5,700,000 American Jews? They certainly don't represent me! I deny that they have a monopoly on truth. Those of us who are so dissatisfied with the profile [the Conference of Presidents] is projecting must get together and have an alternative voice so that we can demand the proper credibility. . . . Unless we speak out loudly and clearly, we're not doing our job as Jews."

Earlier this year in Jerusalem, Prime Minister Yitzhak Shamir lectured a mission of the presidents conference on the "moral duty" of diaspora Jews to support Israeli policies and called on "responsible" Jewish leadership in America "to clamp down" on any "criticism" of Israel.

Had Meyer been in Jerusalem that day, as he often is, it is safe to say that he would have been quick to object to such patronizing treatment. "I don't think the Jew of the diaspora is a second-class Jew," he says, adding, pragmatically, "I would suggest that anybody who really wants to look more than 10 years down the road has to realize that Israel . . . is always going to be surrounded by several hundred million Arabs and there has to be peace or else there will be a hundred-year war, which Israel will not withstand and cannot withstand and I resent the fact that the voice of the American Jewish peace camp is not given the proper coverage. It's important that people know that everybody isn't clapping and applauding Mr. Shamir and Mr. Sharon."

Meyer sees Israel's continuing drift to the right as leading to a terrible schism among Jews—both in the diaspora and in Israel—with the Gushniks and colonists on the West Bank taking up arms against the Israeli Army, the army itself divided and civil war a possibility.

Of course, the scenario is farfetched, as the rabbi admits. But what if he's right?

Closer to home, Meyer charges much of the Jewish establishment with having turned its collective back on a host of issues, beginning with Jewish gays and lesbians, whom, if it has viewed them at all, it has viewed negatively.

B'nai Jeshurun, on the contrary, has gone out of its way to welcome gays and lesbians into the congregation, and last June hosted the premiere of "Evening Liturgy of Consolation," a cantata composed by Louis Weingarden, who has AIDS, for the benefit of the AIDS Resource Center, Hale House for Infants and the B'nai Jeshurun AIDS Committee.

Meyer shakes his head when asked about New York Mayor Ed Koch's remarks about Jesse Jackson and Israel during the New York Presidential primary last April. "It was the same type of hateful and very dangerous rhetoric that I had heard in Argentina. I find a certain Jewish arrogance with regard to how *powerful* the Jewish vote is, how *powerful* the Jews are. Some 10 million Christians live in Greater New York as well. There is so much healing required between blacks and whites, specifically between the blacks and the Jews, and it has to be addressed on the highest level."

While the highest level is pondering the issue—or praying that it will go away—Meyer has taken a first step toward solution by trying to bring his synagogue closer to a black church. B'nai Jeshurun's social action committee recently visited the church and is planning an evening of song with it. "No speeches, no politics," Meyer says eagerly, "just their church choir singing along with our congregation."

Meyer talks about the work that needs to be done with the Hispanic community. "It's close to my heart—after all, my kids are Hispanics!" Soon, he will ask his congregation's board to vote on involving the synagogue with the sanctuary movement, which provided asylum for Central American political refugees. "I think it will go through," he smiles. It probably will. Two days after the arrest of John Fife, the Presbyterian minister from Tucson, Arizona, who started the sanctuary movement, he spoke from B'nai Jeshurun's pulpit.

Meyer had been going nonstop since early in the morning when he took two calls from Buenos Aires. Later, a Hollywood producer phones. All day children from the Abraham Joshua Heschel School had been running overhead, back and forth, back and forth. He soon had to leave for another engagement. His head hurt. He had been speaking about the Orthodox Jewish community and the orthodoxy within all parts of Jewry. That alone made him sigh.

There is a great deal of pomposity on the part of many of his colleagues, he was saying. "They feel they are God's right hand, they're so *positive* they know exactly what God wants. So many people speak in the name of God that I think they have a little difficulty trying to listen to the echo of God's real voice, what the Bible calls 'a soft, murmuring voice' that we catch if we're very, very attentive, that drives us on to more spiritual accomplishment rather than material accomplishment, that drives us on to risk love, to learn how to deal with life and death, how to sanctify the profane, how to make a difference in a very dark world, how to light that candle."

He had gradually lowered his voice, more out of fatigue, it seemed, than for drama, so that at the end he could barely be heard. It must have been a rare moment in Marshall Meyer's life.

Hugh Nissenson

Diane Cole

ynthia Ozick called him "the first American Jewish writer to step beyond communal experience into the listening-places of the Lord of History"; literary critic Alfred Kazin wrote, "His closeness to some secret genius in Jewishness has found its narrative voice." Other reviewers have praised his laconic literary style and his ability to dramatize the social and moral dilemmas facing the Jews of Israel and America. The novelist Johanna Kaplan, author of "O My America!," perhaps described his gifts most eloquently: "Hugh Nissenson's unique lyric voice confounds the boundaries of fiction. His spare, haunting, melodic cadences propel us into distant times or dark, yet familiar places of the heart so that all these are made wholly new—an illumination. His rhythms and images remain in the brain, and like dreams, unbeckoned, come crying out in full dress in the midst of ordinary life."

Tall and silver-haired with wide, animated eyes, Nissenson, 52, has produced only five books, but each has transported readers to a different world. His memoir, "Notes From the Frontier" (Dial Press, 1968), takes us to an Israeli border kibbutz before and after the Six-Day War in 1967. "My Own Ground" (Farrar, Straus, Giroux, 1976), Nissenson's first novel, thrusts us into the squalor of immigrant tenements on the Lower East Side. Two collections of short stories, "A Pile of Stones" (Scribners, 1965) and "In the Reign of Peace" (Farrar, Straus, Giroux, 1972), carry us to Warsaw's Jewish community at the turn of the century, contemporary Jerusalem, New York today.

Most surprising is the territory this self-described Jewish-American writer has staked out in his latest novel, "The Tree of Life" (Harper & Row)—the stark wilderness of Ohio on the eve of the War of 1812. Yet, Nissenson tells me, in an interview at his Upper West Side apartment in New York City, "I could not have written this novel *except* as a Jew." But, I remind him, the plot turns on characters who are hardly familiar with Judaism: a former minister-turned-Yankee trader who has lost his faith; an Indian who believes his soul to be inhabited by a Satanic spirit, and, surprisingly, the real Johnny Appleseed, who turns out to be a Swedenborgian mystic. So how does Judaism fit in?

"The book describes the war between Hebraic and pagan elements— one of the great dramas of the Western soul," he explains. "It asks the question, 'Are you a Hebrew-Christian, or are you a pagan?' Tom Keene, the main character, calls himself an infidel, a man who has lost his faith in the risen Christ. He acquires faith, instead, in love, paternity and, of course, art. He is, after all, an artist."

The central image of the novel—the tree of life—is an image shared by Jews and Christians, he adds. Indeed, says Nissenson, who began studying world mythology during childhood, "the tree of life appears as a symbol in almost every religion in the world." He then enthusiastically traces the symbol's manifestations in one culture after another. So it is perhaps fitting that he uses this universal image to bridge the gap between the different cultures and characters that inhabit his imagination.

True, though their religions differ, the characters in all his books suffer similar crises of faith: In the Israeli kibbutz of "Notes from the Frontier," in the Lower East Side tenements of "My Own Ground," and in the makeshift cabins on the Ohio frontier of "The Tree of Life," Nissenson depicts tormented souls who renounce all belief in God, or declare themselves followers of the god of pure chance. A frail, mad rabbi in "My Own Ground" prays for a redemption that will come only when the world has sunk to the lowest level; in "The Tree of Life," we meet his unlikely counterpart, the demon-driven Indian Tommy Lyons, whose bestial raids mire his frontier world in blood.

Besides demonic characters, Nissenson also portrays idealistic dreamers. In "My Own Ground," a fervent socialist prays for political utopia, and in "The Tree of Life," John Chapman (otherwise known as Johnny

Appleseed) speaks to dead spirits he believes await him in a Utopian afterlife. Mystics abound in all Nissenson's works, but while his previous books explored the mysticism of Gershom Scholem, Nissenson's new novel delves into that of Swedenborg. "As always," he says, "I am fascinated by the mad religious figure, the prophetic religious figure. John Chapman is the Protestant version of a figure that has haunted my imagination all my life—the crazy old man."

"The Tree of Life" contains both a deepening of Nissenson's traditional theme and a departure from it. But his primary departure, he believes, is his form—he uses the daily diary entries of Tom Keene to unfold his tale.

Surely, other novelists have used the diary form, but "The Tree of Life" uses a special model—"Notes from the Warsaw Ghetto," Emanuel Ringelblum's searing account of his community's destruction. "I wanted the sense of excitement that that books conveys, the sense of a diary written at the moment that things are happening," Nissenson says.

In calm, spare entries, Tom Keene faithfully reports everything happening at the moment—not only every frontier brutality, but his every purchase, sale or trade. One soon knows, Nissenson comments, "This guy is a Yankee trader, and no matter what happens, he is making a 'total' " because he's a businessman, and the business of America is making money.

Many entries include Keene's brief lines of verse. Like William Blake, the British poet and engraver to whom Nissenson likens his character, Keene does not merely write but also paints visionary images that form an integral part of the text—the most striking one being "Our Mother Death," a stark, black and white painting of a skull dressed up in a bonnet and scarf. (Nissenson has actually painted renditions of his character's visionary images, which could easily be mistaken for the primitive Indian art of the novel's time period. The A.M. Adler Fine Arts gallery in Manhattan displayed them in a Nissenson one-man show this fall.)

With its attention to detail, its crafted prose and its striking imagery, "The Tree of Life" reads more like history than fiction, a narrative poem rather than a novel. Yet Nissenson's concern with authenticity links "The Tree of Life" to his previous works. Cynthia Ozick has commented that many of his stories could have been translated from the Hebrew; another critic has suggested that some of his tales could have been translated from the Yiddish. And now a document not from the Israeli but the Ohio frontier.

"I wanted to do something wholly original," he says, "to get back to the original meaning of the word 'novel'—something new. That's what gives me the greatest sense of pride."

Nissenson displays a different sense of pride as he guides a visitor through his study filled with relics of his latest artistic journey. High on one wall hangs a buckskin suit worthy of Davy Crockett; beside it, a white dress shirt, a bullet bag, assorted hunting and powder horns, a tomahawk—every item a man might need to hunt, or dress for church. The honey-colored skin of a mountain lion is sprawled on one chair; on another, a blank-eyed bear's head. One could spend days cataloguing the items in this cramped, miniature museum of early Americana, which also contains the head of a European wild boar, a stuffed American raven and American wild turkey, two Indian masks and a stark white human skull dressed in a black pigtailed wig with feathers and Ben Franklin glasses. For seven years, Nissenson entered this room each day, working to recreate the brutal frontier world of "The Tree of Life." In his next project, a childhood memoir, he will "wrestle with what it means to be a Jew," he says. Not as an Israeli, or as an immigrant living on the Lower East Side at the beginning of the century, but as a Jew "growing up scared to death—and I mean terror!"

Born in 1933, Nissenson grew up on Manhattan's Upper West Side "in an intensely anti-Semitic time," he says. His first words, he explains, were "Mussolini" and "Ethiopia." Whenever his parents spoke of European Jewry, he recalls, they had "the 1,000-yard stare, a phrase used to describe GIs who had seen too much combat duty."

He identified intensely with the stories he heard and the newsreels he saw of the destruction of European Jewry, and quickly came to the conclusion that "being an American is the most precious thing in the world." However, he adds, "you could never be sure that you were secure as an American, because if Gentiles were on the rampage killing Jews in Europe, how could you know it wouldn't happen here?

"Whenever I walk down West 82d Street, past the Roman Catholic church there, I think back to the Easter when I was 12, when a gang of Italian and Irish kids beat my head against the red brick wall, shouting 'Christ-killer!'"

Only a block away, at a Reform synagogue on 83d Street, Nissenson had become bar mitzvah. "The rabbi there," he remembers, "a man with an immensely powerful and mellifluous voice, berated these Jews, all of us, during the war and afterward, for our passivity in the face of what was happening. And yet, when I asked him at my bar mitzvah, 'How can you believe in God after the murder of the six million?' he turned on me and said, 'Be quiet! Don't dare ask these questions.' "

Nissenson pauses, then goes on in a hushed, agitated voice, "I grew up in a world where human beings went from the use of poison gas in Ethiopia to Zyklon B in the gas chambers. . . . And I must say that the atom bomb did not come as a surprise to me. No, it did not! A bomb the size of a pea destroys a whole city? All my life had been a progression of watching slaughter and atrocity.

"And I thought, 'The human race is crazy, man! And it's very dangerous to be a Jew, because you seem to be the victim.' . . . And I've spent a lifetime obsessed by history, because Jews suffer history. If history happens, the Jews get it."

Nissenson's obsession with history, and with Jewish history in particular, led him to cover the Eichmann trial in Jerusalem for *Commentary*, an event that "changed my life completely. I never recovered from those four months of sitting in a courtroom with such palpable evil . . . It was the determining factor in my eventual loss of faith. It was impossible to believe there could be a God, given such terrible evil. And such evil had a human face—he was not a devil, but a human being."

As someone who possesses what he describes as a "classic religious personality," who obsessively studied the world's mythologies and religions from an early age but today lacks religious faith, Nissenson admits to being caught in the central paradox that permeates both his thinking and his work: the conflict between his longing to believe and his skepticism. "It is in this struggle that the fuel to my fires is to be found," he says. "And if you are an artist, you must discover within yourself that which gives you the most conflict. It is out of these paradoxes, out of these irreconcilable differences, that the creative response comes."

Nissenson dramatized such "irreconcilable differences" most poignantly in the voices of the inhabitants of Kibbutz Maayan Baruch, on the Lebanese border, in his first-hand, non-fiction account, "Notes from the Frontier." One Israeli is a fanatical believer in the religion of Marxism; another seeks meaning in his archaeological collection. Others, who believe in a traditional Judaism, find the Jewish homeland devoid of religious meaning.

The political landscape of Israel today also arouses troubled thoughts in him. Nissenson believes the Israelis "are fighting for their soul . . . wrestling with what kind of nation they're going to be. Are they going to be a democracy, a repressive regime, pluralistic, all these things? . . . I find it extraordinary that the Jews are so preoccupied with the morality of their position. They are tormented by this, and of this I am immensely proud." After all, he says, how many nations in world history have been aware that moral issues were at stake?

A frequent visitor to Israel, Nissenson is hesitant either to criticize or to offer advice: "I can do nothing but relate to [their political problems] from a distance," he says. "No matter how deeply involved I am with the people who live there, I'm not living there."

Like his artist-protagonist Tom Keene, Nissenson believes that redemption lies only in the act of creation, illuminating both the beauty and the horror of the human heart. So his task remains to cultivate, in his imagination, the tree of life that bears knowledge, truth and art.

Amos Oz

Richard Kostelanetz

> I became a Socialist because my parents were right-wingers, and became a
> kibbutznik because my parents were town-dwellers, and probably became
> a novelist because my father was a scholar.
> — Amos Oz, to an interviewer in 1973

Kibbutz Hulda is in the valley between Jerusalem and Rehovoth, closer
to the latter. Like other kibbutzim in the area, it contains acres of cotton
fields, several large factory buildings where chick-peas and transformers,
among other things, are produced, smaller structures for recreation and
dining, numerous multi-unit living quarters, and a swimming pool. What
makes Kibbutz Hulda different from its neighbors is the fact that since
1955 it has been the residence of Israel's best-known and most respected
young novelist, Amos Oz.

Born in Jerusalem in May 1939, the only child of Yehuda Arieh
Klausner, a prominent scholar and right-wing Zionist, Amos Oz was a
precocious, headstrong youngster, not unlike the bright child in his
book, *The Hill of Evil Counsel*, published in English in 1976. At fifteen, he
bolted from the family home to live in Hulda, a few miles from what was
then the Jordan border. To further distance himself from his family, he
took another name, his present one, pronounced Ah-mos Awz (not like
the Wizard's name).

At the beginning, while he finished secondary school, Oz worked in

Hulda's cotton fields. In 1957, the year when, at eighteen, he became a full member of the kibbutz, he was inducted into the army. He served for three years, in the Nahal (a military-agricultural division of the army) establishing new kibbutzim. In his spare time he wrote—initially patriotic poems, detective stories and other relatively light works. In 1960 he made his professional debut with a few poems and a story in an adult literary magazine.

Since Kibbutz Hulda has been such an integral part of Oz's life, it seemed best for me to meet him there; the drive from Jerusalem took less than an hour. I went to his studio in a bungalow block of four small apartments, ideally suited for single people. At the door, Oz—a short, slight man with brown hair, warm blue eyes and a ready smile—greeted me with a firm handshake. Wearing loosely hung jeans and a work shirt, he reminded me of the American actor, Paul Newman; photographs on his book jackets scarcely do justice to his good looks. He offered me coffee with powdered cream, or tea. On that hot day I wanted cold soda pop, but he said apologetically that his studio had no refrigerator.

In the anteroom, roughly five feet by eight, are a cot along one wall and an exercycle, of all things, in the middle. We sat and talked in a backspace, perhaps eight feet by twelve, his work room. This contains a desk in front of the sole screened window, a wall full of books in English and Hebrew, a cabinet holding cookies and extra copies of his own books, another cot, a large radio and two plain easy chairs. There is no telephone; neighbors wanting to talk to him generally come to the window.

Oz speaks English easily, if imperfectly, with a British-Israeli accent; he favors direct, simple sentences—much like a high school teacher, which he is. That day he had been at work since 5:30 a.m., which, he remarked, "wasn't especially early on a kibbutz," where farm workers are in the fields at 4:30.

Early in 1961, he told me, he returned to Hulda and married Nily, who was born on the kibbutz. Her father had emigrated to Palestine from Bessarabia in the second stream of settlers in 1930. That year, Oz fathered a daughter named Fania, worked in the cotton fields and wrote in his spare time. One Saturday evening, the kibbutz assembly—one adult, one vote—selected him to attend the Hebrew University for two years, because Hulda needed a teacher. He points out that the kibbutz sent him for only two years rather than the full three "because they did not want me to get a degree. They probably thought that, if I took a degree, I would run away. I fooled them twice, taking the degree in two years [in philosophy and Hebrew literature] and coming back."

Beginning in 1963 he taught full time, six days a week through the long Israeli mornings, writing in the evenings and on the Sabbath. Since he had begun to receive public recognition for his stories, he applied for one day off every week; this was granted at the end of 1963. Two years later he published his first book, *Artzot Ha'tan* (*Where the Jackal Howls*), a collection of stories which has not appeared in book form outside Israel, though parts of it appear in English now and then in magazines and anthologies. It won him both the Holon Prize and two days a week off from teaching—illustrating what Israelis call "creeping annexation."

In 1966, he published *Elsewhere, Perhaps*, a portrait of kibbutz life that in my judgment is the most interesting of his three novels. Needless to say, the book stirred up discussion and argument among his kibbutz neighbors. As he remembers it, the responses ranged from "How dare you?" to "At long last, someone is telling the truth." In Oz's opinion, "It is useful to live in such an immediate and frank milieu. I'm surrounded by people I know well, who know me well, who don't withhold judgment on my writing."

Most readers suspect that in *Elsewhere, Perhaps* Oz was writing about his own kibbutz, but certain details suggest otherwise. The fishponds that are prominent in the fictional Kibbutz Metsudat Ram do not exist at Hulda, and there is no analogue for the part-time poet, Reuben Harish. "I never use living models," Oz explains. "If I did, it would be difficult for me to remain here." He paused to light a cigarette. "Besides, people have such high opinions of themselves that, if you portrayed them as they are, they would not recognize themselves."

The technical achievement of *Elsewhere, Perhaps* is Oz's handling of the richly developed major characters, ranging from Harish and his attractive teenage daughter Noga to the kibbutz truck driver Ezra Berger, his wife Bronka and his brother Zachariah (also known as "Siegfried"), who has left the kibbutz to earn his fortune in post-World War II Germany.

Oz accomplishes remarkable feats with the book's narrative voice. In most of the novel the speaker is the kibbutz itself, an omniscient voice speaking as "we"—analogous to the chorus in Greek tragedy, as Oz sees it. From time to time, however, each of the seven principal characters speaks in the first-person singular; this shifting point of view is, per se, a technical tour de force. Oz acknowledges that his fictions begin with characters and thus with characteristic voices. I think he is far more skilled at characterizations, often swiftly rendered, than at plots. When I suggested that the character of Ezra Berger "takes over the book, because he initiates no wrong, although wrongs are done to him," Oz concurred, saying Ezra "is the only mature character and thus in a way dearest to me."

Controversial though the book was in Hulda, Oz did not feel any pressure to leave. "I've always been a good waiter in the dining halls, and that's what counts around here," he commented lightly. "That's how people know me. I also still do my turn as a night-watchman." He lit another cigarette. "With a submachine gun in hand, you patrol the fields and feel heroic from eleven at night to six in the morning. And when I'm between things, I go out and work in the fields, picking apples and driving the tractor."

The kibbutz collects all Oz's royalties, which now amount to more than $20,000 a year. "Every penny I earn, I sign the back of the check and hand it over to the treasurer. Everything I need for my work, even a stay in a hotel away from here, I can get. All I need to do is ask the treasurer to pay for it. I never had to rely on publishers' advances. I never had to commit myself to a deadline. I don't fill out income tax forms. I have no mortgage."

In return, Oz gets a studio, board, another apartment for himself and his wife, lodging and education for his family (which now includes two daughters and a son), a workroom for himself and even the Europa cigarettes he chain smokes. He remembers that the director of the "work rota" once offered to assign two elderly members as secretary-assistants, "with an eye to increasing my productivity." Oz refused; he was not the cottage factory some colleagues wanted him to be.

Had *My Michael*, his second novel, not been finished just before the Six Day War in 1967, it might never have been done. Oz, by then a reservist, went to fight in a tank unit in the Sinai. (During the Yom Kippur War he fought in the Golan Heights.) This book sold exceedingly well—more than 60,000 copies in eleven printings in Israel alone. (Given Israel's population of three million, this would be the equivalent of four million copies in the United States.) To this day, most Israeli readers identify it as the Oz novel they've read and like best. Oz says its success remains a mystery to him. "The book has no fighting, no sex, no nothing. It must have touched an open nerve somewhere." It has been translated into English, French, Spanish, Catalan, Dutch, Italian, Swedish, Norwegian, Finnish, German and Japanese.

A strange, deceptively simple novel, *My Michael* is dominated by its narrator, Hannah Gonen, a young housewife who tells in a dry voice of her disillusionments, dreams, depression and eventual breakdown. Her husband Michael is an inordinately considerate and patient graduate student in geology who seems unable to relieve his wife's funk. Some of the novel's best passages deal with Jerusalem, especially as it was in the 1950s when Oz still lived there. Oz thinks the novel is about "the morning after," not only for a marriage but for Israel itself in the fifties, after the initial fervor to establish the country had died down. Soon after *My Michael* was published, he was given another day off from teaching, this reducing his kibbutz work week to three days.

In 1969, "out of the blue," he received an invitation from St. Cross College, Oxford, to be writer-in-residence for a year. He accepted, taking his family with him—their first trip outside Israel. "It was my first meeting with European weather, a foreign language, Gothic architecture and an organized sequence of time," he recalls. "You could look at a building and see several strata of history."

At Oxford, Oz first met an Englishman who has since played a consequential collaborative role in his fiction's career—Nicholas de Lange, five years younger than he, who is now a lecturer on post-biblical and medieval Hebrew literature at Cambridge University. Familiar with classical Hebrew, de Lange asked to read Oz's work in its original language. Then he produced a sample translation which was so successful that all of Oz's English editions have since been "translated by Nicholas de Lange, in collaboration with the author." Oz declared: "That's a lie. It is translated by de Lange with interruptions by the author." Actually, he said, "We work together like best enemies—reading every word, every sentence, every paragraph. The English translation is the only one that can hurt me."

Oz wrote two novellas, "Crusade" and "Last Love," at Oxford; they were published in 1971 as *Unto Death*. "Crusade" is a nasty, gruesome story about Christian crusaders who steal and kill in a vain effort to reach Jerusalem. "Last Love," which I regard as Oz's single greatest piece of fiction, is a profoundly penetrating monologue by a sixty-eight-year-old kibbutz-circuit lecturer, Shagra Unger, a veteran agitator whose talk mixes petty problems with cosmic perceptions as he expresses his fears about his career's end, which he paranoically blames on hidden Bolsheviks.

"Most of my characters believe in something which I don't believe," Oz says, referring particularly to the stories in *Unto Death*. "They believe in some simple formula, be it 'elsewhere' or 'violence.' Or 'love,' whatever some of them mean by that word." By this point, the structures of his fiction were becoming sharper and more concise. The narrator of *My Michael* took an entire novel to tell her story, that of "Last Love" only a novella; later works develop even more swiftly.

Touch the Water, Touch the Wind, the third novel, published in 1973, is considerably shorter than *Elsewhere, Perhaps,* even though its materials belong to a much longer work. Oz describes it as "a problematic substitute for a 19th century family saga. The crux is an uncle of mine whom I've never seen, my father's brother David. When my father came to Palestine, his brother preferred to remain in Vilna, where he was a lecturer on comparative literature at the university. He was a devoted European, when everyone else was a communist or a nationalist patriot. He refused to accept Zionism or any other chauvinism. When the Nazis came, they killed him, his wife and his son, my cousin Daniel. Throughout my childhood, I was told that Uncle David was too clever to die, that he would show up." This myth informs the principal character of *Touch the Water*.

Oz's intentions notwithstanding, the novel suffers from a preposterous surface and is generally regarded as his least successful effort. Professor Robert Alter, perhaps Oz's most attentive American critic, calls it "unpersuasive, especially when compared with the genuinely hallucinatory intensity of his best writing."

His most recently translated book, *The Hill of Evil Counsel* (which was published, in de Lange's translation, in England and the United States in 1978) marks a return to excellence. Three interrelated novellas deal with Jerusalem in the mid-1940s during the British Mandate. The Hill of Evil Counsel of Oz's title was the location of the British High Commissioner's office. "The Jerusalem of my boyhood was a nuthouse. There were more madmen there than anywhere else in the world. Everyone was a messiah. Everyone was a redeemer. Everyone had a formula for universal redemption in one go," Oz said.

He paused to light another cigarette. "Jerusalemites in those days secretly yearned to crucify and to be crucified. They thought the world needed urgent redemption—redemption in violence, pain and bloodshed. They all had the same urge: purify, get purified. Redeem the world through bloodshed in one way or another. Either kill the bad guys to help the good guys or kill oneself, in order to cause a shock that would change the world."

There is more Oz to come. A juvenile story, *Sumchi*, issued in 1978 by his Tel-Aviv publisher, Am Oved, will appear in this country later this year. Dan Omer, literary columnist for *Haolam Hazeh*, regards it as Oz's very best fiction. Last summer his first book of non-fiction appeared in Israel—a collection of essays on literature, politics, kibbutzim and social-ism. He expects that a selection of these will soon appear in English. On his desk is a long novel on which he has been working for several years. He would not say when it will be done, nor would he tell me about it. ("Just say I'm superstitious.")

Oz writes in longhand, initially in intense spurts at a place away from the kibbutz, with its scheduled demands. He begins with characters which come to him in dreams, or as voices, or as "mannerisms I can identify." He edits his material down to its final form. "Three thousand pages then become four hundred," he says, perhaps implicitly referring to his work in progress. He types the final draft himself, mostly with his two index fingers on the Hebrew typewriter in his workroom. He confesses to having started more fiction than he finished, mostly because "I often don't like what I am doing."

Like other kibbutzniks, he wants to show a visitor his home. So we walk through the children's houses, going first to the nursery to see his son Daniel Yehuda Arieh, now two years old, named for his cousin and his father. He points with pride to the intercom microphone-speaker in every child's bedroom, attached to a central listening station, where a woman on watch spends every night. The system was purchased in 1965, Oz tells me, with the proceeds of the Holon Prize. While his royalties are fed into the kibbutz treasury, he can use prize money in Hulda as he wishes.

From the nursery we move to the fives-to-sevens house, where thirty screaming youngsters remind Oz that "I owe them a story. One of my Sabbath duties is telling stories to children and I began one for them that got interrupted." We go on to the next age group and finally to his elder daughter, Fania, a short, slight young woman. Now eighteen, she is completing her "matriculation exams" at high school. Then we tour the kibbutz chick-pea plant and the transformer factory, which Oz says is particularly profitable. We observe the cotton fields extending in one direction as far as the eye can see and in another to the hill from which, prior to 1967, came Jordanian artillery fire and infiltration. He takes me to the kibbutz movement archive where his wife Nily works, cataloging publications about the movement, as well as such documents as minutes of early meetings and personal diaries. Nearby is the auditorium where the kibbutz amateur theatrical group performs and where films are shown twice a week. The building also houses a library with 4,000 volumes in several languages, and "our version of a British pub," where free beer and coffee are dispensed every evening. At the entrance to Hulda we see the road that runs from Jerusalem to Rehovoth. Since Oz can get a kibbutz car only if he registers for it several days in advance, he customarily hitchhikes to the nearby cities.

He knows when everything was built, and gives a friendly nod to everyone we see. Nobody inquires about his novel-in-progress, perhaps because no one cares, or because everyone knows he is working hard on it—or because, as Oz insists, he is more appreciated at home as an ace waiter than as a writer. "It is impossible to act like a celebrity when you happen to live on a kibbutz," he confides. "Hulda is as close to an extended family as you can get in the world. If I lived in New York City, I wouldn't have such an intimate acquaintance with four hundred different people. I'm not William Faulkner, but whatever he could find in one town in the deep South of the States, I can find here."

We return to his study after lunch for another round of conversation. He speaks of the Israeli literary scene as "the most fascinating, perhaps not the best, in the world today, because of the compression of development. We have symbolists and realists, surrealists and dadaists, all converging in a small country. There are a hundred writers in Israel, working in a tremendous variety of styles, tendencies, concepts of literature, manners of writing. There is not even a vague consensus of what literature is about. It is possible to be in the right Tel-Aviv cafe, at the right time of day, to get the John Donne, the Lord Byron and the Allen Ginsberg of Hebrew poetry, all alive and kicking—not on speaking terms, but on screaming terms." Among the currently interesting Israeli writers he mentions are fiction writer A.B. Yehoshua and the poet Yehuda Amichai—both already well-known in the United States—and then Amalia Kahana-Karmon, whom he characterizes as "remotely related to Virginia Woolf—never translated and perhaps opposed to it."

He admires the Hebrew language for its variety of accents and national styles (Russian immigrants speaking it perceptibly differently from, say, Americans), and for the opportunities it offers for invention. Since the language is young, so to speak, it is possible for an author to coin new words or invent fresh constructions, he declares. "Hebrew is very hard to translate. Translating Hebrew into a Western language is different from translating French into German. It is traveling a long, long way."

He speaks of writing novels out of "a delight in comprehensive organization—hierarchy, priority, interaction. Now organization is, as we know, a religious experience." He paused to light another cigarette. "When I fail to tell a story, or to write a novel, or when I have a direct and unambivalent message, then I write an essay. To put it in simpler terms, when I totally agree with myself I write an article."

Remembering his extensive military experience in battle and in the reserves, I ask why he has not yet written a war novel. "It is impossible," he replies. "Those who have been on the battlefield know what it is like, and those who haven't don't know. Tell a monk what it is like to make love. War is made of smells and stenches—burning rubber, gunpowder, burning metal. There is no way to convey this in words."

Oz is as well known in Israel for his political opinions as for his novels. His position is customarily classified as left-wing Zionist. He has a different definition. "I'm an evolutionist, rather than a revolutionist, in everything—story-telling, socialism, sex. Though I've often been presented as 'radical' in Israeli politics, I think I've never been radical in anything. Regarding the Israeli-Palestinian conflict, I've always believed in an inconsistent compromise. Both sides have a solid, well-rounded case that turns the Israeli-Palestinian conflict—not the Israeli-Arab conflict, which is something else—into a tragedy, rather than a Wild West film. Heroes of tragedy, obsessed by an obsession for justice, destroy and annihilate each other. So people die, and justice prevails.

"The only way of surviving a tragic conflict is an inconsistent compromise. Politically speaking, two people regard this country as their one and only homeland. So the only way to survive is to divide it. Practically speaking, that means two independent states, in land hardly big enough for one. I agree that in principle, in theory and in historical practice, there is no difference between East Jerusalem and West Jerusalem, Hebron and Haifa, Nablus and Jaffa. We also know that the Palestinian sense of identity, of uniqueness, is largely a by-product of Zionism, but we cannot change that. Palestinians and Israelis alike have perfect claims, each legitimate. Either they divide it or they destroy one another.

"I've never been enthusiastic about national states altogether. The concept of civilizations waving flags attached to territories strikes me as archaic and murderous. In a way, we Jews have demonstrated for millenia what I should like to see as the next phase of history – a civilization without territorial boundaries; two hundred civilizations without a single nation-state. But as a Jew I cannot afford this anymore. I have set an example for two millenia, but nobody followed." He has espoused these positions since the end of the 1967 war.

The day is hot and dry. Though Oz seems cool and relaxed, his chain-smoking notwithstanding, his visitor is beginning to wilt. Oz suggests going to the Olympic-sized swimming pool, which suits me fine. However, his schedule requires him to take care of kibbutz business, perhaps returning some of the telephone calls that collect in its central office. At 4 p.m. he customarily sees his children and the family stays together through dinner, in the Oz apartment or in the communal dining hall. By 8 p.m. or so, the senior Ozes will retire to their small single bedroom apartment, where he will read into the night and sleep prior to another day as a kibbutz writer, which is not a literary term but a sociological one – a definition of one contemporary master's singular professional existence.

Cynthia Ozick

Diane Cole

---

er stories are the stuff that rabbinic dreams are made of: a rabbi turns "pagan" and begins to worship nature; a spinster civil servant summons a female golem to life and becomes the mayor of New York; a writer's lust for material leads her from an abandoned synagogue in Brooklyn to a charlatan rabbi to a Jerusalem haunted by the spirits of the Hebrew poets; a virile poet turns out to have cribbed his lines from his elderly, impoverished immigrant aunt.

The dreamer of these tales is Cynthia Ozick, author of the novel *Trust* and three highly praised volumes of short stories—*The Pagan Rabbi and Other Stories, Bloodshed and Three Novellas,* and most recently *Levitation: Five Fictions.* There would be one or two more volumes to her credit were her essays to be collected, for she has brooded on subjects ranging from the novels of Edith Wharton to the rights of Jewish women. She has invented a "new" Yiddish, examined the teachings of Gershom Scholem, and railed against terrorism and anti-Semitism, in magazines as varied as *The New Leader, Commentary, Lilith, Esquire* and *The New York Times Book Review.*

Fierce passions of the mind and soul animate these works. But when, her eyes to ground, Cynthia Ozick steps to the podium to read before an audience, the short, motherly, middle-aged figure in blue moves more like a kitten than a lion. With a nervous, high-pitched giggle, she smiles and brushes the bangs of her shoulder-length, simply cut pepper-and-salt hair from off her forehead. She blinks at the applauding audience as if she wants to find some way to hide behind her small, dark-framed glasses. Then, as the words begin to pour forth, her eyes slowly widen, her fist clenches in dramatic emphasis, and soon all that remains is the low, riveting voice of the storyteller and the story itself.

On this night, she reads from a novella still in progress, "Puttermesser and Xanthippe"—the story of the spinster civil servant and the golem she brings to life. Afterwards, Ozick wonders out loud if she has gone too far in detailing the history of the golem—in Jewish folklore, an automaton magically given life by the use of Holy Names. A questioner in the audience asks, "Miss Ozick, isn't the writer the golem-maker?" Ozick's laugh is an infectious staccato burst as she replies, "I think that the writer *is* the golem!"

But if that were true, what imagination gave birth to Cynthia Ozick?

Cynthia Ozick's own story began in Pelham Bay, the Bronx, where she was born in 1928 and where she grew up. As the hard-working proprietors of the Park View Pharmacy, her parents (and she and her brother) managed to struggle through the Depression, but there was time nevertheless for the daughter to read and for the son to build and operate his own ham radios.

Because old school hurts are never forgotten, one of Ozick's earliest memories is of going to Hebrew school only to be dismissed by the rabbi, who instructed her grandmother in no uncertain terms, "A girl isn't supposed to learn! Take her home!" The story has a happy ending, however: The grandmother persisted, Ozick began her studies the next day, and the rabbi eventually went on to praise her "*goldeneh keppel.*"

But after her early years at *cheder*, Ozick says, she "plunged into P.S. 71 and discovered that I was a Christ-killer and deeply, deeply tainted by everything, including a hopeless stupidity." As a result, "I assume, always, as the first premise, that I'm dumb."

Cynthia Ozick dumb? To escape from P.S. 71, she won entrance to Hunter High School for Girls. Later, she became a Phi Beta Kappa graduate of New York University, and from there she went on to earn a master's degree in literature from Ohio State. Her awards include a 1982 Guggenheim fellowship, an earlier fellowship from the National Endowment for the Arts, an American Academy of Arts and Letters Award for Literature, three O. Henry first prize awards for the best short story of the year, and multiple awards from the Jewish Book Council of America.

But for Ozick, the most cherished laurel of all may be the Distinguished Alumni Award given her by her alma mater, Hunter High School. "To me," she beams, unable to hide her excitement, "it's like getting the Nobel Prize."

At one time, Ozick would have given her own personal Nobel Prize to Henry James. As a graduate student who was self-admittedly "besotted with the religion of literature," Ozick wrote a master's thesis on this, her master. And as she read and reread Henry James, she recently confessed at a meeting of the Henry James Society, she actually "became Henry James . . . though I was a near-sighted twenty-two year old young woman infected with the commonplace intention of writing a novel, I was *also* the elderly bald-headed Henry James. Even without close examination, you could see the light glancing off my pate; you could see my heavy chin, my watch-chain, my walking-stick, my tender paunch."

She worshipped literature at the foot of Henry James, and it was not until the age of 25, when she discovered the Jewish philosopher Leo Baeck's essay on "Romantic Religion," that she began "to Judaize" herself, she says, by reading steadily and voraciously in Jewish history and philosophy. A self-described autodidact, she seems to have consumed everything, for few writers possess her depth and range of knowledge not just of the world's literature, but of the world's religions, and the texts and teachings of the Jewish religion in particular.

As she progressed with her personal curriculum, Ozick continued to write—an "apprentice" novel which she labored over for seven years, and which has never been published; and another novel, *Trust*, which also took seven years to compose.

Of *Trust*, published in 1966, she says, "I began it as an American novelist, and ended it as a Jewish novelist." The description is apt. It is a poetic, very Jamesian novel, whose most intriguing character, a prophet-like figure named Enoch Vand, is a master of assimilation. Yet at the book's close, he renounces his worldly, political successes to devote himself to the study of Torah and Talmud—he begins to "Judaize" himself and, it is implied, to redeem himself as well.

Given Ozick's unbounded admiration for Henry James ("I just re-re-re-re-read *The Europeans*," she says), it is perhaps no surprise that he figures prominently in her vision of her own afterlife. Like her character Puttermesser, she will sit comfortably beneath a tree, devouring fudge by the pound, and reading everything she had had neither time nor patience to read in the present life. Unlike Puttermesser, however, she has a plan: she will convert Henry James to Judaism.

"I also have a plan now for Samuel Johnson," she says. "Oh, yes, everything in his mentality is so completely Jewish, if he but knew it. The thing to do is to introduce him to the Rambam. That should take about half-an-hour to convince him—though, of course, we don't know how many eons half-an-hour is, paradise-time."

The time she allots for an interview flies quickly, though, in spite of her initial self-consciousness at the thought of talking about herself before a tape recorder. "When you write something down on paper," she says, "you think about it, you can erase—everything is provisional." And so, a shy, engaging woman, she is eager at first to find ways to divert attention from herself—to an anthology called *Modern Women in Love* that she discovers on a bookshelf, to the bookshelves themselves—and she begins at one point to reverse roles and interview the interviewer.

The modesty is sincere, the interest genuine, and that is part of Cynthia Ozick's charm. If she is known for her encouragement of other writers, it is perhaps because after all her accomplishments she still wonders, "How is it that *I'm* not the beginner? How astonishing!"

Ozick "began" with her 600-page novel *Trust*. "I feel I shot my bolt with it," she says. But few readers of the three books of stories that came next would agree. *Newsweek* book critic Peter S. Prescott, for one, predicts that "when the chroniclers of our literary age catch up to what has been going on (may Ozick live to see it!), some of her stories will be reckoned among the best written in our time."

These stories usually focus on American Jews, but contemporary family life and the immigrant experience provide only the backdrops to Ozick's fiction. And while Jewish tradition, ritual, and history are merely touched on in many Jewish-American novels, Ozick frequently places these at the very center of her characters' consciousness. In "Bloodshed," for instance, a rebbe, a survivor of the Holocaust, instructs a skeptical, nonobservant American Jew about the moral burden which he, too, must bear. In "A Mercenary" and "Levitation," other Holocaust survivors confront the Christian world with the facts of history. And in "Usurpation (Other People's Stories)," a writer goes in search of stories and finds herself faced with a spiritual dilemma—can she create "graven images" in fiction and still be Jewish?

These themes, stated in the abstract, may not sound like the stuff of fiction, but Ozick invests her ideas with passion, drama, and humor. Flights into the supernatural, fantastical metamorphoses of women into sea nymphs or trees into dryads, and satirical inventions such as a "sewing harem," where women seal with needle and thread the passage leading to the womb, abound. Ozick's stories are bright, shiny gems which simultaneously delight and provoke—provoke you to laughter as well as to thought.

But if Ozick's readers and critics can find much humor in her work, she herself cannot.

"I *know* I have no sense of humor," she insists. "I *know* I'm way too serious. And whenever someone goes so far as to say I'm a comic writer, this is a great puzzle to me. But there's a story by Somerset Maugham called 'Jane' and it's about a country cousin who comes to London and makes a great social success as a wit. Everyone tells her, 'You are a great wit,' and she says, very seriously, 'Well, I didn't know that, and I'm sure I'm not, but it seems to me that I just tell the truth.' She struck everyone in her new, sophisticated circle in London as a comedienne when she just told her country truths. And that's what I think of when I hear anyone tell me that I said something funny."

Cynthia Ozick has a habit of speaking and writing what is on her mind, whether the subject is literature, Judaism, feminism, or politics. In *The New York Times* in March 1978, for instance, Ozick wrote an impassioned, open "Letter to a Palestinian Military Spokesman." Ozick's 14-year-old cousin Imri, a clarinetist, had just been murdered in a Palestinian terrorist attack, and his father, a professional flutist, had had his hand shattered in the same incident. This is for Ozick a deeply personal loss, but she sees it in a wider context as she addresses an anonymous Palestinian spokesman:

> On our battered planet there are always, after all, two armies—the army of guns and the army of clarinets. Death flies out of one and beauty from the other. Imri is a fallen soldier in the army of clarinets, and in the end your intractable stumbling block, your deepest contest, will have to be not politics, or your Soviet arms suppliers, or land . . . or your hatred of Jews. . . . or your vow to dismantle Israel. . . .
>
> No. You will have to grapple with what you know to be your chosen enemies—rank after rank of the singing clarinets in the army of civilization. . . . Civilization is more tenacious than the death you bring. Paperbag trees, and Keats in a garden near an airport, and the long, long voice of the flute, and the singing

clarinets—these are the soldiers you will have to defeat. If you can.

More recently, in 1980, Ozick wrote a lengthy article for *The New Leader* on "Carter and the Jews" because she felt it her "personal obligation as a Jew," she said, "to stop Brzezinski." Although Carter and his adviser *were* stopped by the American voters, Ozick only shakes her head now when asked her opinion of President Reagan. "I'm very angry," she says in a muted voice. "And Weinberger is a partner of Brzezinski. He's a part of this same selling of the Jews."

Will Ozick then commit herself to more political essays? In response to this question, she quotes Chekhov: "Artists and writers should engage themselves in politics only enough to protect themselves from politics." Then, in true midrashic fashion, Ozick comments on Chekhov's comment: "The question that raises is in the crucial phrase 'only enough.' Suppose, as a Jew, the writer doesn't *choose* his engagement in politics, as Chekhov did, but is, rather, chosen by it? How much, then, for a Jew is 'only enough?' There are times when the answer can only be 100 percent."

Ozick goes on: "A man called me up, wanting me to do some political writing, and he said, 'You know if you really worked at it, you could be the Ben Hecht of our generation.' If he had only held me up to Agnon! But I felt, what is one supposed to do? I think that if one wants to make a midrashic literature, that is also good for the Jewish people. And I feel guilty about not being more activist, but at the same time, I want to dream, I want to do Jewish dreaming, and I can't always."

In her fiction, Ozick's dreams frequently center around the conflict between the pagan and the holy. Ozick titled an unpublished volume of poetry "Greeks and Jews," and in her best known story, "The Pagan Rabbi," the follower of Moses falls prey to the Greek god Pan, is ravished by a dryad, and in despair hangs himself from a tree in a public park.

In spite of its supernatural overtones, this story was inspired by a passage from the Ethics of the Fathers: "Rabbi Jacob said: 'He who is walking along and studying, but then breaks off to remark, 'How lovely is that tree!' or 'How beautiful is that fallow field!'—Scripture regards such a one as having hurt his own being."

Concerning this story, Ozick remarks that, "In Judaism, the natural life is pagan." Why? Nature worship—or the worship of any god, whether it is the god of Art or Success or Power—is idolatry and abomination.

Reading Ozick's stories, one cannot help but identify her with the young, angry Abraham, who destroyed the many idols made by his father, Terach, and banished them from the household.

Yet Ozick will often take herself and her craft as a writer more heavily to task than other idolators. In her preface to *Bloodshed and Three Novellas*, for instance, she asserts that the story "Usurpation" is "an invention directed against inventing—the point being that the story-making faculty itself can be a corridor to the corruptions and abominations of idol-worship, of the adoration of magical events."

If that is the case, then how can Cynthia Ozick—or anyone for that matter—be a "Jewish writer"?

"It really is a great confusion," she admits. "On the one hand, it's a contradiction, an oxymoron, to say 'Jewish writer' because the writer deals in images, and when you invent or create a little universe of your own, you put yourself in the place of God. You're in competition with the Creator—a parallel, a rival creator."

And it is true, one remembers, that in "The Sewing Harems," Ozick does create a new planet, which she dubs Acirema. In another story, "A Mercenary," she takes it upon herself to invent an imaginary black African nation and endow it with a language, religion, mythology, and poetic literature of its own. In her role as Abraham, the destroyer of idols, would Ozick deny us these parallel worlds in fiction?

She shakes her head. "But then there's another sense." she goes on, "in which you want to create a midrash—and that would be an extension in art of the liturgical impulse. So these are two separate and opposite points of view, and I hold them both! Once I was passionately in the oxymoron position, thinking that writing was truly the most reckless idolatry. Now I'm beginning to think perhaps not, but I don't know how long I'll stay. You know," she sighs, "given my age, I really ought to have arrived at some opinion, some subtle certainty, but I haven't."

Ozick fancies that the first Jewish fiction writer was the author of the sixteenth-century *Tz'enah u-Re'enah*. The title, taken from the Song of Songs, means "Go forth and see, ye daughters of Jerusalem."

"The book is essentially Scripture, retold with commentary and homily for women," Ozick explains. "My Bubba used to read it to me when I was little, and it was like having fairy tales read to me. It was just pure story! And so my theory is that the author wrote for women because that was the only way that the first Jewish novelist could get to express imagination. He couldn't write for men because they were bound to the text itself. But the women were not, and so under the pretext of offering help towards piety, he found a way to make things up and still be Jewish and pious."

Ozick herself is observant of ritual, celebrating the Sabbath and the Jewish holidays, and keeping the dietary laws. She and her husband of thirty years, Bernard Hallote, a lawyer, belong to an Orthodox congregation near their home in New Rochelle, New York, and their teen-aged daughter Rachel goes to an Orthodox day school. Nevertheless, Ozick says, "I cannot offer myself as an Orthodox Jew."

"You see," she explains, "I don't even like the phrase 'Orthodox.' I think they should just dump it. It's a Christian word—'Or-tho-dox,'" she enunciates emphatically, "meaning right belief. And how are those words—right belief—Jewish? They just aren't."

Further, Ozick says, "the thing that really enrages me" is that the boys in her daughter's class—because they are boys—are called to the Torah to read, while the girls—because they are *not* boys—have to "sit there like a bump on the log."

Ozick thinks that women rabbis are "fine," and regards the *mehitza*, or partition, used to hide the women from the men's view during services, as "shaming in the most literal way."

"It's shaming to Jewish men because all of Judaism is based on restraint and saying no," she says. "You don't eat meat with milk, no matter how much you may want to—you're so trained that you don't even *want* to, so it's not even restraint. But the rationale for the *mehitza* is that the males have this sexual passion which is uncontrollable at all time. I mean, you control yourself from handling money on Shabbos, and you control yourself from eating on Yom Kippur. In fact, *all* of Jewish life is self-control. So why must you fence in the objects of your uncontrollable lust?

"Then the *mehitza* also assumes that women are not sexual creatures," she goes on, "and of course they are. But what if men *were* the ones who had the uncontrollable passion and the women none? Well, you put sick people in the hospital and crazy people in the mental institution. So obviously it's the *men* who should be warehoused and fenced in, since the problem is self-admittedly with them."

A feminist since the day the rabbi sent her home from *cheder* because she was a girl, Ozick nevertheless finds some of the current directions in feminism "appalling."

"Classical feminism wanted access to the great world for women," she asserts, not the self-imposed segregation that some feminists today have favored. "And classical feminism wanted to knock out phrases like 'woman writer,' " she continues heatedly, "a label which I desperately despise. That's a loathsome phrase."

For the word "woman," she points out correctly, is not an adjective, but a noun. Further, gratuitous allusions to a writer's sex only feed into stereotypes of what a "woman" writer, as opposed to a "man" writer can produce, and also assumes that the sex of the writer determines the content and quality of the work more than the writer's mind itself.

As a *writer*, Ozick is concerned with language. And as a Jewish writer (this phrase, she says, does not describe a category, but rather a profundity), Ozick is concerned with the translation of Jewish ideas into English, a language which she believes is a Christian language. "There is no way to hear the oceanic amplitudes of the Jewish Idea in any English word or phrase," she wrote in her preface to *Bloodshed and Three Novellas*. In fact, "Judaism itself is a Christian term," she wrote, "descriptive of something meanly sectarian and inferior: one 'ism' out of many."

But paradoxically, English has also become for most Jews the "new Yiddish," Ozick believes.

"I think sixty percent of all Jews alive now speak English as their first language," she says, "and in that respect English is now our *mamaloshen* — it's our mother tongue." But the difference between the "new Yiddish" and the "old Yiddish" is that the new Yiddish is not an in-group language. "Now we have listeners," she says, "and everybody can understand us.

"And although we address ourselves inwardly," she continues, "by virtue of the language, we also address ourselves outwardly. We have ears that are not Jewish listening, and I think that we inevitably, consciously, address ourselves to those ears, too. And that's not because we are looking to please them, but because we are assimilated. Because insofar as we use the language of their culture, we also belong to it."

We belong to the English-speaking, Western culture, Ozick says. But nevertheless, "it bothers me very, very much that I know everything about Whitsuntide and Michaelmas and Epiphany, and nobody knows anything about Rosh Hashana."

As an example of this lack of understanding she tells the following story: "I remember one Rosh Hashana, sitting in the sun parlor window of my parents' house. It was a warm afternoon, the window was open, and a very kindly neighbor of ours passed by, and with all perfect good will she raised an imaginary glass and said, 'Hic! Happy New Year!' And though this may not be the best example, this stands for me as an American symbol of the total lack of comprehension of what the main sensibility of Jewish intellectual, ceremonial life is. Who would misunderstand Good Friday, or Easter, or Christmas? Who?"

Who would misunderstand Cynthia Ozick? She is an artist for whom ideas are passions, and those passions are her life. She translates those passions into stories full of drama, verve, and wit, but her hunger for knowledge will not imprison her in a scholar's cloistered study. For Cynthia Ozick also knows that the artist who worships art alone is merely pagan. In choosing the God of Moses, she chooses life. And for the true artist, like Cynthia Ozick, that final choice gives life to art itself.

Rabbi Hailu Moshe Paris

Marcia R. Rudin and A. James Rudin

In the faded photograph a three-year-old black child clings to the hand of an elegantly dressed man. They are posed at the door of a hut in a compound surrounded by a high, spiked wooden fence.

The child is Hailu Moses ben Abraham, an Ethiopian Falasha, and he is standing with his cousin in front of his home for the last time, waiting to be taken to a new home and new parents in faraway America. It is 1936. Ethiopia has been overrun by the Italian Fascists, who have killed his parents.

Hailu Moshe Paris—he took the last name of his adoptive family in the United States—always carries this photograph in his wallet, along with another, of a handsome Falasha priest, a religious leader of the community, wearing a traditional turban. He also carries a card which states: "Rabbi Hailu Moshe Paris is a member of the American Association of Hebrew Professors," a professional organization of Hebrew teachers.

These three items tell the story of the boy's life—born into the Falasha tribe, which practices an ancient, pre-Talmudic form of Orthodox Judaism, he continued to observe his Judaism as a black man in America, and yet has retained deep emotional ties to his native land.

Eudora Paris, Hailu's eighty-six-year-old American mother converted to Judaism in the 1920s under the influence of Arnold J. Ford, a dynamic, black, self-styled rabbi who preached a black nationalistic form of

Judaism to his followers, most of whom were West Indians. From the age
of eleven, Hailu went with Mrs. Paris to services at the Commandment
Keepers Congregation of the Living God in Harlem, founded and led by
Ford's disciple, Rabbi Wentworth A. Matthew.

It was Rabbi Matthew who helped Paris to discover and maintain his
identity as a black Jew and prepared him for his bar mitzvah. Matthew
also later ordained him as a rabbi. In the 1950s Hailu and his mother
attended B'nai Israel, a synagogue at Lenox Avenue and 120th Street,
one of many small black Jewish groups that spun off from Matthew's
congregation.

Paris attended De Witt Clinton High School in the Bronx and went
on to the City College of New York, but soon dropped out. A few years
later, though, he received a Mizrachi scholarship to study in Israel, where
he spent two years at Yeshiva Daroma in Rehovot, concentrating on
Hebrew literature. On his return to the United States he was admitted to
Yeshiva University, where he completed his bachelor's degree in 1968
and worked toward a master's degree in Jewish education, which he was
granted four years later. All this time he was working as a supervising
counselor in the city's Spofford Detention Center.

From 1972 to 1975 he taught American history, Jewish studies and
black studies at prestigious, private Horace Mann High School in
Manhattan. Supporting his ailing and now nearly blind mother, Paris
currently works in a CETA-funded city program as an administrative
consultant in the New York City Sanitation Department.

All the same, at night and on weekends, Hailu Moshe Paris has for
years pursued what he considers his real career as a rabbi, even though he
has never been able to earn his living from it. He started his rabbinical
life in 1958, after his return from Israel, heading the Harlem congregation
where he and his mother had worshipped. In 1964, while he was
attending Yeshiva University, he went to the Orthodox Mount Horeb
Congregation in the South Bronx, serving as assistant to West Indian-
born Rabbi Albert J. Moses. He took over when Rabbi Moses died in
1971. Three years ago, after the area had become infested with drug
peddling and crime, Mount Horeb moved to a small building formerly
occupied by a branch of Young Israel, in Laurelton in the borough of
Queens.

The Mount Horeb Congregation of about fifty black Jewish families is
Orthodox. Men and women sit separately during the services, the men
on the main floor, the women in a balcony at the rear. Their ritual,

liturgy and music are based on the Sephardic tradition; they use the Sephardic prayerbook edited by the late Rabbi David de Sola Pool. Following Sephardic custom, the congregation faces the Holy Ark in an easterly direction while Beni Israel, the cantor, chants the service in his clear, powerful voice. Israel, a tall, handsome man who always wears a white turban, earns his living as an insurance salesman and was the cantor in a black congregation at 110th St. and Broadway for twenty years before coming to Mount Horeb.

The group has no religious school since many of the children attend the Brandeis Day School, a Queens yeshiva, during the week. But the synagogue maintains a heavy schedule of religious and social events, with special emphasis on celebration of the Jewish holidays. One of its major activities is its constant campaign for admittance of Falashas into Israel from Ethiopia, where the tribe is currently caught in the crossfire in a civil war and has always been under strong pressures from Ethiopian Christians to convert to Christianity. Along with the traditional Jewish hymns "Adon Alom" and "Ayn Kaylohaynu" sung by other Jewish congregations, the black Jews of Mount Horeb Synagogue sing:

> Twenty-one cents each working day
> Is all Falashas earn for pay.
> Extricate them from this hell,
> Transport them to Is-ra-el.
>
> Twenty-eight thousand souls who yearn
> To exercise Law of Return
> Help them live in dignity,
> Help them become Is-ra-el-i.

Rabbi Paris, a tall, solidly built, gregarious man in his middle forties, with horn-rimmed glasses and an ever-present yarmulke, speaks almost incessantly in the clipped West Indian cadence of his foster family. His lively mind moves so quickly that he talks in a kind of perpetual rush to keep up with his thoughts; a listener has the feeling that he's being left far behind. Yet after a short time one senses that beneath the exuberant surface there is a deep sadness within this man, reflecting his tensions and frustrations.

He is a bachelor. Has being both black and Jewish anything to do with this? He laughs, says his search for a mate has been difficult. "The wrong person could take you away from your Judaism."

There are tensions in being black and Jewish, he says, but "They are social tensions rather than internal. I am, after all, fighting both the Christian society and the white society. I felt less conflict between blackness and Jewishness in Ethiopia than in America, because Ethiopia is a Semitic society and of course everyone looks like me. Everyone there is black. And in Israel there is less prejudice because there are many dark-skinned Jews from Yemen, North Africa and Asia. But in America if you're black you have to work ten times harder at being a Jew."

What about Paris' relationship with the non-Jewish black community? "I'm not that well known in the general black community," he explains. "I don't have that much contact with the grass roots blacks. When I came to the United States as a refugee I was a symbol of the Ethiopian war. Most of my contact was with people like those who ran the *Amsterdam News*, the black newspaper. They were the ones who were concerned with the war, who supported the Ethiopians. Later I was known mostly as a contact with the Ethiopians and the Falashas. I seldom worked in the total black milieu."

Paris admits that occasionally he meets blacks who express curiosity about him. "But," he says, "on the whole nobody makes a big thing of it. At my job, they know I'm taking off the Rosh Hashanah and Yom Kippur holidays, and that's it. The only time I am regarded as special is when I am in a directly ecumenical situation, when I am functioning specifically as a Jew." Looking back, he thinks that growing up in Wentworth Matthew's closed community was very supportive. "It helped. There was curiosity, but it wasn't traumatic for me. For others it might have been."

What about the black Jewish community's relationship with other blacks? All in all, Paris finds, "The numbers of black Jews are so small that there is no problem with the general black community. We might be attacked if there were an attack on Jews who are visible in yeshivot and in marginal communities. And, by the way, such hostility results from a cultural breakdown, not from the European type of anti-Semitism. But there is no special feeling about black Jews as black Jews in black neighborhoods."

Actually, Paris declares, "The black Jew's problem is not anti-Semitism, but rather how to maintain his Jewishness."

Most black American Jews are Jewish as a result of intermarriages between blacks and Jews or because they or their ancestors converted. Many such conversions—perhaps not carried out to the satisfaction of Jewish religious law—took place in urban centers in the 1920s, when some black nationalists turned toward Judaism under the inspiration of charismatic leaders such as Arnold Ford and Wentworth A. Matthew in New York, "Bishops" William Crowdy and A.Z. Plummer in Belleville, Virginia, and "Prophet" Cherry in Philadelphia.

However, some blacks claim they can trace their Jewish ties to the days of slavery, when their ancestors were either converted by or intermarried with or cohabited with Jewish masters in the American colonies or the West Indies. Other black Jews believe that their forefathers became Jewish while they were still in West Africa and brought their religion with them when they came to America as slaves. (There are many such interpretations. Some scholars believe that a significant number of African blacks were converted to Judaism by Jewish refugees, merchants, or soldiers who traveled from Israel to North Africa during ancient times. These Jewish blacks then migrated elsewhere in Africa where they became victims of slave traders. Still other historians believe many Africans were converted to Judaism by European Jewish merchants who came to Africa in the 14th and 15th centuries.) Hailu Paris' distinction is that he is one of the few black Jews in America who stem from the Ethiopian Falashas.

A decade or so ago, according to Rabbi Paris, there were about 10,000 black Jews in the United States, with the largest concentration in the New York City area. Now he cannot provide a likely estimate of the numbers. Many "have simply stopped being Jewish," he explains sadly. "They took down their mezuzahs. Those blacks who had never really absorbed the feel of Judaism were turned off. To all intents and purposes they dropped out. Even those who had gone to Jewish schools for many years dropped out. And some of their children also went to recognized yeshivot for years—so the charges that they didn't have enough education to be Jews are untrue. We have lost that generation. The entire Jewish community has paid a high price."

Contemporary New York blacks who have clung to their faith worship in Paris' congregation, in black synagogues in Cambria Heights and South Jamaica, Queens and in a few small synagogues in Harlem. Some have joined white congregations, primarily in Sephardic synagogues such as Manhattan's Spanish-Portuguese synagogue, which, according to

Paris, are more receptive than Ashkenazic institutions. Others worship at Ohel Israel, a large Yemenite congregation in Brooklyn. And Robert Coleman, a black convert to Hasidism, founded an Orthodox black synagogue and rabbinical training center in Borough Park in Brooklyn.

Why does the white Jewish community deny recognition to this group — and to men like Hailu Paris as religious leaders? Is it a matter of racism?

The official Jewish position is quite clear, religious leaders say. Rabbi Solomon B. Freehof, dean of American Reform rabbis, states: "There is no race distinction in Judaism." Rabbi Ahron Soleveitchik, a prominent Orthodox teacher, agrees: "From the standpoint of the Torah there cannot be any distinction between one human being and another on the basis of color." Rabbi J. David Bleich, a leading Orthodox authority, says: "Judaism is color blind; skin pigmentation is unknown as a halakic concept. The problem of determining the status of the various communities of black Jews is totally unrelated to color. The sole issue is that of Jewish identity. The question of recognition of black Jews as members of the Jewish community must be seen within that context; as such it is simply an instance of the much broader question: 'Who is a Jew?'"

Paris and other black Jews are very discouraged about their attempts to gain recognition: "Black Jews are just not high on the agenda of American Jewry," he points out. "They have Israel and Soviet Jews to worry about. And there is this tradition within Judaism of no mass conversions. They may be afraid that they would be opening up the doors to the goyim."

On a broader level, he declares: "Most of the New York black Jews are very negative about the Jewish community ever trying to make any alliance on whatever level, be it biblical or historical or political or cultural. There is just this block, this tremendous block. Any way you look at it, it's a negative. In the twentieth century, which has been such a devastating one, you would think the Jewish community would be more sensitive. They seem to be less rather than more so."

Recalling his people's decades-long endeavor to integrate into the white Jewish community, he relates how these efforts were intensified in the 1960s when blacks were gaining acceptance in some quarters. "I lectured a lot in many, many synagogues in the Northeast. We thought," he says mournfully, "that with integration, talk of civil rights and the rest, we could make headway in the Jewish community."

Efforts to integrate black Jews into the white Jewish community

climaxed with the establishment in 1964 of an integrated youth movement in New York City known as Hatzaad Harishon (First Step), an
attempt to break down barriers between whites and blacks. But the
organization fell apart over the issue of whether or not the blacks should
be required to convert ritually. The blacks believed they were already
authentically Jewish and therefore did not need to convert. The white
Jews, however, maintained that only a small number of blacks—perhaps
5,000—who had officially converted had the right to be considered Jews.
In 1970 the group disbanded in an atmosphere of great bitterness.

The demise of Hatzaad Harishon dealt an almost lethal blow to hope
for integration. Three years later, when Wentworth A. Matthew died,
his congregation—already deeply troubled because the white Jewish
community would not accept them as Jews and by economic and racial
pressures felt by the entire black community—disintegrated. Even Matthew's grandson, David L. Dore, who graduated from Yeshiva University in 1977, couldn't hold it together.

The passing of strong leaders such as Matthew, Paris asserts, left a wide
gap in black Jewish life. "Matthew was from the old school," he reflects.
"He had strong religious beliefs. He was structured. Nobody is that way
now. My generation has lost its religious roots. There is an emptiness."

And there is no central organization of black Jews to help fill the void.
Every attempt to organize themselves has failed. He blames the black
Jewish community itself—for using the wrong tactics, approaching the
wrong people, not producing a strong leader who could unify the group
and deal effectively with "establishment" Jews. "They don't understand
power," he reflects. "They don't know how to use it."

On an individual basis some black Jews are still trying to integrate,
largely by attending white synagogues and by trying to get blacks into
established rabbinical schools. "But," Paris explains, "nothing seems to
satisfy the white Jews. Every potential black rabbinical student who has
applied to Hebrew Union College has been rejected. Why? There was
always a reason. They weren't up to par. And when a black Jew comes to
the authorities and says 'I have been converted by Rabbi so-and-so,' they
say 'I've never heard of him.' They don't even bother to check it out. You
see, the problem is first, 'Who is a Jew?' and then, 'Who has the power to
make you a Jew?'"

Some black Jews and observers of the community argue that discrimination exists in various forms, in both the United States and abroad.

Joel Hawkins, Mount Horeb's vice president and editor of its newsletter, was halakically converted to Judaism in the early 1950s in Wichita Falls, Texas. "One day," he relates, "I went on a picnic with the Jewish congregation there. Remember, they still lynched people then. The sign at the picnic ground said 'Whites Only,' but I went in and we had a fine picnic. There I wasn't considered black because I was a Jew. When I returned to New York City I went to Shabbat services at a white synagogue and afterward the rabbi said 'I think you would be happier with the black Jews in Harlem than with us here in Queens.' Strange, but in New York I wasn't considered a Jew because I was black."

Hawkins reports that today his ten-year-old son who attends a yeshiva on Long Island is "still called 'nigger' by kids there." When there was a theft at a yeshiva, Hawkins recounts, "the only student who was searched was a black girl."

Like their rabbi, Mount Horeb members have grown weary of attempting to gain acceptance from the white Jewish community. Turning inward, they are focusing their energies almost exclusively on saving the Falashas. They have formed an independent Committee to Aid Ethiopian Jews because they distrust the white-run Pro-Falasha Committee.

Paris cites the failure of the Israel government to take more than a trickle of Falashas and the virtual silence of most of world Jewry on the Falasha issue as yet another example of racism. "The Jewish world still refuses to recognize them as Jews," he points out, "even though the Sephardic chief rabbi of Israel has officially ruled that they are Jews. How do the Israelis know that a Russian Jew is really a Jew? Because when the Russian government stamps 'Jew' on his passport, they accept that he is a Jew. But they don't accept the Ethiopian government's word that the Falasha is a Jew."

Cantor Israel echoes his rabbi's demands, declaring: "For years during the regime of Haile Selassie we were told that things were being done at the highest level, that we shouldn't rock the boat. But nothing was done. Now with a revolutionary government in Ethiopia we are told the same thing. Only a few Falashas have been brought to Israel. If the Israel government is willing to take on the Soviet Union, why not the Ethiopian government? The answer is apparent to everyone: racism!"

Paris avoids flatly accusing white Jews of racism, but admits there may be at least a "racial carryover" from the American society.

"The problem is, do they want an ordained rabbi who is black?" he asks. "It's not a question of me or anybody else, but do they want a black rabbi? It seems to be a big problem, a very big problem."

His voice fades and he muses, "Maybe in another generation. Maybe in another time, another place . . ."

Martin Peretz

Robert Leiter

The minute you step into Martin Peretz's sleek, modern office at *The New Republic*, you see it—the cover of the August 2, 1982 edition of the magazine framed in clear plastic.

On it, in bold white letters against a maroon background, are the words that began an immediate and wide-ranging controversy throughout the country: "Much of what you have read in the newspapers and news magazines about the war in Lebanon—and even more of what you have seen and heard on television—is simply not true."

It is fitting that some part of "Eyewitness Lebanon" occupy a place of prominence in Martin Peretz's office. The controversy continues to rage over many of the article's major accusations: that news reporting from Lebanon was biased; that TV cameramen were after only the "hot" images—bombed-out buildings and rubble-filled streets; that we were allowed to see the smoke of Israeli bombs but not their targets; that the casualty figures were wildly exaggerated.

Not surprisingly, "Eyewitness Lebanon" was praised by Zionists and fiercely criticized by Peretz's fellow journalists at *Newsweek* and the *Washington* and *Columbia Journalism Reviews*, to say nothing of the left-wing press.

Whether the article changed any minds or settled any scores is now irrelevant. "Eyewitness Lebanon" is important because it is an expression of what Martin Peretz has been striving to achieve since the late 1960s—

and what he hopes to accomplish in the pages of *The New Republic* every week: truth in journalism.

To understand this, one must know something of Peretz's political history. Born in New York City on July 30, 1939, he did his undergraduate work at Brandeis University, where he made a reputation for himself as a brilliant and outspoken student. From there Peretz went on to Harvard, earning both an M.A. (1965) and a Ph.D. (1966).

At that time, Peretz and his wife, Anne Farnsworth (a Singer heiress), both of whom had been active in the civil rights movement, began contributing substantial sums of money to such New Left organizations as Students for a Democratic Society and *Ramparts* magazine.

But Peretz's disillusionment came earlier than most in the counterculture. In 1968, he took sharp exception to an article in *Ramparts*, after the magazine, like many other journals of the left, had grown increasingly critical of Israel following the country's victory in the 1967 Six Day War.

Peretz broke with *Ramparts*—and discussed the issue at length in an article he wrote for *Commentary*, where he characterized Warren Hinckle III, the *Ramparts* editor, as having "an intuitive feel for what he (Hinckle) calls the 'flippy.' Now flippiness has its merits," Peretz continued, "particularly if one is intent on stirring up cauldrons. But it also entails a sacrifice of intellectual rigor."

Peretz described the *Ramparts* article as "the most carefully selective and skewed history of the [Arab-Israeli] conflict to come from any source save possibly the propaganda machines of the respective parties." Though the *Ramparts* piece occasionally mentioned "Nasser's calculating politics," it ended by placing the onus upon Israel for everything that was wrong in the Middle East.

By these standards, Peretz wrote, "Israel and Israel alone must bear the responsibility for the future." In his final paragraph, Peretz described the course of action he planned to follow. He wrote: "The attitude of so many on the left toward Israel and the Arab world has brought a welcome end of innocence to many other American radicals who will from now on be somewhat more skeptical of all nostrums of the *engagés* which have been so readily and thoughtlessly accepted—as the desperation bred by the [Vietnam] war and the riots in our cities intensifies. It remains to be seen whether out of the intellectual and moral debacle of these past months, a sensible movement with sensible perspectives for peace and human rights can at last emerge."

Sixteen years after these words were written, Martin Peretz, who, with his shaggy beard and intense manner resembles more a stern rabbi than the editor-in-chief of one of America's most prestigious journals of opinion, could discuss his break with the New Left—what he likes to call the first in "a history of breaks"—with dispassion.

"I realized quite fully in 1967—though I had sensed it much earlier—that in the American left there were strands of anti-Semitism, not least among Jews. And not least among Jews who held what they believed were universalist ethics. These Jews were uncomfortable with Jewish particularism, and with Jewish economic and professional success. These types are not, unfortunately, new to us. But I also came face to face, for the first time, with black anti-Semitism.

"The Italian novelist Ignazio Silone wrote an essay entitled 'The Choice of Comrades.' The title of the piece refers to what Silone considered the single most important decision an individual makes as a member of a community. In 1967, I looked around at my comrades and said, 'They are not mine. We do not share a moral unity.' Of the two collectives of which I am a part, my comrades were antagonistic toward both. They did not feel the patriotism that I, as a child of immigrant Jews, felt then and now about America. And they were also contemptuous of the Jewish collective.

"After the break, I went into a kind of decompression chamber for about a decade, and it was sometimes very painful for me. Now when I look upon the individuals with whom I was associated and consider some of the things that I believed in with such fervor, I'm not certain whether I did more harm than good. To have thought of myself as a comrade of Stokely Carmichael's was something that, for a long time, made me wake in the night in a cold sweat."

Peretz was also angered by much of the media reaction to his break with the left. "The public likes everything explained to them in cliches," he comments. "And so, newspaper and magazine articles began saying that Marty Peretz broke with the left because the left passed a resolution against Israel. But, you see, I can live with resolutions against Israel. What I witnessed in the late '60s was a much deeper and much uglier process, and I suppose that if I'd been wiser and had known more about history—if by that time I had really integrated the long Jewish view of history into my life—I might not have made such mistakes. But I hadn't, and so I did."

Today, Peretz is certain of the place that Judaism plays in his life. "I feel very comfortable about being Jewish," he tells me. "It's part of my way in the world, in the same sense that I feel comfortable about reading books. I'm not trying to set up a false parallel here—but I know that there isn't a day when I don't pick up a book. And there isn't a day when I'm not touched by something, or attracted by something, or want to affect someone else, by a Jewish experience or sensation or thought. It's part of my way of living."

He illustrates his point with an anecdote about a young man who attended the seminar Peretz teaches at Harvard.

"He asked me out to lunch, and I accepted. Not that we had ever been close, but when a student asks you to lunch, you go. In the course of the meal, this tall, blond athlete tells me that his grandfather had two fortunes, two treasures. He had made a lot of money—'and my father squandered that fortune,' my student explained. 'But I'm going to be a psychiatrist and have no financial worries. However, my grandfather was also a learned Jew—and my father squandered that fortune too, *that* treasure. So, you see, I am ignorant. Can I retrieve this second fortune? Is it possible for someone to live in a secular world and still identify as a Jew? I've come to you because I feel that you do live this way.'

"Well, you know, that discussion was one of the most touching experiences of my life because the whole thing came from someone I didn't know very well. I didn't even know he was Jewish! And so I felt sort of high for weeks afterwards because here was a kid who said, 'Hey, it works for someone.'

"You see, some people in this world are nervous Jews, and they carry that around; and some American journalists are nervous Jews, and they carry that around. But I'm not a nervous Jew, and I carry *that* around.

"I would like to have a world in which I didn't feel so driven to write about the Jews. But that would be a world in which the perils to the remnants of our people would be less."

His awareness of these dangers compelled Peretz to write "Eyewitness Lebanon." Now, more than a year after the article's appearance, he remains assured—despite the extensive criticism—of the accuracy of his reporting. "In answer to any of my accusations, no one came out and said, 'That's just not so,' " he declares.

Peretz's critics liked to paint him as an apologist for the Begin government; most of them failed to recall that, prior to Lebanon, *The New Republic* had been harshly critical of the prime minister. And, though Peretz found the invasion of Lebanon justified, he still opposes many Likud government policies.

"We at the magazine would like to see Labor people back in power in Israel," Peretz makes clear. "But, as you may have realized, *The New Republic* hasn't published much about Israel since Lebanon. And that's because I'm not certain it's part of the magazine's role to do so. I'm more interested in what's happening *to* Israel at the hands of the world media than I am about what's happening *in* Israel. I would like the public to know that many members of the American press rarely look at anyone's history, that individuals come before them full-blown and fresh.

"But there's another factor at work here. Certain powerful journals and institutions in our country—I'm thinking particularly of *Time* magazine and the liberal Christian churches—have never thought a hell of a lot of the Zionist enterprise from the start. Why *The New York Times Magazine* feels compelled to publish the same type of article about Israel every three months or so is beyond me. The articles are always about the death of ideals.

"However, I imagine that *if* oil really becomes more plentiful and the scarcity issue erodes; and *if* the Arab oil producers begin to have budget deficits rather than surpluses, as Saudi Arabia is now going to have; and *if* the people who have been inclined to be friendly to the Arabs actually see that in their desperation the Arabs cannot get their act together, then the Palestinian question may not become as boring as the Kurds but it will no longer absorb peoples' minds to the extent it does now. It's clear to me that in Washington the concentration on the Middle East—the pandering to and for the Arabs—has lessened. And it's not simply much less than during the Lebanon war, it's also much less than during the previous two years.

"What must be kept in mind about Israel is that the country is now going through a very painful transition period. Part of what is going on is simply the normalization, or routinization, that comes with any revolution. Zionism now works, and one goal of Zionism has been accomplished—that is, the partial normalization of the Jewish people. Because of this normalization, there are now all sorts of political and social pathologies at work in Israel.

"Someone said to me the other day, *'Begin hat mazel'* [Begin has luck]. And he does. Whether the Jewish people have luck—well, that's another matter. Is it lucky for Israel that there will be seven little bivouac camps around Nablus? I don't think so.

"If the Arabs had wanted peace in 1967, none of this would have happened. If they'd wanted peace between 1967 and 1977, very little of this would have happened. During those years there were only a few settlements. And if the Arabs had come forward at Camp David, a lot of this wouldn't have happened. Now it's happening. Israel is not obliged to wait forever. Whether what is happening now is good for Israel—I think that's a whole other matter."

Few magazines in this country, other than strictly Jewish publications, take the kind of interest in Israel that *The New Republic* does. And it does so by design.

Several years after his break with *Ramparts*, while searching for a new forum for his evolving political philosophy, Peretz told Gilbert Harrison, then owner and editor of *The New Republic*, that if the occasion arose he would be interested in buying the magazine.

Peretz purchased *The New Republic* in March 1974, at a price of $380,000. And, according to an article in *Newsweek*, a contractual clause was worked out prior to the sale, allowing Harrison to remain as editor until 1977, "with final control over hiring, firing and manuscripts."

That arrangement was destined to fail. As one staff writer put it, "How could it last? The new guy wanted to exert his influence and the old guy wanted to keep his autonomy." Differences could not be worked out. "Two people running a magazine doesn't work," Peretz admitted at the time. "There was little for me to do." And, considering Peretz's interests and energy, such idleness must have been comparable to his living in exile.

Others have said that the Peretz-Harrison rift came about after Harrison heavily edited a long piece Peretz wrote about the United Nations. The article eventually appeared in the magazine as three paragraphs without a byline.

But, whatever the reason, it is also clear that Peretz wished to mold *The New Republic* in his image. What had basically been a one-man operation would be run on a more "collegial" basis. Then, as now, Peretz distrusted the world of professional Washington journalism and planned to look to the universities for new writers and ideas.

In Peretz's opinion, his magazine is now the voice of the liberal center. It regularly publishes articles critical of *all* shades of political thinking. He explains: "We at *The New Republic* believe not only that a hard-line foreign policy and a generous domestic policy are imperatives, but that they are prerequisites, one to the other."

"Reagan is unable to pursue a foreign policy," Peretz continues, "because he has destroyed the sense—or, more to the point, hasn't reestablished a sense—of a national community. He's too tied to avaricious interests. And people really feel a kind of existential alienation from whatever public purpose he establishes.

"Despite what the Reaganites think, you cannot have a strong and forward-moving foreign policy if you don't have a community of common interest to support it. You cannot have a strong society at home, feeling confident in itself and in its ability to expand and enrich its people, when a country as big and as powerful as ours feels itself becoming increasingly helpless abroad.

"It goes without saying that we are part of the opposition to the Reagan administration—but we're also part of the critical opposition to the Democrats. That's the corner of the political landscape we've carved out for ourselves."

Peretz also believes there is far too much sentimentality among left-wingers about their pasts. "We at the magazine would like to fight the legacy that considers any liberation movement as in and of itself good. And that's because we know from history that too much innocent blood has been spilled for such causes. We have placed ourselves in an adversary position vis-à-vis the left and the right—but also to Israel and Zionism, because those who love Zion must by necessity take a critical stance toward it."

Considering the importance of *The New Republic* in Peretz's life, it is surprising to learn that, on the average, he spends only one day a week at the magazine's offices.

(This is not to imply that Peretz does nothing else. In addition to lecturing at Harvard once a week, he is director of the Dreyfus Fund, chairman of the board of directors of the Jerusalem Fund, a trustee of Brandeis University and a member of the board of governors of the Hebrew University of Jerusalem. He is also an entrepreneur with holdings that, in addition to his magazine, include a television station.)

On his *New Republic* days, Peretz flies to Washington from his home in Cambridge, Massachusetts, arriving at the magazine offices by 9:30 in the morning. The wide windows in his office overlook busy 19th Street and give the modest-sized room an airy feeling. The walls are covered with framed photos of his wife and children at various ages, in addition to etchings of Golda Meir and Theodor Herzl and a satiric drawing by George Grosz. As might be expected, books are everywhere. They are crammed into the bookcase and spill over on endtables and chairs; they fight for space with the magazines, newspapers and letters crowding Peretz's long oak desk.

The morning hours are hurried and filled with the sounds of voices calling to Peretz from offices down the hall or coming through the intercom system. The phone is rarely silent. And at any moment, any one of Peretz's staff—Hendrik Hertzberg, Dorothy Wickenden, Morton Kondracke, Jack Beatty, Leon Wieseltier or Ann Hulbert—may appear at his door, which is never closed. And Peretz makes requests of his secretary every thirty seconds or so.

"I have a rough draft for a 'Diarist' that I want you to type," he informs her. She retrieves a mass of yellow, legal-size sheets of paper covered with a nearly illegible scrawl.

A staff member appears at the door with a drawing that will appear on the cover of the next magazine. Peretz shrugs, not particularly impressed.

Then, to his secretary: "Find out the name of Sy Hersh's last book for me." And, after a moment: "And check on the circulation of *U.S. News and World Report.*"

He reads over the galleys of his reply to the *Columbia Journalism Review* about "Eyewitness Lebanon" and is angered about several excisions that were made.

From there he moves on to *The Washington Post*, which he thumbs through quickly, paying careful attention only to the world news reports and the editorial page.

A phone call comes, and there is talk of oil and stocks. "Are you buying or selling anything interesting?" Peretz asks.

Another call comes from author Nick Eberstadt. "I like your 'Diarist,'" Peretz tells him. "It might be a little short. We'll set it in type and then we'll see."

Using his intercom, Peretz calls each office on the floor, trying to locate the two remaining volumes of a three-volume *History of the International Working Class Movement*, which have been sent to the magazine for review. No one has seen the books.

In one corner of Peretz's desk sits a large ceramic bowl that fairly overflows with newspaper clippings. Peretz takes out one clipping at a time and reads down the columns rapidly, as if scanning ticker tape announcing the latest stock results.

Then, returning to the intercom, he reads a news item to senior editor

Leon Wieseltier, in which Peretz has been described as "polite." They both laugh, agreeing that this must constitute a first.

Peretz calls in his secretary. He tells her he will be leaving that afternoon for New York City to deliver a speech and that on Friday he will be teaching at Harvard. He plans to spend the following week with his wife in Palm Beach.

Then Peretz dictates two letters. The first, to the Philip Morris Company, is about their advertising in *The New Republic*. The second, to Saul Bellow, concerns the Committee for the Free World, whose newsletter attacked Leon Wieseltier's long *New Republic* essay on deterrence. There have also been attacks in the neo-conservative publication on *New Republic* contributing editor Michael Walzer's egalitarian views. Peretz is writing to say that such criticism of veteran anti-totalitarians such as Walzer smacks of an ugly sectarianism.

Peretz goes to Ann Hulbert's office, where he discusses the next cover and techniques to enliven it. Everyone agrees that using a celebrated name on the cover—like John Updike's (he has written a piece on the Fairfield Porter exhibition at Boston's Museum of Fine Arts)—will help. There is also talk of using color reproductions with the Updike article to enhance its effect.

Then it is noontime. Peretz has scheduled what is known as a "*New Republic* lunch"; today a young man from the National Security Council has come to discuss government policy in the Middle East. Lunch, served in the conference room, is an informal affair: cold cuts, rye bread and rolls, sodas, dessert and coffee.

The discussion, amid much eating, is free-wheeling and lively. Leon Wieseltier argues that the Reagan administration is playing into the hands of the wrong Arabs. "The screws should be placed on Hussein," he insists. All the staff members agree that pressure is being placed on the Israelis, not on the Arabs. "Why," Wieseltier asks, "should the victors act like the vanquished?"

Charles Krauthammer, another senior editor, takes exception to the views of those in Reagan's cabinet who insist that the West Bank must go to Hussein, when the United States can't even produce him at the peace table. "You can't produce *any* Arabs," he asserts. "You would instill more confidence in the Israelis if you showed them that pressure was being placed on other game players." Krauthammer contends that the enormous public pressure directed toward Israel will, in the end, achieve the opposite of what Reagan wants.

After lunch, and an amicable parting with the Security Council representative, the staff members remain in the conference room for the weekly editorial meeting. Peretz sits at the head of the table, leading the discussion.

A future cover story on the Roman Catholic Church and social issues is considered. "We'd like to show that on social issues the Church is as retrograde as ever," Hendrik Hertzberg, the editor, states. "On political and economic issues, it's a bit more advanced. But the piece would attempt to show that, theologically, the Roman Catholic Church is divided within itself."

"Let's plan on having a sidebar about the Protestant churches," Peretz suggests.

Hertzberg makes a note.

One of the magazine's young interns discusses doing a piece on Washington's homeless. "I'd like to find out who takes care of these people. I'd like to look at the whole question of volunteerism. Are the suburban matrons doing their share?"

"But figure out what the facts are before you decide what you want to say," Peretz cautions him.

There is a discussion about "the back of the book." Literary editor Jack Beatty lists an impressive number of upcoming reviews. Besides Updike, he has scheduled Henry Fairlie on social critic Randolph Bourne, Leo Bersani on Baudelaire, Samuel Haynes on a Robert Graves biography and Patricia Meyer Spacks on women in literature.

Peretz then moves on to long-range ideas. He suggests an article about America's new billionaires. The angle would be that the word "billionaire" doesn't suffice to describe this kind of wealth. "We would be talking about people who are worth a couple of hundred billion dollars. The piece could show how the old rich made their money through speculation—in oil or real estate. These people were politically conservative and politically well mobilized.

"Today we have what you might call the 'High Tech Rich.' These tycoons have a certain counterculture thrust to their lives. The article would also investigate the different ways there are for getting rich today. Is it related to the hyper-inflation? However, for the piece to succeed, it would have to be done by a really sharp financial writer."

Someone else suggests that there might be a story in the decline in the quality of science and math teaching.

"As far as I'm concerned," Peretz says, "it's always time to do an education issue. Let's think about it."

Other ideas are aired: What about a piece on financier Felix Rohatyn? Or one about single-parent families?

Peretz says that he would like a lead article about the Reagan budget cuts. Jack Beatty suggests that there might also be an accompanying "note" discussing New York Governor Cuomo's budget cuts. The emphasis would be on humane cutbacks. "Cuomo is taking from Westchester to give to the Bronx," Beatty says, "which isn't in any way politically expedient."

Peretz feels that Beatty should use Cuomo's state budget to talk about the Reagan budget. "But if you find that no one here can do it," Peretz adds, "I'd even be willing to go outside the magazine and get someone else."

From the conference room Peretz goes to his office, stopping at his secretary's desk to check about messages. Then he tells her he is leaving, as scheduled, to catch a plane for New York.

He begins to stuff books and papers into his briefcase. Leon Wieseltier appears at the door, holding a copy of Peretz's letter to Saul Bellow.

"In your letter to Saul," Wieseltier says, "I don't think you should say that your thoughts are incoherent—because they're not."

The two men discuss the matter briefly, Peretz not completely convinced of Wieseltier's opinion, and he then excuses himself and dashes off to give his speech in New York.

Peretz has several reasons for lecturing at Harvard and speaking to various groups. He finds great satisfaction in teaching. "I always do a little undergraduate seminar," he says. "Last year the subject was ideology. This year I'm doing a seminar on nationalism. I enjoy doing them because students still prod the mind in ways that journalists don't. And it's also important—for me, at least—to have enough sufficient and different kinds of activity so that I don't begin to think that Washington is the center of the universe. There are people in this city who think it is the center of everything."

As for public speaking, Peretz does that because there are, he believes, truths to tell, facts that must be added to the record. (He often begins his speeches with two quotes. One is a Yiddish saying: "The truth leads a hard life." The other is from Brecht: "The telling of simple truths takes great courage.")

Peretz likes to consider himself a spokesman within the Jewish community, but a spokesman of a special sort. "There are few people with independent positions of status who involve themselves in Jewish communal life. One of the things I worry about is the intellectual and moral caliber of Jewish leaders. You're a leader in this community only if you're a businessman or a rabbi.

"This was not always the case. The prime example is Louis Brandeis, who was a Boston lawyer and a leading Zionist. He was a truly titanic figure. But we really don't have such leaders anymore.

"That is why I speak as often as I can. I like to think of myself as an independent spirit who doesn't find organized Jewish life debilitating. And I feel compelled to tell my part of the truth as often and as clearly as I can."

Gabriel Preil

Jeremy Simcha Garber

On Walton Avenue, down the street from the Bronx County Courthouse and three blocks from Yankee Stadium, lives Gabriel Preil, a Hebrew poet who has been included in every major anthology of Jewish poetry of the last twenty years, including the recent *Voices Within the Ark*. The Jewish Publication Society is now including a bilingual volume of his poetry in their series, Twentieth Century Jewish Poets.

The small synagogue next to his apartment has gone the way of most of the neighborhood and is now a Pentecostal church. Preil, however, still warms himself by the embers of Jewish life in the area. He greets me at his apartment dressed in a suit and tie, and as we leave he puts a hat on his balding head. We pass by a park dominated by clusters of drug dealers and he points out the statue of Lorelei, now a double amputee, who was a creation of another Jewish poet, Heine. We dine at the kosher Courthouse Deli, turkey sandwich on rye for him and hot pastrami on rye for me. After lunch, we head down the street to the G & R Bakery where he chats with the owner in Hebrew while buying a challah. Our walk ends at the Nedicks at the foot of 161st Street, a plastic reincarnation of the Jerome Avenue Cafeteria which stood on that site for many decades. After ordering a Sanka and a coffee, we look for a table where we won't attract the attention of the frog-voiced, belligerent old Jewish

263

woman or the garrulous black alcoholic, formerly a *shammes*, whom we had encountered on previous visits.

J.G. "How long have you lived here?"

G.P. "Only about eleven years. I am very sensitive to external stimuli; the heat, the cold, natural beauty. Why don't I move from here you might ask? Perhaps the only force stronger in me than sensitivity is sloth."

J.G. "Where are you from originally and how did you happen to become a Hebrew poet?"

G.P. "I was born in 1911 in Dorpat, Estonia. My family was from Lithuania, but my mother had gone to Dorpat a few months before my birth because of the excellent medical facilities at the university there. We soon moved back to Lithuania, near Kovno, and when I was old enough I started going to Tarbut schools and Hebrew secular schools in Maryampol and Virbalis. I was different from many of my contemporaries because I never went to *heder*. And in answer to your second question, I grew up with Hebrew. We spoke Yiddish at home, but I began writing Hebrew at a very early age. I did publish a volume of my Yiddish poetry in 1966, but these were mainly translations and reworkings of my Hebrew poems.

"My father was a druggist and not long after he died my mother and I came to America. I was twelve. My father was self-taught and I became one as well. I dropped out of the Rabbi Isaac Elchanan Teachers' Seminary, the forerunner of Yeshiva University, before I received my high school diploma. I lived in Williamsburg in Brooklyn then and continued to live there for forty-four years until 1967."

J.G. "What stimulates you to write poetry?"

G.P. "Much of my verse has been created from things external, like landscapes. They provoke me. I often must imbibe from such sources to create from within. I would say that my poetry is generally reflective and lyrical, with a special emphasis on imagery."

J.G. "In the course of your career, have you been challenged by critics who wanted your poetry to be more socially relevant or ideological?"

G.P. "No. However, there was a time when I was not understood or appreciated in American Hebrew circles because I was too modernistic. I suppose I was the Hebrew parallel of the English language imagistic poets and in this sense I was a pioneer. In a significant way I was an influence on young Israeli poets of the late forties and early fifties like Yehuda Amichai and Natan Zach. They began to accept me as one of their own.

Even the middle generation of poets like Leah Goldberg and Abraham Shlonsky, and the older generation including Ya'akov Fichman, Ya'akov Cahan and Yitzhak Lamdan either wrote positively about me or at least printed my poems in their journals. Interestingly enough, my first poem in any language appeared in Yiddish in the late 1930s in the *New Yorker Wochenblatt*, a weekly. Afterwards I was published in *Inzich*, the magazine of the Yiddish avant-garde, edited by Glatstein, Leyeles, and Minkov."

J.G. "Was Yiddish more open than Hebrew to avant-garde influences?"

G.P. "During the period of the twenties and thirties, yes, especially in the United States. Neither literature was very daring until *Inzich* came along. I was influenced by their manifesto, which was similar in a way to the credo of the imagists Amy Lowell and Ezra Pound. It declared that the subject of the poem doesn't matter. What *is* important is bringing out ideas and emotions through unsentimental imagery. In retrospect, I would say that for me it was hard to toe the line and remain completely detached."

J.G. "And what was your connection with the Hebrew cultural circles of New York?"

G.P. "I was involved with the Histadrut HaNoar HaIvri (The Hebrew Youth Organization) which existed in the late 1930s and '40s, and which was revived for a short time in the fifties. We published a little magazine called *Niv* (Expression) as well as sponsoring literary, dance and dramatic activities. We were related to the Histadrut HaIvrit Be'America (The Hebrew Organization of America) which publishes *HaDoar (The Post)*, the weekly Hebrew journal."

J.G. "What is it like to be a Hebrew poet writing in America?"

G.P. "It's a strange situation. I am now, with the exception of Eisig Silberschlag, the 'Last Mohican' of Hebrew poetry in America. If not for my literary contacts with Israel, I would have been lost here. I don't mean to slight *HaDoar*, edited by Yitzhak Ivri, or *Bitzaron*, edited by Haim Leaf, both published in New York, but I lead my tangible literary life in Israel."

J.G. "Cynthia Ozick, the American Jewish writer, wrote a story, 'Envy,' about the jealousy and resentment of some Yiddish writers toward a colleague of theirs who penetrated the huge English reading audience with great success. How do you feel about the recognition given to I.B. Singer, Elie Wiesel, Saul Bellow and other widely read Jewish writers?"

G.P. "My preoccupations lie so far from the writers mentioned, I am so completely different from them, that I have no reason to be jealous. I am a poet. I am not their competitor. Apart from their writing, I would like to know Bellow and Wiesel more intimately. But we are not similar, so how can I be envious? They are read in English, I in Hebrew; they write prose, I write verse. I will admit, though, that every writer may at times be envious of someone else, though he may be unaware of it."

J.G. "I understand that your first and second books in English translation appeared in 1980: *Autumn Music*, edited by Howard Schwartz (St. Louis: Cauldron Press) and *Gabriel Preil—Selected Poems*, translated by Robert Friend (London: Menard Press). And now the Jewish Publication Society is including a bilingual volume of your selected works in its series of 20th century Jewish poets, which includes Benjamin Mandelstamm, Chaim Nahman Bialik and others. Do you think American Jewry is ready for your poetry in translation?"

G.P. "In general, poetry is read by few people in America, and if you are discussing American Jewry the number grows even smaller. Even if I were to gain a thousand new readers, though, I would be pleased."

J.G. "Can you explain what happened to Hebrew in this country?"

G.P. "At one time there were a number of Hebrew writers here and the language was more potent, but that time has passed. The older writers died or moved to Israel and almost no young writers have arisen to take their place."

J.G. "Is the United States unable to sustain a viable Hebrew movement?"

G.P. "Maybe this phrasing is too sharp, but I am afraid so."

J.G. "And where would you lay the blame?"

G.P. "There is very little secular Hebrew education provided here. The Hebrew education that does exist involves Bible and prayer but hardly any modern literature. It's not a question of blame, though, but simply a recognition of the realities of the situation. The dominant culture is very strong in the United States, in contrast to Lithuania, for instance, so that it is difficult for a small culture to survive."

J.G. "Yet doesn't Hebrew literature in Israel also contend with strong external cultural influences?"

G.P. "Certainly. There are those critics who lament the decline of specifically Jewish influence and tradition on Hebrew poetry. I see it as inevitable. A Turkish poet writes like an English poet if they are both moderns. The world literary culture is one. On the other hand, the very nature of the Hebrew language tends to preserve allusions to the Bible and tradition. Still, one can never tell what the future may bring. Perhaps one day a gifted poet will emerge from out of the Hebrew institutes of learning here. It is possible but highly unlikely. However, it is probable that scholars, historians and researchers of Jewish studies will continue to develop in America."

Reconstructionism

Diane Levenberg

For much of its brief history, Reconstructionism was misunderstood and thought of as the most confusing branch of Judaism. Many Jews joked that a Reconstructionist was a person who prayed "to whom it may concern." In the last decade, however, Reconstructionism—as practiced by a growing number of adherents, and taught at the Reconstructionist Rabbinical College in Wyncote (a suburb of Philadelphia)—has come to be a significant part of American Jewish life.

What is Reconstructionism and what constitutes its growing appeal for American Jews? I find one answer in the tiny library of the movement's rabbinical college, where a woman has been diligently studying the philosophy of Reconstructionism.

"You mean," she says out loud to no one in particular, "after all these years thinking I was just a lapsed Orthodox Jew, I'm really a Reconstructionist?"

"That's the secret of Reconstructionism," answers a female rabbinical student wearing a yarmulke. "Dig away at the ideological layering of most American Jews and you'll discover that their attitudes conform more to Reconstructionism than to any other branch of Judaism."

Simply put, Reconstructionism argues that every generation of Jews has the responsibility to fashion its own interpretation of Judaism. Rabbi Jacob Staub, the editor of the magazine *Reconstructionist* (and a graduate of the Reconstructionist Rabbinical College), leans back in his chair, tries to ignore the clutter of work that threatens to overwhelm him and attempts to clarify this Judaism to which he has devoted most of his adult life. "Judaism has always been changing, evolving. What is constant is the Jewish people, and the centrality of peoplehood is what is central to Reconstructionism. In the past, there was a single belief or practice, rather than a reflection of a people's ongoing quest for meaning and transcendence. Just as things have changed in the past, so must we adapt to new and unprecedented circumstances. These include political emancipation and ideological challenge."

Staub explains political emancipation. Formerly, he says, Jewish communities were organized so that Jewish law was enforced and education was basically Jewish. Now, Jews no longer live in self-governing communities but in the wider society. Being Jewish today is optional, and the ideological challenge is to reformulate the insights of our ancestors into our own idiom. They spoke in supernaturalistic terms; we need to develop our own terms, including nonsexist language, a way to address a God who resides in this world rather than beyond it. And, he continues, Reconstructionism affirms that Jews live in two civilizations and have much to learn from modern democratic society. American and Jewish values, for example, can be harmonized, but only if we can reconstruct Judaism in ways that allow us to confront it with intellectual integrity so that it activates our lives and helps us dedicate ourselves to divine purposes.

Staub is eager to clarify another point. "You know," he says, "contrary to what is often portrayed, this is not a secular agnosticism. Rather, Reconstructionism is an attempt to find a transcendent presence of God in interpersonal relationships, in natural processes, in movements of social change and in ritual observance."

Reconstructionism was founded by Mordecai Kaplan, a man who is referred to by some as the first American Jew to make a career of not believing in God. Kaplan arrived in America, in 1889, as an 8-year-old immigrant, accompanying his father who had been invited to join Rabbi Jacob Joseph in establishing a rabbinical court of law in New York. As befitted the son of a Hebraic scholar, Kaplan studied in a yeshiva. Showing early signs of rebellion, he went on to a public high school where he learned perfect English. After graduating from the City College of New York, Kaplan entered Columbia University, where he read widely in sociology, anthropology and psychology. Eventually, his work would reflect the influence of John Dewey and Emile Durkheim.

A prodigious scholar, Kaplan, at the age of 21, was ordained at the Jewish Theological Seminary by the renowned Talmudic scholar Solomon Schechter, who took Kaplan under his wing. Kaplan's career seemed to be blossoming.

Kaplan became the first seminary graduate appointed to a New York congregation—Kehilath Jeshurun, the wealthiest Eastern European congregation of its time. Although the congregation was Orthodox, its hiring committee, to satisfy the younger congregants, went to the seminary to find an English-speaking rabbi. But the Union of Orthodox Rabbis decreed that Kaplan's ordination was not acceptable. Soon after his arrival, Kehilath Jeshurun caved in and changed Kaplan's title from "rabbi" to "minister." A few years later, on his European honeymoon, Kaplan received *smicha* (Orthodox ordination) from Rabbi Jacob Isaac Reines, the founder of the Mizrachi organization.

An intellectual thinker regarded for his impeccable integrity, Kaplan was unhappy as a pulpit rabbi. At times, overcome by spiritual questions and in doubt about the answers, he said that he might serve society better by selling insurance. At the seminary, influenced by Arnold Ehrlich, a biblical scholar and radical secularist, Kaplan renounced his Orthodox beliefs. Solomon Schechter came to his rescue and appointed him professor of homiletics—the first such position the seminary ever offered a graduate of an American university. Kaplan, believing that his role was to teach the proper content of a sermon, used his classroom as a platform for his radical beliefs. Later, in 1947, while also directing the seminary's Teachers Institute, he became professor of philosophies of religion.

Some of his students would say that for 30 years Kaplan was the dominant intellectual force at the seminary. Others would disagree: After World War II, his popularity declined. But each of his students would concur that until he took a course with Kaplan, the seminary was a very disenchanting place.

Only Kaplan tried to wrestle with the reconciliation of Judaism and modern thought. Only Kaplan would admit, in class as well as outside, that he did not believe God had dictated the Torah to Moses. And only Kaplan tried to formulate a philosophy of Judaism that might include a concern for the problems of economic justice and a program of social action. For those students at the seminary interested in rational philosophy, Kaplan's courses were the only game in town.

Kaplan's position at Kehilath Jeshurun grew increasingly untenable. When it came to religious matters, he was liberal. On labor issues, however, he was most punctilious – accusing the board, for example, of treating synagogue employees unfairly. In 1922 he resigned, taking with him 23 families to found the Society for the Advancement of Judaism in New York City.

To disseminate his ideas, week after week, Kaplan now had the more liberal pulpit of the society. Then in 1934, he published his "Judaism as a Civilization," and Rabbi Ira Eisenstein, his son-in-law and right hand at the society, declared the birth of the Reconstructionist movement.

The *SAJ Bulletin* had grown into the *SAJ Review*. The *Review* evolved, in 1935, into the *Reconstructionist*, the movement's magazine. Now the movement began to develop a program, to describe its practices and to define its ritual standards.

In its first platform, issued in 1935, Reconstructionism defined Judaism as a civilization and affirmed the necessity for reinterpreting traditional beliefs and revising traditional practices. A civilization, as part of its culture, must express a political viewpoint. Reconstructionism, therefore, emphasized its love of cultural Zionism and its commitment to social action.

A civilization must also have religion, and religion entails a belief in God. However, for many Jews the "Kaplanian" definition of God is confusing and controversial. In *Future of the American Jew*, Kaplan called God the power that makes for salvation – defining salvation as the "progressive perfection of the human personality and the establishment of a free, just and cooperative social order." Rabbi Arthur Green, the new president of the Reconstructionist Rabbinical College, explains that Kaplan believed in a "transnatural God not quite natural and not quite supernatural. To him, God was a power that operated in the universe but only through human agencies."

According to Kaplan, the desire for salvation is the life force of Judaism. "We sense," said Kaplan, "a power which orients us to life and elicits from us the best of which we are capable or renders us immune to the worst that may befall us."

As for the concept of Jews being the Chosen People, Kaplan believed that every nation has a calling. For Jews, it is to develop Jewish civilization in a way that enhances the life of the individual and leads to ethical communities that manifest godliness. While Kaplan took great pains to refute the idea that Jews are superior, he did believe that the idea of "chosenness" emerged from a profound psychological truth: A people has no right to live for itself and the Jews in particular have always been imbued with the desire to perform some important service for humanity. By working toward the universal establishment of peace based on justice and freedom, Kaplan believed, Jews, along with other nations fulfilling their calling, would bring on the messianic era.

Orthodox Jewry at first tried to ignore the "heretical" rabbi. However, when the Sabbath Prayer Book appeared in 1945, deleting references to Jews as a chosen people, and omitting, as well, the concept of a personal messiah, it was burned in a public ceremony by a group of Orthodox rabbis. Like Spinoza, Kaplan, by fiat of a *herem* imposed by the Orthodox rabbinate, was excommunicated — officially excluded from the Jewish community.

Kaplan, for his part, continued to be loyal to the seminary, remaining on the faculty until his retirement at the age of 82. Convinced that Reconstructionism would inevitably capture the hearts and minds of Conservative rabbis, he saw no reason to inaugurate officially his own separate movement. Although, at Ira Eisenstein's urging, Reconstructionism developed structures that set it apart from the Conservative movement, it did not, until 1960, declare itself a separate branch of Judaism. Finally, with the organization of the Federation of Reconstructionist Congregations and Havurot, Kaplan, sensing Eisenstein's prescience, began to refer to Reconstructionism as a movement.

As early as 1945, the federation encouraged the development of *havurot*, small fellowships, in a program that began to flourish in the late 1950s. As Reconstructionism grew, it began to recognize local chapters too small to call themselves synagogues, and in this became the actual creator of the *havurah* movement. Though the smallest branch of Judaism in America, it has grown considerably in the last five years. In 1969 there were 10 congregations; in 1980, 23, and in 1987 there are 60 congregations and havurot.

At the age of 102, Kaplan died in 1983. He was one of the great thinkers of modern Judaism, but despite his brilliant and fertile mind, his ideas might have slowly withered in the aftermath of the Holocaust. In his rational, nonmystical way, Kaplan wanted Jews to understand God as Process, which leads men and women toward goodness and righteousness. His thinking appealed to pre-Holocaust Jews, inclined toward secularism anyway. After the Holocaust, Jews had trouble seeing God as a force in the world that might lead to Goodness. "And," explains Arthur Green, "while Kaplan believed in the rationalism of science, today we understand that technology is the terror."

In addition, many of Kaplan's critics cite as a problem his failure to understand the true nature of evil—the shadow side of individuals and nations. He believed in humanity's essential goodness—harboring the hope that all nations could be ethical. Other critics fault him for his rationalist approach to theology. According to Susannah Heschel, editor of On Being a Jewish Feminist, "Like many other modern Jews of his day, Kaplan attempted to reconcile Judaism with prevailing intellectual secular trends. For him, these trends are primarily the challenges of scientific knowledge and an abiding belief that reason could control the world. Spiritual traditions within Judaism, such as Hasidism and Kabbalah played almost no role in his thought, and he was distinctly more concerned with community organization than with piety, meditation and prayer—the nonrational modes of religious experience."

In postwar America, Kaplan's Judaism needed some reconstruction of its own. The rebirth of Reconstructionism began quietly enough in an unassuming brownstone building in one of Philadelphia's inner-city neighborhoods—the first home of the Reconstructionist Rabbinical College, which today is the center of Reconstructionist thought and growth.

The year was 1968 and the timing was perfect. The Jewish renewal movement was also about to begin. Young American Jews were, after the 1967 Six Day War, proud of their Jewish identity. They had learned the art and effectiveness of dissent in the anti-Vietnam War and civil rights demonstrations. And with the growth of feminism, the second sex was becoming stronger every day. Put it all together and you have the recipe for Jewish renewal. Using Kaplan's ideas, you have not only a methodology, but a mandate for synthesis.

That first year, 50 men applied (only 13 were accepted) for admission to this school that would train them as rabbis who need not be bound by the authority of halakhah. They were attracted also by the simultaneous Ph.D. they would receive from neighboring Temple University.

While Ira Eisenstein, the college's first president, tried to maintain its classically Reconstructionist structure, the college was radical in some of its innovations. For his own daughter, Kaplan, in 1922, had created

American Judaism's first bat mitzvah, and now the college was the first rabbinical school in America to accept women with the intention of ordaining them. Sandy Eisenberg Sasso entered the second class and was ordained—the first Reconstructionist female rabbi—in 1974.

Another innovation was the college's course of study. Adhering to Kaplan's definition of Judaism as the evolving religious civilization of the Jewish people, Eisenstein organized a five-year core curriculum not around Jewish texts, but around each major period of Jewish civilization.

"In its early years," writes peace activist Arthur Waskow in *These Holy Sparks*, "R.R.C. had few faculty members who could act out the vision of the founders. In a sense, only the Jewish renewal movement itself could create such teachers." Understanding that this might be so, the college, in 1981, appointed Ira Silverman president.

Silverman, then 36, had taught government at Princeton University and administered special projects for major Jewish organizations. He saw his role as fulfilling and extending the work of Kaplan and Eisenstein— renewing American Jewish life.

Open to new ideas and radical dreams, Silverman looked to the Jewish renewal movement for his faculty. He hired Rabbi Zalman Schachter, a Kabbalist and professor of religion at Temple. Waskow, historian of the Jewish renewal movement, joined the faculty. Rabbi Max Ticktin, one of the founders of the Fabrangen Havurah in Washington, D.C., came to teach modern Hebrew literature. Silverman also made room for several feminist thinkers such as Shulamit Magnes and Rabbis Rebecca Alpert and Linda Holtzman. The college is proud of keeping its own; along with Alpert and Holtzman, a third of the faculty and staff are graduates.

In an important move, a year after his appointment, Silverman helped the college acquire the former Curtis Mansion, a redbrick, slate-roofed Georgian mansion in Wyncote. The college now had an imposing facade, the look of an Ivy League campus. (In October 1985, eight years early, the college retired its mortgage.) "Institutional growth is one thing," says Silverman. But the school's main purpose is the "education of leaders for Jewish life in the future."

The larger facility allowed the college to reach out to the community in several important ways. The new Kaplan Institute for Adult Jewish Studies, founded in 1984, sponsors seminars on ethics, economics and feminism. It recently hosted a poetry conference, bringing to the campus several outstanding Jewish-American poets (Allen Ginsburg and Stanley Kunitz among them) to study Jewish texts.

The Wyncote campus is also home to two unusual institutions, one religious and the other secular. The Reconstructionist Congregation is open to college community members and to Jews in the Philadelphia area who are looking for an egalitarian alternative to traditional congregational life. And the Shalom Center, founded in 1984 and developed by Silverman and Waskow, is a broad-based national resource center offering Jewish perspectives on preventing nuclear war.

The college itself is a model of synthesis regarding the training of rabbis. Reform's Hebrew Union College-Jewish Institute of Religion is very much a professional school and makes practical rabbinics the central emphasis of its program. The Conservative Jewish Theological Seminary sees itself as an institution for training Jewish scholars and has an excellent program in Talmud and rabbinic studies. The Reconstructionist Rabbinical College, while taking practical rabbinics very seriously, is not focused primarily on rabbinic texts. According to Rabbi Albert, "the college is more interested in how those texts work in the context of Jewish history."

For example, college president Rabbi Arthur Green teaches a class in modern Hebrew literature. Skillfully, he asks probing questions and is careful to translate difficult Hebrew words. His own fluent Hebrew is descriptive and literary. He is completely at home in the classroom, and it is obvious that he loves to teach. His students, as often as possible, answer thoughtfully in Hebrew. Is it possible that the 16th-century Kabbalist Isaac Luria could practice phrenology, read flames, study palms and understand the language of birds? Students find themselves back in a quieter, more mystical age and ponder these questions.

It is a small class—only five students—and in that it is typical of the college. What is unusual is that this is one of the few courses conducted, at Green's insistence, almost entirely in Hebrew.

This year, the college boasts an enrollment of 60 students; it adds about 10 students with every incoming class. The college is also proud of its extremely low attrition rate, losing perhaps only one student a year. "It's a good program, and we have older students who arrive already knowing what they want," explains Alpert, the dean of students.

The faculty consists of 3 deans who all teach, 6 core directors and 25 part-time teachers. These teachers represent every approach to Judaism, from Orthodox to Reform. "We want the students confused," says Alpert. "We want them to struggle with being Jewish—to fight with each other."

Reconstructionist rabbis are trained to be teachers and resource people, empathetically guiding their fellow Jews as they struggle with contemporary spiritual dilemmas. Most of the students find their training demanding and stimulating.

Jonathan Kligler of New York transferred to the Reconstructionist college from Hebrew Union College. He is a dance teacher, a mime, a musician and a carpenter. Unlike most of the students here, however, his family is supporting his education. "I see that my major role in life is to facilitate groups of people in celebration. I have a gift for that," he says. The college is proving to be just what he hoped for. "H.U.C. was set up to make me a Reform rabbi," he explains. "This allows me to try it [the rabbinate] on."

Barbara Penzner came to the college from Kansas City, Kansas. She is 29 and, while still a student, served as rabbi of the college's congregation. "It was a great job," she says. "Just what I wanted to do—live out Reconstructionist principles." Since this is a new congregation—only in its third year—Barbara saw herself as a pioneer. "Creating a congregational community takes a lot of education," she explains. She was also president of the college's student association and proudly admits that she believed in recruiting new candidates.

What criticism does she have of the college? She's in the middle of a lunch on the run, but she puts down her cup of tea to consider the question. "Because there is so much pluralism, it's hard to focus from year to year. But my definition of Reconstructionism is Process. This offers a lot of leeway in regard to other people's ideas. The hard part comes when people start to question that process. It's not easy to give everyone an equal vote in spite of differences."

Every week, the college convenes for a community meeting that deals with an issue important to the entire community. Anyone can raise a topic—subject to approval by the president of the student body and the dean of students. Recently, the meeting was a symposium on lay-rabbinate relations. Trustees of the college, who had been upstairs attending a board meeting, dropped in to hear questions regarding Kaplan's idea of democracy. Who is the final authority—the congregation or the rabbi?

Kaplan's views on Judaism have opened the door to a wide range of perspectives and provocative interpretations. Feminist theologians, for example, embraced Kaplan's idea of God as Process. While a traditional view is that God is static and stationary, the feminist view is that God is dynamic and changing. Searching for a maternal, nourishing God, Jewish feminists are attracted to a Reconstructionism that, in the words of Rebecca Alpert, "posits a God who is not omnipotent, who does not cause the death of a young child to punish the child of its parents, but who can be said to suffer with those parents as they deal with their anguish."

Rabbi Zalman Schachter, in his teachings at the college, tries to bridge two worlds—the intellectualism of Mordecai Kaplan and the mystical, emotional Hasidism of Abraham Joshua Heschel. Schachter explains the difference between the approaches of these two important theologians. Kaplan, he says, tried rationally to see how God works in the world; Heschel tried to capture the awe and wonder of God's working in the world.

Understanding all too well Kaplan's idea of living in two civilizations, Schachter explains Process this way, using the symbols of the zodiac: In the Age of Pisces, God revealed Himself as totally transcendent. Now, in this new Age of Aquarius, God is immanent—more in the world. This way of reinterpreting Judaism so that it meets the needs of contemporary Jews and infusing Judaism with the "nonrational modes of religious experience" is at the heart of Schachter's neo-Hasidic approach to Reconstructionism. When he saw Jews living in a spiritual wasteland crying out for an experience of ecstasy, Schachter created P'nai Or, an innovative, egalitarian "New Age" havurah.

P'nai Or, in nearby Mt. Airy, is the havurah at which many of the college's students pray. In experiencing their own Judaism, they experiment, move their bodies when they pray, and use breath, dance and music to feel, as proof of their energy within, some sense of God's presence. Often, the prayers are chanted as poems, and in contemporary English they take on new meaning. There is no sermon, and the reading of the week is discussed by everyone, which results in the creating of a collective modern midrash—an up-to-the-moment commentary on the text. Some of the female students have also joined a women's minyan where they experiment with feminine God language—addressing a feminine God by using prayers and rituals they themselves have composed and created. These rabbinical interns then try to infuse their congregations and the college student body with these elements of nonrational, experiential neo-Hasidism.

Last year, Ira Silverman left the college to head the 92nd Street Y.M.-Y.W.H.A. in New York City. He was president for five years, having accomplished much of what he set out to do. The campus has a new look, the school is on a much sounder financial footing, and he helped to make it a place where Jewish renewal is lived out on a daily basis.

"Part of the Reconstructionist outlook," Silverman says, "is to seek to transcend the religious denominationalism which divides us. Our particular organizational talent is encouraging Jewish renewal. And that takes leaders and ideas. At the college, those are the two focal points: producing leaders and ideas.

"At the same time that they are educating rabbis, they are seeking to become a center of Jewish thought. I had in mind the creation of centers to direct attention to Jewish ethics. I would also like to see there a center for Jewish art—to stimulate music, graphics and dance in synagogues and elsewhere. It might be a kind of Shalom Center of the Arts."

As the new president of the college, Arthur Green is helping to expand its horizons. Why had he given up a tenured professorship to come to the college?

"I spent 10 years as a professor at the University of Pennsylvania teaching undergraduates. I'm not sure that that decade of life was very well spent. I came to R.R.C. because I think one of the most important things one can do in the Jewish community is create a new kind of Jewish leadership.

"I want to create a serious alternative to Orthodoxy for thinking Jews . . . where serious Jewish thinkers can find a place within the Jewish community. Now I'm helping to train a new kind of rabbi who will serve the Jewish community in ways it hasn't been served until now."

In 10 years of advising graduate students at Penn, Green awarded only two doctorates (two more are in the works). He brings these rigorous standards to the college. To the joy of many students, he is launching a major curriculum change. Students will no longer need an additional graduate degree from another institution. Until now, maintaining exhausting schedules, they studied at the Reconstructionist school, took courses at local colleges and universities to obtain either a master's degree or a Ph.D. and worked as rabbinical interns. They will now spend four years at the college itself. For one year, they will also study in Israel.

"Much of the way Judaism is developing is happening in Israel," explains Green. "I would like us to be the place where Jewish theology and Jewish intellectual history are best taught. And though I hope the student body will grow, I wouldn't want the college to exceed more than

75 students. If it does, I'm in favor of opening another branch." (Since its opening, the college has ordained 80 rabbis).

A graduate of the Jewish Theological Seminary, Green had gone there to study with Heschel. He brings to the college his love of Hasidism and a way to synthesize it with Reconstructionism. If Green and Kaplan could talk today, what would they say to each other?

"As I see it," Green answers after a thoughtful pause, "Hasidism is moving towards an abstract notion of God as a transcendent mystery which also fills the world in an all-embracing and ever-present way. God as Personality is but one such manifestation.

"Kaplan was not open to mysticism—that was his cultural prejudice. He was a Litvak, with the dedication to rationality of a *misnagid* [non-Hasid]. He was trying to save Jews who came to America—children of immigrants, intellectuals, atheists. 'Look,' he said, 'here's an honest approach to Judaism, something you don't have to feel intellectually sleazy about.' If he were my age today, I think I could win his grudging assent [to the idea] that there was this abstract notion of Divinity in Hasidism that wasn't so different from some of the things he was talking about. We would probably meet somewhere in the middle over the issue of Process theology. We would agree on the importance of Jewish culture and about creating an organic Jewish community."

Green smiles. "Many of the things that Kaplan said and taught have been so widely accepted that the battle is over."

Gershom Scholem

Richard Kostelanetz

J ewish scholars and Jews in general had more or less forgotten about Jewish mysticism until Gershom Scholem began to publish his researches, initially in German in the 1920s and then in Hebrew and English. Today, though himself not a mystic, Scholem is the world's principal authority on Jewish mysticism. He is widely known and respected as a teacher, a writer and one of the great intellectual historians of this era.

His self-definition goes thus: "I am a specialist, a historian of religion. My subject has been Jewish mysticism. I wrote purely scholarly work before I dared to come out with general reflections. I tried to make a scholarly basis for understanding the phenomenon of mysticism within Judaism. If you go into one thing in a deep way, it branches out in many ways. At the beginning, I thought I would be writing for fifty people. I was surprised that after thirty years the books have thousands of readers."

Scholem's books, which began to appear in 1923 when his edition of *Das Buch Bahir* was published, and now number more than thirty works, have single-handedly revived a lost tradition and made him the most prominent scholar in his particular field and, many believe, the towering figure in all modern "Jewish studies."

These works are remarkable not only for the quantity of Scholem's pioneering research but for the depth of his understanding and the quality of his expository style. The material he chose to study—the tradition and teachings of the Kabbalah—includes some of the strangest, most impenetrable books ever written, among them *Book Bahir* (1180), *Sefer ha-Zohar* (1280–86), *Avodat ha-Kodesh* (1531), and *Ha-Nefesh ha-Hakhamah* (1608), among other formidable texts.

Such works were produced by mystics, whom Scholem defines as people "favored with immediate, and to them real, experience of the divine, or ultimate reality, or who at least strive to attain such experience." For him, mysticism is in essence a radically conservative endeavor, reinterpreting the traditional content of a religion for the sake of tradition, and advocating spiritual renewal. "The mystic's experience tends to confirm the religious authority under which he lives; its theology and symbols are projected into his mystical experience, but do not spring from it," Scholem writes.

The Kabbalah, in Scholem's definition, is "the sum of Jewish mysticism," as distinguished from the predominantly rationalistic tradition of Jewish thought that extends from the Torah to most modern Jewish theology. He points out that in Jewish tradition the Kabbalah represents a continuing attempt to portray unfathomable dimensions of human experience, particularly man's relationship to God and the cosmos. Thus, Kabbalistic texts present "symbols of a very special kind, in which the spiritual experience of the mystics was almost inextricably intertwined with the historical experience of the Jewish people." Scholem made a herculean, largely successful attempt to make this tradition comprehensible. It is a measure of his success, in this respect, that reading him on Jewish mystical thought is considerably less difficult than reading the originals.

Perhaps his best-known book is *Major Trends in Jewish Mysticism*, published by Schocken in 1941, which has sold some 40,000 copies in the United States alone. But the distinctiveness of the Kabbalah is most tellingly portrayed in a smaller volume, *On the Kabbalah and Its Symbolism*, published in German in 1960 and in English translation (Schocken) in 1965—and, like other Scholem books, sprinkled with footnoted references to a library of esoteric materials. (Both books are available in American paperbacks.) In the later work are the succinct definitions quoted here, as well as Scholem's most comprehensive generalizations about the character and function of mysticism.

In *On the Kabbalah*, Scholem also reveals the key polemical purpose behind his research—making Jews aware of a tradition that had been suppressed, if not forgotten. He says: "From the start this resurgence of mythical conceptions in the thinking of Jewish mystics provided a bond with certain impulses in the popular faith, fundamental impulses springing from the simple man's fear of life and death, to which [rationalistic] Jewish philosophy had no satisfactory response. Jewish philosophy paid a heavy price for its disdain of the primitive levels of human life. It ignored the terrors from which myths are made, as though denying the very existence of the problem. Nothing so sharply distinguishes the philosophers and Kabbalists as their attitude toward the problem of evil and the demonic. By and large, the Jewish philosophers dismissed it as a pseudo-problem, while to the Kabbalists it became one of the chief motives of their thinking."

Scholem's monumental biography, *Sabbatai Sevi: The Mystical Messiah*, originally published in Hebrew in 1957, appeared sixteen years later in America (Princeton University Press, 1973) to favorable reviews and surprising popularity. The initial hardbound edition sold out at $25 per copy; a paperback edition, whose even thousand pages are priced at $9.95 continues to sell briskly.

No one but Scholem could have written such a book, the product of decades of dogged, if not obsessive original research on the principal Kabbalistic leader of Jewish history. Sevi was the self-proclaimed messiah who emerged from Smyrna, in southwestern Turkey, in the middle of the 17th Century. Aided by a devoted and effective publicist known as Nathan of Gaza, and capitalizing upon the popular expectation that 1666 would be a turning point in human history, Sevi inspired a messianic, pietistic fervor that converted millions of Jews. Believers in faraway Poland, Holland and Yemen closed their businesses and packed their belongings, waiting for Sevi to call them to Jerusalem. However, the Turkish sultan, recognizing political challenge, had Sevi arrested and then summoned him to Constantinople, offering the options of death or conversion to the Muslim religion. Sevi chose the latter, taking an Islamic name (in 1666, no less).

Though his movement all but entirely disintegrated, Sevi's spiritual influence persisted among many Jews. "No doubt this faith had been humiliated and discredited," Scholem concludes. "Its hope had been vain and its claims refuted, and yet the question compounded of pride and sadness persisted: Was it not a great opportunity missed, rather than a big lie? A victory of the hostile power rather than the collapse of a vain thing?" Acknowledging this as a crucial episode in Kabbalistic social history, Scholem analyzes Sevi and his movement from several perspectives—among them history, psychology, theology and literary criticism—producing a grandly scaled, spectacularly detailed biography that, despite its scholarly appurtenances, is still quite readable for the layman.

Another, his latest, titled *On Jews and Judaism in Crisis*, and just published by Schocken, contains some of his recent essays as well as a long, informative interview.

When I telephoned Scholem in Israel to request an interview, he inquired in German-accented English if I knew Hebrew. "No," I reluctantly replied. He then asked how closely I had read the *Zohar*. "Not very," I said. There was a heavy pause. "Mr. Kostelanetz, you are not well prepared." It was clear at the beginning that this was a formidable, testy man, scarcely predisposed to either flattery or journalism.

I went to the second floor of a semi-detached house on a tree-lined block in the Rehavia section of Jerusalem where Scholem lives with his wife, Fania. He came to the door—a courtly European gentleman, dressed in Continental-style blue suit, black shoes and maroon tie, so different from the informal Israeli attire. He looked like scores of other elderly Jewish men—medium in height and build, with a long nose, his face clean-shaven to the tops of his temples, a crown of white hair and long ears. But he was considerably more spry than his contemporaries—and indisputably more voluble. Speaking English fluently, yet pausing occasionally to find the precise word, he invited me into the front sitting room, adjacent through an open doorway to another room graced by a large desk. Sitting in one easy chair, inviting me to take another, he told me that he and his wife have lived in this comfortable, carpeted, sunny apartment for forty years.

Books lined all the visible walls, from floor to ceiling. He said that the other room is filled with books of and about Jewish mysticism. The bookcases in the room where we talked are devoted to Christian mysticism, Sufi mysticism, studies of the Old Testament. Bookshelves containing works of modern literature and Christian theology also dominated the dining room. In the hallway, shelves ran perpendicularly from one wall to the other above our heads, with the books' spines facing out in both directions. On one long shelf were copies of his own books, originally published in German, Hebrew and English, along with numerous translations into other languages. Kafka, he told me, is his

favorite modern author; the late S. Y. Agnon, who was also a close
friend, the best Israeli writer.

Born in Berlin, December 5, 1897, Gershom Scholem grew up among
four brothers, each of whom distinguished himself in a different way. He
described their father, who was in the printing business, as "a typical
German petit bourgeois," saying: "Papa worked on Yom Kippur and
didn't go to synagogue. We were not rich, but we were not ever hungry."
Nonetheless, the sons went through the ceremony of *bar mitzvah*,
because "everyone Jewish in Berlin did in those days."

Young Gerhart, as he was then known, discovered Judaism for
himself, deciding to study Hebrew seriously and calling himself a Zionist.
Religion, curiously, was his form of teenage rebellion. "I signed up at the
Jewish community library in Berlin, and I started reading Judaica. That
was a big step for me."

In 1915, he purchased a three-volume edition of the *Sefer ha-Zohar*,
which he asked his father to rebind with interleaving white sheets, so
that he could make abundant annotations. Springing up from his sitting
room chair, he pulled down a fat book, bound in red leather, to show me.
It was this volume, now in my hands, with page after page of annotations, that had kindled Scholem's interest more than sixty years before.
In order to read the *Zohar* in its original language, young Scholem had to
learn Aramaic, a precursor of modern Hebrew. (He remains critical of
the principal English-language edition which, he says, "left out many of
the most important parts.")

By 1917, soon after one of his brothers was arrested for Communist
activities, young Gerhard was thrown out of his father's house. "He sent
me a registered letter ordering me to leave his household by March 1,
1917. He said, 'It's all the same—socialism, Zionism. It's all anti-
patriotic.'" When Germany entered World War I, Gerhard was faced
with the threat of military service, which he evaded with an insanity
plea. "I put on an act without knowing what I was acting," Scholem once
said. "I spent six weeks in a lunatic asylum where I had been sent for
observation and checkup. There they ruled me totally insane. Papa had
to take me back because the doctors made him."

Not wanting to stay at home, young Scholem attended the University
of Jena to study mathematics, his initial academic specialty. He eventually earned a German state diploma, the equivalent of an American
M.A. He went to Switzerland in 1919, there beginning his intensive
studies of the Kabbalah. "I had to teach myself, because there was no one

to teach me." In 1920 he returned to Germany to take his doctorate in Semitic languages in two years in Munich, with a thesis on the Kabbalah. "I can still quote in Arabic the verses on which I was examined," he said, smiling engagingly. "All my life I've had an uncanny memory for superfluous things—dates, years, numbers."

At this time he also began to publish essays in Martin Buber's periodical, *Der Jude,* and to teach adult education courses on Jewish mysticism. By then he had established himself as a singular figure in German-Jewish cultural life—as he remembers it, "a freak phenomenon—a Jew from a non-observant family who doesn't want to put on *tefillin* and all that, but who is sitting and studying Hebrew and busying himself with Judaism, and wants to know what it's all about, and is a passionate Zionist."

Acting on his Zionist convictions, Scholem recalled, he emigrated to Palestine in September 1923. Soon after his arrival he had two job offers—one teaching mathematics, the other as the Hebrew librarian of the nascent Jewish National Library. He took the latter. "Since the Zionists are always bankrupt, then as now—nothing has changed—I was paid from the *schnorrkasse,* from money collected from tourists' donations. I was paid in cash—ten Israeli pounds a month, the equivalent of ten English pounds—unlike everyone else, who collected pieces of paper. Pay was often delayed for several months in those times. We all lived on credit. Today everyone would go on strike if they were not paid on time."

When the Hebrew University was founded in 1925, Scholem was among the first to be appointed to the faculty. He had already published scholarly researches on the Kabbalah and resurrected forgotten texts in new editions, and in 1927 compiled a *Bibliographica Kabbala.* He spent twenty years in the wilderness of minutiae before the 1940s, when he began writing the more general books, such as *Major Trends,* on which his public eminence is based. "Without this spadework, all generalizations are useless," he told me. "They are hypotheses of a charlatan." He then named several recent books about the Kabbalah which, in his opinion, had dubious, insubstantial origins.

He has written exclusively about Jewish thought and the Jewish people, rarely mentioning other religions. "I realized how difficult it must be to understand a religion not one's own when I read even serious Christians writing about Judaism. They have little feeling for, how you say. . . ." The ends of his fingers shook, a tense inch apart from each other. "I was careful not to repeat the same mistakes. I have stuck all my life with things I know. It was difficult enough to get a deep understanding of Jewish things." He paused, ever formal, to adjust his tie. "In general, we should be very careful of what we read about other religions—Far Eastern religions, especially—if it is written by outsiders."

The telephone rang; his wife answered it. The caller was an academic colleague with a bibliographical query. "Yes. I have the book," Scholem declared impatiently, pointing to a particular tree in the forest of shelves. "Tell him I'll call him back."

Scholem then told me that he came to Israel as a spiritual Zionist who wanted to create a living Jewish society rather than a political state. He began to write in Hebrew and dropped "Gerhard" for "Gershom," the name which he received at his circumcision. (Nonetheless, his wife and old friends still call him "Gerhard." He speaks of himself as "Scholem.")

In the 1930s he was a member of Brit Shalom, a political organization favoring closer Arab-Jewish relations in Palestine, which included Martin Buber and Judah Magnes among other prominent members. The group's political position, he now admits, was naive. "It has come out that almost all dual-national countries explode from within. Forces tear them asunder. I don't say I'm glad about this; history shows this. That was the only political group I ever belonged to." The phone rang again, with another call to return.

Although he retired from the Hebrew University in 1965 at the age of 68, Scholem has been active in many other spheres. From 1968 to 1974 he served as president of the Israel Academy of Sciences and Humanities. In 1975 he became a member of the newly formed Israel Institute of Advanced Study. Late in 1975, he was Boston University's first Visiting Andrew W. Mellon Professor, teaching a course on Jewish mysticism and conducting a seminar on Jewish messianism. He lectures frequently around the world. Most of his recent books are collections of previously published essays—not only *The Messianic Idea in Judaism* (Schocken, 1971) and *On Jews and Judaism in Crisis*, but three volumes in German, titled *Judaica I-III* (1963, 1970, 1973) and a large new one in Hebrew which sold out its initial printing of 5,000 copies in a few months. He usually copyedits and proofreads translations in all the languages he knows.

The most elaborate bibliography of Scholem's writings appears, in a Hebrew frame, in the *festschrift* prepared for his seventieth birthday, *Studies in Mysticism and Religion* (Magnes Press, Hebrew University, Jerusalem, 1967).

Scholem describes himself as a procrastinating writer who spends most of his days "doing nothing" – which is a busy writer's euphemism for reading voraciously and making notes. As a deadline approaches, he harnesses his energies and writes in a rush. "Then," his wife told me, "there is no night and no day, no food and no people." Most of *Sabbatai Sevi*, for instance, was written in a matter of months, in London in 1954; two more chapters were later added in Israel. One major Scholem book still unavailable in English, though translated into French and German (the latter by Scholem himself, who expanded it to three times the original Hebrew length), deals with the origins of the Kabbalah. Another in German, published in 1975, relates Scholem's friendship with the legendary German writer Walter Benjamin, who died in 1940 at the age of 48. "That is an important book," he exclaimed, pointing his finger at me and then pausing as he recollected my ignorance of other languages. "It is a great pity that you cannot read it."

Having discovered his ultimate subject at the beginning of his scholarly career, he applied his enormous energies to mastering it. "What interests me is the inner workings of Judaism – understanding Jewish history and Jewish thought," he declared, accenting the crucial terms. "What forces were contributing to making Judaism survive? I could see a dimension of Judaism which, in the Nineteenth Century, in the emancipated countries, was forgotten. Forgetting Jewish mysticism was one of the prices that European Jewry paid for its enlightenment. They were proud in their time to demonstrate that Judaism could be a rational thing, a left-wing Protestantism." He paused, looking at me over the top of his glasses. "I was neither for Kabbalah nor against Kabbalah, but I knew it was of relevance to understanding Judaism as a living thing."

Is his work related to the general revival of interest in mysticism? "Consciously, my work was not connected," he said. "My initial interest was solely in Judaism. Of course, there is *zeitgeist*. There are things which structurally have some affinity to Kabbalah – decidedly, in my opinion. William Blake, for instance, can describe a world which resembles that of the Kabbalists. In his own time, he was considered a scandalous atheist. To a modern man who studies the Kabbalah, Blake's world is very familiar.

"Mysticism is a certain stage in the development of a religious system. Therefore the mysticism of Christianity reinterprets its tradition much as Jewish mysticism does. They are similar in form, but not in content. The next question is what are the cognate structures that have appeared, without historical connection, in several times and several religions, not only in Judaism and Christianity, but in Hinduism, Sufism?

"Do you see those six books?" he exclaimed, pointing to uniform editions on a top shelf. "They were written by Jacob Boehme, an uneducated shoemaker, a Christian who lived around 1600. They are as close to the Kabbalah as anything can be." He paused to punctuate his next point. "We know very little, very little, about the workings of the human brain. We are just beginning to discover. That has been proved by the successes and excesses of psychoanalysis, which set us thinking about the limits of our knowledge. There are now several schools of psychology which are all working on shaky grounds—no less shaky than the Kabbalah, which is also an attempt. I consider religion the center of everything—more so than, say, the social sciences."

No one questions the quality of Scholem's scholarship; the more serious critics are contemporary Kabbalists who doubt if a nonpractitioner can best interpret the sacred texts. On the other hand, Stefan Moses, a professor of comparative literature at the Hebrew University, himself a devout student of Kabbalah, recommends Scholem's books to his own students, as simply the best guides there are to the subject.

In his recent essay on *Kabbalah and Criticism* (1975), Harold Bloom, the DeVane Professor of the Humanities at Yale, cites Scholem as the only sure authority on the Jewish mystical traditions, stating that "he has made himself indispensable to all rational students of his subject."

Scholem is religious, though not scrupulously observant. He works on Saturday (though never on Yom Kippur) and no longer attends synagogue regularly, though he once did. His bald head is bare; his wife has never kept a kosher kitchen. "If I had had children," he said, "I would have been more observant. It is important that such traditions get passed on. I try to behave as somebody who believes that God exists. Of this I am sure. I never was an atheist. I do not understand atheists—how they can live with a set of values, without being troubled by the nonsense of it. I do not understand how they can stand up to a nihilistic scheme of values, where there is no guarantee of conscience other than brutal power." By acknowledging the existence of God, Scholem also accepts the importance of faith apart from reason, and thus the aspirations and activities of people with extreme faith—the Jewish mystics.

Nonetheless, the primary paradox is that this sane, largely rational man has spent more than sixty years tenaciously studying the most extraordinary bunch of eccentrics who ever called themselves religious Jews. The second paradox is that most mystical thought implicitly disapproves of scholarly bookishness such as Scholem's. "Anyone who concerns himself seriously with the thinking of the great Kabbalists," he once wrote, "will be torn between feelings of admiration and revulsion."

In his new book, Scholem reprints a long essay, originally written in German, which severely criticizes Martin Buber, Scholem's early editorial benefactor and then a colleague at the Hebrew University. Buber's best-known books deal with the later Kabbalistic writings of Hasidic Jews. In his essay, Scholem questions Buber's scholarship, his intellectual structures, his piety, his language, his influence—a rather comprehensively devastating polemic. "Buber was an artist," Scholem explained over lemonade and his wife's cakes, "but he hated to be called one. His approach was esthetic. He was not interested in analytical understanding. He had a sound mistrust of philology." From his stance as a scholarly writer, committed to academic empirical standards, Scholem regards Buber's books about Jewish mysticism as more valid as literature—"poetry," he says—than as scholarship.

I asked Scholem about the current "relevance" of his work. "I despise that question," he shouted, both index fingers pointing forbiddingly. "Scholars should not work for relevance to others, but because they think it worth being done. This question has two dimensions—for yourself and for the mood of the times. I do not care about the latter. One may be alone; one may have thousands of readers. Had I written my books in 1840, when Jews were trying to forget these things, nobody would have cared. They would have called the books 'irrelevant.' They would have said that there is a crazy Jew in Berlin who likes such things."

Scholem supports the separation of church and state, even in Israel. He objects to laws that enforce the Sabbath, even though most Israelis are not observant. "Jewish religion would mean much more to most of us and to younger people if it were not part of the political machinery, which uses religion to win support in exchange for political and material favors. If the religious in Israel did not have this political support, they would be weaker materially but stronger spiritually." He mopped his brow with his handkerchief. "Religious experience doesn't lie down. Religion is extremely forceful." In more respects than one, Scholem remains a spiritual Zionist, particularly concerned with the quality of mental life in Israel, among Jews.

Harold Schulweis

Sheldon Teitelbaum

I n 1952, Rabbi Harold Schulweis left New York for the West Coast, where he hoped to be beyond the reach of the religious establishment that had ordained him.

For nearly four decades, Schulweis was left to do as he wished. As senior rabbi of Valley Beth Shalom, an influential Conservative synagogue in the upscale, largely Jewish San Fernando Valley town of Encino, Schulweis busied himself with systematically chipping away at the conventional structure of the American synagogue. Eventually he came to regard the process of decentralization and democratization he had launched as "Jewish *perestroika.*"

Among Schulweis's accomplishments: the creation and transformation of the *havurah* into the basic subunit of progressive American Jewish congregational life; the establishment and training of a cadre of hand-picked "pararabbinics" and family counselors vested with decision-making powers normally deemed the sole domain of the rabbi, and periodic attempts to undermine the fatalism and xenophobia, characteristic of some ultra-Orthodox circles, which he believes have infected the Jewish mainstream.

In the course of his pursuits, Harold Schulweis has achieved national stature—rarely attained outside of Orthodox circles—both as a congregational leader and a thinker of consequence.

290

Lately, however, he has become increasingly ill at ease. He has lived through a number of major earthquakes during his sojourn in southern California. But it is not the incessant shifting of tectonic plates underfoot that worries him. Schulweis's internal seismograph is tuned, rather, to the rumbling of a more militant Judaism that he fears could bury those who have embraced pluralism as a basic Jewish value.

Unless the Jews both here and in Israel who are not part of the ultra-Orthodox community imbue themselves with the strength, will and savvy to fend off the coming spiritual onslaught, he believes, a cataclysm will result. The warning signs, for Schulweis, are plain. In Israel, for instance, ultra-Orthodox and allied religious parties have achieved hitherto unimaginable parliamentary strength. Inevitably, he believes, they will force a change in the "who is a Jew" statute, to the detriment of non-Orthodox and secular Jews everywhere.

In California, meanwhile, astute Agudath Israel politicos stalk the halls of legislative power, seeking to become the arbiters of Jewish law on the West Coast. In Los Angeles, the Lubavitchers, or Habad, have successfully established themselves—in the eyes of many non-observant Jews and not a few Hollywood stars—as one of the few authentically Jewish activist organizations deserving funding.

These days, Schulweis, a liberal, a religious humanist and a spokesman for Conservative Judaism who professes a distinct sympathy for Reconstructionist principles, sometimes seems to stand with his back to the proverbial sea. Theologically certainly, Schulweis is far to the left of most of his colleagues. He is by no means alone in his alarm at the in-roads made by the ultra-Orthodox, but he says he was one of the first to realize they could never be appeased—that ultimately he would have to take a public stand against the values and tactics they have adopted.

"Fundamentalist Orthodoxy is practicing apartheid against us," Schulweis says. "There is a real danger now of a Karaite/Sadducee split within the Jewish people. Push is coming perilously close to shove. I myself have never spoken out on the pulpit against the Lubavitch for their cultishness and their anti-goy sentiments before. I think it's important to do so now.

"Once and for all," he adds, "non-Orthodox and secular Jews—here and in Israel—are going to have to take religion seriously. The issues I address in my sermons are not just matters of philosophy. Ideas have consequences. Theology has teeth."

Born in 1925 in the Bronx, Schulweis felt the intellectual teeth that bite and the claws that scratch early on. His father was a Socialist and a Yiddishist. The Schulweis household teemed with visiting Yiddish poets, writers and actors. The talk at the kitchen table was of the great Jewish thinkers.

"And the popular world had greats like Abba Hillel Silver and Stephen S. Wise," recalls Schulweis. "I remember going with my father to hear them at Carnegie Hall and being greatly attracted to their heroic stance. These people spoke in prophetic terms—there was a love of language and a lack of embarrassment at dealing with lofty, global Jewish concerns you don't see much these days."

Of course, Schulweis realizes that times have changed, that the ringing rhetoric of a bygone era—when the Nazi onslaught could be addressed forcefully and with great moral clarity—would now sound false.

"Things are muddier now. They've been that way since 1945—there are no open-and-shut cases. And that's true of Judaism and Israel as well. Not because of a failure of nerve, though—there is simply a general revulsion against absolutism."

Moreover, says Schulweis, the Protestantization of the American Jewish community mitigates against ideologically motivated calls to action. "There has been a tremendous amount of acculturation by American Jews—not to another religion, but to the commercialism, materialism and hedonism of what I think of as T.V. culture. But it isn't merely a Jewish phenomenon. We've all been seduced by the garden of Gucci."

Living in New York during the 1950s, one could still avoid being overwhelmed by a crass mass culture, Schulweis says. Apart from everything else it has always been, New York was a city of ideas. During his years as a graduate student in philosophy at New York University, Schulweis learned that students didn't simply take courses—they took sides. "Sidney Hook didn't teach political philosophy," he says. "He offered a program, a way of life. N.Y.U. was like that."

Schulweis's grandfather on his mother's side, however, was an Orthodox Talmudist. And he enjoyed some success in turning his grandson away from the determined secularism that pervaded his father's household. Schulweis's undergraduate degree in 1945 came from Yeshiva University, his Ph.D. in theology from the Pacific School of Religion some 30 years later.

Schulweis would not characterize himself as a maverick, but youthful rebellion did play a part in his decision to seek ordainment. He had never responded well to authoritarianism—neither his father's nor his religion's. His God, consequently, was a friend, not the tyrant many others envisage. "There are various ways in which we express our Oedipal resentments," he explains. "One is to become a rabbi."

On June 21, 1950, shortly after his ordination at the Jewish Theological Seminary, a small item in the *New York Times* caught Schulweis's eye. The story noted that Agudah rabbis had recently gathered to excommunicate Mordecai Kaplan, the founder of Reconstructionism, and to burn his prayer book.

"That excited me," recalls Schulweis. "Even before meeting him I was in his camp."

Schulweis was drawn to Kaplan's steadfastness. Here was a genuine rebel, a thorn in the side of organized Judaism. And eventually Kaplan's program sparked Schulweis's intellectual sense of wonder. The young rabbi liked the naturalism in Kaplan's approach to religion. Kaplan espoused a Judaism without supernaturalism. Rather than sanctify a glorious mythic past, he emphasized human choice and the collective experience of the Jewish people, placing a greater premium upon the present.

"I have always been attracted to the heroes of religious audacity," says Schulweis. "My earliest religious recollection is of Abraham and Moses quarreling with God—and getting away with it. I have a basic fear of subservience, of learning that the purpose of religion may merely be obedience to God."

Schulweis's first two years as a rabbi were unhappy—as an assistant rabbi at Temple Emmanuel in the Bronx neighborhood of Parkchester. "As an assistant rabbi," he recalls, "you really are what the title implies, whether you like it or not. You can't make your own decisions—there are so many channels to go through for every little thing and in the end it boils down to a practical veto by the senior rabbi."

Schulweis also found the setup too adversarial for his tastes. "If you preached a successful sermon," he says, "the senior rabbi died a little bit. If not, you caught flak. I really hated it."

Meanwhile, New York was beginning to pale for Schulweis. True, there was a continuity within the Jewish communities along the Eastern Seaboard that Schulweis learned to value. In places like Baltimore and New York, Jews had the depth of generations of Jewish life to draw on for identity and sustenance. People could talk about their grandparents having been active in one organization or another, and it meant something special to them. "There was a transmission," says Schulweis, "of sentiment and pieties which I have always treasured."

But the East Coast, he believed (and still does), was where the institutions of Jewish power resided. You could feel them looking over your shoulder. And when it comes down to that, he thought, it is time to get out.

In 1952, responding to rumors of greater spiritual freedom out West, Schulweis left New York for Oakland, where he became leader of Temple Beth Abraham, a largely middle-class synagogue of some 500 souls. The relief he felt there was palpable. California was still pioneer country—a rabbi could be inventive, could loosen up his services in a fashion that would have been unthinkable back east.

During the 1960s, Schulweis, a supporter of the N.A.A.C.P., involved himself in the civil rights movement. And as the decade progressed, he found himself identifying with the hippies of Haight-Ashbury as well. These were gentle rebels, kindred spirits. One Passover, he instructed his synagogue's sisterhood to host a second seder for the Jews among the hippies in the basement of a neighborhood Protestant church.

"It was a sight," says Schulweis. "Here were these kids with their long hair, their bangles and beads, and we all sat around singing 'Had Gadya.' "

Some time later, the University of Judaism in Los Angeles asked Schulweis to fly down to deliver a series of weekly lectures on Jewish philosophy. Schulweis liked what he saw.

Los Angeles was teeming with Jews and they seemed more intensely Jewish than their counterparts to the north. Yet L.A. was even more open to experimentation than Oakland. When Valley Beth Shalom, a small, demoralized congregation reeling from a spate of unsuccessful rabbinical stewardships, sought his services, Schulweis headed south in 1970.

His first concern, he recalls, was with the country club atmosphere he found in the synagogue, which had few qualms about excluding those who could not afford minimal dues. He consequently appealed to wealthy congregants to double and even triple their membership dues in order to pay for these people.

To his surprise—Schulweis says one of his failings, which it took him years to overcome, was a pronounced bias against the wealthy—they came through, and have continued to do so for the last 18 years. With this matter settled, he launched the shake-up of traditional religious observance he believed would never have been conceivable in the East.

It began relatively inauspiciously, with small, mostly symbolic changes. For instance, Schulweis dispensed with the rabbinic robe. It put too many barriers between himself and the congregation. He introduced Hasidic clapping to break up the somber, cathedral-like ambience of the Sabbath service. The Zeitgeist of the times, he believed, weighed against formality. Schulweis, hoping to introduce some joy into the Sabbath services, brought in an accordionist on Friday nights and, after services, encouraged his congregants to dance.

In 1973 Schulweis told a skeptical Rabbinical Assembly convention in New York's Catskill Mountains that it had dawned on him from the start that his new congregation was comprised of a new breed of Jew who required special treatment.

His grandfather, he told them, had been a religious Jew. The rhythm of his private life had been synchronized by his daily prayers, his sense of community honed by his devotion to upholding the commandments of his religion. His father, though irreligious, had not surrendered his ultimate fidelity to the Jewish people. He was, said Schulweis, an ideological Jew, as were those who became Zionists and Bundists, Socialists and atheists.

The people in Schulweis's congregation, many of them accomplished me-generationers decades before either the practice or the term gained currency, lacked an ideology to sustain them. Indeed, these "psychological Jews," as Schulweis characterized them, regarded community with as much suspicion as they did religion. The only reason they deigned to join a synagogue at all was that they figured it might benefit their children to grow up slightly less jaded in their Jewishness than they were.

In the process, however, Schulweis's congregants, neither atheists nor believers, neither Zionists nor assimilationists—merely passionless and spiritually unencumbered—had inadvertently turned their synagogue into a crass reflection of themselves.

The synagogue existed, it often seemed from their attitude and behavior, for their own private, individual enjoyment. Which is why, says Schulweis, Shabbat *Minhah* Bar Mitzvahs became the rage at Valley Beth Shalom. By holding the ceremony in the early evening when the other worshipers were safely in their homes, the parents had relieved their son of the burden of learning a haftorah, and themselves of having to throw a kiddush for a bunch of freeloaders.

On the eve of his first Rosh Hashanah at Valley Beth Shalom, convinced that he could not do business on this basis, Schulweis had a heart-to-heart chat with his flock. It was clear, he said, that they meant little to each other. They met in boardrooms, in social halls, but how many could say they had even been in one another's homes? Schulweis realized this privatism was endemic to southern California. But if they did not know each other, if they weren't friends, how could they be expected to pray, to learn and to act together?

Schulweis's remedy was the havurah. He divided those of his congregants willing to participate in his experiment into groups of 10 families, striving in each to attain a balance of social, cultural and celebratory ingredients. The task of each havurah, he said, was to teach itself, through discussions and shared readings, what it meant to be Jews; to break down the walls between them, and to coax the tremendous, pent-up lay energies contained within them.

This grand experiment proved eminently successful. People who might once have been strangers found themselves regularly sharing Sabbath meals, building sukkoth, administering *hanukot bayit*—housewarmings—and visiting the sick and bereaved.

"During an economic depression in the aerospace industry in the 70s," says Schulweis, "a number of engineers within our synagogue found themselves suddenly unemployed. I know of *havurot* which drew together to help their *haverim*, making contacts for them with employers in related fields, assisting them in the writing of résumés, offering counsel and support to the families involved."

For years, however, the "havurization" of the American synagogue was regarded with considerable trepidation within the non-Orthodox rabbinical community. During his speech to the Rabbinical Assembly Schulweis noted that many rabbis feared they and their synagogues would become superfluous as a result. If people could live Jewish lives on their own, why bother with synagogues and rabbis?

Schulweis argued that, in fact, the havurah would eventually increase the importance of the rabbi. "The rabbi becomes important to the community," he said, "only when the community itself shares his interests and participates in the sancta of our tradition."

The "Jewish distance" between the rabbi and the psychological Jews, he said, made the rabbi indispensable as a functionary but insignificant as a guide. Unfortunately, the psychological Jew needed the latter far more than the former. True, as a functionary the rabbi became indispensable. But in the process, said Schulweis, "he became less relevant."

Perestroika did not stop with the havurah. These had done wonders to personalize the synagogue, but there was more to Judaism than self-affirmation, and whatever that was, Schulweis's congregants—spiritually unsophisticated, overpowered by mass culture, their families no more immune to institutional erosion than any others in America—needed it badly.

"Outreach," complains Schulweis, has become the great Jewish slogan of our times, a panacea for all the community's organizational ills. "About 10 years ago, however," he recalls, "I realized that we didn't have a delivery system. Outreach is fine, but you have to ask the obvious question: Who is going to do the reaching out?"

Again, Schulweis looked to his congregants for an answer. The solution was to handpick members who, with suitable instruction, could be relied upon to counsel the others on Jewish matters. Schulweis had noticed, for instance, that many of his congregants knew little about the rites of passage so integral to Jewish life. A son is born, and suddenly the parents start scrambling for a *mohel* (a circumciser), for a suitable name for the child, for someone to tell them what might be entailed by the *pidyon ha'ben* (redemption of the first-born) ritual. The child approaches 13, suddenly there is the matter of a Bar Mitzvah. The parents have no clue as to what the ceremony is about or how to throw a reception that isn't tawdry but actually adds something of moral value to the event.

After training them for two years, Schulweis dispatched his pararabbinics and *mechanchei ha'mishpacha*, or family counselors, to the homes of his congregants, where they were empowered to provide information and counsel.

Thus a parent intent upon splurging on expensive floral centerpieces for a Bar Mitzvah might be persuaded to consider purchasing books instead, each to be signed with the names of those seated at their respective tables and then donated to a deserving institution, such as an orphanage or a library for the handicapped. Parents planning a lavish wedding might be urged to contribute 3 percent of the money earmarked for the *simcha* to Mazon, a locally based national program to feed the poor and homeless, Jews and non-Jews alike. Members of a family struck by the death of one of its members could receive help in choosing a cemetery, selecting a casket and arranging a service.

And at a more mundane level, Schulweis's emissaries went into the homes of families, offering parents something of Jewish value to impart to their children. "It has been my experience," says Schulweis, "that many of my congregants had nothing Jewish to say to their children. They had been struck dumb by the dominant culture. We tried to provide them with the resources—stories, songs—to restore their Jewish voices."

Of course, there could be no ignoring the psychological needs of his "psychological" Jews. Often they came to him with personal problems he as a rabbi was hard put to address. Schulweis therefore set up a counseling center at the synagogue. The counselors staffing it were members of the congregation who had been trained by professional psychiatrists and psychologists. In existence some dozen years now, the center currently assists about 100 troubled members of the wider Jewish as well as non-Jewish community each week.

Next Schulweis went to work on what he perceived as his community's warped perception of its place in the larger, non-Jewish world.

It had been his lifelong observation that Jews lapsed easily into a view of the world as implacably hostile. Not even Schulweis's affluent congregants could escape the recognition that the world appeared, as a matter of course, to detest even them.

Schulweis never has denied that anti-Semitism remains a threat in the world. But rational reasons accounted for irrational anti-Semitism— reasons ranging from jealousy and envy of Jewish success to the hatred generated by the great, terrifying Christian myth of deicide.

"But to believe that Jew-hatred possessed ontological properties," says Schulweis, "is to adopt a terminal cynicism, to withdraw from the world in the fashion of a Shimon Bar-Yochai or to assimilate in a desperate attempt to escape from this leprous community of ours. I understand Jewish resentment and anger and contempt for Western civilization," he says. "I just think it's suicidal."

Around 1960, Schulweis came across a book, *Their Brother's Keeper*, by Phillip Friedman, which documents the travails of European Christians who protected Jews from their Nazi tormentors during World War II. "As the years progressed, I realized that Friedman had only scratched the surface. Estimates now are that between 50,000 and 500,000 Christians either actively protected Jews or collaborated with those who did."

In 1962 Schulweis established his Institute for Righteous Acts, in Oakland, to undertake the empirical study of such apparent altruism and its philosophical significance for Jews. If the world could truly not abide its Jews, how could one account for so many people—even those not entirely well-disposed toward Jews—risking their lives and property to save them?

Some 25 years later, Schulweis became aware that many of these rescuers had, in fact, suffered greatly for their compassion. Many, particularly in Eastern Europe, discovered after the war that they had become pariahs in their own communities for having assisted Jews and were forced to emigrate to North America. Today, says Schulweis, most of those still alive are old, sick and impoverished. Yet the Jewish community, which was quick to set up Holocaust centers to bring Nazis to justice, has never invested nearly the same energies in helping these people.

Schulweis's response was to establish, in 1987, the Jewish Foundation for Christian Rescuers. Its mandate, he says, "is to do a Klarsfeld and Wiesenthal with these people. We have hunted out the war criminals. We have not undertaken a systematic, active search for those who helped us. It is important that we seek them out and, where necessary, try to sweeten the remainder of their lives. And it is incumbent upon us to further study this phenomenon of altruism, to discover whether it can be transmitted, perhaps even curricularized."

[The foundation is run out of the New York offices of the Anti-Defamation League of B'nai B'rith and is chaired by New York lawyer E. Robert Goodkind, whose fund-raising success has enabled the organization to provide financial and medical assistance to needful Christian rescuers, in some instances arranging urgent medical care for them, in others, getting them into Jewish homes for the elderly. The foundation has also been able to mete out regular stipends to rescuers living both in the United States and abroad. "The response within the (Jewish) community," Goodkind told me, "has been tremendously heartening."]

Schulweis recalls the mayhem not long ago in the West Bank village of Beita, where a confrontation between Arab villagers and a group of Israeli children ended in the killing of a teenage Jewish girl. The Israeli military authorities attributed the death to the accidental firing of an automatic weapon carried by one of the children's guards. (See *Present Tense*, March/April 1989.)

"An important thing happened there," says Schulweis. "Some of the Palestinian women inside Beita tried to protect the children from the mob. If we could go back in time to the Spanish Inquisition, I'd bet we'd find a fair number of ordinary people who did the same. I'm sure that this kind of thing happens all the time.

"I think our moral salvation and that of our children is dependent upon being able to face up to this. You can't preach that he who saves a single life saves an entire world and then refuse to recognize this extraordinary self-sacrifice, simply because it is more comforting to retreat inward."

Yet with few exceptions, the Jewish community has remained indifferent. Schulweis takes a jaundiced view of this insularity—he calls it "a form of chosenness that is poisoning Jewish sensibilities." And he has no doubt that the ultra-Orthodox Jewish community, and particularly Habad, which he calls a xenophobic cult fearful and disdainful of the non-Jewish world, obsessed with spiritual as well as corporeal purity, is riddled with this sense of chosenness.

Schulweis compares the unease he felt during a recent encounter with a Lubavitcher with the dread felt by Jacob while meeting his brother Esau, after wrestling an anonymous man beside the Jabbok tributary.

Esau reputedly greeted Jacob with a kiss on the neck. But biblical commentators argue that there is some ambiguity suggested in the markings over the Hebrew word "kissed." This expression of brotherly love, they think, may instead have been a long-repressed bite.

Like Esau, the *Habadnik* gripped the hapless rabbi in a bearlike embrace, professing fervent love for his *Yiddishe neshama*, his eternal Jewish soul. With regard to Schulweis's interpretation of Jewish life and law, however, the bearded rabbi was less charitable. The Lubavitcher rebbe had clearly instructed that one could neither love nor accept heresy—one could only mourn its occurrence and take steps, wherever possible, to root it out.

But what, asked Schulweis, if the rebbe were wrong in dismissing his brand of Judaism as heresy? Surely the Rambam himself would have been loath to render so drastic a judgment. "I'll tell you the truth," said the Habadnik. "I'd rather follow my own rebbe when he is wrong than follow you when you're right."

The Habadnik then kissed Schulweis on the cheek, asked that he not take offense and left. Schulweis has been doing a slow burn ever since.

Schulweis was offended because he believes this kind of thinking threatens to obliterate a pluralism that lies at the heart of Judaism.

History, not just tradition, is what makes Judaism, Schulweis believes; no text alone, however sacred, can offer the final word on it.

At first, Schulweis thought that his friends within the Orthodox community would ultimately repudiate the divisive disdain expressed by the ultra-Orthodox. But it never happened. People who were delighted to discuss Jewish issues with him over coffee and cake refused to appear on his pulpit or to share in prayer with him at his synagogue. Like the Catholic clergy before Vatican II, they feared that doing so would bestow legitimacy or equality upon his own brand of observance. "The moderate Orthodox have remained silent over attempts to delegitimize us because they fear the ultra-Orthodox may turn on them as well."

Indeed, Schulweis recalls from his seminary days an inclination within the Conservative movement to appease the Orthodox. It was clear to him then, he says, that they would never succeed at this, no matter how reverential their behavior.

Eventually, Conservative Jews learned the lesson only now becoming apparent to the modern Orthodox. Ultra-Orthodoxy is inherently exclusionist. Even the Hasidic movement finds itself divided over the proper interpretation of the word of God. Within the cloistered world of the ultra-Orthodox, the sight of a knitted *kipa*, or skullcap, which the non-Hasidic Orthodox favor, can inspire suspicion and delegitimization. Within the ultra-Orthodox world today, there is, for instance, mounting unease with the Zionist component of modern Orthodoxy. Some believe that Zionist nationalism has undermined other, traditional Jewish values. Ultimately, believes Schulweis, the modern Orthodox movement will find itself singled out. It, too, will learn that there can be no appeasing such true believers.

Today Schulweis rarely talks the shallow rhetoric of unity among the Jewish people. Today he appears to believe that Jews will do better to preserve the "space in their togetherness" than to achieve "a smothering intimacy that obliterates all differentiation."

"So many of the problems we regard as external are really internal," Schulweis says. "American Jews are so naive, they think that by contributing money to Habad or other institutions ostensibly urging Jewish unity, they are helping to ensure the survival of an 'authentic' Judaism. What they don't realize is that money talks, and that in this instance it speaks for divisiveness."

Schulweis hopes that the most recent flap over the proposed redefinition of "who is a Jew" in Israel will, in fact, sensitize the non-Orthodox to the dangers they face. "Perhaps now they will understand that the ultra-Orthodox are not merely eccentric and idiosyncratic."

The fundamentalist Orthodox, Schulweis believes, face an even greater internal danger, engaging as they do in what Schulweis calls "exclusionary split thinking." He says, "Split thinking is a disease. When you do it you lock yourself out of a tremendous reservoir of history and ethos, ritual and charm and beauty."

Schulweis recounts a marvelous anecdote to illustrate his fear of Orthodox exclusivity, which he argues is based upon an inherent metaphysical racism. The story tells of two Lubavitchers. One of them explains: "The whole world is divided between 'them' and 'us.' No point speaking about 'them.' Among 'us,' the world is divided between Ashkenazim and Sephardim. No use talking about Sephardim. Among Ashkenazim, the world is divided between Hasidim and Mitnagdim. No use talking about Mitnagdim. Among the Hasidim, the world is divided between the Satmar and the Lubavitcher. No use talking about the Satmar. Among the Lubavitcher there are the intellectual and the *farbrengen* types. No use to talk about the latter. Among the intellectuals there are you and me. And you know how little you know."

In the end, however, not even Schulweis has been able to escape the lure of split thinking—at least not with regard to the question of Palestinian nationalism and the *intifada,* or uprising, that it has provoked. Schulweis was outspoken in criticism of the massacres at the Sabra and Shatilla refugee camps in Lebanon; he has given his pulpit over to Hanna Siniora, the editor of the pro-Palestine Liberation Organization East Jerusalem newspaper *Al-Fajr* (and to speakers for the right-wing Americans for a Safe Israel as well); but he has remained unusually silent during the intifada.

Though against split-thinking, Schulweis stands foursquare behind *havdalah*—separation, or in the case of his own silence on this matter, the distinction between what he calls dissent and intervention.

Despite the belief among a growing number of Jews in this country that diaspora Jewry must be moved to criticize certain Israeli policies— that it alone is in a position to do so safely and rightfully—dissent does not, says Schulweis, appear to be absent within Israel itself; nor is it in danger of fading from the scene.

As proof he notes that the Israeli Supreme Court recently overruled the military censor and even the Mossad, Israel's external intelligence agency, in the matter of the publication of an article critical of the Mossad's former chief. Lieutenant General Dan Shomron, the Israel Defense Force's Chief of Staff, has testified at a closed-door session of the Knesset's Defense and Foreign Affairs Committee that he does not see much chance for the army to quell the intifada, and this, says Schulweis, has been bandied about freely in the Israeli press. Senior I.D.F. officers have repeatedly warned of the adverse effects the policing of the occupied territories is having on the army's morale and its training schedules, and their concerns are shared by a majority of Israelis.

Still, says Schulweis, the diaspora dissenter's problem is not so much that there is no dissent in Israel, but that Israeli dissent has not succeeded in forcing a turnabout in foreign policy.

Between Israel and the diaspora, Schulweis believes, there is, at best, a limited partnership—one in which Jews outside Israel assume few of the risks of their Israeli counterparts. Schulweis has a son who lives on a kibbutz and who serves in *miluim*, the army reserves. He pays taxes and has—says Schulweis—won the right to participate in the public argument over the proper course of Israeli foreign affairs.

In contrast, he notes, people like Stanley Sheinbaum—one of five American Jews who went to Stockholm last December to meet with P.L.O. chairman Yasser Arafat—intervened in the affairs of a sovereign state of which they are not citizens. Convinced of their judgment, they have "infantilized" the Jewish state in the manner of a father who imposes his will on a foolish child who must be saved from endangering itself.

And what if critics are not correct, asks Schulweis? "What life and death consequences for diaspora Jewry follow upon the interventionists' endangering decisions?" Indeed, he says not even the death of an average of one Palestinian youngster a day will force him to intervene in a situation he believes is far more complex and morally shaded than that depicted in the media. Not if it goes on for one more year and not for another 10.

It's not a question of numbers or age, and it's not a question of time," says Schulweis. "I just don't know what to say, and I think it can sometimes take as much courage to shut up when that is the case as many assume it takes to speak out in dissent. I'm not at all sure that silence is always a mark of cowardice and dissent the mark of moral heroism.

"I think the bottom line, for me, is that I have a feeling for the sincerity and morality and democratic character of the Government elected by the people of Israel. My take on Israel is that they're all scared as hell. I don't think they enjoy this intifada. Their fear is genuine and justified, and they are in the process of working it out. Until they do, I am not going to use whatever political clout I may have to pressure them to do something they might think is against their interests."

So how come Harold Schulweis pulls out the stops when it comes to the "who is a Jew" imbroglio?

"For all its intensity," says Schulweis, "in no way does *this* intervention affect the safety and security of Israel. Moreover, the amendment directly affects the status of diaspora Jews and their religious institutions. Nor is there any question here of dealing with the state's sworn enemies.

"The fact is that there is no duplicity in joining the dissent on one issue and opposing it on another. All dissent is not rolled up into one package."

Ariel Sharon

Matthew Nesvisky

Not long ago, Ariel (Arik) Sharon was the second most powerful man in Israel. As Prime Minister Menachem Begin's health and spirits declined, Sharon appeared to many observers to be the cabinet's driving force. He had concluded the war in Lebanon—which was being perceived as "Sharon's war"—and was busily engaged in negotiations for a peace agreement with the Lebanese. Some Israelis thought that both the invasion and the diplomatic efforts could enhance the likelihood that Israel would retain the West Bank, an objective which Sharon had aggressively espoused. In short, Sharon and his views were riding high in the winter of 1982–1983.

Today the 56-year-old ex-general with the boyish cowlick has been reduced to what, by any measure, must be considered an ignominious position. He is still in the government, but, as a minister without portfolio, he has no specific duties. His chief supporter, Menachem Begin, is no longer in office, and Prime Minister Yitzhak Shamir apparently doesn't quite know what to do with Sharon.

Shamir has good reason to keep Sharon on, for a government that survives no-confidence motions by only one vote needs all the support it can get. But, because Sharon is quarrelsome in the cabinet and unpopular with a large segment of the public, many in the government no doubt secretly wish that Arik Sharon would somehow just go away.

In this contentious nation, which has never lacked controversial leaders, few have sparked the passions Sharon has aroused. Only two have inspired street demonstrators to chant their names along with the title of "King of Israel"—Menachem Begin and Arik Sharon.

But even Begin never inspired the kind of vituperation the news media have visited on Sharon. He has been called a psychopath, a lunatic, an egomaniac, a McCarthyite, a war criminal. Those who admitted to grudging admiration for his bold military exploits likened him to General George Patton; others saw Sharon only as a target for pitiless criticism.

Much of this name-calling is conveyed in Israel's feisty press, and the news media became something of an obsession with Sharon, and he has begun to give as good—or as bad—as he gets. Last fall, with no other duties than occasional fund-raising efforts abroad, Sharon was given the job of supporting the Likud government's candidates in mayoralty elections, and he spent weeks haranguing crowds in cities and development towns all over the country. He rarely addressed the issues, and usually said little about the candidates. Instead, he attacked the news media.

It was the press and television, Sharon said again and again, that were undermining morale in the army and among civilians. The media, he said, were riddled with "leftists," "liars," "fifth columnists," "anti-Zionists" and "poisoners of the nation." It was the press, Sharon charged, that had damaged the spirit of Menachem Begin. It was the press that was serving enemy interests. It was the press that was going to lose the achievements of the Lebanon war and the security provided by the West Bank and the Gaza Strip.

While these attacks on an easily identifiable adversary as the source of the country's ills were popular with some Israelis—mainly dissaffected youths in poor neighborhoods—Sharon's behavior appalled much of the public and, of course, newspeople themselves.

Last September, the Jerusalem Journalists Association took the unprecedented step of declaring that it would not report on Sharon's activities or speeches, or even print his name. The journalists soon reversed this decision as ill-advised and counterproductive, but believed they had made a point. On the other hand, Sharon also scored when he said that a boycott by "the lying press" could only be to his benefit.

Several weeks after this episode, I called Sharon's office to arrange an interview for this article. I had no sooner introduced myself than

Sharon's spokesman, Uri Dan, launched into a long, ear-blistering denunciation of the media, describing all reporters as "vermin, liars, cheats, word-twisters, assassins, sensationalists." The fact that I had never written a word about Sharon didn't count; I was a newsman and therefore against the interests of the state. Further, Dan pointed out, I work for *The Jerusalem Post*, a publication that "never once printed a true word about Arik," and "broadcasts its libels throughout the world." Finally, he told me I could call back in a few days—but a dozen calls to Uri Dan and other members of Sharon's staff proved fruitless.

Ariel Sharon is not the first Israeli politician to criticize the press. (Labor Party leaders did so when they were in power, as Likud leaders do today.) Nor are the scrappy Israeli news media always models of journalistic responsibility, especially when they unloose the charged rhetoric that is frequently flung at politicians of the right. Still, when a public figure repeatedly makes blanket condemnations of the press that smacks of a desire to slay the messenger for bearing ill tidings. In the end, in assessing his behavior, one image appears to suit Sharon—that of an injured animal blindly striking out in all directions.

Indeed, Sharon has reason to feel injured. His present problems arose largely from the Lebanon war and its aftermath. At the beginning, the invasion was recognized as a classic Sharon steamroller offensive, but the quick initial successes gave way to the prolonged siege of Beirut, the Sabra and Shatilla massacres and the occupation of part of the country. Then, both local and foreign criticism inevitably focused on the man who personified the war and the policies behind it.

The Kahan commission of inquiry into the circumstances of the massacres strongly suggested that Defense Minister Sharon should resign. Some of his cabinet colleagues let it be known that they thought Sharon had misled and deceived them during the course of the war. Much of the press and the public questioned whether Sharon had been allowed to go too far.

Just as he had always done in his army career, Sharon met attack with counterattack. He insisted that the war had not gone badly, that the "perverted" press merely made it seem so. He eschewed any responsibility for the massacres, charging that when the Labor Party was in power it had worked hand-in-glove with Lebanon's Phalangists, who slaughtered Palestinians in 1976. As for resigning, Sharon maintained that he would not be made a scapegoat, and in effect challenged the Prime Minister to fire him. In the end, he agreed to give up his post as Defense Minister, on the understanding that he would remain in the cabinet.

Unquestionably, a disappointed and frustrated public is likely to seek out an individual on whom to heap blame just as an individual under attack would strongly defend himself. But, all that aside, where does that leave Arik Sharon today?

Sharon has had two careers, in the army and in politics. The first ended in the sort of cul de sac he seems to have reached. It's somewhat surprising to recall Sharon's failures, because for more than a generation he was for many people the symbol of the quintessential Israeli farmer-soldier. In fact, it is generally believed that Sharon was the model for Ari Ben-Canaan, the indomitable hero of Leon Uris's blockbuster novel, *Exodus*.

Like the fictional character, Ariel Sharon was born on a farm—in Kfar Malal, a cooperative village in the Sharon Plain, which was established by his Russian-born father, Shmuel Scheinerman. Shmuel taught his young son to use firearms to fight off crop-stealing Arabs; while still a teenager, Arik joined the Haganah, the pre-statehood underground army. As a platoon commander in the 1948 War of Independence, he was severely wounded in the battle of Latrun. Nevertheless, he returned to combat and by the end of the war had earned a reputation for imagination, initiative and absolute fearlessness.

Such attributes made Sharon the natural choice to command the elite volunteer Unit 101 in the early 1950s. Operating like the World War II Desert Rats, this special outfit was formed to respond to terrorist infiltration, which by the middle of the decade had produced more than 1,000 Israeli casualties. The unit's task was to mount deep-penetration reprisal raids across the borders into Jordan and Egypt.

At first, Unit 101's actions gave the young nation a sorely needed boost in morale. But Sharon soon appeared to be overly zealous. In 1953, for example, after a raid on an Israeli village, he had been instructed to attack fedayeen (Arab commandos) in the Jordanian village of Qibya. Sharon's raiders blew up many houses and a school, and left sixty-nine Jordanians dead. Sharon denies knowing that people were in the houses. Still, international criticism of this action proved highly embarrassing to Prime Minister David Ben-Gurion. Government and military leaders alike began to be concerned about this brash young officer.

But a pattern had been set that would be repeated again and again. In the 1956 Sinai Campaign, Sharon's troops captured the strategic Mitla Pass in a lightning maneuver, thus assuring victory for the entire army. But four of Sharon's battalion commanders charged Sharon with perhaps the most serious accusations that can be leveled against a commander: exceeding his orders and fighting an "unnecessary battle." The four demanded that Sharon resign; he firmly refused. Then Sharon was put in charge of training programs and given study leave.

In the 1967 Six Day War, Sharon commanded a division that captured all the strategic points in the Sinai—again using stunning tactics.

Eventually, Sharon was given the task of pacifying the Gaza Strip, which was plagued by Arab terrorists. He pacified the area, but his methods apparently shocked many of his men, and upset his superior officers. An investigation cleared Sharon of the charge of using excessive force, but he was pulled off the job. "But I got the job done," he said. "The terrorism was stopped, and the Arabs and the Israelis lived in peace."

By 1973, Sharon apparently became convinced that he had advanced as far as he could in the army, and that the coveted position of Chief of Staff would never be his. In what must have been a heart-wrenching decision, he resigned from the army to take up a career in politics.

Before the Knesset elections could be held, however, the 1973 Yom Kippur War broke out and, as a reservist general, Sharon was mobilized. Once again he performed brilliantly, this time crossing the Suez Canal and cutting off the Egyptian armies from Cairo.

In the December 1973 elections, Sharon gained a seat in the Knesset. And when the Likud came to power in 1977 he was named Minister of Agriculture. His four-year tenure in this post was almost as stormy as his career in the army.

For example, because of his single-minded concentration on building settlements in the West Bank, Sharon was accused of allowing Israel's once-proud agricultural economy to collapse. Moshavim (cooperative farms) went bankrupt, vegetable and flower exports tumbled, and the nation was treated to the spectacle of farmers plowing under citrus groves that had been productive for years. To be sure, the entire economy suffered in the period after the Yom Kippur War—but that was small consolation to farmers who believed that their minister saw settlements only in terms of security and politics, and thereby denied them funds they insisted should go to them.

Equally controversial were the armed "Green Patrols" that Sharon established to keep Bedouin goatherders off state land. The patrols were repeatedly denounced for bulldozing Bedouin shacks and carting off women and children to resettlement camps.

At the same time, Sharon's own farm, the largest private landholding in the country, became a perpetual source of embarrassment to the Begin government. All other cabinet ministers complied with regulations, divesting themselves of personal business interests. Sharon alone refused to do so, and his legal maneuvers to forestall giving up the farm went on for years before a compromise was worked out.

Controversy about Sharon's tenure as agriculture minister pales in comparison to the tempests that blew up during his stewardship of the defense portfolio. For as long as he could, Begin held the defense portfolio himself, but finally he acceded to coalition demands and relinquished it to the ex-general. If Begin did not later regret this decision, many others inside and outside the government did.

The first opposition to Sharon after he became defense minister in August 1981 came from the defense establishment itself after he announced plans for a sweeping reorganization. His proposals included a top defense post for his old friend, Arye Genger, an Israeli who had been living in the United States long enough to acquire American citizenship and become a millionaire businessman. Such moves, and especially the heavy-handed manner with which Sharon attempted to implement them, led to the first strikes in the history of the defense establishment.

Another storm raged over Sharon's creation of "civil administration" in the West Bank—which, despite its name, was mainly staffed by career army officers. Then, during Sharon's attempts at rapprochement with Arab residents there, Israel witnessed the worst period of violence since the territories were taken over after the Six Day War. To observers who recalled that he had opposed the Camp David accords and had termed the autonomy plan a "trap," the turmoil on the West Bank under Sharon was hardly a surprise.

All this was eclipsed in the summer of 1982 by the invasion of Lebanon. What may have appeared at first as a justifiable attempt to assure "peace for Galilee" ended, many believed, as the costliest, least defensible and most demoralizing military experience in Israel's history. Long before the war, novelist Amos Oz had warned that "an evil wind of Unit 101 adventurism" was sweeping the land.

It would seem that, just as Sharon went as far as he could in the army, he has reached a similar dead end in his political career. While he remains popular with former supporters and young men who still revere him as a brilliant field commander who can rout any Arab army, they hardly make up a wide enough base to be considered true public support.

Sharon stands on equally shaky ground within the cabinet. Despite any doubts Begin may have had about Sharon, he always backed him publicly—but Begin is gone. Deputy Prime Minister David Levy has long been Sharon's most outspoken critic, and recently Sharon has made enemies by provoking clashes over the Likud's economic policies and bitterly attacking Moshe Arens, his successor as defense minister.

Whether Prime Minister Yitzhak Shamir will give his contentious colleague another post is an open question. Sharon has suggested that he would like to become the minister in charge of settlement in the territories. But Science and Development Minister Yuval Ne'eman, certainly no less committed than Sharon to promoting the Jewish presence on the West Bank and in Gaza, currently handles that task. Another suggestion is that a post be created making Sharon "Minister for World Jewry." Some diaspora figures have greeted this idea with a shudder.

Is Ariel Sharon, then, effectively finished? Presumably he will always have a home on the political right—and his political fortunes may be linked to the future of the West Bank. Should another Israel government prove more yielding on the territory issue than the present one, and should the Israeli public feel that territorial compromise jeopardizes its security, many would be likely to rally around the man who, for all his faults, has never wavered in his defense of the state.

However, few signs of territorial compromise are evident, and the conventional wisdom is that no government which wants to survive will opt for it without broad public endorsement.

Meanwhile, a man once widely admired for his tactical genius, courage and personal charm is now engaged in the rather unseemly business of railing against "the enemy within"—claiming that Israel's problems stem "not so much from the Arabs as they do from the Jews." Labor Party Knesset member General Mordechai Gur says Sharon is "unbalanced, adventurous, dangerous," but this is regarded as opposition party hyperbole. But today Ariel Sharon clearly is behaving very much like an angry man.

Rabbi Joseph Dov Soloveitchik

Sylvia Rothchild

Т he most important thing I learned from the Rav is that Judaism doesn't give you peace of mind. It just gives you the strength to struggle," a student said.

Everyone stands respectfully when Rabbi Joseph Dov Soloveitchik enters the dining hall of the Maimonides School in Brookline, Massachusetts. His Saturday night lectures, free and open to the public, attract large audiences. Members of his local community, yehiva students, Harvard undergraduates, rabbis, teachers, young and middle-aged couples, and curious outsiders come to experience his Torah lessons. His listeners include members of the *chevra chas* (men who study the Talmud), the group who invited him to Boston in 1932 to be their teacher and—a title, rather than a position—their "Chief Rabbi."

His reputation as a Talmudic scholar and philosopher of *halakhah* is worldwide, but he is spoken of simply as "the Rav." Those who follow his Saturday *shiyurim* (lessons)—an extraordinary mixture of service, Talmud class, philosophical exploration and poetry reading—find themselves in the presence of a complex and fascinating man.

The long white beard, thick spectacles and tentative public smile suggest the traditional rabbi. He gave his talks in Yiddish during his early years in Boston, but now he speaks in a flowery, academic English with a Yiddish accent, making points with familiar Talmudic gestures. A product of both Jewish and Western scholarship, he uses images from mathematics and physics; he quotes Plato, Aristotle, Kierkegaard and Kant as well as the Jewish sages.

The Rav, a man of many faces and voices, can be warm, personal and move his listeners to tears. He can also be aloof, formal, impatient, a little forbidding when he puts down questions that interrupt his train of thought. His voice is deep when he reads from Hebrew or Aramaic texts and high-pitched, almost a falsetto, when he speaks English.

His talks usually begin with a few lines from the Bible, the Psalms or the Prayer Book. He develops them like a composer with a musical theme, variations, repetitions, fugues, codas and cadenzas presented without concern for the hour or the attention span of his listeners.

The Saturday *shiyur* starts at nine and may continue until long after midnight. The audience relaxes, dozes, takes notes. An artist sketches as he listens. The Rav provides a spiritual focus for his followers; they say they come to him for "spiritual nourishment," for "recharging." In the midst of a society which ignores the *halakha* that governs their lives, they have a need to be in a room full of people who value and respect the same traditions. For them the Maimonides School, which Rav Soloveitchik created, is a kind of home.

His prestige as a visible figure of authority is very important to them. They are aware that he has the respect of Reform rabbis, secular academics and intellectuals. They express a sense of privilege that this famous interpreter of Jewish law is their teacher and rabbi. They speak with pride of meeting Orthodox Jews in other parts of the world who envy them their opportunity to hear the Rav's lectures.

The students respond with special warmth and enthusiasm. They anticipate the Rav's arguments and the development of his favorite themes. There are whispers of "Now he will say," and some finish his sentences *sotto voce* before he does.

"One grasps the wisdom of the Omnipresent," says the Rav, "when one understands *halakhah*." He teaches that *halakhah* is a way of thinking as well as a religious system of behavior which forbids some actions, permits others and requires still others. He speaks of the *halakhah* rather than of Judaism — sometimes of "a *halakhah*," a single law, sometimes of the general idea of the Law, a divinely ordained discipline, a blueprint for an ideal existence, which is more concerned with the sanctity than the dignity of man.

His interpretations discourage divisions between the sacred and profane aspects of life. His objective is to integrate the secular and religious in a unifying religious system of behavior. His explanations reveal considerable flexibility and concern for human weakness. He stresses that the *halakhah* demands a great deal, but also offers possibilities for atonement and forgiveness.

Many of Rav Soloveitchik's lectures deal with humility and the need for repentance. Jews who accept the *halakhah* are expected to subordinate their own desires to the "will of God." The Rav often reminds his followers that the purpose of the *halakhah* is not to make men happy but "great of spirit" and "aware of the Divine."

As he talks, one perceives his determination to clarify each concept, his effort to extract every drop of meaning from the lines he chooses. In the process, understanding and believing become one. Abstract ideas evolve into religious consciousness. Modern insights seem to develop naturally out of ancient wisdom. The lines between prophecy and prayer, prayer and action, study and prayer almost dissolve.

In an interview with Rav Soloveitchik at his daughter's home in Brookline, I found him worldly, charming, easy to talk to. He reminisced about the deep religious experiences of his childhood, which underlay all of his community's life in Eastern Europe, and the difficulties he'd had in recreating them. He referred to the Sabbaths and holidays, the real preoccupation with repentance on Yom Kippur and the real sorrow of Tishah B'Ab that are unknown to most American Jews.

In his teaching, he is obviously concerned that holy days be *experienced* rather than *observed*. Nothing is sacred, he says, until man makes it so, and the decision to make time sacred is a human responsibility—a destiny that can be chosen. But, he recognizes, problems arise between making the decision and carrying it out.

On Tishah B'Ab, a fast day of mourning in memory of the destruction of the Temple in Jerusalem, Rav Soloveitchik tries to recapture his own feelings and share them with his followers. The sanctuary at the Maimonides School becomes a place of mourning. The day is spent on the literature of sorrow and suffering. The Rav reads from the Book of Lamentations, commenting on the text as he goes along. Young men in jackets and sneakers (a sign of mourning) sit on the floor with prayer shawls wrapped around their heads. A father sits with his children on his lap. Other families spend the day listening to the Rav and praying together. At sundown they break the fast together.

The Rav has had his greatest influence as a professor of Talmud at Yeshiva University in New York City. He has held this post since he succeeded his father, Rav Moshe Soloveitchik at the Rabbi Isaac Elchanan Theological Seminary in 1941. Many generations of rabbinical students who have known him as a teacher in the last thirty-six years continue to accept him as the supreme religious authority.

While Boston has been his place of residence since he came to this country, Yeshiva University keeps him in touch with young rabbis and his large, far-flung community of fellow scholars. His need to continue commuting between the two cities at the age of seventy-four is evidence of the importance both communities hold for him. In addition to his teaching, Rav Soloveitchik gives Talmud lectures to the general public in New York City at Congregation Moriah in midtown Manhattan and sometimes at the 92nd Street YM-YWHA, but Boston provides a more intimate community. He lives close to his daughter, Dr. Atara Twersky, the wife of Rabbi Isadore Twersky, who holds the Harry Wolfson Chair in Judaica at Harvard, and his grandchildren.

In summer, Rav Soloveitchik conducts classes on the patio of the Maimonides School, a modern building in a quiet neighborhood of large Victorian houses with ample lawns and huge shade trees. Yeshiva students from New York, Harvard majors in philosophy and psychology, recent graduates of the school and a handful of retired men, members of his original *chevra*, study Talmud in a New England atmosphere.

The yeshiva-trained young men fall automatically into the habit of rocking back and forth as they study. Young men in tattered jeans and beanies instead of skull caps look like secular Cambridge types, but their concentrated attention during a discussion in Aramaic shows a kind of devotion rare in secular study.

On a pleasant summer day when the tennis courts, swimming pools and beaches are crowded, the Talmud classes at Maimonides seem at first glance to be in another world totally separated from anything happening in Brookline—or the rest of America, for that matter. But, listening to the discussions, a visitor might find surprising connections between the commentaries of the sages and current news headlines. For example, one afternoon he discussed the commentaries on a few lines in Deuteronomy (13-18). They dealt with the problems of separating true from false prophets, sorting out those who try to mislead others from those who succeed, and considering the difference between misleading a single individual and a multitude. Contemporary affairs were never mentioned, but impossible to ignore.

In the class was a Harvard undergraduate who had studied with the Rav for four years and was enjoying a last immersion in Talmud study before going on to his secular studies. He spoke of Rav Soloveitchik with great affection and respect. ("The best thing about him is that he's such a nice guy—an absolute genius—no one has done more to bring intellectuals and Talmud scholars together.") He was especially taken with the Rav's "ability to squeeze every shred of idealism out of the Gemara" and "go deeper than anyone else to reveal the best minds of all time."

A student in computer science from New York told me he came for the summer classes with the Rav because he was "the best Talmud analyzer in the world. I'm not here because of his personality," he declared. "It's his method I come for. If there was someone better, I'd go study with him wherever he was." He confided that he studied with Rav Soloveitchik at "great economic cost," because the time he spent on Talmud limited his ability to earn money. In his early twenties and single, he said he would marry only a girl who would accept his passion for Talmud study.

The Rav's class is not like a university seminar. He poses questions and answers them himself. He doesn't like to waste time on student opinions. His objective is to get them to understand the words of the sages. He reminds them that Torah logic is not the same as Western logic, that Torah can be interpreted in various ways and that conflicting interpretations can be equally correct.

When the class is over, he relaxes. He greets his students one by one, touching an elbow or shoulder to establish contact. He apologizes for not spending more time with them, though the class has been in session more than four hours.

A rabbinical conference at the Maimonides School last August brought a few hundred Orthodox rabbis to Boston to study with Rav Soloveitchik. With them he spoke in practical terms, discussing specific laws and customs, celebrations of holidays, proper observance of the 613 commandments. When questions were asked, the answers were sought in Maimonides and Rashi. The Rav said it is understood that guidance must come from the sages, not from personal opinion or common sense. Study is absolutely essential in order to know what is permitted and forbidden.

A few weeks later the Rav lectured to a conference of psychiatric social workers on the *halakhic* concept of community. He described his vision of a "covenantal community," the highest form of social organization. In the act of praying together, he explained, pain is shared and sympathy evoked. He described the best community as one in which prayer becomes action. He reminded his listeners that the teaching community is the most developed and that the central figure in Jewish history was not a political figure but Moses, the teacher.

Rav Soloveitchik spoke of his concern about the dual role of man as a lonely and relating being, and about the connection between freedom and loneliness. One of his listeners, troubled by the formality and didacticism of his presentation, at first thought he wasn't relating to his audience because he read from a paper. Later she said she had not been prepared for the intensity and seriousness of his teaching. "He went deeper than any speaker we ever had," she said. She was not aware of how carefully he had prepared his message to respond to the needs of an audience of social workers.

Rav Soloveitchik has written a great deal but published very little. His reputation as the leader of enlightened orthodoxy was acquired as a teacher and lecturer. An annual discourse at Yeshiva University on the anniversary of his father's death attracts thousands of people and is a major academic event for American Orthodox Jews.

A descendant of a long dynasty of great Talmudists who were committed to an oral tradition and left little in print, the Rav claims that his wish for perfection makes him reluctant to publish his essays. There are rumors that some of his work will be published in the near future. Meanwhile his followers bring tape recorders to his lectures and try to reconstruct his messages. *The Jewish Advocate* in Boston has printed a few reconstructions of his lectures. *Hanevaser*, the official student publication of the Jewish studies department of Yeshiva University, published *A Conspectus of the Public Lectures of Rabbi Joseph Dov Soloveitchik* in 1974. It offers some clues to his subjects, but naturally cannot reflect the charisma of his delivery.

Three essays the Rav was willing to publish were "Man of Halacha" in *Talpioth* in 1944, "Confrontation" in *Tradition* 6 in 1964 and "The Lonely Man of Faith" in *Tradition* 7 in 1965.

In these works, as in his lectures and discussions, he expresses his fascination with man as a divided creature, passive and active, both cause and effect. His vision of man is not as an orderly, rational being but as a contradictory and paradoxical one, ravaged by conflict and crisis, attracted and repelled by the mystery of divinity. He believes men and women are capable of childish innocence and faith, no matter how outwardly sophisticated they may appear to be. His conceptions are closer to the thinking of some Catholic theologians than to that of liberal Jewish thinkers. One of his students at Harvard said that the Rav is often quoted as a neo-Kantian, which is no surprise since the subject of his doctoral dissertation was the metaphysics of Hermann Cohen, a disciple of Kant.

The Rav's concern for the conflicting forces in man seems to be related to his experiences in several different worlds. He was born in Pruzhan, Poland in February 1903, into a family which had been famous for Jewish scholarship and accomplishment since the middle of the 18th century. The *Encyclopaedia Judaica* contains several pages on the accomplishments of this dynasty of great Talmudists.

He has continued the scholarly line of his grandfather, Rav Haym Soloveitchik, known as "the Brisker Rav" (because of the time he spent in Brisk) who revitalized Talmudic study with a technique of scientific classification and rigorous analysis. His son, Rav Moshe Soloveitchik, the present Rav's father, introduced the Brisker method as a rabbi-teacher in various East European communities—and Joseph Dov, in turn, brought the method to American rabbis and students.

The "American" Rav Soloveitchik spent his childhood in Khoslavitch, a White Russian town, where his father was the rabbi. He studied in the local *cheder* (Hebrew school) under an elderly Habad Hasid until his mother, a learned daughter of a rabbinic scholar, became alarmed at the inadequacy of his education. Beginning at the age of twelve, his father supervised his training according to the Brisker method, a process that demanded a high degree of intellectual, moral and religious discipline. His father also guided his study of the Maimonides *Mishneh Torah*. His mother, meanwhile, introduced him to the writings of Ibsen, Pushkin and Bialik, among other secular authors. Until he was twenty-two, he prepared to enter the University of Berlin with the help of a series of private tutors. He entered the university in 1925, studied mathematics, physics and philosophy, and received his doctorate in 1931. He then married Dr. Tonya Lewit, who had a Ph.D. in education from the University of Jena. A year later the Rav, his wife and their firstborn child emigrated to Boston.

Rav Soloveitchik, born into a tradition that emphasized the intellectual responsibilities of the rabbinate, was prepared to be a student, scholar and teacher. He had, however, experienced Hasidic teaching as a child, rigorous Talmud study with his father and the secular intellectual life at the University of Berlin. He knew both the pious and impoverished life of Orthodox Jews in Eastern Europe and the formal, restrained atmosphere of Orthodox Jewish life in Berlin. None of those experiences prepared him for Jewish orthodoxy in America in 1932.

He spent his first years in the United States in a profound state of culture shock. Though he had found the Berlin Jews too proper, too rational and too concerned with appearances, Boston Orthodox Jewry seemed by comparison lacking in education and sophistication. The High Holidays in Berlin were dignified and elegant occasions. In Boston he was shocked by the policemen who stood at the synagogue door to collect tickets. The noisy selling of *aliyoth* (honors) and the lack of decorum in the congregations made him feel that attendance at services were social occasions rather than deep religious experiences.

American congregations have always seemed to him like clubs for rootless people rather than places for religious sensitivity and spontaneity. His concern for prayers as, in his words, "a mirror of human behavior rather than a hollow decorum," set him in opposition to those who were mainly interested in esthetic services. His sense of prayer as an awakening of the self to moral obligations rather than a removal from reality—his conviction that the true sanctuary is created by the forms of daily life, by study and observance of the law—made him unsympathetic to the fashion for pulpits, vestments, stained glass and pipe organs.

Rav Soloveitchik seems uncomfortable with the tone of Jewish communal life, with the emphasis on fellowship and fund-raising. He still speaks bitterly of the failure of American Jews to save more of European Jewry during the Hitler years. He speaks warmly of American-Jewish support for Israel even though he doesn't encourage settlement there, in part because he sees a future for orthodoxy in America.

In 1959, after the death of Israel's Chief Rabbi, Isaac Herzog, Rav Soloveitchik declined an invitation to succeed him as Ashkenazi Chief Rabbi. Though Orthodox Israelis are still troubled by his refusal to join them, his American followers find it easier to understand his preference for the *Galut* (exile) experience. His concept of exile, described in a lecture at Congregation Kehilath Jeshurun in New York in 1972, is that it began with Adam upon his expulsion from Paradise. He believes the experience of exile to be "the essence of the Jewish people."

In "The Lonely Man of Faith," Rav Soloveitchik described himself as "a stranger in a modern society that is technical-minded, self-centered, self-loving." He wrote: "My doctrines are not technical. . . . My law cannot be laboratory-tested. What can I say to a functional, utilitarian society?" There are many references to his feelings of loneliness and homelessness in his lectures and essays.

In spite of his feelings of isolation, which he admits are psychological, he has had a rich public life and a warm private one. His wife was an inspiration and helpmate until she died in 1967. The Rav's annual memorial lecture in her memory keeps her name and accomplishments alive.

The Rav set himself the task of creating a constituency with a knowledge of Torah as soon as he came to Boston. Though he found few peers who shared his education and outlook, he made himself available to young Talmudic scholars and organized an informal institute with regular Talmud lessons, weekly lectures for laymen and occasional lengthy public discourses.

He immediately recognized that the children of the *chevra chas* members were not following in their fathers' footsteps, and founded a school to help save another generation for orthodoxy.

The Maimonides School opened in Roxbury, then the largest Jewish neighborhood in the Boston area, in 1937. It was the first Hebrew day school in New England and one of only two such schools outside New York City. The Rav wanted to combine serious Jewish study with the highest standards of secular education. He was interested in training Jews, not necessarily rabbis. He believed that young American Jews should not be separated from other Americans by dress, accent or mannerisms.

Though such thinking is common in 1977, it was quite unusual forty years ago. Leaders of the Combined Jewish Philanthropies in Boston, more interested in Americanizing Jews than in strengthening their faith and identity, opposed the venture and gave it no support. The Rav admits today that he didn't know whether the kind of day school he planned was a good or bad institution, but he didn't see how there could be another Orthodox generation without the kind of rigorous Jewish education that only such a school could offer.

He began with no money and six students meeting in the basement of a synagogue. The Rav went out to solicit funds, which came in single and five-dollar bills. Recalling those days, he says he might not have dared to go ahead without community support if he had not been so young and enthusiastic. Smiling wryly, he told me: "It is well sometimes not to be too practical and to act on the spur of the moment in an ecstatic mood."

The school that began so modestly as an elementary school now has an enrollment of 400 boys and girls from kindergarten through high school. It offers science, mathematics, history, French and social studies, as well as Hebrew, Talmud in original text, Prophets, Oral and Written Law, and Daily and Holiday Prayers. Boys and girls start the day with compulsory *davening* (prayer) at 7 a.m. and take classes together. The boys wear skullcaps and are also expected to wear *tsitsit* (ritual fringes) under their shirts. The principal says, "It's a living lie to come here without them," but no one checks on the boys.

In recent years, even the Combined Jewish Philanthropies in Boston has come to its support and Rav Soloveitchik no longer solicits funds — but, like other schools, Maimonides is always struggling to meet its expenses.

Over the years, Roxbury Jews moved to Brookline and more distant suburbs of Boston, and blacks took their places. The area underwent considerable change. So, in 1961, the high school department went to a new building in Brookline and the elementary school followed in 1965. Students travel to the school from all the suburbs, some spending more than an hour getting there.

The student body has changed considerably. At the beginning all students came from Orthodox homes. In the 1950s, about 20 percent were from homes characterized as not *strictly* Orthodox. During this decade, parents told me, half the students have come from truly observant homes, and the principal, Rabbi M. J. Cohen, said 30 percent are really Orthodox.

The most Orthodox parents are concerned about possible dilution of the Orthodox atmosphere. The non-Orthodox — or, as one father described himself, the "bad Orthodox" — often change their life-style to maintain a consistent value system for the sake of their children. Though the Rav speaks of Judaism as "a way of thinking," Maimonides students and parents are deeply concerned about the dietary laws and Sabbath observance. High school-age daughters have been known to take over their mothers' kitchens. One young woman said earnestly, "I had no choice. My mother is very careless. I wanted my friends to be comfortable in my house."

The Rav's school, as some parents call it, is committed to preserving an authentic Orthodox environment in spite of its heterogeneous student body. It is also committed to what Rabbi Cohen describes as a synthesis of Western and Jewish learning. What actually takes places seems more like a form of coexistence. The teachers of religious subjects are required not only to be expert in their fields but to be observant Jews. Teachers of secular subjects are chosen only for their competence.

Parents praise Maimonides for producing "good, square kids with a strong sense of identity and purpose . . . with respect for authority," as one told me. They see it as a sanctuary from drug problems, early sexuality and intermarriage, stressing that no graduate has yet married out of the faith. Some also praise it as an outstanding prep school, from which 98 percent of the students go on to college.

The Hasidic Jews in Boston accuse Maimonides of being too intellectual and insufficiently religious. Conservative and Reform Jews complain that it is too rigid and authoritarian. No one, however, asks whether an Orthodox Jewish day school has a place in America.

Rav Soloveitchik has succeeded in creating an alternative to the traditional yeshiva. Maimonides, now being administered by his students and admirers, has not only trained young people to follow the traditions of their parents but also has trained those who didn't have traditional parents to follow. His daughter, Dr. Twersky, who heads the school committee, is regarded by parents and faculty as a representative of the Rav, a guardian of his standards and goals.

Orthodox Jews generally speak of themselves as in "the mainstream of Judaism." In the Boston area, where they make up only 2 to 5 percent of the Jewish population, they regard themselves as part of a majority in time, a historical community that is in touch with the wisdom of the sages and separated from contemporary heresies. They divide themselves into Orthodox, more Orthodox and most Orthodox.

Rav Soloveitchik has played a strong role in the development of new generations of Orthodox Jews. There is no single successor waiting in the wings to carry on his scholarship and family traditions. Haym Soloveitchik, the Rav's son, is the dean of the Bernard Revel Graduate School at Yeshiva University. The Rav has grandchildren in Brookline and in Israel, and many students and disciples. He was the product of an extraordinary time in Jewish history, as well as an extraordinary family. A new time may encourage other scholars and leaders, other styles and commitments.

The Rav is a unifying influence, a conservative man who is thought to be more liberal than most of his followers. His intellectuality separates him, however, from most people. He is not the kind of rabbi a simple man would dare approach with his problems. His frequent refusals to involve himself in thorny political and religious issues have made him a subject of controversy in both America and Israel. (One of these was his refusal to rule on the status of the Ethiopian Falashas as Jews.)

He has served as a bridge between the East European and the American experiences. The respect and adulation he receives are not only for his own scholarship and teaching, but also because he is a representative of a distinguished rabbinical family and of a world that exists mainly in memory.

Jacobo Timerman

Mario Diament

Toward the end of March 1977 Jacobo Timerman called me to his office. He had just returned from a trip to Spain, and this was our first chance to talk. I was then the executive editor of *La Opinión*, the morning newspaper that he edited and had founded in 1971. The first thing I noticed was that he looked worried and exhausted.

"I think the military are going to arrest me," he said.

"Why?" I asked, alarmed.

"Because of the investigation into the Graiver affair."

David Graiver, an Argentine financier who died in mysterious circumstances in October 1976, had been accused by the military Government of General Jorge Rafael Videla of having managed some $10 million worth of funds for the terrorist group, the Montoñeros. The funds were the product of ransom payoffs following a series of spectacular kidnappings of business executives.

"Are you involved?" I asked.

"Graiver owns a small share of the newspaper," Timerman said. "But that's not the reason, it's the pretext."

"So why don't you leave the country?"

"Because I'm a Jew. If I were anything else, I would leave. But I can't give them the satisfaction of having a Jew run away."

I was accustomed to certain theatrical attitudes from Timerman, but

324

the moment did not lend itself to games. In April 1977 the military junta that had overthrown the Government of Isabel Perón had been in office one year. Kidnappings and disappearances had become daily events. Therefore, no one dared to play the hero in such a climate.

Timerman was arrested on April 14, 1977, but public reaction was not what he had expected. The military Government was quick to make known the contents of interrogations conducted by General Ramon Camps, Chief of Police of Buenos Aires Province, who was in charge of the Graiver case. Allegedly, Timerman had confessed during the interrogation that he was a "leftist Zionist," had founded La Opinión "to capture a leftist readership" and admitted that David Graiver was a business partner in the newspaper. Argentine newspapers docilely reproduced this information without questioning its origin or under what circumstances the "confession" had been obtained.

The presumed "confessions" and the deliberate use of terms such as "leftist Zionist," "Marxist" and "capture of minds" were intended to create suspicion in public opinion of the existence of a "Judeo-Marxist conspiracy," and were effective enough to paralyze public reaction. In my conversations with leaders of the Jewish community and officials of the United States Embassy, I found similar reservations: How much truth was there to what the papers published? Had Graiver been the Montoñeros' banker? Were Graiver and Timerman business partners?

It was useless to argue that these were not the issues, and that what was in question was the illegality of Timerman's arrest (the operation had all the earmarks of a kidnapping), the suppression of his civil rights and the probable use of torture during interrogation. In the atmosphere smothering Argentina at that time, an arrest or a disappearance was ipso facto proof of guilt. People were afraid and nobody wanted to take risks.

The amazing thing is that many of the arguments used by the military junta and the collaborationist press to neutralize testimonies denouncing terror and anti-Semitism in Argentina were repeated by eminent American intellectuals in 1981, when Timerman's book Prisoner Without a Name, Cell Without a Number was published in the United States.

The Reagan Administration had come to Washington convinced that President Carter's human rights policy had seriously impaired the standing of the United States with friendly countries. Reagan's response was what he called "silent diplomacy," a euphemism for his policy of not interfering in anti-Marxist dictatorships. The United States Ambassador to the United Nations, Jeane Kirkpatrick, had devised a subtle distinction between dictatorships, arguing that while those on the left were "totalitarian," those on the right were merely "authoritarian."

Consequently, many within the Administration and particularly those in the neoconservative camp, accused Timerman of having concealed his association with Graiver and of playing into the hands of the radical left. (One year later, the pro-Israeli lobby would join the critics, outraged over Timerman's criticism of the Israeli invasion of Lebanon in his book, *The Longest War*.)

A series of articles began appearing in the American press, questioning Timerman's credibility, his motives, and, above all, rejecting the charge that the Argentine military regime was anti-Semitic. The arguments were curiously similar, as if they had been inspired by the same source. Had Timerman been arrested for being a Jew, or because his newspaper had antagonized the military regime? Why was there no mention of Graiver in his book? Was he not exaggerating his descriptions of the nature of anti-Semitism in Argentina? Weren't his claims of the existence of "concentration camps" in Argentina a fabrication?

In an article published in the *Wall Street Journal* on May 29, 1981, Irving Kristol, professor of social thought at New York University and a prominent neoconservative, impugned the validity of Timerman's statements and asked why, if his case was so clear, he had been treated with "reserve" by the "most liberal" press in Argentina, as well as by the Argentine Jewish community. And in an essay published in the July 1981 issue of *Commentary*, Mark Falcoff, a historian of Latin America then teaching at the University of Oregon, went to the extreme of justifying "repression," contending that "as it is necessarily the case in any urban setting where the forces of order must contend with the virtual invisibility of the enemy, a blanket repression is often the only means which offers any hope of success. In such situations—let us not mince words—the distinction between terrorist and suspect, between sympathizer and activist, indeed, between innocent and guilty, is often lost—but in the end the job can be done, if the will is there to do it."

Later, the anti-Timerman front widened to include those troubled over his book on Lebanon, and the accusations attained unusual virulence. A prominent Israeli journalist even depicted Timerman as "a Latin-Polish pocket-size edition of Bruno Kreisky," an obviously unfriendly description. And others—especially outside of Israel—profoundly resented his public criticisms of the invasion.

What was, in reality, the Timerman affair? Was it an anti-Semitic episode or a political event? Is Timerman a human rights advocate or a fraud?

Jacobo Timerman was never much loved in Argentina. Respected yes, but rarely loved. His personality is too overbearing, his observations often humiliate and his ideological trajectory is often sinuous. The journalistic milieu in Argentina abounds with anecdotes about his legendary rebuffs and sarcastic remarks, a mix of wit and perversity.

On one occasion, he summoned the editor of La Opinión's literary supplement, who had just printed a long article on the difficulties poets faced in getting their work published. He snapped at him: "Instead of using up all that space to explain why poets can't publish their work, why don't you publish them?"

At the height of the military dictatorship, he returned a letter from a high-echelon Air Force officer, advising him, "I don't like the tone in which you address me."

When he became enraged over an error in the newspaper or because he felt one section or another did not meet his standards, he would shoot off short memoranda, typewritten on yellow paper, with such insulting remarks as, "If you had a speck of dignity, you would resign," and "Your section is the mirror of your mediocrity."

Virtually every journalist who has worked for Timerman has an anecdote to recount, but not even his most hardened enemies dispute the prodigious talent that permitted him to create publications that have made history in Spanish-speaking journalism.

Jacobo Timerman was born in the Ukrainian city of Bar in 1923, but his parents emigrated to Argentina when he was 2 years old, and he grew up between two influences: that of Eastern European Jewish tradition and that of the Argentine cultural ambience.

From his youth he was initiated in Jewish journalism, as a militant of the leftist Zionist organization Hashomer Hatzair, and he participated in the creation of publications such as Vida de Israel (Israeli Life), Comentario and Nueva Sion (New Zion).

In 1953 Timerman went to work for Agence France-Presse and in 1957 he joined the political section of the newspaper La Razón, a conservative evening newspaper, where he began to distinguish himself as an incisive and original columnist. Several colleagues from that period recall that he would enter the press room of the Interior Ministry and greet the other accredited journalists, "Good morning, mediocrities."

At that time he had his first contacts with Arturo Frondizi, who would be Argentina's constitutional President between 1958 and 1960, until he was overthrown by a military coup. Much of Timerman's future trajectory can be analyzed in terms of this connection.

His first great journalistic success was the magazine *Primera Plana* ("Front Page"), a weekly modeled on *Time* and *Newsweek*, which came out in 1962. The magazine, an instant success, adopted an irreverent literary style that forever changed the face of magazine journalism in Argentina. *Primera Plana* had a formidable influence. Its critics became dictators of the arts, film and stage, raising up gods or demolishing them. Writers like Julio Cortázar and Gabriel García Marquez and Carlos Fuentes were discovered in Argentina thanks to *Primera Plana*.

Politically, the magazine backed a sector of the army that called itself *azules* (blues), in opposition to the rival group *colorados*, or reds. The colorados had overthrown Frondizi in March 1960 and put in his place the Senate's Provisional President, José María Guido, in order to keep a facade of constitutionality.

The *azul* faction was led by General Juan Carlos Onganía. This group, which favored a return to legality and military professionalism, emerged victorious from a military confrontation with the colorados that took place in September 1962. After assuming power, the azules announced elections for the following year.

The confrontation between azules and colorados left deep scars in the officer corps, and the rivalries and resentments were to continue for several years, even after many of the generals and colonels who took part in the confrontation retired.

The winner of the 1963 elections was Arturo Illia, a humble medical doctor from Córdoba, Argentina's second largest city, who was a candidate for the social democratic Unión Cívica Radical del Pueblo (People's Civic Radical Union). But his triumph was marred by the fact that Peronism, the majority political power, had been excluded from the elections and its sympathizers had protested by casting blank ballots. Illia assumed the presidency with 25 percent of the votes.

Although Illia restored freedom and democracy, his administration was sluggish and inefficient, and was being sabotaged by the Peronist unions and the opposition, as well as by sectors of his own party. Timerman was among those who began to plot his overthrow, arguing that the exclusion of the Peronistas from the election was unconstitutional and that no government could claim to be representative of the people with 25 percent of the electorate's votes. In 1965, with a group of investors supporting General Onganía, he founded *Confirmado*, a magazine meant to help bring an end to the Illia Government.

Illia was overthrown on June 28, 1966, and Juan Carlos Onganía became President, amid the silent approval of most political parties. But far from transforming Argentina into a modern and efficient society, Onganía revealed himself as a messianic nationalist bent on banning political activity and imposing rigid morality. (In 1967, for example, he prohibited the opera *Bomarzo*, by the distinguished Argentine composer Alberto Ginastera, because a ballet scene contained a simulation of a sexual act.)

Timerman retired from *Confirmado* and from journalism at the end of 1966, disillusioned by the turn the military Government had taken. (Years later, he would admit his mistake in having supported the coup against Illia.) In partnership with a retired air force general he created a financial consulting firm. It was then that he met a magnetic young Argentine Jewish banker named David Graiver. In 1971, with Graiver as his business associate, Timerman began editing *La Opinión*, a morning paper inspired by the French daily *Le Monde*.

La Opinión brought together a group of brilliant journalists and writers, but as would later become evident, many of them belonged to the leftist branch of Perónism and some eventually became activists in terrorist organizations. In many ways, *La Opinión* was a typical Timerman product. It began by opposing the Government of army Commander in Chief General Alejandro A. Lanusse, who headed the coup against Onganía in June 1970. Soon, however, the paper veered to his favor. ("Lanusse changed, not me," Timerman later explained.) Then, for a brief period, the paper enthusiastically supported the government of Juan Perón when he attained the presidency of Argentina for the third time in October 1973. His third wife, Maria Estela Martinez, better known as Isabel Perón, was Vice President. But, again, the paper soon began to press for his replacement.

Isabel Perón became President following the death of her husband on July 1, 1974. Although *La Opinión* played a decisive role in her overthrow in 1976, the very day after installing itself in the Casa Rosada, or presidential palace, the military junta led by General Videla began its harassment of the newspaper.

The military leaders had never concealed their contempt for Timerman and *La Opinión*. They considered him untrustworthy and unmanageable, and the newspaper pro-Marxist and "Freudian." (When *La Opinión* was finally seized by the generals in August 1977, four months after Timerman's arrest, General Teófilo Goyret, who took over its editorship, said: "Many people think that the most dangerous thing about *La Opinión* was its sympathy for Marxism. I don't think that was the worst. The worst was its sympathy for Freud.")

During the first months of the military Government *La Opinión* had given it cautious support. Years later some critics charged Timerman with having editorialized in favor of the military on repeated occasions, and in one instance Timerman offered in the newspaper's pages to undertake a personal tour abroad to respond to accusations of human rights violations in Argentina.

The fact is that in the Argentina of 1976 and 1977 a newspaper's priority was to survive, and *La Opinión* tried to maintain a delicate balance between formal support for the Government and a denunciation of its abuses.

All the same, when evidence of the kidnappings and disappearances began to surface and the families of the victims presented themselves before the civil judges to demand their return, *La Opinión* and the English-language Buenos Aires *Herald* were the only newspapers to print their demands. The stratagem was to print the writs of habeas corpus as a way of establishing the fact that a disappearance had occurred.

For Timerman, this was probably his moment of truth. The Minister of the Interior had warned him to stop publishing the writs but, although less frequently, the newspaper continued to do so. Timerman's moods alternated between a profound depression and an obstinate determination to confront the regime's brutality. When Edgardo Sajon, technical director of *La Opinión* and former spokesman for the Government of President Lanusse, was kidnapped by the military on April 1, 1977, Timerman devoted a portion of the front page to counting off the days "since the disappearance of Edgardo Sajon." (Sajon has never reappeared or been accounted for.)

Consequently, when the military thought it had a case against the Graiver family (David Graiver had died in October 1976 in a plane crash in Mexico) for its alleged connection with the Montoñeros, and when it became known that Graiver was a partner in *La Opinión*, the generals thought that, at last, they could settle their old score with Jacobo Timerman.

He was arrested in the early hours of April 14, 1977, covered with a hood and taken to a police cell in the city of La Plata, 30 miles south of Buenos Aires, where he was interrogated and brutally tortured. His properties, including his apartment, his car and the publishing company of *La Opinión*, were confiscated by a decree of the military junta. He was tried by a military court that had to concede his innocence after a year and a half of deliberations. But the military Government refused to set him free. Finally, in September 1979, after a second order by the Supreme Court demanding his liberation on the ground that no indictment was filed against him, Timerman was stripped of his citizenship, expelled from Argentina and put on a plane to Israel.

Timerman returned to Argentina toward the end of 1983. He had lived in Israel for two years. After arriving in a blaze of publicity in 1979 following his expulsion by the Argentine military Government, he left Israel virtually as a pariah after the publication of *The Longest War*. ("The taxi drivers refused to take me when they learned I was Timerman," he told me in 1984.) He settled for a time in Spain and lived briefly in New York, but he wished to return to Argentina. He felt encouraged by the prospects for change opened up by the democratic Government of Raúl Alfonsín, and was flattered by the offer of friendship the new President extended to him. He arrived in time to see his persecutors put on trial, and to testify about his ordeal.

In 1984 he took charge of *La Razón*, where he had begun his career. *La Razón* had systematically supported all the military coups, and Timerman gathered together a group of young journalists and changed the image and spirit of the paper.

What he had not anticipated was the degree of animosity that he still awakened in many Argentines. Although his return caused a stir in journalistic circles, the public still harbored old resentments, some of them created by the venomous campaign unleashed against him during the years of dictatorship. There was also a new generation of readers for whom the name Timerman did not mean very much.

After struggling with a declining circulation, Timerman withdrew from *La Razón* in 1986, declaring he would return to the United States. He was tired and discouraged. As with many of his drastic statements—

in 1982 he had vowed never to return to Argentina—this new exile would also prove short-lived.

In 1987 Timerman was finally recompensed by the Alfonsín Government in the sum of $5 million for the loss of *La Opinión*. These days, he divides his time between Buenos Aires, New York and the Uruguayan resort of Punta del Este, where he is building a luxurious villa. His book *Chile: Death in the South* appeared recently in Argentina, where it did not arouse much interest, and in the United States (Alfred A. Knopf). He is working on a book on Cuba, about which he will not give advance word, although it is rumored that it will be strongly critical of Fidel Castro.

One suspects he is often bored. When I went to see him, he told me of the drink he'd had in New York's Algonquin Hotel with William Shawn, the legendary former editor of the *New Yorker*. They spoke of nostalgic matters, until Shawn commented: "I miss the excitement of publishing a weekly magazine."

"And I miss the excitement of a newspaper," Timerman confessed.

Seven years after the appearance of *Prisoner Without a Name, Cell Without a Number* and its attendant polemic and controversy, all the elements of this tragic story have been substantiated. The evidence against the junta proves that Timerman did not exaggerate in describing the conditions of his captivity and the aberrant excesses committed by the military. According to a report of the National Commission on Disappeared Persons, a panel created by President Alfonsín to investigate the horrendous events at the time of the dictatorship, conditions in the concentration camps were comparable only to those of Nazi Germany. Witnesses and victims, Jews and non-Jews, confirm that in the hell of the illegal prisons Jews were accorded an extra dosage of sadism and perversion.

In the winter of 1985, General Camps, Timerman's torturer, was convicted by a civilian court for violating human rights, assassination and torture. He is serving his sentence of 25 years in a provincial prison, and suffers from cancer.

The nine members of the three military juntas that governed Argentina between 1976 and 1983 have also been convicted by civil tribunals and are serving their respective sentences, including life imprisonment for General Videla.

To understand the "Timerman affair," it is necessary to understand what happens to a society that falls prey to fear.

To ask if it was a matter of anti-Semitism or merely a political episode is a tautological question. Anti-Semitism, when it is used politically, becomes a political fact. The Graiver case was a political and economic scandal, but it was also an instrument used by the military dictatorship to introduce the notion of a "Jewish conspiracy" in order to distract public attention from the kidnappings and murders they were carrying out.

The "liberal press," if such exists in Argentina, did not defend Timerman because it has never defended any cause that did not directly affect its own interests. Its role during the years of dictatorship was very far from being honorable. (The National Office of Investigations has recently established that the three leading Argentine newspapers—La Nación, Clarín and La Razón—were partners of the military Government in the illegal purchase of a paper factory that had belonged to the Graiver group.)

The leaders of Argentina's Jewish community were also unable to overcome the consequences of fear. When they should have defended Timerman and denounced the anti-Semitic plot the military was concocting they vacillated, believing, as the generals wished them to, that the Timerman affair had nothing to do with his being a Jew. Indeed, in the climate of terror and confusion that reigned in Argentina in 1977, the Jew Jacobo Timerman repelled the Jews as much as the anti-Semites.

In 1983, while preparing to play the part of Timerman in a television film based on his book, the actor Roy Scheider asked me to explain to him what Timerman had meant to the Argentine military.

I told him that Timerman was not only an independent and talented editor but also a Jew named Jacobo.

"This is an element that must be seriously taken into account," I told him. "Jacobo is not merely a Jewish name. In Argentina, it is the quintessence of being a Jew. It is the unconcealable Jew."

Scheider was pensive for a moment, and then said, "Right. It is as if the editor of the New York Times were called Pancho."

Michael Walzer

Robert Leiter

Michael Walzer's office at the Institute for Advanced Study in Princeton, New Jersey, looks like a suite at the Plaza, and the effect is disconcerting. How can it be that one of the country's foremost socialist thinkers, a committed leftist who espouses equality, works in an institute that is tucked away from the real world and reeks of privilege?

But the youthful-looking 50-year-old Walzer is by no means an orthodox leftist; he thinks of himself as a democratic socialist (he emphasizes the small "d" in democratic) and as a man of the left (but of the *near* left as opposed to the far left). He is many other things as well—a political activist; an editor, along with Irving Howe, of *Dissent* magazine; a former professor at Harvard and Princeton Universities, and now a research fellow at the Institute for Advanced Study; the author of more than a half dozen books. Equally important, Walzer is a dedicated Jew and long-time Labor Zionist.

"I want to be thought of as a theorist and moral philosopher," he explains. "But I want my democratic socialism to inform what I do as a theorist and philosopher. And I want it all to connect in private and public ways with my life as a Jew."

Indeed, all of Walzer's roles seem to connect with his Jewishness. Unlike other Jewish intellectuals, he does not consider American Jewish life to be banal and without content. "I worry with other people that there's been a thinning out of Jewish culture," he says, "that with each successive generation there is a lack of knowledge of the traditions. But I don't only feel that. There also seems a great deal of vibrancy here and potentialities for revival."

In Walzer's view, the proliferation of Jewish studies programs on American campuses, the growth of the *havurah* movement and the debate over the place of women in Judaism suggest that there is some ferment within institutional Judaism and some innovation outside of it.

"What is most important to realize," Walzer says, "is that there are now two centers of Jewish life in the world—America and Israel—not one as Ahad Ha'am had supposed." Walzer believes that Judaism's distinctiveness rests in its ethical traditions, in its emphasis on social justice and worldly pursuits, but that the legacy is now under assault in both America and Israel. "We face a revival of Orthodoxy, or fundamentalist Judaism," he says, "that is comparable to Christian and Islamic fundamentalism. Orthodoxy presents its own version of what is special about the Jews, and it is something we must resist."

He is also troubled by the fact that many American Jews appear to be abandoning the left. "Jews who want to be Jews," he says, "however they understand that peculiar state of being, must cleave to the civil liberties and the liberal and pluralist politics that now make it possible for them to be Jews."

Walzer views contemporary Jewish neoconservatism as assimilationist, an effort to defend only American Jewish material successes. He concedes that "interests sometimes have to be defended, and sometimes fiercely." But he adds: "If we defend only our interests and not our values, if we lose the sense of ourselves as a historic community, a community of shared values, then we have lost too much. Of course, we should protect the positions we have won in a secular world, but if the plural pronoun 'we' is to continue to refer to a people, and not just a collection of persons, we have to protect something else as well."

Walzer is equally dismayed by what is now occurring among Jews in Israel. He describes the political climate there as "very scary." And he says, "Some of us should have anticipated it. I know I didn't. I suppose my own Labor Zionist background didn't include enough knowledge of Orthodox Judaism and diaspora history to see what was coming."

The religious right wing in Israel is offering what Walzer calls a Jewish alternative to democracy, a kind of "theocratic, halakhic, messianic state." For many years, he continues, "there were only two categories in

Jewish political thinking: There was exile and there was redemption. Since Israel isn't exile, then a lot of people think it's redemption. In fact, it is neither, so we need intermediate categories."

In his most recent and widely acclaimed book, *Exodus and Revolution* (Basic Books), published in 1985, Walzer attempts to use the Exodus story in order to arrive at some of those intermediate categories. Exodus, he argues, is an example of evolutionary politics, in which people are liberated, then regress and wander; yet progress is made, a slow forward motion. Exodus politics means "accepting the limits of historical reality," and not looking to supernatural forces to settle complex issues.

According to Walzer, former Prime Minister Menachem Begin is in many ways responsible for Israel's present state of affairs. "We must recognize Begin's achievement in facilitating the peace with Egypt," he says. "Even if Moshe Dayan was the architect, Begin's political presence was of the utmost importance. But Begin must be held accountable for releasing the ideological tensions that have strengthened the settlement movement and have given credence to Rabbi [Meir] Kahane. He's responsible for the Lebanese war and the ruination of the Israeli economy. Begin's government was one of monumental irresponsibility."

Still, Walzer expresses a certain astonishment and pleasure over the fact that Israel's basic democratic institutions have remained intact. "The remarkable stability of these institutions," he says, "is in part the product of British imperialism, the imitation of European examples. The question now is whether they are going to be naturalized within Jewish life, whether they will receive theoretical legitimacy. The country's long-term survival depends on that, it seems to me."

Walzer believes that Israel's future also depends on its neighbors. "If there is some kind of peace process, or relatively peaceful evolution," Walzer explains, "that will enormously strengthen the liberal/left forces within Israel. And if there is a continuing stalemate, continued occupation of the West Bank, continued settlement activities, that will strengthen the forces of the right."

Walzer sees a solution to this dilemma in the establishment of some kind of Palestinian entity in some part of the West Bank, one with links to Jordan. However, he doesn't yet see the political forces, either among Palestinians or Israelis, that would bring about such a peace initiative.

Part of the problem rests with the Palestinians themselves, he contends. "There is a real difference between the Palestinians of the West

Bank," Walzer argues, "and the Palestinians of the diaspora. But these differences have been suppressed by the P.L.O. It's the struggle among the Palestinians to appear as a unified whole that works against the peace process. Of course, any Palestinian who comes forward would be under a sentence of death. Still if [Jordan's King] Hussein and some West Bank groups were to speak out, Israel could hardly resist. In fact, a large part of the Israeli community wouldn't want to resist."

Walzer's greatest fear is that Israel is systematically creating a kind of Northern Ireland or Lebanon on the West Bank. "I used to take a kind of perverse comfort from reading about Irish politics," he says, "because the entanglements seemed worse and less susceptible to resolution than the entanglements between Jews and Arabs in the Middle East. But now I don't seem so certain about that."

Michael Walzer was born in New York City. In 1944, when he was 9 years old, his family moved to Johnstown, Pennsylvania. There his father, who had worked as a furrier, managed a jewelry store.

At that time, Johnstown, located 70 miles east of Pittsburgh, had a small Jewish population that supported three synagogues: Conservative, Orthodox and Reform. "We joined the Reform congregation," Walzer recalls, "which was in some ways the most intellectually lively of the three, chiefly because of the rabbi, who later went on to Chicago and took my parents with him. My mother became the executive secretary of that congregation and my father managed a jewelry store in Chicago."

After what he describes as a typical suburban upbringing, Walzer went to Brandeis University, where he distinguished himself scholastically, became president of the student government and began the political activism that continues to shape his philosophical writings. He organized campus support for the 1954 Montgomery bus boycott against Jim Crow laws and orchestrated the picketing of Northern branches of stores that were being picketed in the South. (Also while at Brandeis, Walzer met his future wife, Judith, with whom he has two daughters, one an undergraduate and the other a third-year law student at Harvard.)

From Brandeis, Walzer went to Cambridge, England, for a year; he then earned his doctorate in political science at Harvard. Throughout the 1960s, his devotion to political activism burgeoned in both the civil rights and anti-Vietnam War movements. Together with Martin Peretz, now the editor in chief of *The New Republic* (of which Walzer is a contributing editor), he founded the Emergency Public Integration Committee, a civil rights group, and joined antiwar groups like TOCSIN and Mass PAX.

Meanwhile, Walzer taught at Harvard for a year, and then at Princeton for four years, from 1962 to 1966. He returned to Harvard and remained there until 1980, when he became a fellow of the Institute for Advanced Study. Though he is not obligated to teach, he has given courses at Princeton, at the New School for Social Research in New York City and at the Hebrew University in Jerusalem. For the most part, however, he "sits around and writes."

He does not consider his many books and essays to be examples of "high" philosophy; no matter how abstract the subject, he says, they all refer to historical and contemporary events. In his opinion, his writings constitute a kind of "reflection in tranquility" on politics.

His first published work, in 1965, was his doctoral dissertation, *The Revolution of the Saints* (Harvard University Press), a study of the Puritan revolution in 17th-century England, and it contains the seeds of many of the theories and ideas he has pursued throughout his career. In Walzer's view, modern political activity began with the Puritans. But theirs was a different revolution from those that followed in France and Russia, which were marked by "an increase in coerciveness and terrorism."

The Puritan revolution, Walzer says, was an example of a "successful revolution," one that establishes and legitimates a new set of social and political relationships. In his next book, *Obligations* (Harvard University Press), a series of essays on the theory of consent published in 1970, he explores the nature of such relationships, specifically the question of what citizens owe to the powers that be. Because of the war in Vietnam, this was a question that had particular relevance for American leftists.

Walzer opposed the war, and was uncertain about what constituted the precise nature of the "obligation owed by an individual citizen to the modern state." He notes in *Obligations* that the authorities say citizens must, if necessary, fight and die for the state, but he adds, "This view of every citizen as a potential soldier has its origin in states and societies very different from our own." Walzer goes on to explain: "The extraordinary transformation in social scale which has occurred in the past century and a half has created a radically different kind of political community—one in which relations between individual and state are so attenuated as to call into question all the classical and early democratic theories of obligation and war. The individual has become a private man, seizing pleasure when he can, alone, or in the narrow confines of his family. The state has become a distant power, never again firmly within the grasp of the citizen."

In his next major work, *Just and Unjust Wars* (Basic Books), published in 1977, Walzer further defends his opposition to the Vietnam War but not from the position of a pacifist. "There are times when it is right to fight," he says. "This is a very important theme in the book. I could not be a pacifist."

But with that said, Walzer makes it clear that "though particular wars can be just and even necessary, war itself is never a good thing. . . . You can't fight a war which is simply a battle between combatants—unless it occurs in some ideal terrain, like the desert. Under modern conditions, you are always imposing great cruelties upon innocent people, and even though you cannot avoid doing that, it is important to recognize that you are doing it. Precisely because war is sometimes a necessary activity, this ought to lead you to limit it as best as you can."

On the basis of his just/unjust war theory, Walzer opposes United States intervention in Nicaragua, a position he expressed in both a letter and an article in *The New Republic* in response to a pro-"contra" editorial in the magazine.

The letter, drafted by Walzer and other *New Republic* contributing editors (including Henry Fairlie, Hendrik Hertzberg and Richard L. Strout), states that the means the Reagan Administration proposed to use—$100 million worth of military aid to the contra rebels—cannot accomplish the ends it envisions. No matter the extent of United States support, the authors submit, the contra army will not be able to overthrow the Sandinista regime and replace it with a liberal democratic government on the order of Costa Rica. The contras, they say, continue to be dominated by antidemocratic supporters of the former Somoza regime, whose human rights violations have been amply documented by Amnesty International and Americas Watch. They fear that when and if the guerrillas triumph, the democratic elements among the contras will be "pushed aside by the thugs who control the guns."

The authors are not certain any American policy—even their own proposed policy—toward Nicaragua could succeed in establishing a pluralist democratic system there. They would "combine political and economic pressure, negotiations, and aid and encouragement to democracies in the region." They consider these measures preferable to the

Reagan plan because they might accomplish one of the United States' goals in the region: "preventing Nicaragua from becoming a heavily armed, aggressive Soviet military surrogate on the American continent."

Walzer believes that intervention in Nicaragua would create a proxy war, and that at this moment it is a citizen's obligation "to think very hard and worry a great deal," because Americans would be pursuing policies on their own behalf and imposing terrible hardships on others. This type of action would be no different, in his opinion, from the Bay of Pigs invasion of the early 1960s – and equally doomed to failure. And while Walzer has never admired Castro and does not think much of the Sandinistas, that would not lead him to support what he considers to be foolhardy policies.

If the contras had a strong popular base, if there were a Solidarity-type movement in Nicaragua, Walzer would favor sending rifles, but not troops. "Without support," he says, "the contras would gradually fade away" – which is another reason why he thinks Americans are foisting war on innocent people.

In the article he published in the April 28, 1986, issue of *The New Republic*, Walzer adds another layer to the argument. "The point of the war," he writes, "is to put off for as long as possible the moment when President Reagan must choose between acknowledging that Nicaragua is 'lost' and sending in the Marines. I don't think that he wants to send in the Marines. Some people in Washington may be practicing their trumpet calls, but Reagan and his chief advisers seem to me entirely honest when they say that the point of aiding the contras is to avoid more direct American involvement. In all probability, the contras can't win, but all that matters is that they not lose. So long as the war continues, the president can say that he is standing tall, fighting communism, defending the Hemisphere (and cheaply too). If some future Democratic president gives up on the contras, he is the one who will have 'lost' Nicaragua."

Walzer was encouraged to write his anti-contra essay not only by the magazine's editor, Michael Kinsley (who, as TRB, has published his own dissenting opinion in the magazine), but also by the magazine's editor in chief Martin Peretz, who is known for his more hawkish stance. Asked whether he entertained the idea of resigning as contributing editor in view of his disagreement with the magazine's editorial position, Walzer says that as long as he is permitted space to state his objections, he sees no reason to break his ties with Peretz. "I'm old enough to remember all sorts of factional fights on the left that did us all no good whatsoever," he explains.

Aside from Nicaragua, Walzer's just/unjust war theory also influences his views on terrorism and nuclear weapons. He argues that terrorism has "to be distinguished from other forms of violence and coercion. It is definitionally aimed at innocent people, the random killing of innocent people. It's easy to be against it; most people are. I've tried over the years to respond to various [apologies] for it, like Sartre's defense of the Algerians or various defenses of Palestinian terrorism. It seems to me to be very important to keep the definitions straight and to maintain a very tough line against that sort of thinking."

As for nuclear weapons, Walzer believes that the United States was wrong to drop the atomic bomb on Hiroshima at the end of World War II. "To kill and terrorize civilians," he says, "without even attempting . . . an experiment [in negotiation] was a double crime." Still, he favors minimal nuclear deterrence. "I don't see much alternative to it," he says, but adds: "It's a policy for which you have to seek an escape; I don't believe that a policy that commits you to the intention of killing millions of people can possibly be morally satisfactory."

Regarding Israel, Walzer expresses understanding of why certain Israeli politicians would like to develop nuclear armaments and at least to threaten their hostile neighbors with their possible use. Granted, he says, there is not a lot of official information about what Israel is doing as far as the development of such weaponry. "But," he believes, "the position of publicly announcing that Israel will not be the first to introduce nuclear weapons in the Middle East seems a good one."

Walzer's *Just and Unjust Wars* ends with the line: "The restraint of war is the beginning of peace." In summarizing his argument in this way, Walzer means to criticize pacifists and unilateralists. "Pacifists think of my enterprise as making war nice," he says. "But restraining war from the inside, rather than just standing and saying 'no' to the whole process, seems to be a more plausible way of working toward peace."

In his *Radical Principles* (Basic Books), a collection of essays published in 1980, and in *Spheres of Justice* (Basic Books), which appeared in 1983, Walzer examines in detail the subject of socialism, which he sees as a strong version of democracy—not as the control of the economy by the state. He concedes that "you can't call yourself a socialist without making a judgment on what some people call actively existing socialism, namely regimes from Bulgaria to China," but he notes that "my conception of democratic socialism is something that lies—to use that old phrase—beyond the welfare state."

Nowadays, Walzer says, "in a period of great social meanness and retreat, it is very important for people on the left not only to define the welfare state, but to keep alive the sense that it can be made better. When I grew up in the 1940s, what was called socialized medicine was a lively option in the United States. Harry Truman was promising to bring Congress a program for national health insurance. We've retreated a long way from those years. But I don't think that we should concede that this is a permanent retreat. . . . One can't look at something like Social Security, say, without realizing what an enormous gain it has been for ordinary people, how much better it has made the lives of aging citizens. I don't like the kind of radicalism that denigrates every material victory because it isn't a total transformation of social relationships.

"What I tried to do in *Spheres of Justice*," Walzer continues, "was to imagine what it would be like if we had a perfect welfare state." The most important aspect of Walzer's proposed society would be that no one social good—money, for example—could be used as a means of domination. Money could be spent on only certain commodities; it could not be used, say, to bribe a judge. "One wants to limit the exercise of power and the exploitation of people," Walzer explains. "That has always been the moral core of socialism. To make everyone exactly the same in material possessions—that doesn't seem to have a lot of moral power, that idea."

Walzer seeks "to avoid both the imperialism of the market and the imperialism of the state." However, he also wants people to resist domination. He says: "I don't conceive of a society where there's some kind of egalitarian ombudsman who goes around protecting people from domination. People have to protect themselves. That's one of the first lessons I learned in my history as a leftist. I think it was Trotsky who said that the liberation of the working class must be the work of the working class. That's true for everybody—for Jews and blacks. You have to do it yourself. People ought to be helped, but no one can do it for you."

Many of these and other theories have been formulated by Walzer in response to the criticism of the neoconservatives. He credits writers such as George Gilder and Charles Murray, among other neoconservatives, for having drawn the attention of leftists to the crucial issue of how the welfare state creates dependency. "This means," he says, "that democratic socialists have to work out forms of welfare—mechanisms and procedures—that will socialize the welfare state, create a participatory system that will use the energies of poor people. In this way, welfare will become a mutual endeavor and not just a check in the mail."

Walzer also credits the neoconservatives with having renewed the cold war from an ideological perspective. "This is a good thing," he says, "something that democratic socialists can agree with. Even at the height of détente, I wanted to stress the ideological disagreements between the West and the Soviet Union."

But if a revival of the cold war comes to mean nothing more than a continuous readiness to fight in other people's countries, then Walzer would oppose such a stance as wrongheaded and dangerous. "Support for the contras," he points out, "seems to me an example of keeping a war alive that helps neither us nor them."

Walzer also criticizes the neoconservatives for what he calls their "old-time leftist tactics." He says, "They have reintroduced a nastiness into public discourse. There is really a Bolshevik tone to many of their publications. Their polemical style is closer to Lenin than to anyone else in the history of politics."

The fact that neoconservative ideas now dominate the American political arena does not bother Walzer; rather, he considers it a special kind of experience. "We [on the left] are both out of favor and personally comfortable, which means that our connection with people who are uncomfortable in this country—the victims, say, of Reaganomics—is necessarily a construction of our will. . . . But it's very important to keep those people in mind, because a great deal of contemporary life is devoted to making them invisible."

Trude Weiss-Rosmarin

Estelle Gilson

I n every institution—whether it is a synagogue, a Hebrew school, a hospital—we find the identical situation. The women members are allotted no say and almost no representation at all when it comes to basic decisions affecting the policy of the institution.

From an editorial in The Jewish Spectator, August 1936

I contend that the pupils of most supplementary Jewish schools heave a sigh of relief after bar and bat mitzvah and stop attending classes because the present system and method of Hebrew instruction has not engaged their capacity of intelligent understanding.

From an editorial in The Jewish Spectator, March 1970

I suggest that UJA contributors who wish to be informed on the programs and finances of the organizations they support through their local Jewish Federation and Welfare Funds, inquire why the information they are entitled to has been assigned "top secrecy."

From an editorial in The Jewish Spectator, Summer 1976

Who is the man of the year? Whoever gives $200,000. Who is the woman of the year? Elizabeth Taylor. Why? Jewish organizations really live for the sake of being mentioned in the New York Times.

From an interview, March 1977

344

The pointed, provocative views of Dr. Trude Weiss-Rosmarin, author, lecturer and editor of *The Jewish Spectator*, reflect a lifetime of fierce intellectual independence and passionate devotion to the ideas and ideals of Judaism. Since strong ideas evoke strong reactions, Dr. Weiss-Rosmarin has many detractors who regard her as a stubborn rebel, an anti-Establishment gadfly, even a "vigilante." Her admirers believe that she has made lasting contributions to Jewish life and that future Jewish generations will honor her as a true scholar. (Dr. Robert Gordis, himself a scholar, calls her "the most Jewishly learned woman in the world.") They hail her as an editorialist whose views were years ahead of her time and a prophet undistracted by desire for gain or personal power.

Her impact is felt in the "Establishment" which has adopted many of her once-maverick concepts and which she continues to attack for waste, censorship, the exalting of material wealth over spiritual wealth and other sins. And she has an affectionate following among young Jews seeking to express their Judaism in ways that bypass established institutions.

A dark-haired woman of middle height with a quick smile, warmth and wit, Trude Weiss-Rosmarin speaks in pleasantly accented tones. Neatly dressed in slacks and a loose-fitting top, her motherly attitude in conversation ("It's raining too hard for you to walk to the subway." "How did she look to you?" "I tell her to lose weight and dress better") and the bookish atmosphere of her living room are in distinct contrast to her abrasive literary style.

Though Dr. Weiss-Rosmarin has written books on many subjects (*Religion of Reason: The Philosophy of Hermann Cohen, The Hebrew Moses, New Light on the Bible, Jewish Women Through the Ages, Judaism and Christianity: The Differences, Jewish Survival*), her primary livelihood comes from lectures and seminars. Some of the latter, where she is rather grandiosely (she is the first to admit it) described as "scholar-in-residence," involve a weekend with a particular congregation and include lectures on Friday evening and Saturday morning, sometimes a "little talk Saturday afternoon," and, along with bagels and lox, a final lecture on Sunday morning. Current topics range from "Israel, Facts and Fictions" to "Jews as 'Overachievers.' "

She is best known, however, for her editorials in *The Jewish Spectator*, a quarterly which she and her husband, Dr. Aaron Rosmarin, originally founded as a newsletter for the School of the Jewish Woman (also their creation) in February 1936. Now past its fourth decade, it was a monthly

magazine until 1974; Dr. Weiss-Rosmarin has been its editor and publisher all that time.

Simple in format and serious in tone, *The Jewish Spectator* has remained unchanged in size and style for many years. Its major titles are
listed simply on the cover; it contains no photographs and few advertisements. Its articles cover practically every aspect of Jewish life. Some focus
on questions of immediate concern, such as Israel's status in the world or
the dilemmas of American Jewish youth; others recall people and events
in Jewish history. It discusses religion, philosophy and psychology—
publishes original fiction and poetry (listed as "verse" on the contents
page)—brings its readers literature of every age, from Hebrew classics to
modern Israeli writing.

What makes *The Jewish Spectator* "must" reading is The Editor's
Quarter, a series of editorials (as many as five or six an issue) that begin
on Page 1 and continue until Dr. Weiss-Rosmarin has had her say,
sometimes overflowing onto back pages. This is her classroom, her
pulpit, the ground she has chosen for her battles. Some recent subjects:
"Is Carter Good for Jews?" "Ten Years After the Six-Day War," "Jewish
Culture Is *Not* Served."

Each editorial is rich in facts, figures, opinions, ideas, disdain for
ignorance and demands for action. Even those who agree with her views
sometimes find the Weiss-Rosmarin style an exercise in overkill. Yet she
often puts into print what other Jews are thinking but cannot bring
themselves to say, for political, social or personal reasons. Even her
critics agree that time and again she has pointed out Jewish problems and
needs before anyone else was aware of their existence, these including
"failures of Jewish education" and "the un-freedom of Jewish women."

When ethical or moral positions are at issue, she troops up the support
of innumerable biblical and traditional citations. From the double-
columned page, italics and bold-face print leap to the reader's eye as
though the word cannot be trusted to do its work unarmed. A piece
called "The Right to Criticize" is literally mined with biblical quotations
(I counted twenty-two) to explain what is needed of modern Jewish ethics
in terms of ancient Jewish ethics.

Few women of Dr. Weiss-Rosmarin's generation attempted independent
careers and none but she has succeeded in sustaining a publication
without Establishment ties. Many of her peers are the Establishment
now. At age 70 why does she continue to fight? One admirer suggests it

is because her heart and mind are illuminated by *ahavas Israel*, love for the Jewish people.

But that is only part of the answer.

Trude Weiss-Rosmarin's earliest recollections of her involvement with Judaism are painted with anti-materialist, anti-establishment colors, and with pride. "I was a black sheep . . . I was a dropout . . . I was a runaway . . . we were rebels, but rebels with a cause . . . we were of that generation of young German Jews who discovered Judaism and were intoxicated—I couldn't use a better word—with it."

Dr. Weiss-Rosmarin's family, German for four or five generations, was "religiously" but not "culturally" Jewish, she said. Her parents arranged for religious school training (in Frankfurt, where she grew up, there was released time once a week), but joining the "Jewish kids with the rabbi turned me off," she recalls. She found a way to have herself excused and began studying Hebrew on her own. "Starting at the age of 10 or 11, my day went like this: Home from school at 1:30 or so. Homework—well, homework for school was done quickly. Then all afternoon, way into the evening, far beyond my bedtime, they had to drag me away, I was sitting with a Hebrew book, with dictionaries—or I went to the Hebräische Sprachschule." This was a non-Establishment school where Yosef Yoel Rivlin, "who gave all and demanded all," taught Dr. Weiss-Rosmarin, who calls herself a good teacher, to be "strict, demanding and concerned."

During those years, she was also learning Yiddish at a "forbidden" place, the synagogue of the Eastern Jews, where no self-respecting German Jew would be found. "I just loved to hear the Polish Jews talk," she remembers.

When she was about nine, she joined the Blau-Weiss movement, a young Zionist group with Wandervogel (German youth movement) overtones. In 1922, Gershom Scholem, the distinguished scholar, who was then nineteen, attacked the group as "fascist." But young Trude who relished the hiking, singing and outdoorsy Jewishness, wasn't bothered by the organization's authoritarian structure. "Scholem, I suppose, doesn't like physical exercise," she observed drolly.

At 14, a committed Zionist and fluent in Hebrew, Trude Weiss-Rosmarin ran away from home to clean stables, milk cows and teach Hebrew at a *halutz* training farm near Berlin. She wasn't cut out to be a farmer and ended up desperately ill and at home once more.

But teaching still appealed to her, and in Frankfurt, at the Freie

Jüdische Lehrhaus, which Franz Rosenzweig had founded, she formed further ideas on education, many of which she still holds. Rosenzweig, a noted thinker and author, was a man of incredible devotion to Jewish learning, whose memory Dr. Weiss-Rosmarin still reveres. A touching sketch of a religious service at the home of the then-paralyzed, speechless and helpless Rosenzweig appears in her article on Frankfurt in the Fall 1976 issue of *The Spectator*.

What mattered above all in the Rosenzweig school was "the spirit," she said. The essence of that spirit was an urgency to share with others the importance and beauties of Judaism which the young teachers had discovered for themselves. It led her, at 17, to abandon formal studies and to organize a Hebräische Sprachschule in Duisberg. And the spirit is still within her, judging by her reaction to a question about teaching children Hebrew, asked after she lectured at Congregation Beth El in South Orange, New Jersey, some months ago.

"Ah, well," she exploded happily. She stepped back from the lectern. Her arms began swinging rhythmically at her sides. Her head was high and tilted slightly back. Her feet were tapping. You could feel the excitement churning up in her. "Now, the Hebrew language," she began.

Recounting anecdotally how she had learned Hebrew, how she had taught it to others—explaining, expounding and provoking her listeners to think about the three root letters of the familiar word *shalom* and words derived from it, she soon had them believing it would be easy to go home and learn Hebrew. But whether they understood roots or not, no one could mistake the message of Dr. Weiss-Rosmarin's style. "Learning Hebrew is good, easy, exhilarating, important. I did it, he did it, children can do it, you can do it. Do it!" The lesson was topped off with a witticism. "Look, you don't learn Hebrew to order breakfast in your hotel in Israel. The waiter is in a hurry. He hasn't got time till you figure it out. Order your breakfast in English. But read Hebrew!"

After her "drop-out" years, Trude Weiss-Rosmarin resumed her studies. She prepared privately for university admission, and by the time she was 22 had completed her doctorate. Her dissertation, the title of which she translates as "The Mention of the Arabs in the Assyrian-Babylonian (in the Cuneiform) Texts," was later published in the United States by the Society for Oriental Research. Then she married Aaron Rosmarin, a Russian-born American citizen, and came to this country with him in 1931, hoping for an academic career.

"I wanted to teach Assyriology. If I had stayed in Germany I would have become a *privat* [unsalaried instructor of the lowest academic rank]," she said recently. "When I came here I wrote to Cyrus Adler. I wrote to this one, I wrote to that one. But there was no room for it."

Her interest in the exotic field persisted—in those days she read papers regularly at meetings of the Society of Biblical Literature—and forms the basis of one of her contributions to today's Judaism. "She was the first to show us how to cope with traditional biblical scholarship," said Rabbi Wolfe Kelman, executive vice-president of the Rabbinical Assembly (Conservative).

If there was no school that would hire the young scholar, she and her husband were not long in forming their own. In 1932, under the auspices of Hadassah, they created the School of the Jewish Woman on West 100th Street in New York City. Recalling those days, Dr. Weiss-Rosmarin said she'd suddenly realized: "I established the first woman's school in New York. I've toyed with the idea of telling someone at the city's present Woman-school that it is not an unprecedented venture. I've always been a woman's libber, if you want to call it that. My variety of woman's liberation is equal opportunity, equal access. Nowadays I don't even write about that anymore because everyone is writing."

Dr. Weiss-Rosmarin modeled the school after Frankfurt's Lehrhaus. Courses were accredited by the Board of Education for what was then called "teacher alertness credit," and the students learned Hebrew, Bible, Jewish history and Yiddish. The association with Hadassah was short-lived. The Lehrhaus had had no official auspices. Hadassah, with its own established program and policies, created problems for the young and unconventional director. She recalls vaguely that "They wanted their people or courses. I ignored them, let's put it that way. I'm not such an angel when it comes to dealing with organizations. Maybe they were right. But you can't make a school under auspices where people interfere with you—do it this way, do it that way." The school lasted until 1939 when, according to Dr. Weiss-Rosmarin, the outbreak of World War II distracted both teachers and students, and it was closed down.

In December 1935 the students received Volume 1, Number 1 of a monthly school newsletter. By February 1936 the newsletter had acquired the title of *The Jewish Spectator*, and began an uninterrupted critical observation of the American Jewish scene. Later that year another aspect of the Weiss-Rosmarin career began to take shape, when *The Spectator* published a notice that "Dr. Trude Weiss-Rosmarin accepts lecture engagements."

The focus of the magazine became more personal when Dr. Weiss-Rosmarin assumed sole editorship in 1943, after she and Aaron Rosmarin were divorced. ("It's never good to be in business with your husband," she declared.) Though early issues tinkle thinly in graceless English with social news ("Mr. Saul Elman [father of Mischa] comes almost daily to the School. He loves Hebrew so much that he even likes the girls who speak it"), and jokes ("Bella—'Don't you care that your husband is a stutterer?' Mae—'Why should I care? Do you think he has a chance to talk a lot?' "), they are as Beethoven's "Für Elise" to the orchestral force of the Fifth Symphony. For in Jewish matters the Weiss-Rosmarin style, themes and tonalities are already discernible.

A list of the authors published over the past four decades would be boringly encyclopedic, but in its first year alone *The Spectator* brought its readers such writers as Ludwig Lewisohn, Franz Werfel, Jakob Wasserman, Judah Halevi, Stefan Zweig, Heinrich Heine, Ibn Gabirol, Arthur Schnitzler, Chaim Nachman Bialik, Louis Golding, S. Y. Agnon, Joseph Opatoshu, Iser Tolush, I. J. Singer and Cecil Roth.

From the beginning, Dr. Weiss-Rosmarin stressed the importance of Jewish literature for the survival of Jewish culture; she published numerous articles on how to bring Jewish books and people together. Writing about the *New York Times* Book Fair in 1937, she asked: "Where is the Jewish book? If we want to arouse the interest of the American-born Jews in Jewish culture we must give them a chance to find it in the places they choose to frequent, and not in those of our own choice." Among such places she recommends kosher butcher shops.

Above all, she seized on questions of importance and arrived at particular and often unique conclusions. Through insistence and sheer repetition, she became completely identified with certain issues.

Do Diaspora Jews have the right—perhaps even the duty—to criticize Israel? Dr. Weiss-Rosmarin's answer is "Yes." She points to Israeli newspapers which criticize the government freely in terms that, she says, American Jews would never dare to use. "There is no freedom of speech in Jewish publishing in America," she says, predicting that her statement will never see print.

"This business of Masada" is another favorite subject. She believes the defenders of that historic outpost did not commit suicide rather than surrender to the Romans.

She finds the "Masada complex" deplorable and unbelievable in the context of Jewish law and history. "There has never been a case between Christians and Jews, anybody, where a large group of people who were fully armed, who were not starved, who had a lot of food and water and a strategic advantage. . . ." She left the thought unfinished. "Well, you fight." She discounts Josephus, the contemporary Jewish historian of the incident, as unreliable, and asserts that archeological evidence can be interpreted to support her views. She presented them in a paper in Jerusalem in 1973, to be published in the Proceedings of the Sixth World Congress for Jewish Studies.

Terrorists have to be talked to, according to Weiss-Rosmarin. She refers to the horrors of the terrorist attack a few years ago on the village of Ma'alot where, she says, Israeli children died under Israeli gunfire because of Moshe Dayan's refusal to negotiate with the terrorists. "With a terrorist you have to negotiate. That's Jewish law. You don't storm, you tire out. You wait three or four days. Terrorists? I will tell you something — terrorists always win in the end. Then they become tame."

Dr. Weiss-Rosmarin long ago concluded that Israel must make peace with the Arabs. As far back as 1967, when she wrote a pamphlet, *Toward A Jewish-Muslim Dialogue*, she said that Israel must turn toward her Arab neighbors to develop fully and in conformity with her history. Today, her view is that Israel cannot assimilate the growing Arab population inside its borders and has been morally weakened because cheap Arab labor has made physical work demeaning for Israelis.

She has been an ardent advocate of Jewish day schools ever since 1946, when she wrote a pamphlet called *An Open Letter to Jewish Parents* which was published by Torah Umesorah, a national organization dedicated to that cause. "In those days," she recalls, "if you spoke of a Jewish day school for children, you were un-American. You wanted to ghettoize the Jews."

For forty years *The Jewish Spectator* demanded that Jewish women be granted equal rights and equal opportunities in marriage, divorce, education, employment. This ceaseless drive helped pave the way for some of today's gains — for example, women studying at yeshivas, participating fully in Jewish rituals, serving as executives of international Jewish organizations.

Another four-decade issue, which Dr. Weiss-Rosmarin still pursues, is "accountability"—an accounting of how charitable funds are raised and spent. The Jewish Agency is a particular target of her attacks. She says tartly, "The money collected here for charity is being eaten up by superfluous functionaries here and everywhere of the Jewish Agency. Where I write a letter of inquiry, they fly across the ocean. A rabbi, when he was elected to the Actions Committee of the Jewish Agency, said, 'Listen, congratulate me, at last I've become a member of the free Jewish travel club.' "

As Dr. Weiss-Rosmarin presents it to her lecture audiences and in the pages of *The Jewish Spectator*, this question transcends mere budget juggling. She avers that many of Israel's ills—the low level of *aliyah*, the lack of housing, the demand for abortions, the poor education of Yemenite Jews—derive from the wasteful administration of charitable dollars. "If all the money collected in this country over all these years were spent on the purpose it was raised for, you wouldn't have any Israelis coming here," she told me.

"Accountability" is probably the most intractable of all the questions she's tackled. Until recently, the response to her accusations was dead silence on all levels. It's still difficult to find someone in an official position to talk for the record about her charges.

But some people are beginning to ask for budgets—for accountings—and some organizations are beginning to respond. Dr. Weiss-Rosmarin's role in the process was recognized in a resolution adopted by the 75th Rabbinical Assembly in April 1975, which read in part: "For many years now, only one responsible Jewish voice has been raised in questioning certain fund-raising procedures most of us took for granted. Dr. Trude Weiss-Rosmarin, in her magazine *The Jewish Spectator*, has consistently hammered at the lack of accountability in fund-raising drives. She was roundly denounced for it, but recent headlines bear her warnings out. The absence of strict public accountability apparently leads, or at least permits, disorders and serious losses. The American Jewish community owes Dr. Rosmarin a vote of thanks for her warnings."

Most individuals and agencies subjected to Weiss-Rosmarin's fire don't respond for several reasons: they prefer not to engage in public disputes; they are convinced that she would end up having the last word in her pages; they believe her charges to be irresponsible. Some have asserted that her abrasiveness, her unwillingness to listen to another point of view and her systematic shooting down of one Jewish organization after another are counterproductive.

Even those who agree with her position on many issues cringe at the vehemence of her style. Her words cast harsh light on the scene she is illuminating. Behind them the Bible, the Talmud, all of Jewish history are often quoted and referred to at length. Before them the path of future error reflects her chilling prophecies.

Despite all the pyrotechnics, Trude Weiss-Rosmarin is personally unpretentious and accessible, particularly to those who are studying, teaching, writing about "her" kind of Judaism. She is regarded with respect and fondness by men and women in all the generations. Rabbi Kelman recalls times during his Canadian boyhood when his elders talked about the remarkable woman in New York—the teacher, lecturer and writer on Judaism, and wife and mother, whose exemplary life was dedicated to *torah in derech eretz* (combining the highest Jewish ideals with a worldly occupation).

Rabbi Joseph Glaser, executive vice-president of the Central Conference of American Rabbis (Reform), remembers reading her editorials when he was a young student in California, and, after he'd settled in New York, his pleasure at picking up the telephone, hearing "This is Trude," and having a half-hour of intellectual conversation.

Blu Greenberg, a writer on contemporary Jewish affairs, disagrees with Weiss-Rosmarin on some questions but calls her "a prophetic voice" and points out that "she identified issues before others knew of them" and "has been proven right many times."

Last June, Dr. Weiss-Rosmarin and *The Jewish Spectator* moved to Santa Monica, California, which, she says, is closer to the fastest-growing Jewish communities where people are interested in her kind of seminars and lectures. Why not Israel? *The Spectator*, so uniquely an American Jewish publication, would probably not survive transplantation.

Whether she is in New York or California, producing *The Spectator*, teaching university courses, lecturing, participating in seminars, or writing books and articles, her goal has remained constant: to disseminate the truths of Judaism as she interprets them. Beginning with the concept of one God, one mankind, one justice, and the premise that "Judaism is a way of life," she takes the reader from sage to sage, to search Jewish ethics, morals, history, politics for those truths.

Elie Wiesel

Morton A. Reichek

At midday on the first floor of City College's Shepard Hall, in uptown Manhattan, in a corridor that passes as an annex to the student lounge, a dozen or so students were enjoying the final moments of their luncheon break. Gathered around a portable radio perched on a chair, they danced boisterously to ear-shattering rock 'n roll music.

A few hundred feet away, sealed off from the revelry in a small office, fourteen students, eight of them young women, were assembled for Jewish Studies 155, a course on Hassidic literature. The professor: author Elie Wiesel, who has been on the faculty since 1972.

Wiesel sat with his back to his desk, the students seated informally around him. In Hebrew, Yiddish and English, they read and discussed passages from a story by Rabbi Nachman of Bratzlav about seven beggars—a tale that deals allegorically, among other things, with the virtues of humility. A legendary Hassidic rabbi renowned for his imaginative philosophical discourses—Wiesel regards him as Kafka's literary progenitor—Nachman lived in the Ukraine during the late 18th and early 19th centuries.

Analyzing the symbolism in Nachman's story, Wiesel injected references to Camus, Proust, Jung, Kant, Pascal and Spinoza, often lapsing into the sing-song chant of a Talmudic scholar. He had a look of rapture on his face, as if enjoying the thrill of discovering a new truth. "The dialectical problem for the Hassidic masters was how to be both great and humble," he said. Wiesel linked that dilemma to contemporary Israel. "On the one hand, the Israelis have to boast that they have tanks and generals and are strong on the battlefield—to deter the Arabs," he declared. "But when they come to the United States and the UJA to beg for money, they have to tell how poor they are. As Levi Eshkol said after the 1967 war, 'We are a *nebachdiche Shimshon* [a Samson to be pitied].' " He chuckled at Eshkol's Yiddish observation, and called him Israel's "nicest" prime minister.

A gentle, soft-spoken man who has written six novels, an autobiographical memoir, a play, a book of Hassidic stories and three volumes of essays, short stories and reportage, Wiesel has become something of an American Jewish folk hero. Distinguished Jewish scholars have called him "the conscience of contemporary world Jewry," "the high priest of our generation" and "a modern Job." For a rapidly growing number of Jews in this country, especially younger people, Wiesel generates the same kind of emotional excitement that the Reverend Billy Graham does for fundamentalist Protestants and Bishop Fulton J. Sheen for American Catholics. But Wiesel's charisma comes across on a much lower key, without theatrics and with a much stronger intellectual tone. His lectures—he delivers twenty to thirty a year, largely to Jewish community and student groups—are sold out in advance, often attracting standing-room-only audiences. His name adorns the letterheads and mastheads of major Jewish organizations and publications. He is in constant demand to grace Jewish communal meetings with his presence. In short, he is now both a religious and a cultural luminary in the nation's Jewish establishment.

He has also become a major force in American literature. Critics have compared him to Sartre, Camus and Malraux. His novels tend to be more theological parable than realistic fiction. His primary theme—seeking faith in a world so insane and absurd as to make faith difficult if not impossible—has attracted the serious attention of Christian theologians, particularly those with an existentialist bent.

Wiesel, who will soon leave City College to become Andrew W. Mellon Professor in the Humanities at Boston University, had invited me to sit in on his Hassidic literature class. He has deep personal roots in Hassidism, whose legends and traditions he celebrates in much of his writing and lectures. Earlier I had attended his other course, "Moral and

Ethical Issues of the Holocaust." I was struck by the incongruity between the raucous, almost festive scene in the corridor and the intensely studious, yeshiva-like tableau that Wiesel had created in his tiny classroom. The contrast was so absolute, so improbable, it seemed contradictory that the two groups of students could gather in such proximity beneath the same roof at the same time.

But the contradiction was somehow appropriate. Not unlike Rabbi Nachman, who is one of his heroes, Wiesel is surrounded by incongruities and paradoxes. "I am not afraid of contradictions," he likes to say.

He was a teenage inmate of Auschwitz and Buchenwald, and his fame rests largely on his identification as a survivor and chronicler of the Holocaust. In his work, he speaks with the voice of an Old Testament prophet, projecting a sense of moral fervor that makes him the Holocaust's most vivid witness for many American Jews. Yet Wiesel insists that he "does not write or speak directly about the Holocaust." The only exceptions, he says, are his first book, *Night,* a terrifying account of his year in the Nazi death camps, and *Ani Maamin* (Hebrew for "I believe"), a cantata set to music by Darius Milhaud, which grapples with the Messianic question and its relevance to Jewish suffering. Says Wiesel: "The Holocaust cannot be described, it cannot be communicated, it is unexplainable. To me it is a mystical event. I have the feeling almost of sin when I speak about it."

That statement reflects Wiesel's penchant for metaphysics and his own intensely mystical outlook. But Wiesel the mystic is also a pragmatic political activist. His causes are Israel and civil rights for Jews in the Soviet Union and in Arab countries. His 1966 book, *The Jews of Silence,* helped publicize the plight of Soviet Jews, and he is a leader in the movement fighting for their right to emigrate.

His admirers range across the spectrum of religious opinion from the Orthodox to the secularists. A well-known American rabbi has described him as "the leading spiritual personality in the American Jewish community." But Wiesel belongs to no synagogue, although he supports several yeshivas, and does not attend religious services regularly. Nor does he espouse any profound new or radical philosophy.

The essence of his philosophy is that despair can be transmuted into a positive force, and can be overcome through compassion and communal solidarity. It was best summed up in an electrifying speech he delivered in December 1973, shortly after the Yom Kippur War, when he said: "Those who went through the Holocaust, they are the strongest Jews on earth.

Oh, they are vulnerable. But yet nothing, nothing can crush them. For whatever can be done to them has already been done to them. And if they faced it and they came out of it, and if they still remember it, they can turn this despair into a tremendous power. And from this experience and this power and this despair, a Jew can draw more reasons, new reasons, to hope.

"To me, therefore, that is the real meaning, the most timeless meaning of being Jewish. To have reasons to be angry, but not let your anger destroy the image you have of yourself or distort you. To have reasons to hate, but not to hate. To have reasons to despair, and not to despair."

When I phoned to arrange our first meeting, he said to me shyly: "I have a question that I am embarrassed to ask you. Are you familiar with my work?" I assured him that I was. My interest in meeting Wiesel had been stimulated by my son's reaction to *Night*. When he read the book last year, Jim was fifteen, Wiesel's age when he was shipped to Auschwitz. In this book, only 119 pages long, Wiesel describes the horrors of the concentration camps—a pious boy surrounded by a mound of corpses, accusing God of abandoning His creation.

I had encouraged my son to read the book, pointing out that if his great-grandparents had not been fortunate enough to flee Russia and Poland shortly after the turn of the century, the fate of the boy in *Night* might have been my own. The book had a stunning emotional impact on Jim, whose normal reading diet leans heavily to sports literature. "While I read it," he told me, "I tried to think it didn't really happen, that it was only a story someone made up. But when I paused, I realized that it wasn't fiction. Is he a sane man now?"

Sanity, in fact, is a subject with which Wiesel is obsessed. As a student at the Sorbonne in Paris for almost three years, he specialized in clinical psychology. The New York Society of Clinical Psychologists has honored him for his perceptive treatment of the insane in his writing. Madmen figure prominently in nearly all his novels as symbols of what Wiesel regards as the failure and betrayal of rationalism. "I believe that reality disappointed us so much," he explains, "that I seek something in another reality. So what is the other reality? Madness. I believe that anyone who was in the camps came out deranged. There is the basis of madness in every person who survived. When you have seen what they have seen, how can you not keep some madness? This in itself would be mad—to remain normal."

Elie Wiesel (pronounced ALE-ee we-ZELL) was born in 1928 in Sighet, a Hungarian-speaking enclave under Rumanian rule. The only son of a Hassidic storekeeper, he led the cloistered life of a Talmudic student. Only in later years, for example, did he become aware that there had been Zionist and Communist groups among Sighet's Jews. "To me," recalls Wiesel, "Rabbi Akiva [a Talmudic sage who lived some 1,900 years ago] was more alive than Ben Gurion."

In 1944, Sighet's 12,000 Jews—nearly half its inhabitants—were deported. Wiesel's father died before his eyes at Buchenwald. His mother, a younger sister and other members of his family were killed in other camps. When he was liberated, he asked to be sent to Palestine, but was barred by British immigration restrictions. Refusing to return to Sighet, Wiesel was sent with about 400 other Jewish orphans to France. For two years, he was the ward of a French Jewish welfare agency, continuing his religious studies and learning the French language. (He writes in French today.) He discovered that his two older sisters had survived the death camps only when one sister, who was living in Paris, spotted him in a newspaper picture of Jewish refugee children. Now a widow, she still lives in France. The other sister subsequently migrated to Canada and died in 1974.

Wiesel entered the Sorbonne in 1947, supporting himself as a Hebrew teacher and as Paris correspondent for a Tel Aviv newspaper, *Yediot Achronot.* He wrote a doctoral dissertation comparing Jewish, Christian and Buddhist concepts of asceticism, but never submitted it. In fact, he has never earned a formal academic university degree, although he has collected a large number of honorary doctorates. During Israel's War of Independence in 1948, he tried to join the Jewish army, but was rejected because of poor health. So he went to Israel as a correspondent for French newspapers. He returned to Paris after the war to resume his studies and work as a correspondent for an Israeli newspaper.

In 1956, he arrived in New York. To supplement his modest earnings from the Israeli paper, he became a staff writer for the *Jewish Daily Forward*, a Yiddish newspaper, and a correspondent for *L'Arche*, a French magazine, performing a linguistic tour de force that must be unique in the annals of journalism. He became a U.S. citizen in 1963.

Wiesel is a frail, ascetic-looking man with brooding eyes, a melancholy face, and sharply chiseled features. His first name, a diminutive of Eliezer, means "my God" in Hebrew—a fitting name for a man as preoccupied with the question of the Divinity as he is. He speaks excellent English, with a curious blend of French and Yiddish accents and perhaps a dash of Hungarian. When he speaks, he gesticulates busily with his long, bony hands, frequently punctuating his conversation with the sighs of one who is obviously weary of the suffering he has endured and observed. He lives with his Viennese-born wife, Marion, a four-year-old son and a sixteen-year-old stepdaughter in a sprawling, elegantly furnished apartment on Central Park West.

Last year, Wiesel wrote a widely discussed article for the *New York Times* in which he argued that Jewish survival was once again being threatened by "a certain climate, a certain mood." The manifestations, he said, were the loss of American and world sympathy for both Israel and Jews in other lands. "I feel threatened," he wrote gloomily. "For the first time in my adult life I am afraid the nightmare may start all over again."

During my first visit, we discussed his anxiety, which has become a persistent theme in his current lectures. I asked for his view of why anti-Semitism has been such a durable force in history. "We always disturb people," he said. "I would even say we represent the artistic form in history, the conscience of history. That's why we disturb them. Imagine Abraham or Moses coming out of a society full of murder and saying, 'Don't kill.' And 'There is only one God.' So from the very beginning, there was something in Jewish history that opposed us to the others. We were the forerunners. We said no. No to the present. No to the circumstances invading the present.

"Then we became objects of hate because we did not yield. Man and mankind wanted to destroy the Jew, and the Jew refused to be destroyed. The Jew wanted to improve man and mankind. Man and mankind refused to be improved. Inevitably, this aroused resentment between us particularly in strongly Christian environments. It was either/or. Either Christ was the Messiah, and we were wrong and had to be punished. Or he was not. And how could the Christians accept the idea that he was not? So they *had* to persecute us in order to be able to believe that Christ was the Messiah. The end, of course, came one generation ago."

The Holocaust initially served as a shield against anti-Semitism, but its significance has been degraded in recent years, Wiesel believes. Says he: "That is why today Christians no longer feel guilty. For twenty-five or thirty years, the Holocaust shielded us. It wasn't nice to be anti-Semitic because automatically the person who hated us was in the same class with Hitler. But when you distort the past, when you devaluate the experience

and cheapen it, the shield becomes useless. And today it has already
become very easy for a person to come out and say, 'I'm against Israel.' To
me that means, 'I am against three million Jews in Israel.' "

Our conversation was interrupted when Wiesel's little boy, Shlomo
Elisha, walked into the room. He had just awakened from a nap. "Hi,
Elisha," Wiesel said lovingly. I asked Wiesel what the child's primary
language is. He whispered to Elisha in French, then in English, and asked
him to recite the Hebrew alphabet for me, proudly displaying the boy's
multilingual talents. He then asked the child to leave the room and close
the door. Elisha refused. Wiesel turned to me and said laughingly:
"Already the rebellion starts." Gently he escorted the child out of the
room and called for his Jamaican nursemaid.

What does Wiesel mean by the "devaluation" and "cheapening" of the
Holocaust? "There is so much vulgarity on the subject," he told me. "The
subject is being betrayed." He is distressed that the Holocaust had been
overexposed to institutionalized and frequently superficial study by what
he regards as intellectual diletantes, that it is being exploited for fund-
raising ventures and that it has become a commonplace—almost commercial—subject for books, articles and speeches. Wiesel was hesitant to
expound on such a sensitive question for fear of "hurting other people's
feelings."

But, I asked, "If we are to remember what happened, how do we teach
or learn about the Holocaust and escape the trap of 'vulgarization'?"

"I don't know," he replied. "It used to be a sacred topic. It must be seen
as a special event, meaning a special event which requires a special style,
a special approach, a special level, a special sensitivity, a special tone of
voice. When we speak of anything related to the subject, a certain
trembling goes through us. It must not become simply a subject among
other subjects."

That is why he insists that he writes and speaks *around* the Holocaust
and not *about* it. The distinction is a significant one for him. His books
generally avoid the clinical details of the physical atrocities associated
with the Holocaust. Instead, he focuses on the survival of his heroes and
on their agonizing search for a rational God who permitted the horrors
of the Holocaust to occur.

"I say certain things not to say other things," he said. "I write a page
and the absence of the Holocaust in it is so strong that the absence
becomes a presence. My books are about the impossibility to write about

the Holocaust, the non-communicability of the Holocaust. Something happened during the Holocaust, and we don't know what. God, we never will know what. We cannot even talk about it. What I try to show is that one cannot write about the event. I try to show the incommunicability of the experience."

Nevertheless, I protested, "You do communicate—and very eloquently—about what happened. You confuse me. You raise more questions than you answer for me."

"I hope so," he said. "For me it is enough if I can heighten sensitivity. Don't think that because you have read some of my books or have heard some of my talks that you know what happened. Nobody knows. Only those who were there. Of course, there is a terrible contradiction. While I know that I want to transmit, I also know that I cannot transmit. Nobody can. We are a caste apart. Only those who were there will ever know really what happened. The others are removed, one generation removed. They may hear the echo of a song. They may see a spark of the fire, but not the fire. And that's why I speak about the mystery of the Holocaust."

He paused for a moment, his brow furrowed. "But maybe we—those who saw the events—have become too sensitive," he said sadly.

We discussed contemporary Israel and its inability to argue its case more effectively in world councils. I criticized Israel for failing to gain more support from the Third World countries by not emphasizing the Afro-Asian origins of well over half its Jewish population, and for allowing itself to be tainted by Arab propaganda as a colonial outpost of white European imperialism.

Wiesel agreed. "Israel has always been poor in explaining itself," he said. "And often I wonder why. After all, we who are the masters of public relations, experts on Madison Avenue. I think Jews can explain everything but themselves. They can explain potato chips, they can explain cars, they can explain any cause you give them. But they cannot explain themselves. They're unable for many reasons. First of all, I always go back to the past. For me, the references are in the past—the Bible, the Talmud.

"Moses is an example. He should have been *the* speaker, the public relations expert. But he stuttered. You can't explain it. And this is still going on. It's a mystery.

"We are the only one of the ancient peoples who in spite of the persecutions and massacres and pogroms have survived. You can't imagine when you study our history for the past 2,000 years, not one generation anywhere without a catastrophe. In my play [*Zalman, or the Madness of God*], I understand the father. Alexey's argument is hard to refute. He says 'I don't want my son to suffer as a Jew, period.' I think of my son. I don't want him to suffer."

Zalman, which was published in book form in 1974, shown on television, and was produced on Broadway, is set in a small city in contemporary Russia. The major character is an aged rabbi. When a group of foreigners visits his synagogue, the Soviet authorities warn him not to communicate with the visitors. Nevertheless, the rabbi delivers an impassioned sermon denouncing the repression of the Jews. The play focuses on the political consequences of the rabbi's action and on the conflict within his own family. His son-in-law, Alexey, is an assimilated Jew who wants to prevent the rabbi's grandson from seeing the old man and from being exposed to Jewish religious practices.

"I see," says the dejected rabbi to Alexey. "Another branch broken from the living tree of Israel. That's what you want. To smother the spark. Silence the song. Is that really what you want? Tell me."

Alexey responds: "Much more and much less. I don't think in those terms. You're thinking of an entire people. I am concerned with my son. I shall break the chain that links him to misfortune. My father suffered as a Jew, and so did his, and so did my great-grandfather and his father before him. How long do you want this to go on? I say: Enough, enough! It must stop. Once and for all. With my son—it will!"

On a subsequent visit I met Wiesel's wife. She is a pretty, vivacious woman in her early 40s. Her family fled from Vienna to France after the Nazis occupied Austria. When France was occupied, she and her family were placed in a detention camp but escaped to Switzerland, where she received most of her education. She and Wiesel met in the mid-1960s and were married in 1969.

Marion Wiesel, who speaks with a slight British accent, is now her husband's primary English translator. He continues to write in French, he says, because French "became more than a language to me. It became a refuge, a home."

I asked him why he has not settled in Israel. "I don't have a clear reason," he said. "There must be many elements in my decision. I belong more to the Diaspora, the segment of our people that is still not redeemed, that is still in pain. I am sure it must have to do with my guilt feelings that every person in my position feels, having survived. There is something wrong with us. Logically, we should not have survived. I don't deserve redemption yet, for the achievement of the ingathering. I am not worthy. I am still waiting. I was more taken by the torment than by the triumph."

He spoke without a trace of pretension or sanctimony. He paused and sighed. "There must have been more practical reasons, too," he said. "It was easier to get a job as a foreign correspondent outside of Israel. But that was not the main reason."

Returning to the Holocaust, he began to explain the purpose of his writing. "You know, for men of my generation, that event should be the yardstick. And once you have this as a yardstick, you don't want to invent. But we try to invent a meaning to events that had none. And we try to reinvent situations and to recreate, to bring back towns that were destroyed. We build ruins on ruins. And, in a way, we are untouchable for we are doing what must be done. We are witnesses in the cruelest and strongest sense of the word. And we cannot stop. We must speak. This is what I'm trying to do in my writing. I don't believe the aim of literature is to entertain, to distract, to amuse. It used to be. I don't believe in it anymore."

That may be why Wiesel's books are often difficult to read. They yield neither pleasure nor relief. His basically exultant and affirmative philosophical message is submerged in the bleak literary landscapes that characterize his fiction. His heroes are invariably trapped or confined men, engaged in protracted soul-searching over the existence of God in the face of human suffering. His writing is crammed with symbolism, melodrama, religious aphorisms and parables that sometimes intrude on his narrative cohesion.

In his work, Wiesel has exposed the unfolding drama of his own spiritual odyssey, employing characters who are almost always Holocaust survivors, and geographic and personal settings that are based heavily on his postwar experiences.

In *Dawn*, his first novel (published in the U.S. in 1961), the protagonist is a survivor who has joined the Jewish underground in Palestine. He is assigned to kill a British officer, a hostage for a captured Jewish terrorist sentenced to death. The book explores the ethical question of the victim becoming the executioner and concludes that all murder is suicide. In *The Accident* (1962), a European Jewish journalist lies in a New York hospital hovering between life and death after being struck by a taxi.

(Wiesel himself was critically injured by a taxi in Times Square shortly after his arrival in this country, and still walks with a limp as a result.) Haunted by his guilt as his family's sole survivor of the Holocaust, he is a rebel against God, but struggles to accept love and life in his search for a meaning.

The quarrel with God is continued by the hero in *The Town Beyond the Wall* (1964), the story of a survivor who returns to his native town in Hungary, which serves as a parable about human indifference to injustice. (A year after the book's publication, Wiesel himself returned to Sighet for a visit.) In *The Gates of the Forest* (1966), the hero is the only Jew to escape the Nazis in his Transylvanian village. He takes refuge with a family servant, assumes a Christian identity, and is nearly killed when, playing Judas in a passion play, he proclaims that Judas and not Jesus is history's victim. Escaping again, he joins a partisan band and ultimately settles in the U.S., where he finds a semblance of spiritual comfort among Hassidic worshipers, having passed from youth to manhood and from hate to love.

A Beggar in Jerusalem (1970), which is probably Wiesel's most popular novel, is a complex and poetic account of the Six Day War as seen by a Holocaust survivor who accompanies an Israeli military unit. Wiesel's most recent novel, *The Oath* (1973), begins two decades before the Holocaust and deals with the destruction of a Jewish community in the Carpathians and the protracted spiritual trial of its sole survivor.

These novels, many of which are now used as texts in college literature and religious courses, represent Wiesel's own metamorphosis from what was virtually nihilism in the autobiographical *Night* to a qualified acceptance of Jewish traditionalism.

"I don't like to speak of my religious beliefs," Wiesel said when I asked how he reconciles the existence of a divine force with evil and suffering. He noted that his wife, whose family was much less religious than his own, now keeps a kosher kitchen and that he observes the Sabbath by not working. "I am a Hassid to this day," he said, "but there are many things I don't do which I should do." He was hesitant to say more. I pressed him to amplify, embarrassed by my own boldness in approaching a question so sensitive.

"In *Night*," Wiesel explained, "I wanted to show the end, the finality of the event. Everything came to an end—man, history, literature, religion, God. There was nothing left. And yet we begin again with *Night*. Only where do we go from there? Since then, I have explored all kinds of options. To tell you that I have now found a religion, that I believe—no. I am still searching. I am still exploring. I am still protesting.

"It's too easy to say, yes, I have faith, and it is too easy to say no. I don't want an easy answer. I have problems. I believe that the tragedy of the believer is greater than the tragedy of the non-believer. I do have questions. Mine is a tragic faith.

"Ahh, it's hard to talk to you about it because, in comparison to the Sabbath observance that used to be mine before, what I am doing today is outrageous. But still, but still . . ." His voice trailed off. He remained quiet for a while. Then as if speaking to himself, he murmured: "I observe. Ahh. Sometimes I don't know why. It's for my son. I want him to have something, even if he wants to give it up later."

Wiesel says that he "feels most comfortable to this day" among Hassidim. He enjoys going to their *shtiblach* (study halls), attending their religious festivals and conferring with their rabbis. One of his closest friends is an aged, Polish-born Hassidic rabbi, Leib Cywiak, who lives in Brooklyn and figures in one of Wiesel's short stories. The two have weekly telephone conversations, and each Passover the old rabbi personally delivers a supply of specially prepared matzos to Wiesel's apartment. The rabbi was the leader of a Hassidic *shtibl* on Manhattan's Upper West Side, close to the apartment in which Wiesel lived when he arrived in this country. The *shtibl* has since closed, and Wiesel will not drive on the Sabbath to other Hassidic houses of worship.

I spoke to Rabbi Cywiak about Wiesel. "I became acquainted with Mr. Wiesel before he became well known," the rabbi said in Yiddish. "But I quickly recognized him as a man with the spark of *emunah* (belief). I saw him as a man who would someday stimulate and nourish the souls of American Jews. He is one who speaks from the heart and what he says excites the hearts of others. A great love has developed between us. I would go through fire and water for him and he would do the same for me."

Another of Wiesel's closest friends was a man whose world was far removed from Rabbi Cywiak's—the late François Mauriac, the noted French Catholic philosopher. While he was living in Paris, Wiesel was assigned by his newspaper to interview Mauriac. The two became friends; Wiesel still refers to Mauriac as his "patron." Mauriac encouraged him to publish his first book. *Night* was originally published in Yiddish in Buenos Aires, under the title *And the World Has Remained Silent*, in 1956.

Wiesel rewrote it in French, and Mauriac helped him find a Paris publisher two years later. The book appeared in the U.S. in English in 1960.

I asked Wiesel if, thirty years later, the world—Jewish and non-Jewish—had learned anything from the Holocaust.

"It's again going to sound contradictory," he answered, "Because on the one hand, I say there is nothing to be learned. At the same time, I say, of course, we must learn when we can. Simple things. The importance of words. We didn't believe in the thirties. And that's why it could happen. If the world had taken Hitler's words as seriously as he did, I think that would have prevented it. Then, we have learned something about solidarity. If mankind had shown more solidarity with the victims, there would have been no Holocaust.

"If the liberals had understood the importance of their own preaching, that when they say freedom for man that includes freedom for Jews, there would have been no Holocaust. And the Jews themselves. If the Jews had shown more solidarity—that, too, is unique. It never happened before. Usually when some things happened in one place, there was always one gate open somewhere. This time, all the gates were closed. So, of course, we learned. Does it apply to the present? I think it does, because again if it hadn't been for the Holocaust, there would have been no Israel. We all have guilt feelings. The parents, because they didn't do enough then. The children, because they say we don't want to be in the position of our parents. That is why there is a response to Israel today. The same thing about the Russian Jews. Had it not been for the Holocaust, there would have been no response to their fight either."

To Wiesel, the development of Jewish nationalism in the Soviet Union after the destruction of half of Russia's Jews by the Nazis, the assimilation of the other half, and the decades of cultural and religious separation from other Jews is a "miracle." "How can it be explained? I don't know. I am very poor at explaining. The temptation to assimilate was tremendous. I understand it. I understand the Communist appeal for the Jews. Communism—I call it messianism without God. Messianism based on man. Beautiful, what a beautiful idea. Granted, it was distorted. But in the beginning? It was a beautiful idea. Change man, change life, change history.

"They even used a theological vocabulary for redeeming man. Beautiful. And I can understand why Jews were taken by it. If God won't help, we shall. If God does not want to help the Jew, then we shall change the non-Jew so that he will accept the Jew. And therefore the Communist movement was stronger than Zionism among Russian Jews."

The plight of Russian Jewry is the subject of a novel on which Wiesel is now working. The book is tentatively entitled *The Return*. It deals with the 1948–1952 period during which Stalin ordered the killing of more than 200 Russian Jewish writers, artists and other intellectuals because of his paranoiac fear of a "Jewish conspiracy." Hundreds of others were arrested and disappeared, most of them loyal Communists. Says Wiesel: "I am haunted by these people whose death was taken away from them. It's not part of Jewish history. We don't know what happened to them. That's what I am trying to imagine."

The hero of his new book is a Russian Jew who manages to flee to Israel to reveal how such noted Yiddish artists as Peretz Markesh, Itzik Feffer and Shlomo Mikhoels had been liquidated by Stalin. Wiesel's hero then mysteriously returns to Russia. "He returns for a purpose," Wiesel says. "I won't say what. But it's sheer fiction."

Two new Wiesel books will be published this year. The first, due out in the spring, will be *Messengers of God*, a collection of impressionistic vignettes of major Biblical personalities, showing what the author calls "their relevancy to contemporary times." It was released in France last October. Based on a series of Wiesel lectures, the book will be a sequel to *Souls on Fire: Portraits and Legends of Hasidic Masters*, which marked a shift in emphasis in Wiesel's work away from the Holocaust theme to a retrospective inquiry into Jewish religious topics. Wiesel plans more volumes in the series—on Talmudic authors, ancient Jewish philosophers and Jewish poets. Like the first, these will be based on his lectures aimed at popularizing Jewish religious history.

The second book is a collection of diaries of *Sonderkommandos*—the Jewish concentration camp prisoners who carried corpses from the gas chambers to the crematoria before they were put to death themselves. Wiesel is now translating and editing the documents, which were hidden in tin flasks buried in the ruins of a Polish concentration camp. "You can't imagine the depths, the mysteries," Wiesel says, describing the contents of the documents with a look of horror on his face. "A man saying, 'Today August 18, 10 o'clock: I have just buried my wife; 10:15: I have just buried my child.' "

Wiesel is inundated by requests for advice, for help in launching Jewish community projects, and for assessments of both Jewish and non-Jewish educational programs. On the morning that I was his classroom guest, I arrived in his office, which he shares with another professor, shortly after 8 a.m. The first of his two classes was scheduled to begin a half hour later.

He greeted me warmly and was immediately interrupted by a long-distance phone call. The caller was a rabbi in Detroit who had a question to ask Wiesel. I walked into the adjoining office to allow Wiesel to talk privately. I returned several minutes later after I heard him hang up the phone.

"I really don't have answers," Wiesel remarked when I commented on his popularity and on the eagerness of others to obtain his advice. "As you've seen, I'm much better at the questions than the answers."

YIVO

Estelle Gilson

On New York's Fifth Avenue stands a cool limestone mansion, twin to the Louis XIII Palais Royale in Paris, which bears on an outer wall an unobtrusive plaque in Yiddish.

Neatly lettered, the plaque announces to the observant passerby that this elegant building is occupied by the Yidisher Visnshaftlekher Institut or Institute for Jewish Research, known throughout the world by its Yiddish acronym, YIVO. The patrician edifice that once housed Vanderbilts and their treasures now contains more exotic and disturbing riches within its marble walls. No butler awaits visitors at the magnificent iron gates. These days it is Faigeleh Lederman, her chestnut hair pulled atop her head, who buzzes them in.

Founded more than fifty years ago in Vilna as an institute for graduate studies of East European Jewry in the Yiddish language, YIVO now conducts its research, teaching and publishing activities, and maintains its library and archives at 1048 Fifth Avenue, in cramped splendor. In this five-story building, which YIVO first occupied in 1955, its archives, containing more than 10,000,000 items of Jewish interest, from 16th Century rabbinical court records in Old Yiddish to Nazi documents, have overflowed into a gilt and mirrored ballroom. The library of more than 300,000 volumes, ranging from ancient, leather-bound Florentine tomes to modern periodicals from all over the world, takes up more than a floor of space.

Opening the door on East 86th Street where the entrance to the building is located, you face a wide, circular marble staircase. In its crook, two or three long-haired girls and bearded boys with and without *yarmulkes* often sit and talk over coffee. Past Faige's switchboard on the left is the magnificently carved and paneled office of YIVO's board chairman and current chief executive officer, Morris Laub.

Seated at his large, curved, polished desk in front of a marble fireplace, he spoke about YIVO's history, its program and plans, occasionally tilting back in his chair to reach across the mirrored mantel for YIVO-published books to show me. Laub, a gray-haired man with curving white sideburns, impeccable in a maroon jacket and bowtie, assumed his duties as executive officer of YIVO on September 1, though his association with YIVO as a member of its board dates back many years. He combines a scholarly background with long experience serving national and international Jewish organizations, having recently retired from his last post as director of the World Council of Synagogues.

What does he hope to do for YIVO? Mr. Laub has no hesitation in finding the answer. "I want to reveal the best-kept secret in American life," he smiles, "YIVO."

Laub feels that the institution and American Jewry have a great deal to offer each other, and he has made it his first duty to find ways to introduce YIVO into Jewish life.

The YIVO staff of about thirty full-time and part-time persons is spread throughout the building. On the first floor, offices are tucked far back in large rooms that cannot be effectively partitioned because the building is under consideration for landmark status. Numerous tiny offices off narrow corridors fill the upper floors. Though telephones ring, typewriters clatter in Yiddish and English, a copying machine whirs, there is no sense of office hustle, no crackle in the air. Are the sounds lost in the large building, one wonders, or is this the rather sleepy pace of scholarly studies?

YIVO's archives are kept in the basement, and tables and desks must be cleared of someone's work before assistant archivist Marek Web can show me any of his treasures. Of the millions of items in his care, he chooses first some material from Vilna—parts of the revered Sutzkever-Kaczerginski archives, figuratively and literally the heart of YIVO, which were hidden away by the poets Abraham Sutzkever and Schmerke Kaczerginski when they worked at the Vilna headquarters under Nazi supervision. One part of this large collection contains pre-Holocaust material accumulated in YIVO's early years. The rest, salvaged from the Hitler period, consists of diaries, documents and artifacts from ghettos throughout Europe, including Vilna, and papers of the Judenräte (Jewish governing councils in the ghettos) and the German authorities.

"How did so much of it survive the Nazis?" I ask. Web answers, "It was buried." "But papers, books, letters, how did they last?" The trim, dark-haired archivist leans back and smiles. "There should be a warm word in Jewish history for the milk can."

But if the heroism of those who saved large amounts of Vilna material is still vivid to Web, he is worried too. Much of it is still not classified, and time is running out. As an example, Web cited YIVO's magnificent Yiddish theater collection. Quantities of photographs, playbills, posters, programs, manuscripts, reviews, phonograph records and sheet music are still to be inventoried. "Who will be left in a few years," Web asks sadly, "to identify these photos, to recall dates and places of these performances?"

But work on old archival material moves slowly at YIVO, where the problems of locating scholars capable of handling it and funds with which to pay them are chronic and can be disabling.

In the reading room at the head of the marble stairs, Dina Abramowicz presides over a multilingual library with its own call system and double-faced English and Yiddish call cards. An eighteen-foot potted palm in the far corner, planted by the poet H. Leivick, author of *The Golem*, on the birth of his first son, evokes the warmth of Biblical legends. The room's elaborate marble fireplace and handsome wood paneling are barely perceptible in the bright clutter of books. The tables are laden with papers, folders and clothes; it is sometimes hard to find a seat. If you need to have a document copied, you may have to wait for someone who can do it to turn up. Books come down on the dumbwaiter from stacks on the third and fifth floors by way of a striped shopping bag, and call slips go up safety-pinned to its handles.

Recounting the history of the library, Abramowicz removes her glasses, rubs her eyes, touches her hand to her gray hair and speaking slowly, softly, intensely says: "After the war, all over Europe, there were millions of homeless books." And before she is done I will learn how the Nazis rounded up books from libraries, homes, schools throughout Europe. Many were burned, others were sent as scrap to paper mills. Some, destined for the future Nazi University or for "research" on Jews, but sent first to YIVO in Vilna for cataloguing, were saved by acts of heroism. "How can I get the facts?" I ask. Dina Abramowicz cites from memory item after item for my reference.

Thirty thousand Vilna books that survived the Holocaust and have been at YIVO for nearly twenty years have not yet been completely catalogued. As with the archives, the work of sorting and classifying them has been done in small batches as the need arose—and when time and money were available.

In October 1975, a library and archive grant from the National Endowment for the Humanities provided much-needed assistance for both divisions of YIVO. Work at the library under this grant is integrated with the Library of Congress, with the ultimate goal of producing a Union Catalogue of all Yiddish books in the country. The great Jewish catalogued collections in the United States today are at the New York Public Library, Hebrew Union College and Harvard University, but YIVO has the largest Yiddish collection in the world. Since YIVO does not use the same cataloguing procedures as the Library of Congress, some problems are anticipated. Also, Yiddish will have to be transliterated into the Roman alphabet. Meanwhile, luckily for present-day scholars, Abramowicz seems to have it all in her head.

The guardians of YIVO's treasure have a deep sense of history and mission. The explanation of every YIVO function begins with tasks defined fifty years ago. The description of every hope begins with the fulfillment of dreams destroyed by the Holocaust. To understand what YIVO is today and wants to be tomorrow, one must go back to the 1920s in Berlin, as Zosa Szajkowski, YIVO research associate, did in recounting YIVO's past. Szajkowski, a gray-haired man who is often seen shuffling slowly through the building, is quietly but passionately attached to YIVO. He knew many of its founders and recounts their history in a thin, clear voice.

Nahum Shtif, a Russian-born philologist, first conceived the idea of an academy of scholars to plan, conduct and publish research on Eastern European Jewry in Yiddish. Shtif, who served as editor of *Yidishe Shprakh*, was a Zionist in his youth and a member of the Zelbshuts, a self-defense organization founded during the 1903 pogroms. Later he helped found the Sejmist party, a Socialist group, and the Jewish Democratic Party. He moved to Berlin in 1922.

Though the idea of a Yiddish academy was new, Shtif's advocacy of

Yiddish scholarship was not. Jewish organizations had begun to collect Jewish source material from *shtetls* and cities some three decades earlier. Eastern Europe was flowering with studies of the literature, music and drama produced over the years by its 10,000,000 Jews. The Jewish Historic-Ethnographic Society, founded by the great historian Simon Dubnow in St. Petersburg, was sending teams of trained scholars to Jewish towns in the Ukraine to collect data on the speech, customs and folklore of the people. Dubnow, who was to become one of the founders of YIVO, was a self-taught scholar and an early follower of Ahad Ha-Am. He taught at the Institute of Jewish Studies in St. Petersburg, but left Russia for Berlin in 1922, remaining there until 1933, when he escaped to Riga, Latvia. In that country, on December 12, 1941, the 81-year-old scholar was murdered by a Gestapo officer who had once been his pupil.

Shtif shared his idea with historian Elias Tcherikover, a native of the Ukraine, who was then also living in Berlin. Four copies of the proposal were copied out by Shtif's and Tcherikover's wives for circulation among Yiddish scholars.

YIVO's fiftieth-anniversary exhibition documented the response of Jewish intellectuals throughout the world to the two men's call for a conference in Berlin in 1925. From Kovno to Buenos Aires, the concept of a YIVO stirred excitement. Tcherikover wrote: "We are a group of cheerful paupers. We are the last obstinate champions of Yiddish."

That the proposal met with such immediate enthusiasm was a reflection of the physical and intellectual restlessness characteristic of Jewish scholars during that period. Shtif, Dubnow and Tcherikover had all left their native country for Berlin, and all were to move again. Tcherikover, the most peripatetic, had been in New York in 1915 and returned to Russia after the Revolution, only to leave again in 1921. Typically, these learned Jews spoke many languages – discovering eventually that only the language of their youth, of their parents and grandparents, gave them a sense of home.

Beyond this, they had been faced with the recurrent problem of Jewish scholars who wish to advance the great ideas of their time, but often find those ideas becoming new weapons in the arsenal of anti-Semitism. Socialism, communism and revolution were in the air in those days, and many Jews were expounding all of them – but also learning bitter lessons. Tcherikover, who wrote a Marxist interpretation of the writer Mendele Mokher Siforim in 1905, was driven, when he returned to Russia after the Revolution, to compile the hideous record of the 1917–1921 Ukraine pogroms. Szajkowski, though somewhat younger than YIVO's founders, recalls in his book, *Jews and the French Foreign Legion*, that in his Communist youth he disrupted Socialist and Zionist meetings and even collected funds for Arabs, "the victims of Zionist imperialism," during the Palestine pogroms in 1929. Perhaps the later reactions of Jewish intellectuals in general and YIVO's founders in particular can best be summarized in the words of ex-Communist Charles Rappaport. Szajkowski writes that Rappaport, having left the Party, was looking through a volume of Heinrich Graetz' *History of the Jews* one day, and was heard to sigh, "What an idiot I was. My entire life I have toiled for strangers."

If Shtif, Dubnow, Tcherikover and the scholars who responded to their call felt that they could serve a Yiddish academy without fear, they were also certain that such an academy would serve them and the Jewish people. YIVO was to be, as it is today, a place where Yiddish is home and home is Yiddish.

The time had come "to organize Yiddish scholarship," as the founders put it. The first question was: Where would the new academy be? It was almost inevitable that Vilna became YIVO's home. Not only were Berlin Jews considered too assimilated and Warsaw Jews too left-wing and politicized, but Vilna had impressive credentials of its own. Known as "the Jerusalem of Lithuania," it was already a seat of Jewish learning. Nearly 47,000 Jews, more than one-third of Vilna's population, were crowded into the city's ghetto in 1921. Jews had lived in the city since 1551; at the beginning of the 17th Century it was already attracting scholars for rabbinical studies. Thousands of Jews poured into Vilna after Russia forbade them to live in rural areas at the end of the 19th Century. Thousands more sought asylum there during World War I.

Through the years unemployment and learning lived side by side among Vilna's Jews. But for every problem that poverty and scholarship raised, there seemed to be a solution close at hand. The study of *halakhah* and *kabbalah* went on everywhere in the ghetto. The Jewish Labor Bund was there, as were General Zionist and Mizrahi groups and organizations (such as Po'ale Zion, the Zionist Socialists and the Sejmists) attempting to bridge the gulf between the Socialists and the Zionists. The Jewish Historic-Ethnographic Society moved there.

Vilna was also the home of the important 35,000-volume Strashun library, founded in 1873 by Matthias Strashun, a Talmudic scholar who bequeathed 7,000 volumes to the community. Half its collection was rabbinical; the rest included 5,000 Yiddish books and Judaica in modern languages. It owned rare incunabula, including books printed in 1477, 1485 and 1492. At the time of YIVO's founding, the Strashun was located in a building in the synagogue courtyard. Though it seated a hundred people it was always crowded; the door was frequently closed to prevent a crush.

In addition to the regular schools, Vilna had separate Hebrew and Yiddish school systems, each with a teacher's seminary. It had five Yiddish dailies and two dozen journals. Fortnightlies, monthlies and streams of books were published by its enterprising Jewish press.

During the decade before YIVO's creation the city's history was a turbulent one, with nine different changes of government. In that brief period, Vilna was ruled by the Russians, the Poles, the Germans and the Lithuanians. The Jews were prey to economic depression, military requisitions, famine, disease, forced labor, imprisonment, plunder and recurrent anti-Semitic attacks. Vilna was once again Polish when YIVO was born in 1925.

The Institute was housed in a three-story building with extensive storage facilities. It was outside the Vilna ghetto, a fact which was to become crucially important later, when the Nazis occupied the city and the building itself, for YIVO's treasures as well as arms were smuggled between the two places.

Almost immediately a flood of material began cascading into YIVO's cellars. It included membership lists, agendas, minutes of meetings and reports of the activities of Jewish fraternal, social, educational and political organizations. There were theater pictures, programs and play-bills, and thousands of photographs, art objects, letters, diaries and manuscripts.

With loving care, Marek Web showed me the second version of *The Dybbuk* in An-ski's own hand. It had been recreated in the original Yiddish from Chaim Nachman Bialik's Hebrew translation by An-ski himself, after he had lost the only manuscript while traveling to Vilna. (An-ski, whose name was originally Solomon Zainwill Rapaport, had been a founder of the Ethnographic Society.)

The YIVO library received quantities of Jewish books, newspapers and periodicals produced by and about Jews all over the world. Within two years it had amassed 1,200 periodical titles. Among them are publications in Russian, German and English, published by Jews in

Shanghai and Harbin, China, including issues of *Israel's Messenger*, "the official organ of the Shanghai Zionist Association," dating back to 1906.

YIVO branches in the world's major cities sent material and money to help the Institute. Sigmund Freud and Albert Einstein were among its supporters. Individual YIVO enthusiasts then, as now, tend not to be rich. YIVO's first donation was a twenty-dollar check from Yudel Mark, co-editor of *The Great Dictionary of the Yiddish Language*.

Today, YIVO is a membership organization but, its administrators say, individual gifts and bequests and private foundation grants are seldom large. It has received two grants from the National Endowment for the Humanities but must find matching funds, which is not easy. It participates in the Joint Cultural Appeal, which receives allocations from Jewish Federations and Welfare Funds in many cities, with the notable exceptions of Washington, D.C. and New York.

In its first half-century, YIVO learned that material flows more readily than money. Still, to find items that might otherwise be lost or ignored, YIVO frequently used agents, known as *zamlers*, or collectors—unpaid men and women, trained and untrained—who helped gather memorabilia of all kinds and undertook local research projects, such as recording life histories and collecting songs. Some later became YIVO scholars. They were a phenomenon that persisted after World War II, when *zamlers*, some of them displaced persons, resumed forwarding material to the new YIVO headquarters in New York. YIVO has letters from some collectors who, though desperately poor, spent their own money to gain precious items for the Institute. There are few *zamlers* today.

YIVO also sought to enrich Jewish life and develop wider understanding of Jewish problems through scholarship and the application of modern methodology in the social sciences. Before World War II, it developed an *aspirantur* training program for about one hundred scholars, the *aspiranturen* receiving rigorous graduate instruction in research procedures and languages, as well as in sociology, political science and economics. They were expected to follow in the footsteps of YIVO's founders.

YIVO's research activity was divided into "scholarly sections," each led by distinguished specialists. The results were published in Yiddish and summarized in English, German and Polish. Intensive work went into standardizing Yiddish speech, spelling and grammar. Dubnow and Tcherikover were in charge of history, with work conducted in Berlin and Paris. (YIVO published Dubnow's *History of the Jewish People* in

1930.) Economics and statistics were directed by Jacob Lestshinski, also with headquarters in Berlin. The education and psychology sections were in New York; philology and literature were led from Vilna by Max Weinreich, the noted historian and linguist. Among the ardent supporters of the language study program was Dr. Zemach Shabad, a physician, Jewish community leader and one-time Polish senator. Max Weinreich was his son-in-law.

Weinreich, partially blinded by a stone thrown in an anti-Semitic assault in 1920, taught Yiddish at the Vilna Teachers' Seminary. So committed was he to the language that he translated Freud and Homer into Yiddish. Almost sightless in his last years (he died in New York in 1969 at the age of 75), he is remembered at YIVO as an "endless source of knowledge," who read constantly with the text an inch and a half from his eyes.

When the Nazis attacked Poland, Weinreich was in Copenhagen on his way to a conference. He managed to get to New York with his family in 1940, and later became a central figure in the transfer of the YIVO headquarters from Vilna to New York and in the Institute's subsequent development. In 1947 Weinreich accepted a post teaching Yiddish language, literature and folklore at City College, thus becoming the first professor of Yiddish at an American university.

Weinreich's son Uriel, born in Vilna in 1925, an internationally known linguist of dazzling talents, was professor of Yiddish studies and chairman of the Linguistics Department of Columbia University. Two of his greatest achievements were the textbook *College Yiddish*, published in 1949, and *The Modern English-Yiddish, Yiddish-English Dictionary*, which YIVO published in 1968, one year after his untimely death. His widow, Bina Silverman Weinreich, is a research associate at YIVO.

The Shabad-Weinreich three-generation association with YIVO underscores the strong intellectual and emotional bonds many of its European personnel have with each other and with the Institute. Some, like the Institute itself, survived the Holocaust and have made the task of preserving, sifting and studying its history their life's work. Assistant director Hannah Fryshdorf, Dr. Isaiah Trunk, the chief archivist, Dina Abramowicz and Zosa Szajkowski, all Europeans, have been with YIVO for more than twenty years. Simon Dawidowicz, whose wife, Lucy, was in the Vilna *aspirantur* program, retired in 1975 after more than thirty years of service in the publications department.

Beyond the ties of common experience and interest which bind

longtime YIVO people, there is a spiritual tie. It is rooted in an unspoken
but clearly transmitted, intensely felt belief that they are the keepers of a
treasure, the guardians of a miracle. They guard not only the books and
archives of Vilna that survived the Holocaust, but the fruits of Jewish
scholarship which emerged from that bitter time. The historians, poets,
musicians—the trained and untrained Jews who collected papers, wrote
letters, kept journals while faced with death—were aware that they were
their own archives. Like YIVO's Vilna collections, the poignant scraps,
the prose, the poetry, the yellow Stars of David, the ration books,
everything was worth saving for its intrinsic value. But that they were
actually preserved in ghettos and death camps, that they actually survived bombs and bonfires, pillaging and paper factories, eventually to be
put into YIVO's hands, is testimony to Jewish heroism and determination to record the Jewish fate.

In Vilna, YIVO was housed at 18 Wiwulskiego Street. Past its gate in the
courtyard were laurel and rose bushes, fragrant and lovely in the spring.
Inside, a map of the Jewish population of the world hung over the
staircase, above it an electric clock. In 1942 the clock, by then stopped,
was surmounted by a swastika.

   With the Nazi occupation of Vilna, YIVO had become a depot for
Reichsleiter Alfred Rosenberg's collecting squads. Rosenberg, the vi-
ciously anti-Semitic chief Nazi ideologist, was in charge of Nazi "cultural"
operations. In 1939, by Hitler's orders, Nazi policy toward Jewish and
other "alien" cultural materials had changed. No longer were they
indiscriminately destroyed. Instead they were collected, sorted and
shipped to Germany, to be used for "scholarly purposes." Rosenberg had
squads in every area of Europe gathering material.

   All Jewish items were sent to the Nazi party Institute for Research on
the Jewish Question, located in Frankfurt. Some thirty Jews worked in
YIVO under Nazi supervision, among them Sutzkever, Kaczerginski and
Rachel Pupko-Krinsky, then a young school teacher. With poignant
awareness that both the Jews and the books were in danger of perishing
at any moment, Pupko-Krinsky wrote (in *The Root and the Bough*, a
collection of reminiscences of that period) of the ingenuity required to
smuggle Jewish treasures from the YIVO building to the ghetto, to be
hidden away. "Though spied on regularly," she said, "we seldom left
YIVO empty-handed. . . . Once out of the YIVO courtyard, we had but
a single thought: What was going on at the ghetto gate on Rudnicka

Street? . . . If upon reaching the corner . . . we saw no Germans at the gate, we fairly flew, lest the police or SS Murer himself appear out of nowhere." One evening Pupko-Krinsky ran headlong into the dreaded Murer, while she was carrying a silver beaker Sutzkever had "lifted" from a special exhibit of silver ritual objects, Torah scrolls and valuable books. Murer asked the terrified woman: "Have you got any money?" "No," she answered, as if in a trance. Taking her stony fear for calm, he let her pass into the ghetto.

Later the Vilna workers decided that what they could smuggle out of YIVO was only a small part of what they wished to save. They joined forces in distracting a Polish supervisor for an hour a day, giving him lessons in Latin, German and mathematics, while Sutzkever and Kaczerginski worked frantically to hide objects under the boards of YIVO's attic. Each evening the workers left the building with the fear that they might not return the next day, and were terrified lest the Germans find traces of what they had done.

Kaczerginski's wife had avoided living in the ghetto. The Christian man with whose family she lived smuggled guns and bullets to the people in YIVO, which they in turn smuggled into the ghetto. Once he delivered a machine gun just before a team of German cultural experts was to arrive. While the inspection was going on, the gun was taken apart and hidden under paintings in a display of "Judaized European art." As the officers approached the gun, Sutzkever rushed around the room, waving his hands like a maniac. "If discovered, not only we but the whole ghetto would be destroyed," he wrote in *The Root and the Bough* after the war. The diversion worked. Later the gun was taken to the ghetto and, according to Sutzkever, "On September 12, 1943, it helped us break out of the ghetto, escape to the forest and ally ourselves with the partisan camp." After the Nazis were defeated, Kaczerginski and Sutzkever returned to the YIVO building and the remains of the ghetto to retrieve what they could of YIVO's treasures.

Emmanuel Ringelblum, YIVO member, historian and hero of the Warsaw ghetto, was sheltered by a Polish railway worker. In the bunker where he lay hidden, Ringelblum prepared a lengthy report on partisan activities for YIVO. He wrote almost to the moment on March 7, 1944 when the Nazis found and killed him and his family. The report lay hidden beneath the bunker until it somehow arrived at YIVO in New York. The remarkable journal was published in 1958 as *Notes from the Warsaw Ghetto*.

In the Lodz ghetto, mailman Nachman Zonabend apparently picked up as many or more papers as he delivered. These were internal records of Jewish life in the ghetto, including its newspapers. Zonabend later escaped to Sweden with his collection. Though he remained in Sweden, these materials were sent to YIVO in New York, where they formed the basis of Dr. Trunk's history, *Lodz Ghetto*. (Trunk's *Judenrat*, which won the National Book Award for history in 1973, was also based largely on YIVO archives.)

The books and archives that individuals saved were only a fraction of the enormous haul that Rosenberg's squads collected. In Eastern Europe, 375 archival institutions, 402 museums, 531 institutes and 957 libraries were looted. The Jewish material remained "under study" in Frankfurt until Allied bombings toward the end of the war caused the Germans to move their booty to the town of Offenbach. There, dilapidated, moldy, tarnished, torn, exposed to elements and to thieves, the remnants and artifacts of East European Jewry were found by the liberating armies. There were 276 collections from the city of Vilna alone, and thousands of unidentified photos, bundles of letters from the dead to the dead, Torahs and candelabra from devastated synagogues. And there were books—three million books!

The swift and successful handling of this vast store was an example of American efficiency. Appointed by U.S. military authorities to set up and operate the Offenbach Archival Depot, Major Seymour Pomrenze, an archivist proficient in German, Hebrew and Yiddish, began a three-month operation in February 1946, launching some 200 workers on the monumental task. He was followed by Captain Isaac Bencowitz, also a skilled linguist, who completed the job by the end of that year. Pomrenze remains a YIVO consultant to this day. Thanks to the efforts of General Lucius Clay and the U.S. State Department, much of the recovered material from Vilna—some 50,000 bound volumes and 30,000 folders of archival papers—was forwarded to YIVO.

New York became the site of YIVO's international headquarters in 1940, following the arrival of Max Weinreich and other refugee scholars. They and those who managed to escape from Europe's cauldron in succeeding years galvanized what had been the "New York branch," then housed in the HIAS building on Lafayette Street in lower Manhattan, and later, from 1942 to 1955, in a building on West 123rd Street. YIVO bought the former Vanderbilt mansion in 1955. Up to that time, the branch, established in 1940, had borne only a pale resemblance to its European counterpart, for few American Jewish intellectuals had been interested in Yiddish scholarship. Intrigued by the concept of the "melting pot," most had adopted the immigrant's dream of becoming good English-speaking Americans. Thus both YIVO and Yiddish in New York had been struggling against an opponent unknown in harshest Poland, the pressure for assimilation.

When Tcherikover arrived he brought important historical material from the European YIVO. He soon set to work on a history of the Jewish labor movement in the United States. This was published by YIVO in Yiddish in two volumes in 1943 and 1945, and in an English version in 1961. Tcherikover later became YIVO's archivist and left his personal library to the institution. Jacob Lestshinski of the economic section also left part of his personal collection to the YIVO library, as did Max Weinreich.

The library's periodical collection increased steadily as, unbidden, Jewish newspapers and magazines the world over sent their publications. (They still do.) Dina Abramowicz estimates that 4,000 persons use the reading room each year—the books are not available on loan—and 10,000 receive answers to queries.

The development of the archives parallels that of the library. According to Dr. Trunk, they contain 8,500 linear feet of material, 25,000,000 pieces of paper. In addition to the Vilna archives, YIVO is the largest holder of immigration material in the world. After World War II, it also began collecting first-person accounts from survivors.

Three full-time archivists are employed to handle the inflow of material, which arrives at the rate of two or three accessions a week, and to prepare material for scholars. Holocaust material is still coming in. As recently as last June, YIVO received additional photos of the Lodz ghetto and interviews with survivors of the Holocaust in Poland. Earlier, it was presented with data on a Yiddish school in Vilkomir, private papers relating to Nachum Shtif, the YIVO founder, and valuable additions to the collection of the public correspondence of Herman Bernstein, one-time U.S. ambassador to Albania, whose libel suit against Henry Ford is also documented in its files.

Among other prominent writers, both Irving Howe, author of *World of Our Fathers*, and Lucy Dawidowicz, author of *The War Against the Jews*, made extensive use of YIVO material for their books.

Many items remain to be inventoried. Archivists don't catalogue; they inventory their holdings. That is, they describe them broadly, indicating what a collection contains—e.g., letters, diaries, newspaper clippings— and record its location. But the actual contents of the material are not described, so that each researcher must search through each collection carefully. For example, YIVO records show that it has seventeen boxes (or seven linear feet) of newspaper clippings on Nazi publicist Josef Goebbels.

An impressive part of the archives is made up of material collected by YIVO scholars in Paris and Berlin from 1925 until the beginning of World War II in 1939. These large collections had been given up for lost; their astonishing return is generally credited to Zosa Szajkowski. Szajkowski's thin voice is barely audible when he talks about this period of his life. It is as if he prefers not to talk at all, and indeed, after silently shrugging when asked to provide facts he cannot or will not reveal, he finally says, "I'm still alive. I don't want to talk about it yet." It is known, however, that Szajkowski was born in Zareby, Poland, in 1911, lived in France for many years and then emigrated to the United States in 1941. He was an American paratrooper in 1943. In his own writings which, as he hands me *Jews and the French Foreign Legion*, he says he is willing to have quoted, he states: "Moreover, while in Carpentras I smuggled out from Paris, with the help of French friends, the archives of the Historical Section of YIVO, those of Shalom Schwartzbard [who killed the notorious Simon Petlyura, organizer of pogroms in the Ukraine, and was acquitted], the Simon Dubnow archives and the private archives and library of the Tcherikovers. The latter included the archives on the pogroms in the Ukraine. Some of these archives I was able to send immediately to YIVO in New York via Martinique, the others I had to hide. In December 1944 I obtained permission from the U.S. 82nd Airborne Division to go to Marseilles and get the archives. I found them intact, they had been well hidden, and the United States military authorities consented to send them to YIVO in New York." The full story of the rescue of these documents, YIVO insiders told me, is a saga of courage, perseverance and ingenuity, a book in itself.

Last year the Archives Department began to sort and study art objects which it barely knew it possessed. For years material had come into YIVO too quickly for its meager staff to inventory properly. For example, YIVO knew it possessed a collection of Jewish posters but only recently, when funds were available, was it found to contain 35,000 posters, ranging from election posters to theater posters, reflecting every aspect of Jewish life. Hundreds of other items, from candelabra to an oil painting of a mother and child hauntingly entitled *Madonna à L'Etoile Jaune* (Madonna of the Yellow Star), have been dug out of the basement, to be dusted, sorted and described.

Though many art objects in YIVO's archives are works by well-known artists, their artistic or intrinsic merits are regarded as of secondary importance. For YIVO the vital aspect is that they are part of Jewish history, to be used by scholars and others to make vivid the vast sweep of the Jewish past.

A project that brought widespread acclaim to YIVO was "Image Before My Eyes," a photographic exhibit of Jewish life in Poland from the end of the 19th Century (and the beginnings of photography) to the eve of World War II. This striking exhibit, displayed at the Jewish Museum in New York, was made possible by grants from the New York State Council on the Arts and the National Endowment for the Humanities.

Dr. Lucjan Dobroszycki, YIVO historian and specialist in Polish Jewry, Dr. Barbara Kirshenblatt-Gimblett of the Weinreich Center and Stuart Silver, the designer who prepared the exhibit, told me that publication of two books connected with the photographs is now planned. One, *Image Before My Eyes*, will contain more than 300 photographs from YIVO's collection of more than 10,000. Another, a catalogue in Yiddish and English, will itemize the photo collection according to city of origin and will contain approximately 400 photos not previously published.

The touching pictures, so much like those one's parents saved, raise the question "What makes an archive?" In most cases YIVO archivists expect prospective donors to inquire about the suitability to YIVO of material they wish to send in. But where photographs of Jews are concerned, Dr. Dobroszycki is pleased to accept every photo he is offered. If, therefore, your mother says to you, "What will happen to these pictures when I'm gone? You don't even know who anybody was," suggest she do what my mother did: label every one with name, place and date and send them to YIVO.

Both the archives and the library microfilm their collections to the extent that time and money permit. The library has already filmed many early Yiddish periodicals and the archives is microfilming its immigration documents, the latter partly to provide source material for studies which are being undertaken by many universities and private researchers in the United States.

"We've been a *meshpuchah*, but it's changing now. We're missing two generations," Hannah Fryshdorf said, referring to the sharp division in ages that characterizes YIVO's staff. One group is in its 60s and the other in the 20s and 30s. The scholars murdered by the Nazis and those they would have trained to follow them are both absent. The young librarians and archivists with professional skills and knowledge of Yiddish and Hebrew who now work at YIVO have little direct relationship to the European experience of the older staff. Rather, they reflect the revival of interest in Jewish religion, culture and language that began in the 1960s and has spread in the United States and elsewhere.

Yiddish, a thousand-year-old language, is being studied by the linguistic profession and taught in many educational institutions. Increasing religious observance has brought with it increasing use of Hebrew and Yiddish. Many colleges and universities have created Jewish studies courses and departments which stress Jewish history and literature. Large numbers of masters' theses and doctoral dissertations (of which YIVO publishes a record) have been concerned with previously unexplored subjects in these fields.

With this renewed interest as a stimulus, Max Weinreich and YIVO began in the 1960s to develop plans for an institution to train Jewish scholars and advance research in Yiddish into Jewish life and culture. Weinreich, who was YIVO's research director in both Vilna and New York, made a distinction between "scholarly Jews" and "Jewish scholars." Scholarly Jews abound in universities everywhere, he said, but Jewish scholarship requires a special outlook and years of training. In 1968, a year before his death, the Center for Advanced Jewish Studies came into being.

The Center, which was named for Weinreich after his death, now has some sixty students from dozens of universities in various countries (about 10 percent of them not Jewish) and is not a degree-granting institution, nor does it wish to be. It regards itself as an enabling agent, and assists graduate students or those who have completed graduate studies elsewhere to combine work in their specific fields of study, such as music, literature, sociology, with training in Jewish scholarship. Students are required to know Yiddish, Hebrew and an East European language.

(Those who have no Yiddish can learn the language in the Uriel Weinreich Summer Program in the Yiddish Language and Literature, sponsored jointly by YIVO and Columbia University.) According to Dr. Marvin Herzog, professor of Yiddish and of linguistics at Columbia University and acting dean of the Weinreich Center, YIVO hopes not only to train new scholars but also to stimulate an interest in East European Jewish history and culture throughout the world.

YIVO's chief hope rests in the Center. There are no longer 10,000,000 Yiddish-speaking Jews making history. There is no Yiddish scholarship to organize. To perpetuate YIVO's goals, the Center must help Yiddish scholarship to become an academic discipline, and it must train Yiddish-speaking social scientists to replace the Vilna generation.

And the Center seems to be succeeding. Its courses and enrollment have expanded. It attracts excellent scholars and teachers, and its first graduates have begun careers here and abroad.

But despite generous government grants to help establish the Weinreich Center, YIVO must contribute to the Center while carrying on its other activities—and money has been hard to find. A National Endowment for the Humanities grant for 1974–79 for the Center was tied to a matching fund arrangement, and YIVO's campaign to raise the needed money had to be extended, in the hope that the goal would be reached by the end of the year. Similarly, a matching fund drive to supplement the Endowment's library and archives grant still remains to be completed. And YIVO continues to budget heavily from its regular funds for all these programs.

And after the grants?

As an institution devoted to scholarship, YIVO must find a base of support from a sympathetic community. If all goes well, individuals, foundations and, perhaps most satisfying of all, successful alumni will preserve YIVO's treasures and traditions through the next half-century. Meanwhile in a 17th Century French palace on Fifth Avenue "the last obstinate champions of Yiddish" carry on.

Zelda

Benny Morris

She arrived in Jerusalem, an 11-year-old child in an open, horse-drawn carriage, after the long journey from Chernigov, her birthplace in the Ukraine. In one of her poems Zelda compared that first entry into the Holy City at night to an annihilation of the soul:

> The spectacular dark swallowed mountains
> And courtyards, bushes and trees
> And the horses strode on the face of the heavens
> Among the stars.

Later, she became familiar with the equally annihilatory, bright, noonday light refracting off the stones—extinguishing thought, melting boundaries and singularity. Then she wrote:

> Jerusalem entrapped
> My free soul
> I drowned in the light
> I forgot my name.

And, in another poem, she describes Jerusalem in still another way:

> My house is built on the shore
> On the edge of the moon
> And of the stars
> On the verge of dawns and sunsets.

Zelda Schneerson-Mishkovsky, now known to readers of Hebrew poetry as "Zelda," seems to regard her poems as weapons in a perpetual battle to prevent personal extinction.

In her oblique way, she acknowledges that she long ago fell captive to the Holy City, where she has lived for more than half a century, watching it grow from a town of 50,000 to a capital city of some 350,000. She says that Jerusalem "hasn't really changed."

For her, "The air and the hills remain. The city overcomes its inhabitants and what they may try to do to it. New waves of people come. But they too are absorbed and become Jerusalemites.

"Have no fear," she concludes, "Jerusalem will never change." Her voice trails off—"the light, the air, the stones."

Israeli novelist Amos Oz once described Jerusalem as a magnet "for eccentrics and lunatics of every persuasion and from every corner of the globe." Certainly, Zelda is an unusual Jerusalemite.

She is an ultra-Orthodox Jewish poet, scion of a famous Hassidic family, a cousin of Rabbi Menahem Mendel Schneerson, the head of Hassidim's largest Lubavitcher sect. Zelda half-jokingly describes herself as "a Hasid by temperament," though Judaism does not allow women claim to such a title.

Zelda speaks slowly, in short, clipped sentences. She is a word-hoarder, shunning elaboration or explanation, her statements conveying precise meanings. Sometimes, between sentences, there are long, ruminative spells during which she seems completely alone, oblivious to those around her. She responds to questions with disjointed words, quietly dropped into the room's space like telegrams with no particular destination.

Grandmotherly in appearance though she is childless, with a very round, white, Slavic face, Zelda projects benignity. She sits squat, solid and calm in her chair—but somehow closed off, like an African daisy besieged by night.

Zelda is almost embarrassingly modest, shy and self-effacing. Her eyes—deep-set, bright brown, constantly in motion—appear to focus on everything but her guest's eyes. Like butterflies eluding entrapment, they come to rest on walls, the tablecloth, windows, the floor. But every so often she steals a peek across the table, perhaps to see whether her guest is still there. She smiles frequently and sadly. Of herself, Zelda wrote:

> It is strange to be a woman
> Simple, homely, flaccid
> In a fierce generation,
> A generation of violence.
> To be shy, weary
> In a cold generation, a generation of salesmen
> To exist between conquerers
> And the conquered.

Zelda expresses surprise when I ask whether Orthodox Judaism permits a woman to write poetry, especially in the holy tongue. (Indeed, some ultra-Orthodox Jerusalem sects proscribe the use of Hebrew, save for prayer and the study of the Torah, and speak Yiddish as a matter of course.)

Zelda also allows herself to be photographed, which many devout Jews regard as a sacrilege. She has even been interviewed on television—and owns a television set. "It's a recent thing," she tells me, apologetically. "I watch it infrequently."

She says she likes nothing better than the housewifely tasks assigned to women by traditional Judaism. But her poetry, much of it deeply brooding and lyrical, with strong sexual undertones, marks her as a very uncommon believer.

She explains: "I grew up in the Russian tradition. My mother, a devout Jew, was also well read in Russian secular literature. It is the Polish-Jewish tradition which restricts women to the home and to a narrow ethnic outlook."

She herself likes to read the great Russian novelists in the original, as well as modern Hebrew writers. "And I dabble a little in traditional Jewish texts and exegeses," she says.

Since the deaths of her husband, who was a learned Hassid and a teacher, and her mother a few years ago, Zelda has lived alone in a small apartment in an old building at the end of a quiet, eucalyptus-lined street in Jerusalem's Sha'arei Hessed (the Gates of Grace) quarter. Of her childhood home, not far away, Zelda once wrote:

> I bloomed in a stone house
> Without a yoke, without a purpose
> Like a cyclamen in a rock.

She has been composing poems since she was in her teens. For decades, only a handful were published, usually in obscure journals. "I am not very ambitious," she notes.

In the late 1960s, a friend suggested that they collect everything already in print and locked away in her desk, and seek a publisher. Reluctantly, Zelda agreed – and attained instant fame with the publication in 1968 of her first, slim volume, titled *P'nai* (Leisure).

Critics spoke of the "purity, precision and simplicity" of her verse, of its "lyrical heights and spiritual depths," of the elements of "a sustained prayer" and "the obtrusiveness of death."

Since then, three more slim volumes have been published – a scant *oeuvre* for almost a lifetime of writing. "I have long periods of passivity. They too are part of the process," she explained.

In speaking of her art, she refuses to use the word "creation." "It's too big a word," she says, implying that it rightfully applies solely to the Creator.

She writes only poetry. "I once tried a short story, but it turned into a poem," she smiles. "And I feel no desire to write criticism of other people's work."

Zelda recently retired from school teaching, her profession since she graduated from high school in the early 1930s. "I like teaching grownups and the early primary school grades – not so much those in between." Nothing, she says, gives her greater joy than "introducing little children to the Garden of Eden, to Abraham and David and Solomon." She stopped teaching when her husband and her mother died.

Looking back even further, she recalls that her grandfather and father, both rabbis, died within a year of the family's arrival in Palestine in 1926. "We set out from Odessa in the Soviet steamship *Lenin*," Zelda muses.

She has not been out of the Holy Land since that day. "For years, I didn't have the money. Going abroad then was as improbable as travel to the moon. Now," she smiles, and looks down at her wide hips and legs swathed in a dark, flower-patterned floor-length skirt, "I am too heavy." In fact, she rarely ventures outdoors these days.

Her world has shrunk in recent years. Once it encompassed the schools in which she taught, her husband and his affairs, her mother and a wide circle of friends. Now, with the number of friends diminished, Zelda passes most of her days within her three rooms, with her books and poems. She speaks of her poems as of children: "Once they are written and published, they are no longer mine. They have become independent, separate beings, with lives of their own."

The themes of her poetry seldom reflect what might be called the outer ring of existence—the state, politics, society, the Jewish people. Indeed, she refers only infrequently to the inner circle of family, neighbors, friends, the street outside her window, except as accessories to her portrayal of her inner world of feelings and self-reflection.

But Zelda does not think she is either self-absorbed or self-centered. "I am interested in the world," she declares, and refers to her poem (which, she admits, is the only one of its kind she has written) about Levi Neufeld.

Neufeld—a 29-year-old medical student and an Auschwitz survivor who had been deeply affected by his experience—was suspected of having murdered three people with a submachine gun.

He committed suicide in 1963. His body was found in an abandoned Arab house near Jerusalem about a year after his death. An investigation cleared him of all suspicion after it was proved that he had died before one of the murders. Zelda still speaks of the affair with a quiet passion.

"Some of his acquaintances all of a sudden recalled 'his strange ways' and 'his strange eyes.' The affair haunted me like a dybbuk," says Zelda.

In 1964, Zelda wrote in "In the Lap of the Grasses He Wept":

> His curls ran like a secret river like silk, like peace
> When they washed him of muck and blood
> From the dark pit.

Zelda wrote of his death:

> The grasses didn't urge him to live
> The grasses didn't urge him to get up
> The grasses sang
> Of the joy of the soul
> Meeting in the world to come
> Its father and mother
> And its Creator.

Some of Neufeld's friends, recalls Zelda, came and thanked her for the poem which, they said, had shown real understanding of that "tortured soul." Zelda was moved.

Clearly, Zelda is not a very political person. But, like all Israelis, she has political opinions which she is willing to enunciate in her quiet, diffident, but firm way. Though she will not express concrete opinions about the occupied territories—for instance, which to keep and which not, "as that's a matter for experts, generals, strategists"—she says: "We must keep what is necessary for security, for survival, for continued life." Obliquely critical of expansionism on historical-religious grounds, Zelda says: "The paramount consideration must be security. It must determine policy."

She reads newspapers when they come her way. "People in Israel seem to denigrate each other, themselves, the state, far too much. There is a tone of despair, a type of masochism. In fact, things aren't all bad or all good," she says, with grandmotherly reasonableness. "We are no worse than anyone else. We've done nothing to be ashamed of in the sight of others, though perhaps we should be ashamed of some things before each other."

As a firm believer, Zelda writes often about God, the Sabbath, the Day of Atonement, religious artifacts. Nothing that has happened in her lifetime has shaken her belief in God's existence and goodness. And as for Auschwitz: "His intentions and methods are not always fathomable. Sometimes, He seems to us to be turning his face away. That's all that one can really say."

She sits in her old stone house reading her books, weighing her words, visiting with friends, most of whom live in an older, remembered Jerusalem.

Zelda seems to be waiting. Today, she writes often about death, which has carried off almost everyone she has loved. "I met him too often," she says simply.

Meanwhile, she writes:

> I am grateful to a green leaf
> for a leaf is a hand
> Which pulls my soul out of the abyss.

Index

393

About the Editor

Murray Polner, the founding editor of *Present Tense* magazine, has written numerous books, including *No Victory Parades: The Return of the Vietnam Veteran*, *Rabbi: The American Experience*, and *Branch Rickey: A Biography*. A freelance writer and editor, Polner has contributed to many newspapers and magazines.